St Peter's, Cardross

Birth, Death and Renewal

Diane M Watters

with an image essay by Angus Farquhar

Published in 2016 by
Historic Environment Scotland
in association with NVA

Text updated and expanded from
Cardross Seminary, published by RCAHMS, 1997

Historic Environment Scotland
John Sinclair House
16 Bernard Terrace
Edinburgh EH8 9NX

telephone +44 (0) 131 662 1456

Scottish Charity SC045925

British Library
Cataloguing-in-Publication Data.
A catalogue record for this book is available
from the British Library.

ISBN 9781849172233
© Crown Copyright –
Historic Environment Scotland 2016

All rights reserved. No part of this publication
may be reproduced, stored in or introduced
into a retrieval system, or transmitted, in any
form, or by any means (electronic, mechanical,
photocopying, recording or otherwise) without
the prior written permission of Historic
Environment Scotland.

Any person who does any unauthorised act
in relation to this publication may be liable to
criminal prosecution.

Designed by Oliver Brookes
Typeset in Garamond, Helvetica Inserat and
Gill Sans

Printed in Poland by POZKAL

jacket front cover
St Peter's during NVA's *Hinterland* event, 2016
Alaisdair Smith

jacket back cover
Trainee priest at St Peter's, c1966
Gillespie, Kidd & Coia Archive, Glasgow School of Art

spine
Graffiti by Smug and Estum at St Peter's, 2010
NVA

Contents

Beginnings

Introduction		**4**
Chapter 1	Conservatism and Change	12
Chapter 2	Scottish Modern Architecture	20
Chapter 3	The Evolution of Gillespie, Kidd & Coia	40

Birth and Death

Chapter 4	Conception and Construction	68
Chapter 5	The College in Use and in Decline	118
Chapter 6	Salvaging St Peter's	144
Conclusion		**186**

Renewal

The Future of St Peter's by Angus Farquhar, NVA 2016	**192**
Landscape	196
The Ruin	202
The Altar	214
The Clean Up	218
Graffiti	226
Hinterland	234
Hinterland Manifesto	**246**
End Notes	**248**
Timeline	**260**
Bibliography	**266**
St Peter's College: Practice Drawing List	**268**
Achnowledgements	**276**
Editorial Notes	**277**
Index	**278**

Introduction

The story of Cardross Seminary begins in 1946, when St Peter's College in Bearsden was destroyed by fire, and the college moved elsewhere: first, in 1946, to Darleith House, and then additionally, in 1948, to Kilmahew House, Cardross. It was not until 1953 that the concept of a new and massive extension to Kilmahew House, to be designed by the architects Gillespie, Kidd & Coia, was formally endorsed; and building work did not start until 1961. The new seminary that was eventually opened in November 1966, although not completed until 1968, was a large and strikingly Modern design, but was at the same time not without its traditional, even anachronistic, aspects.

Located on a limited, level area set in steeply sloping woodland, the new seminary buildings were grouped in a courtyard or precinct-like manner on three sides of Kilmahew House. This Scotch Baronial mansion was originally built in 1865–8 to the designs of John Burnet the elder, for John William Burns, son of the founder of the trans-Atlantic Cunard Line. Kilmahew was a compact, tower-like design in the tradition established by J Gillespie Graham at Brodick (1844) and Ayton (1851), with a massive arched porch similar to Burnet's Arden House (1867). During the 1959–66 work, this mansion was thoroughly refurbished. Gillespie, Kidd & Coia's new buildings included the main five-storey accommodation block, with bedrooms on the upper floors and the communal spaces of refectory and chapel below; a projecting two-storey wing at one end of the chapel contained a sanctuary and crypt beneath. To the west of the main block, a common-room and classroom block dramatically jutted out over the woodland, while on the north side of Kilmahew House was placed a small, self-contained group of convent buildings. Architecturally, the Gillespie, Kidd & Coia buildings, grouped into varied external forms and internal spaces, and faced mainly in rough harling and concrete, belonged to the late phase of the Modern Movement –

St Peter's College, Cardross, c1968
Gillespie, Kidd & Coia Archive, Glasgow School of Art

St Peter's, Cardross

Introduction

a period, from the late 1950s to the early 1970s, when the simple, crusading faiths of the Modern pioneers were challenged by calls for more complex solutions.

The extended Cardross Seminary only functioned as intended for a few years. It closed in 1980, within fourteen years of its opening, and began its long decline into decay and, ultimately, ruin: the abandoned complex had only one period of active occupation, as a drug rehabilitation centre from 1983 to 1987. In 1995, Kilmahew House was gutted by fire and demolished, leaving the Gillespie, Kidd & Coia additions standing on their own. Over the 30 years since its closure there ensued a long succession of plans for re-use or repair of the derelict complex, and from the mid 1990s, an equally protracted battle by preservationists to save and restore it. The decaying ruin of the former seminary itself sat patiently awaiting its fate throughout. In 2015, a part-restoration scheme for its re-use as a cultural centre, developed by new owners, the public arts-charity NVA, began work on site. The staging of the art event *Hinterland*, in March 2016, officially opened the former seminary buildings to the general public. The restoration scheme is due for completion in spring 2019.

This book explores and documents both the St Peter's College (also known as Cardross Seminary) project itself, and the wider architectural and religious movements of which it formed an important symbolic part. It illustrates, in microcosm, the varied character of both Scottish Modern architecture and postwar Scottish Catholicism. And it highlights the conflicting factors within the idea of a *Modern* religious architecture: the meaning of a religious building, and its ability to communicate with those who worship in it, depend largely on the power, not of newness, but of tradition. The book also traces the way in which religious and architectural change led to the dramatic downfall of the seminary buildings. The extended St Peter's proved to be an anachronism – a built embodiment of ideals which, even as construction proceeded, were turned upside down by the radical Catholic church reforms

Burnt out car sits on the site of the demolished Kilmahew House, 2003
Dan Dubowitz

Introduction

of the momentous Second Vatican Council (October 1962–December 1965). Its viability was then further undermined by the mounting economic and social difficulties of the Church in the following years, and, last but not least, by the prolonged troubles of its performance and maintenance.

This book, then, records the story of the slow decline of the abandoned seminary, including the demolition of the main building that was its focus; but from the late 1980s, the complex's fate and reputation was also affected by the beginning of the re-evaluation of Modern architecture as a potential subject of heritage. The seminary ruin then entered into a new life as a heritage artefact, and became increasingly divorced from its own religious and architectural history. The misfortunes of the college highlight today's conservation quandary, of how to re-use, or even just to maintain, the more spectacular creations of Modern architecture. This preservation-orientated narrative then finally shifts to examine the story behind its transformation into a permanent art installation. Perhaps a secure long-term future is at last in prospect for St Peter's.

The former seminary during NVA's *Hinterland* event, 2016
Alaisdair Smith

St Peter's, Cardross

Beg

innings

The Chapel of Notre Dame du Haut, France, by Le Corbusier, 1954
Jacqueline Salmon / Art Edia / VIEW

Chapter 1
Conservatism and Change

The project for a new seminary at Cardross, although prompted by the destruction of the existing Bearsden building, was also an expression of the general confidence of postwar Catholicism in the West of Scotland. In that region the Church establishment had embarked on a massive building drive, while remaining, on the whole, faithful to religious and liturgical traditionalism. The organisation of the Church's building drive also featured conflicting elements: it combined highly centralised diocesan direction with considerable autonomy at parish level. These paradoxes contributed indirectly to the evolution of a Modern Catholic religious architecture in Scotland, but also at the same time created significant tensions within that architecture – some of which would emerge at Cardross.

Demographic Change and New Churches

In 1945, the Archdiocese of Glasgow stood on the threshold of three decades of momentous change in the social and cultural condition of its flock, which would transform the organisational structure and geographical scope of the Catholic Church in the West. When Donald Campbell, Bishop of Argyll and the Isles, was installed as the new Archbishop of Glasgow in that year (a position he held until his death in 1963), Glasgow was by far the largest diocese in Scotland, boasting three-quarters of the country's Catholics. Despite the dominant position enjoyed by the Glasgow community, the national Church, as we will see, was structured (and restructured) on a strong regional diocesan basis throughout the nineteenth and twentieth centuries. In 1942, the Bishops' Conference of Scotland had been established as the national grouping to represent the diocese of the country. Scotland had no *de-jure* position of primate, such as that held by the Archbishop of Westminster in England and Wales, but the two Archbishops, St Andrews and Edinburgh, and Glasgow, held seniority. The Bishops' Conference also had control over the national seminary provision for the training of priests.[1] Across Scotland as a whole, in contrast to the fluctuating fortunes of the Protestant churches (which witnessed their postwar peak in the 1950s), the number

Gorbals high-rise flats under construction, Glasgow, c1965
The postwar period saw the break-up of many of the traditional Catholic communities in Glasgow. As sections of the old inner city were demolished, people were moved into new homes – like Basil Spence's 20-storey Hutchesontown area C flats, pictured here overlooking St Francis' Catholic Church and Friary – or were relocated to peripheral schemes or New Towns.
HES SC1052236

of Catholics was continuing to grow, reaching a maximum of 15% of the population in the early 1960s.[2] However, as we will see, the rate of growth was sharply diminishing: it was only one-fifth of that at the turn of the century. Irish Catholic immigration to Scotland had declined in the late 1870s and 1880s, but from the 1890s the Church was bolstered by the arrival of Italian immigrants. By the outbreak of the First World War, the Catholic community, some 513,000, had stabilised and accounted for about 11% of the total population. The Archdiocese of Glasgow accounted for two-thirds of that community.[3]

The location and social status of Catholics in the West of Scotland was changing rapidly. In 1918, most had belonged to the unskilled or semi-skilled working-class, had lived in inner city slum areas, and many still regarded themselves as Irish in nationality (mainly from Ulster). There were sharp differences between the Scoto-Irish with not only Protestant society, but also with old-style Scots Catholicism. Still concentrated in the Highlands and Islands and North-East, these indigenous Catholics (with their post-Reformation concern to keep a low profile) had also joined the economic migration to the industrial heartlands of Scotland in the nineteenth century, adding to an emerging heterogeneity in the Scots Catholic community.[4] Although this group was small in number compared with the growing Scoto-Irish community, clerical control remained firmly with the indigenous Scots Catholics. Bishops in the new industrial areas continued to come from the North-East and Highlands, in the nineteenth, and well into the twentieth century. In 1864 a number of Irish priests petitioned Rome for an Irish bishop in Glasgow, but leading Catholic historian McCaffrey concluded that 'despite

Pope John XXIII and Archbishop Donald Campbell
At an audience with the Pope, Donald Campbell, Archbishop of Glasgow, obtained a blessing for the work of building a new college at Cardross.
Archdiocese of Glasgow

overwhelming superiority in numbers it [the Scottish Catholic Church] never became an entirely "Irish" church' and remained 'firmly in Scottish hands' for most of the nineteenth and twentieth century. Archbishop Donald Campbell, Glasgow's postwar leader, was himself a Gaelic speaker from Inverness-shire.[5] A notable exception was the high-profile English aristocrat Charles Peter Eyre, Archbishop of Glasgow from 1878 to 1902, who, as we will see, impacted significantly on the late nineteenth century Catholic architecture of Glasgow.

Especially after 1945, all these stereotypes of the Scoto-Irish community were overturned. Although Scotland had never experienced religious based housing segregation on a large scale, the massive programme of municipal housing schemes, fed by decanting the populations of razed slums, scattered the old communities and left many Catholics with new homes and new (often Protestant) neighbours. The growth in state social bureaucracy and state education, including publicly sponsored Catholic schools (under the provisions of Section 18 of the 1918 Education Act), encouraged the emergence of a new Catholic middle class in and around Glasgow. The 1918 Act was the culmination of a Catholic 'educational crusade' begun after the passing of the 1872 Education Act, which introduced universal primary schooling to Scotland. Scottish Catholics continued, on religious grounds, to maintain their own schools, but received some government grants and paid rates for the newly formed school boards. Catholics used their voting powers to ensure representation on the boards.[6] Twentieth century state-sponsored Catholic education brought the community 'into the life of the nation', and played a crucial role in developing a modern identity for Scottish Catholics. Catholic educational provision became a 'constitutional symbol' for the Catholic community.[7] The general effect of all these broader social factors was to further integrate Roman Catholics, in both the West and East, into Scottish postwar society, and to consolidate their status. A new and more complex 'multi-dimensional identity' was further developing.[8]

This new status of the Catholic community was reflected in a postwar reorganisation of the Archdiocese of Glasgow. In 1947, it became an ecclesiastical province (a grouping of dioceses under the supervision of a metropolitan archbishop), alongside the metropolitan Archdiocese of St Andrews and Edinburgh. The new province was divided into two suffragan sees (the Diocese of Motherwell and the Diocese of Paisley), as well as the Archdiocese of Glasgow proper, whose own territory was now confined to the city and to the county of Dumbarton. This measure, first proposed at the restoration of the Church hierarchy in 1878, was brought into effect by the Apostolic Constitution Maxime Interest.[9] Glasgow, previously the largest archdiocese in Scotland or England, was at once reinforced in status within the hierarchy of the Catholic Church, and cut in geographical size to cope with rising numbers. In 1948, even after the administrative changes, Glasgow Archdiocese was left with a Catholic population of almost 300,000, 298 priests and 58 parishes. The financial situation of the Archdiocese seemed to be highly favourable.

But the Church was at the same time faced with the urgent challenge of the need to relocate and redistribute parishes. Between 1951 and 1977, the population of

Cardinal Gray visiting St Patrick's School, Kilsyth, 1960s
Gray was Archbishop of St Andrews and Edinburgh prior to being made Cardinal. He was indirectly involved with Gillespie, Kidd & Coia through the new churches in his diocese.

eight inner city Catholic parishes in Glasgow collapsed, from 69,000 to 13,000.[10] In response, the Archdiocese mounted an ambitious church building programme in new housing schemes during the years 1945–65. It is estimated that 41 new parishes and churches were established in Archbishop Campbell's time, and thirteen churches were built in existing parishes (some to replace war losses). Temporary church measures and planning occupied the late 1940s, restrained by building restrictions. The bulk of the new churches in the Glasgow area were designed and built during the 1950s, especially from 1953 onwards. The key architect for the Archdiocese in the 1950s was the prolific Thomas Cordiner, and to a lesser extent Alexander McAnally, Reginald Fairlie & Partners, and Gillespie, Kidd & Coia – the last being commissioned periodically from about 1954 onwards. By the early 1960s, as we will see shortly, Gillespie, Kidd & Coia (GKC) had again become the Archdiocese's preferred architects – returning to their interwar status. Cordiner, and at a later stage GKC, also developed a significant niche in the growing Catholic secondary school sector in the late 1950s and 1960s.

On the whole, the new parishes were smaller than the traditional ones had been. Such a concentrated programme had not been witnessed since the construction boom around Glasgow during the mid nineteenth century influx of Irish immigrants. The fairly static location of the Catholic population between the wars (12% of the Scottish population by 1931) had allowed the existing churches and large parishes to cope, but now all this had to change.[11] In the early postwar years high birth rates (and to a lesser extent the arrival of a large number of Polish soldiers who had escaped to fight with the allies), contributed to the early 1960s national population peak of 15%. The 1950s saw a

Housing in Abronhill, Cumbernauld, by Wheeler & Sproson, c1970
The relocation of large portions of Glasgow's Catholic population to New Towns such as Cumbernauld led to new schools, parishes and churches for Catholic communities. HES SC767336

marked increase in economic immigration from Ireland to Europe, and England witnessed further immigration in the 1960s – which led to a Catholic church building boom there in the 1960s.[12] Irish immigration to Scotland in the 1950s consisted mainly of Irish Protestants from Ulster.[13] In postwar Scotland, it was the geographical shift and spread of Scottish Catholics (alongside their population growth and increased adherence) that impacted most on church building. The postwar New Towns had a significant impact on the developing Scottish Catholic community, as did the spread and growth of Catholic communities into small towns, particularly in the east of Scotland. Cumbernauld New Town, for example, estimated in 1957 that it would have a Catholic population of 12,000–13,000, and larger houses were designed to accommodate larger families – integration was seen as essential for the new community.[14] Modern Scottish Catholics in the 1960s and 1970s, some have argued, were abandoning interwar 'insularity' and 'leaving the ghetto behind'.[15]

To whom the credit should be given for the adventurous building drive in Glasgow is difficult to establish. On balance, it appears that the key driving force was not Archbishop Campbell but Bishop James Ward, appointed to the powerful administrative positions of Chancellor in 1947, and Vicar General in 1948. While Ward was strongly conservative in his religious views, he showed great enterprise and vigour in the quantitative push to create new parishes and religious houses. His obituary in 1974 made clear his linchpin role, as well as the status of Cardross as the culmination of the building drive. It recorded, for example, that for each of 62 new parishes he had to attend meetings, and take part in long discussions and negotiations. Maps had to be studied, the areas visited frequently, sites for the churches inspected, and reports made to the Archbishop. The building of new churches (totalling 70) involved even more work – 'Architects' plans had to be scrutinised, alterations suggested, regular visits made to the sites, which were often very difficult of access, and advice given to the priests entrusted with the projects.'[16] We will see shortly that these central controls were combined with a high degree of autonomy at parish level.

As Chancellor, Ward was also responsible for the financing of the building programme. His ability to juggle the finances of the diocese, borrowing from wealthy established parishes to fund the new churches, was admired: 'On at least two occasions there had to be a severe cut in the building programme, and imposing them brought many worries and anxieties. He tackled the problem calmly, but behind the mask of calm his mind was busy devising appeals to be made casually to priests for a further loan, or a timely hint of the need for increasing collection.'[17] This dynamic policy contained elements of future difficulties. The gradual shift from cross-subsidy from wealthy parishes to bank borrowing, as a means of financing the foundation of new parishes, gradually burdened the diocese with rising debt during the years of Archbishop Scanlan (1964–74); the financial issue became a crisis in the mid 1980s.

Ward's control over the church building programme continued through the early 1960s, providing continuity during an interregnum between archbishops. Following the death of Campbell while on a pilgrimage to Lourdes in July 1963, Ward became Vicar Capitular as a temporary measure, until the appointment of James Donald Scanlan as the new Archbishop in 1964. The general running of the Archdiocese appears to have changed little with the new head. Despite coolness between Scanlan and Ward, whom the former saw as Campbell's protégé, in relation to most administrative decisions 'Bishop Ward's judgement was accepted.'[18] Ward's obituary continued that 'over the years, the Bishop built up an invaluable store of experience and knowledge in church building … It was a source of great joy to him that he was privileged to play a great part in the building of the new St Peter's College, Cardross.' But, although Cardross was in many ways the culmination of the building drive, Ward's push to establish the new parishes inevitably took priority over, and delayed, the building of the new seminary.

Catholic Church Renewal in Rome and Scotland

The evidence thus suggests that Ward, with the authority of Campbell and Scanlan, was the key decision-maker in the adventurous church building programme. All these three men were traditional in their theology and their general approach to Church affairs, yet they authorised the building of strikingly modern churches in the 1960s and of the even more ambitious Cardross project. Were these innovative designs driven by liturgical or by architectural imperatives? Here, it is necessary to take a brief look at the radical twentieth century reforms within the Catholic Church, in particular the momentous Second Vatican Council (October 1962–December 1965), and consider how the Archdiocese of Glasgow and its traditionally minded leaders dealt with the resulting changes – bearing in mind, all the time, that the eventual design for Cardross had been proposed as early as 1961. The roots of the liturgical changes which culminated in 'Vatican II' lay in the early twentieth century agitation of Catholic intellectuals across Europe. Their attempts to reconcile their faith with modern rationality provoked Pope Pius X to condemn their efforts as heretical; in 1909 the Oath Against Modernism was imposed upon priests. Between the two wars, Catholicism lived under the impact of both the Modernist crisis, and of new movements within the Church: liturgical, social action, lay and theological. All of these, in their own way, questioned the established hierarchy and nature of the Roman Catholic Church, acting as forerunners of the reforms of the Second Vatican Council, following which they were given official approval. The individual European theologians who were mainly responsible for this progressive thought were Karl Rahner, Yves Congar, Edward Schillebeeckx and Hans Kung.

Eventually, the Second Vatican Council was convoked on 25 December 1961 by Pope John XXIII. Unlike many previous councils, Vatican II was not called to combat heresy or to deal with some serious threat to the unity of the Church. The Pope, in his opening address, explained that the Council's goal was to eradicate the seeds of discord and to promote peace and unity of all humankind. His desire was then to 'open the windows of the Church, and let the breath of the Holy Spirit blow through it'.[19] Sixteen documents, of varying authority, were promulgated by the Council. Three had major liturgical implications: the Dogmatic Constitution on the Church (1964); Pastoral Constitution on the Church in the Modern World (1965); and the Constitution on the Sacred Liturgy (1963). The first, the Dogmatic Constitution, reconsiders the whole premise of the existing Church, and argues that the Church is the 'whole People of God', in whose service the hierarchy is placed. The laity are therefore full participants. The second pronounces that the Church must be a fully integrated part of the world; and the Constitution on the Sacred Liturgy questions the intelligibility of the existing formal celebration of the Church. If the Church is the whole People of God, everyone must be encouraged to participate actively in the celebration of the Eucharist and the other sacraments. Radical liturgical changes ensued, of which the abandonment of Latin as the language of the sacraments and the reversal of the position of the priest (to face the congregation) were only the most obvious.[20]

How were these drastic changes received by the hierarchy of the Archdiocese in Glasgow, by the parish priests, and by the Catholic community at large? On the whole, the climate in the Scottish Church during the decades of mounting reformist pressure was one of conservatism, tempered with an openness to gradual reform. This was hardly an unusual stance in international terms: it would be misleading and anachronistic to paint a picture of backward Scotland and progressive Europe, although clearly debate in a country where the Church enjoyed minority status would differ in character from that in a predominantly Catholic country on the Continent. Resistance to reform was widespread both on the Continent and across the English-speaking world, while not even the liturgical innovators of earlier years could have foreseen the extent of the post-1965 changes in the Church's liturgy.[21]

In Scotland, these conflicts took a less extreme form, with steady change beneath an apparently rigid structure at the top. The Scottish bishops, including Ward, contributed little to the debates of the Second Vatican Council. Yet afterwards, despite obstruction by some clerics, the hierarchy implemented its reforms relatively painlessly – especially after Thomas Winning became auxiliary bishop to Scanlan in 1971 and succeeded as Archbishop in 1974, bringing a trenchant social vision to bear on his tasks.[22] The period saw a steady growth of avant-garde critiques: by the 1960s, some prominent priests, such as John Fitzsimmons, James Foley and Columba Ryan, supported reform, as did many within the growing Catholic middle class. Among a number of groups of lay reformists, two in particular, the Newman Association, and the Scottish Catholic Renewal Movement (SCRM), were especially prominent. The Newman Association, consisting of university graduates, was founded in England in 1942, and had groups in Aberdeen, Edinburgh and Dundee as well as in Glasgow. Originally set up 'to promote the knowledge and application of Christian principles as taught by the Catholic Church', in the 1950s it became a pressure group for change. After a split in 1963, it began to agitate for adoption of Vatican II principles in Scotland, and formed a Scottish council.[23] However, it remained a relatively small grouping of the intelligentsia, whose activities did not impinge on the majority of the laity. SCRM (originally the Scottish Lay Action Movement, and renamed in 1969) posed a greater threat to the traditionalist clergy: from 1968 onwards it organised large ecumenical meetings and debates, and invited leading Continental theologians to Glasgow, including Kung, Rahner and Schillebeeckx. Although some liberal Catholic intellectuals in the 1960s criticised the Scottish 'faithful' for their passivity, in fact among most Catholics the 1940s and 1950s had already seen many quiet changes: for example, a gradual relaxation in practices such as the requirements of fasting and abstinence before Communion. Yet, historian McCaffrey concluded that the main liturgical reforms of the vernacular Mass celebrated facing the people were 'patchily implemented', and some services were still in Latin in the late 1960s.[24]

Monsignor James Ward VG Bishop of Sita, 1960
Strongly conservative in his religious views, Ward was the administrative driving force behind the Catholic church building programme of the 1950s and 1960s.
Archdiocese of Glasgow

On the whole, theologically led reform within the Scottish Catholic Church, especially in the West, was a rather gradual process which achieved significant results only after the mid 1960s – too late to have influenced the reformist architectural tendencies of the 1950s and 1960s. By 1963, Gillespie, Kidd & Coia had already been designing and building churches with radically refashioned, centralised plan-forms for seven years.

The Training of Priests

The generally hierarchical and conservative values of the pre-Vatican II era also applied to the aspect of Church policy most specifically relevant to the Cardross project: the training of priests. Here, too, Scotland was not unusual in international terms. Ever since 1563, the training of Catholic priests had followed the directives of the Council of Trent. These counter-Reformation tenets had, over the centuries, developed into rigid rules, and seminaries had become isolated from the outside world, strongholds of traditional values. By the 1950s, there were voices of dissent against those values within Scotland, but opposition was not yet widespread.

A religious tradition more specific to Scotland was the old West–East tension (in some respects related to the differences between 'Irish' and 'Scots' Catholicism), a tension which, although much abated in the mid twentieth century, still inhibited any idea of a single national seminary. Archbishop Campbell's eventual decision, in 1959, to proceed with the new Cardross project was in many ways an expression of confidence in the West in a future of continuing Church expansion, within generally traditional religious and social structures. Despite an architectural form which in some respects was bold and innovative, the new seminary was highly traditional in its conception as a self-contained retreat; Campbell had argued at the Fifth Synod of Glasgow in 1949 that 'the archdiocese must have and will have a seminary in keeping with its dignity and traditions'.[25] Chapter 4 will discuss in greater detail the Church's possible motives for the building of the new seminary, and for its architectural form.

Almost immediately, events would begin to undermine the confidence of the 1950s. The number of student priests, after reaching a peak in 1959–60, would begin an inexorable decline in the face of the social, cultural and economic changes of the 1960s. And following the Second Vatican Council, a new Decree on Priestly Formation would begin to enforce the new ideals of an outward-looking Church. The consequences of those developments for the success of the reconstructed Cardross Seminary would be far reaching.

Chapter 2
Scottish Modern Architecture

Postwar Catholicism of the West of Scotland combined traditional theological outlook and a readiness to meet the challenge of demographic change through a large building programme. This programme concentrated at first on new parish churches, but culminated in the ambitious seminary project at Cardross. Within the organisation of these building schemes, there were highly centralised elements – notably, the coordinating role of Bishop Ward. But there was also considerable potential autonomy on the part of individual parish priests in organising and financing their own church projects.

It will be seen that the implications of this for the course of Catholic religious architecture were indirect. Owing to the inherent power of tradition as a motivating force within religion, the pressure for the building of large and prestigious new churches would hardly, in itself, encourage architectural innovation, or the adoption of Modern rather than Traditional styles. The important factor in the spread of a Modern and liturgically progressive Catholic architecture was not active Church encouragement, but the permissive effect of the relative autonomy of individual church projects. This could be exploited by a determined Modern architectural practice. On the basis of a longstanding and successful relationship with both the Archdiocese and individual priests, the firm of Gillespie, Kidd & Coia was able to evolve, and build on a large scale, new design concepts. But the conception of the Cardross project as a traditional 'closed' institution conflicted with some of these new, open-ended social-architectural Modernist concepts.

Traditionalism – The Beginnings of Modern Architecture in Scotland

The new religious and secular architectural trends formed part of the Modern Movement, which established itself in Scotland gradually and, by comparison with the Continent, somewhat late, in the years around the Second World War.

Proposal for St Mary's Cathedral, Edinburgh
Alexander D Bell's drawing (1966) for T Harley Haddow and Partners' proposed St Mary's Catholic Cathedral on the planned new inner ring road (unexecuted).
Harley Haddow Ltd (consulting engineers since 1950)

The Modern Movement claimed to have achieved a far closer integration with the modern world than had any of the previous phases of architecture. It celebrated the wider cultural trends towards a disciplined or collective society which would reject nineteenth century laissez-faire ideas. Where previous architectural phases had tried to express the new building types and techniques of industrial, urban society through the recipes of historic-based styles, Modern architecture rejected nineteenth century society and its architecture and instead put forward more abstract forms and varied ideas. Such ideas ranged from a completely individualistic freedom of form, to a complete acceptance of external social constraints. The main social ideal of Modern designers, community, was based on the idea that collective identity could be created by the design of new buildings. Different variants of community applied to religious and secular buildings.

Some of these ideas had already emerged in the architectural movements that immediately preceded the establishment of the Modern Movement in Scotland. These used broadly historic forms, but in a free manner not conforming to precise styles. Among these movements, there was a marked architectural division between the West and the East of Scotland. In the East, the movement of Traditionalism, using forms broadly based on the Scottish Renaissance, called for a community which could be based on the whole nation and its traditions, and opposed to cosmopolitan Continental Modernity. Leslie Grahame Thomson (later McDougall), a leading figure of interwar Traditionalism, and prominent Protestant church architect, condemned 'rabbit-hutch' flat roofed Continental Modern design as 'sheer bunkum … an international mess of pottage'.[1]

St Molios' Church, Isle of Arran
J J Burnet's design for St Molios' (1886) references traditional castle forms.
HES SC1167896

Protestant church, Canna
Peter MacGregor Chalmers' island church (1912–14) had a clean, unadorned design employing a single volume space. HES SC1499331

Tradition and Modernity in Church Design

Traditionalist church architecture, whether Catholic or Protestant, tried above all to be 'national', adopting simplified, massive forms, often loosely Romanesque and Scots Renaissance in character.[2] Scotland's pre-Reformation medieval Gothic heritage was evoked, but nineteenth century revived ecclesiastical Gothic was, on the whole, avoided. It was a generation of turn-of-the-century architects, most notably the Glasgow-based Peter MacGregor Chalmers, who introduced a scholarly revival of Romanesque and Celtic church design for the Church of Scotland.[3] The modest Church of Scotland, Canna (built 1912–14), illustrated his interest in the pre-Gothic with its simple *cella* (small single space) and Irish type pencil-shaped tower – also employed at St Leonard's Parish Church, Dunfermline (1903–4). The Traditionalist preoccupation with a sober 'simplicity' and evocation of national qualities was most dominant among architects in the East and Highlands of Scotland. Within Catholic architecture, this impulse may have been bound up with a desire to evoke or perpetuate the Scottish Catholic tradition (ever since the post-1560 proscriptions) of simple or modest church exteriors.

Reginald Fairlie was the most prominent and prolific Catholic architect of the early twentieth century. His family were of 'strong Roman Catholic old gentry background' (originally from Ayrshire) and his Scots Catholic connections formed the 'bedrock' of his practice.[4] His key works demonstrated a remarkable knowledge of medieval and Scottish Renaissance architecture. These included Our Lady of the Assumption and St Meddan, Troon (1909), laden with historical allusion with its Holy Rude Stirling-style semi-polygonal apse and raised crow stepped choir, and the Immaculate Conception Church, Fort William (1933–4), with Iona Abbey-inspired capital details. Fairlie's rubble tower-house steeples evoke Scotland's secular castellated heritage: in the 1880s J J Burnet had adopted this castle form in his church designs, for example at St Molios', Arran (1886). Fairlie's modest, harled Our Lady Star of the Sea, Tayport (1939), referenced seventeenth and eighteenth century octagonal based towers, as found at the nearby Fife parish churches of Leuchars and Elie. Fairlie stayed faithful to this scholarly Traditionalist style throughout his career.[5] Stylistic continuity is perhaps best seen with his work at the Abbey Church of Fort

Church of Our Lady Star of the Sea, Tayport
Reginald Fairlie's Our Lady Star of the Sea (1939), evoked seventeenth and eighteenth century forms with its modest harled exterior and octagonal tower.
HES SC386335

St Mahew's Chapel
While Ian G Lindsay's restoration was underway at this fifteenth century chapel, plans were already being considered for the new St Peter's College two miles away. HES SC1540989

Augustus in the Highlands, carried out in two main phases over a 40 year period. Only the foundations of Pugin & Pugin's 1890s Gothic scheme had been built, and in 1914–17 Fairlie designed and built on the foundations a Romanesque inspired choir and tower, and in 1949–56, a high nave in a more stripped neo-Romanesque style. In 1963 Charles Gray added a gabled west narthex (porch). A small inter-connected grouping of Catholic activists, interested in church design and scholarship, emerged in the interwar and early postwar years around Fairlie. Among these were architects Archibald Macpherson and Charles Gray (the latter in partnership from 1948 as Reginald Fairlie & Partners), Catholic convert writer George Scott-Moncrieff, and sculptor Hew Lorimer. In 1959 architect and critic Patrick Nuttgens compiled a monograph on Fairlie, and Scott-Moncrieff and Lorimer contributed memoirs (Nuttgens himself was later to narrate a BBC television programme on the new St Peter's College in 1966).[6]

Traditionalist church architecture was also bound up with the beginnings of architectural preservation, especially in the work of the architect Ian G Lindsay (also acquainted with Fairlie), whose interest in historic churches would eventually lead to the publication of *The Scottish Parish Kirk* in 1960, and would inspire Traditionalist postwar designs for the Church of Scotland. Lindsay cleverly straddled both Catholic and Protestant worlds, and was an Episcopalian himself. At St Finnan's Roman Catholic Church, Invergarry (1938), Lindsay collaborated with Peter F Anson, a convert and prominent Catholic historian, to design a simple, harled, white-washed building 'in the traditional eighteenth century style of Scottish architecture'.[7] Whereas Lindsay looked back to the eighteenth century for aesthetic effect, Anson was interested in this period for historical and political reasons. Scottish studies in Catholicism had, in the late thirties, increased under the influence of the pioneer Fathers Stevenson, Pollen and Forbes Leith. Studies in religious architecture were undertaken by Anson, the Catholic medieval historian Father David McRoberts, and writer George Scott-Moncrieff.[8] These individuals formed part of a new intellectual base of historians and clergy in the 1950s, which led to, among other things, the first publication of the Catholic journal *Innes Review*.[9] Lindsay was again involved with the Catholic

Church in the scheme to restore the fifteenth century chapel, St Mahew at Kilmahew, Cardross, in 1953 – a scheme in which McRoberts played a prominent role. Preservationists had become a prominent grouping within Traditionalism in the 1930s with the formation of the National Trust in 1931, and the founding of the Saltire Society in 1936. Although the movement's initial leader was the (Catholic) 4th Marquess of Bute, after 1945 Lindsay would eventually become the dominant figure. St Mahew's was opened by Archbishop Campbell in May 1955, and was hailed as 'an act of pietas for all who shared in it'.[10] Father McRoberts was an important figure in the early development of the project for the new St Peter's College at Cardross which was later built only a few miles from St Mahew's Chapel. At the same time as his work on the restoration of the chapel in 1953, he was also drawing up his own preferred architectural proposals for the new building at St Peter's College, which involved a kind of conservation scheme, in the form of the re-use and extension of the nineteenth century Kilmahew House.

In the early postwar years, these pre-war historicist-inspired white harled forms were simply adopted and developed along more modern lines by an older generation of church architects. Lindsay's work continued as before: at Colinton Mains Church, Edinburgh (1954), he adopted, in plan and style, the white harled traditional Caithness and Sutherland seventeenth century church types. The source for the high square tower here was that at Dunnet Parish Church, Caithness, with its diminutive lights, and the source for the long thin nave windows was perhaps Strathnaver Church, Sutherland (1774). Utilitarian versions of the same theme included Hall Kirk, Livingston (1949–50). Traditionalist Leslie Grahame Thomson abandoned the decorative Lorimer-inspired style of his Reid Memorial Church, Edinburgh (1929), for a highly personalised white harled church-type with round-arch detailing and red tiled or copper roofs, as at Longstone Parish Church, Edinburgh (1951), and Christ's Church, Dunollie, Oban, Argyll (1954–7). He willingly

St Finnan's Church, Invergarry
Lindsay's St Finnan's (1938) was a white harled building 'in the traditional eighteenth century style of Scottish architecture'. HES SC979668

St Francis Xavier, Falkirk
Fairlie & Partners' monumental classicism at St Francis (1958–61) harked back to Fairlie's early 1930s design for the National Library of Scotland.
HES SC1541815 Shillabeer Collection

returned to a more sombre stone Traditionalism when given the opportunity, as at the round-arched Moncur Memorial Church, Isle of Stronsay, Orkney (1945, executed c1948–53).[11] Similarly, Reginald Fairlie & Partners (now under C Gray and C R Conlon) adopted its own postwar white harled vernacular for the Archdiocese of Glasgow at St Laurence, Drumchapel (1954–57), and St Augustine's, Milton, Glasgow (1954), but these lacked the antiquarian instinct of Fairlie's work. The historicist 'hangover' in church design in the 1940s and early postwar years proved particularly resilient in the east. Some churches were almost indistinguishable from the turn-of-century revivals, such as J F Matthew's ecumenical Lorimer-inspired rubble Robin Chapel at the Thistle Foundation, Edinburgh (1949–52), and H O Tarbolton's St Salvador Episcopal Church, Edinburgh (1939–42), whose bold entrance tower adopts a traditional seventeenth century steeple form, such as that found in Rutherglen, Glasgow.[12] In the Catholic Church the power of tradition remained strong, as witnessed in

St Andrew's Parish Church, Edinburgh
St Andrew's (1954–8), designed by Basil Spence, provided a Modern vernacular model for the Church of Scotland. HES SC1030849

the monumental stripped stone classicism of St Francis Xavier, Falkirk, by Reginald Fairlie & Partners (1958–61), which harked back to Fairlie's earlier design for the National Library of Scotland, Edinburgh (from 1937).

Yet within this broad Traditionalist grouping, there were a number of innovative and individualistic modern designs which, it was argued at the time, might be adopted as models for the postwar era. The 1938 Empire Exhibition's Catholic Pavilion by Gillespie, Kidd & Coia (designed by Warnett Kennedy) was heralded in this way. White, roofless in part, with intersecting curved and rectangular forms, it sat on a rubble base, and was decorated with external mural paintings. In 1939, historian Peter F Anson argued that the pavilion 'may mark the beginning of a new epoch in Scottish Church architecture'.[13] Similarly, Basil Spence's unbuilt early 1950s design for SS Ninian,

Martin and John RC Church, Whithorn (commissioned by the Catholic Diocese of Galloway, but abandoned in 1954), adopted a harled curved chapel like the hull of a ship, said to be inspired by the legend of St Ninian first worshipping in a sea cave in the fifth century.[14] Similarly, Alan Reiach's modest Easthouses Church, Dalkeith (from 1953), provided a vernacular hall church precinct grouping with a rubble walled bell-tower.[15] And again Spence provided a postwar Modern vernacular model in the mid 1950s, this time for the Church of Scotland at St Andrew's, Clermiston View, Edinburgh (1954–8). Adopting a native rubble vernacular, it evoked a rural Scottish steading, but had a Scandinavian-influenced clarity within: it was set on a raised rubble podium accessed by a broad flight of steps. All these forms were adopted ad hoc in later 1960s Presbyterian designs, but Spence's Scottish church designs often sat outwith mainstream developments.[16] In his early 1960s article 'Eleven New Churches in Edinburgh' historian and critic Colin McWilliam celebrated the 'living tradition' found in these new designs (which included

Colinton Mains, Easthouses, Longstone and St Andrew's). In these churches, according to McWilliam 'direct tradition … is so skillfully handled that there is no possible hint of archaism'.[17]

Monumental Modernity – Catholic Church design in the West of Scotland

Whereas a Traditionalist orientation was dominant among architects in the East and Highlands of Scotland, a very different set of values prevailed among those of Glasgow and the West. There, ever since the pioneering late nineteenth century efforts of J J Burnet and J A Campbell, a cosmopolitan Beaux-Arts outlook of rationalised modernity had prevailed. This showed a logical, un-sentimental concern to deal with the essential purpose and structure of a building, and to clad those requirements in simplified, historically based forms, usually of a classical kind. At the same time as this (the years of mass Irish immigration), religious architecture in the West had seen the start of a type of church architecture very different from the demure Scottish Catholic tradition beloved of the Eastern Traditionalists, and more like the Continental Gesù tradition of roomy interiors and monumental facades.

The first expression of this new and more assertive Catholic church architecture in and around Glasgow was not directly connected with the wider Beaux-Arts developments. This was the series of standardised, hall-like, red sandstone Gothic churches built across the West by the English architects Pugin & Pugin. Examples in Glasgow included St Francis (rebuilt 1878–95), St Patrick (1898), and St Alphonsus (1905). The Archbishop of Glasgow, Charles Peter Eyre (1878–1902), was Pugin & Pugin's chief patron. Eyre was English but had been in Scotland from the late 1860s. Already an Archbishop, he strove to bring the Scottish Church into line with the mainstream English-speaking Roman Catholic world (especially England and Wales). This culminated in the re-establishment of the Church hierarchy in 1878 (see Chapter 1).[18] From the early 1870s Pugin & Pugin successfully imported their own neo-Gothic rock-faced rubble church designs.[19] Jack Coia later explained that in his 1930s designs 'I was anxious to break with the grey-stone neo-Gothic' which typified Glasgow's turn-of-the-century Catholic architecture.[20]

St Anne's, Dennistoun, Glasgow
GKC's St Anne's (1931) was a model example of interwar red-brick Italianate church architecture in the West of Scotland. HES SC1370415

In the interwar years, this tendency of roomy interiors and monumental facades became more closely linked up with the Beaux-Arts tradition of rationalist design, in the form of a growing movement of neo-Romanesque, Italianate, and to a lesser extent neo-Byzantine, churches with Latin cross or basilican plans and hall-like interiors whose volume was enhanced by innovative structural design and art. At the turn of the century, P M Chalmers had built several neo-Romanesque designs for the Protestant churches in Glasgow and the West. Alongside traditional Scottish sources he introduced Continental detailing at his stone-built St Margaret's Episcopal Church, Newlands, Glasgow (1908–10), and a massive gable entrance tower at St Nicholas, Prestwick (1908). The neo-Byzantine played a more limited role in Traditionalist Scottish architecture. An important early historicist model was Robert Rowand Anderson's fittingly named St Sophia's RC, Galston, Ayrshire (1884–6). Greek-cross in plan, and built of bright pink and red brick, it had few direct imitators among Scottish architects. H F Kerr returned to rubble faced stone at Dalziel North U F Church, Motherwell (1915), where fifth and sixth century Byzantine sources dominate, in particular Hagia Sophia in Constantinople

St Ninian's Church, Gretna
The substantial neo-Byzantine St Ninian's (1917–18), by C E Simmons, offered an appealing model for interwar Modernists.
HES SC1230863

(as in the case of Galston). But English architect C E Simmons' design for St Ninian RC Gretna (1917–18) provided a more appealing neo-Byzantine model for interwar Modernists. Robert Lorimer heaped praise on the cruciform-plan brown-brick church, with its English Arts & Crafts qualities, arguing that 'if a man has a feeling for rhythm and proportion and fitness, and is able to handle his materials, quite excellent results can be obtained by the knowing use of ordinary brick and plain white plaster'.[21] For the Catholic Church in England it was the prestigious neo-Byzantine polychrome-brick Westminster Cathedral, London, by England's leading nineteenth century Catholic architect John Francis Bentley (from 1895) which provided an exceptionally influential model for its church architects well into the 1950s.[22]

Scotland's interwar Catholic Italianate and neo-Romanesque inspired churches combined a general modernity, in their up-to-date structure and materials, with a traditional hierarchy of decoration and stateliness: the front facade and the sanctuary were the most imposing and ornate parts, just as they had been before the war. These churches were often now built of facing red brick. Significantly cheaper than traditional stone, it was a material favoured by Beaux-Arts Glasgow designers (an early example being J J Burnet's St Philip's Episcopal Church, Edinburgh, 1908). Also in the east, Catholic architect Archibald Macpherson had been using brick for his hybrid early Christian and Gothic inspired historicist St Matthew's, Rosewell (1925–6), and Our Lady and St Ninian's, Bannockburn (1927).

The foremost exponent of this interwar trend in the West was Gillespie, Kidd & Coia. Coia's first church, St Anne's, Dennistoun, Glasgow (1931), was typical of the new red-brick type in its Latin cross plan, and

Nuffield Transplantation Unit, Edinburgh
Nuffield Transplantation Unit (1965–8), designed by Peter Womersley, reflected the more individualistic and poetic forms of Late Modernism. **RIAS, licensor Scran**

impact of Modern architecture was fully felt in Scottish religious and secular building, bringing in its train new Continental concepts of liturgy as well as more general ideals of design for community.

The first effects of Modern architecture, with its emphasis on design for defined social needs and standards, had naturally been in social housing and planning, in the 1940s and 1950s. A new generation of state-employed designers was led by Robert H Matthew. He, often working in collaboration with Alan Reiach, pushed through a series of influential guidelines and projects of Modern community-building in Scotland, including the Westwood Report 'Planning our New Homes', 1944, the Clyde Valley Plan (with Patrick Abercrombie, 1946/9), the planning of East Kilbride

New Town (from 1947)and the first of the Gorbals redevelopment schemes using tower blocks (Area B, from 1958). All of these adhered to the mainstream International Modern faith in the possibility of building new communities using assertively new and boldly geometrical shapes. These would be set in open space and greenery, and designed in accordance with scientifically determined standards – the concept of Functionalism. In general the picture was one of unprecedented and boldly unified forms, and of departure from tradition. Even Traditionalists such as Leslie Grahame MacDougall began to concede that 'the battle is won and modernism is accepted as the order of the day … structure, clean lines, new materials have all been allowed to have their say'.[27]

However, this Modern Movement optimism proved short lived. As early as the late 1950s, criticism started of its basic ideologies. International groups such as Team 10 argued that Functionalism was too rigid to sculpture (or triple round-arched windows), were simply continued, as seen at Immaculate Heart of Mary RC Church, Springburn (1950), St Mary's Chapel, Duntocher (1952–4) and St Thomas the Apostle RC Church, Riddrie (1954). Cordiner displayed an awareness of contemporary English 1950s red-brick Catholic design, and its technical innovations, perhaps best seen at his 'A'-framed Church of the Immaculate Conception, Maryhill, Glasgow (1955–6).[23] Triangular-fronted churches were scattered throughout Scotland in the 1950s including the early St Margaret's RC, Davidson's Mains, by P Whiston & McRobie (1950), St Teresa's RC, Dumfries, by John Sutherland (1956–8), and Park Parish Church, Ardrossan, by James Houston & Son (1958–9). Cordiner's most innovative Modernist work came in his social educational projects, such as Lourdes Secondary School, Glasgow (1951).

The grandeur and sumptuousness of these brick Catholic churches in the 1950s were highlighted by comparison with the very different policy pursued in the same years by the Church of Scotland in new parishes. Very often the latter's new churches were built as modest, dual-use 'hall churches' comprising a community hall with sanctuary at one end.[24] In response to new interwar housing schemes it raised funds (in the region of £180,000) for the creation of nearly 40 new parishes before (from the 1920s) and after the war. Similarly, the Scottish Episcopal Church formed a 'Home Mission Appeal' and built ten new churches in late 1920s: the postwar 'Home Mission Crusade' programme built another five.[25]

The Church of Scotland's twentieth century 'Home Mission', as it was called, was carried out by the National Church Extension committee (in the 1930s under the leadership of Very Rev. John White). It was centrally controlled, sites were chosen and financed from the national headquarters in Edinburgh, and the brief given to architects specified only costs, seating, stage, and the requirements of badminton. Unlike traditional congregations which had been established at grass roots level and grew towards independence, these new missions were settled by committee, and in time became self-governing. In the postwar period, a similar pattern was

Lanark County Buildings, Hamilton, constructed 1960–4
The office block and circular council chamber exemplified mainstream International Modernism in their juxtaposed geometrical forms. HES DP230701

Calderwood, East Kilbride
The emergence of the New Towns provided a new context for Modernist church architecture in Scotland. **The Scotsman Publications Ltd, licensor Scran**

adopted for New Towns such as Glenrothes and Cumbernauld, but now the renamed New Charge Development. The dual social-liturgical role of these modest hall churches of the 1950s, according to church architect Peter Whiston, had 'a baneful effect on modern church design', but reform came chiefly through the more explicitly Modernist New Town churches of the early 1960s.[26]

The Architectural Context of Cardross

These interwar, pre-Modern Movement developments in Scottish architecture set the main themes for the work of Gillespie, Kidd & Coia until the late 1940s. But the Cardross design of 1959–66 was conditioned by the phase which followed: the ascendancy of Modern architecture in Scotland, from the late 1940s to the late 1970s. It was in the late 1950s and 1960s that the

broad light centralised space, flanked by narrow arcades. St Anne's, although adopting neo-Byzantine interlace detailing, had an overall grand Italianate style, with broken pediment and massive consoles, perhaps inspired by Alberti's Santa Maria Novella, Florence (begun 1458). Here Coia was arguably referencing his own Italian heritage.

Gillespie, Kidd & Coia's interwar and postwar church designs will be examined in more detail, but a brief overview of church design (Catholic and Protestant) in the pre-Modern Movement 1950s, a period when the firm received only a small number of commissions from the Archdiocese of Glasgow, is required at this point. After the Second World War, the monumental red-brick architectural trend for Catholic church design continued, and remained dominant until the late 1950s. Many, still with Beaux-Arts overtones, adopted a more rigid geometry and bare aesthetic under obvious postwar cost restraints. This style became the main vehicle for the Glasgow Archdiocese's ambitious programme of new church building from the early 1950s. There emerged a number of rivals to Gillespie, Kidd & Coia, in quantitative output of commissions, including Thomas S Cordiner and Alexander McAnally, who adopted an eclectic mix of stripped neo-Romanesque with hints of Gothic. At St Teresa of Lisieux Church, Possilpark (1956–8), McAnally produced a massive red-brick Romanesque basilica with stylised stone detailing. But it was Cordiner who was the Archdiocese's preferred architect of the 1950s for churches and schools. At Christ the King Church, King's Park (1957–60), and St Margaret Mary's RC Church, Castlemilk (1959), he adopted gable end central towers, a standard Scottish feature from the seventeenth century onwards. Many of the interwar formulaic patterns such as triangular pedimented entrance fronts, big expanses of red brick enlivened with simple crosses or low-relief stone

St Teresa's, Possilpark, Glasgow
McAnally, along with Cordiner and GKC, was a significant architect in postwar Catholic church building. He worked on St Teresa's over the period 1956–8. **HES** SC441345

Church of the Immaculate Conception, Glasgow
Cordiner was the primary architect for the Scottish Catholic Church's schools and churches in the 1950s. The A-framed Church of the Immaculate Conception (1955–6) was perhaps his most innovative. **HES** SC440081

adequately reflect the complexities of postwar European society. Young Scottish critics joined these debates: John L Paterson described Functionalism as 'mechanistic' and 'logic carried to the brink of insanity'.[28] The result of these criticisms was to radically modify the idea of Modern architecture as a unified movement. Reflecting the growing divergences within the movement, some, as we will see, advocated greater concentration on the reflection of social complexity in design. Others argued for more individualistic or poetic form, echoing the postwar work of overseas architects such as Le Corbusier or Louis Kahn. The most trenchant Scottish advocate of this principle was Peter Womersley, in works such as Nuffield Transplantation Unit (1965–8) or the Bernat Klein Studio, Selkirk (1969–72). Others, such as Robert Matthew's younger design colleague John Richards, continued the search for rational concepts of modernity, but in a more restrained fashion, as at Stirling University (1966–73). By the early 1960s, with the onset of this Late Modernism, in Scotland as throughout Europe and America, there was no longer any single dominant theme. The optimistic totality of the original Modern Movement concept was now fragmented into different strands – the social, the rationalistic and the formal – which were combined in different ways within different building types or contexts.

The large and complex Cardross commission related to two of these elements within Late Modern architecture. The first was a tendency within secular design which advocated the building of multi-purpose groups based on new concepts of community. The second related directly to the new trends of expressive form and liturgical reformism in Late Modern religious architecture. Potentially, there was a conflict between the two: between the growing insistence on flexibility in secular architecture, and the continuing acceptance in religious architecture (following Corbusier and others) of the unified artistic statement.

Within Late Modern secular architecture, perhaps the most prominent trend in design from the late 1950s was a reaction away from International Modern patterns of closed, geometrical shapes – now criticised as crude or mechanistic – towards more complicated, less sharply differentiated patterns of homes and social buildings. The new ideals of complexity were clearly related to the projects of the Smithsons in England, as well as to lesser

Heron House, Glasgow
The concrete megastructure (1967–71) by Derek Stephenson and Partners relates skilfully to Alexander Thompson's St Vincent Street Church. HES SC724616

Cumbernauld Town Centre, c1967
Designed by Geoffrey Copcutt and built between 1963 and 1972 to serve a community largely displaced from Glasgow, the Centre was a multi-functional megastructure and was internationally acclaimed when completed. **HES** SC968209

known designs by Le Corbusier, such as the Roq et Rob project of 1948. For dwellings, low patterns were favoured, either uniformly carpet-like or more spine concentrated. For public buildings, the tall slab block was rejected in favour of a more variegated monumentality, often expressed in the form of a megastructure: a structure, pierced by communication arteries, which could flexibly accommodate all sorts of community functions. The established ideal of community was reformulated. New housing and community projects were no longer to be conceived in isolation, or in terms of a total break from the dense forms of old towns towards light and open space. Old was no longer necessarily bad.

The set-piece of this approach was Cumbernauld New Town (built from 1956), where low but dense housing areas were closely grouped around a massive and avant-garde Town Centre (built from 1963), whose design was described by Modern Movement historian Reyner Banham as 'the canonical megastructure'. The visionary architect of the Centre, Geoffrey Copcutt, produced a multi-function structure of transport, parking, shopping, offices and housing stacked on top of each other in open-ended fashion, with motorways and pedestrian access running through the heart of the structure. However, other architects of large, complex Late Modern community buildings, such as Gillespie, Kidd & Coia, did not follow the megastructural ideal of adaptability and flexibility.

Within religious architecture of the same period, there was no direct equivalent to Late Modern secular architecture's quest for 'complex community'. Instead, there was a continuing emphasis on the unified 'artistic statement'. This difference stemmed from the distinctive history of religious architecture in the twentieth century.

Because religious architecture, as a rule, depends for its force on the power of tradition rather than innovation, when innovation comes it often takes an extreme form. The early and mid twentieth century, in Continental European church architecture, was just such a time, in which rapid liturgical change had been expressed through more centralised plans, and unified, abstract forms. Especially famous were the Modern churches of France and Germany in the 1930s and 1940s: one of the key innovators had been Rudolf Schwarz, in centralised designs such as Corpus Christi Church at Aachen, 1930. Throughout this period, Modern church design in the Continent was a hot-bed of discussion and deliberation.[29]

The effects of these innovations were felt in Scottish architecture from the mid 1950s. In the case of Protestant churches, the break with the past was less abrupt, as centralised *Predigtkirche* (preaching-church) planning had been a prominent theme since the Reformation. The modest hall churches of the 1950s were rejected for more ambitious parochial centres within new housing areas and designs shaped by investigations of church functions. The architect Anthony Wheeler, at St Columba's Church, Glenrothes New Town (1960–3), designed a square plan, with separate ancillary buildings, following consultation with academic theologians including Professor James Whyte of St Andrews University.[30] At St Andrews in 1961, Whyte organised a conference by the New Churches Research Group (NCRG), an inter-denominational organisation dedicated to the establishment of a 'truly modern' rationalistic church architecture based on liturgical and social research by architects, theologians, historians and clergy. The group was opposed to 'new dramatic effects of religious expression', and instead favoured 'plain brick boxes with no tricks', influenced by the earlier work of Schwarz.[31] The central figures in the NCRG movement were architects Robert Maguire and Keith Murray, who both edited the influential magazine *Church Buildings Today* (later *Churchbuilding*) from 1961.[32]

Although the NCRG's main work was in England, its ideas had some effect within designs for the Kirk: for example, at Alan Reiach's Kildrum Parish Church, Cumbernauld (1960–2, with Stuart Renton), with its use of pine wood and plain brick, and its highly lit clarity

St Columba's Church, Glenrothes
Designed by Wheeler & Sproson (1960–3), this square-plan church was at the heart of the New Town. **Newsquest (Herald & Times), licensor Scran**

of form. Kildrum also featured a detached bell-tower: free-standing towers and campaniles, rejected in post-Reformation Scotland, now suddenly became fashionable again.[33] New churches (of all denominations) in the New Towns reinvigorated postwar Scottish church design. In 1956, Peter Whiston lamented 'If we examine dispassionately the many churches which have been built in Scotland since the war, except in a few cases, we cannot but be shocked at the appalling poverty of their design, atmosphere and quality.' New Town church design did much to answer these criticisms, and Gillespie, Kidd & Coia played a significant role. Cumbernauld New Town's Protestant churches, for example, were on the whole liturgically innovative. St Mungo's, Kildrum (1963–6, again by Reiach) had a dramatic single-volume square-plan interior. Even the

Kildrum Parish Church, Cumbernauld
Cumbernauld New Town was a hot-bed of innovative church design. Alan Reiach's Kildrum (1960–2) introduced a 'Scandinavian' Modernism to new Protestant architecture. **RIBA**

Kildrum Parish Church interior
HES SC446634

St Mungo's Parish Church, Cumbernauld
Reiach's bold square-plan church (1963–6) just north of Cumbernauld Town Centre. **HES** SC440084

smaller congregations within Cumbernauld initiated reform. Its first town church, Church of the Holy Name, Muirhead (1960–2), was designed by Cumbernauld's chief architect and planner Hugh Wilson – a small but ingenious Modernist buff-brick broad-planned church and hall complex set in an open grassy residential square. The Cumbernauld Free Church, Carbrain (1969–70), by John Davison, Russell Diplock Architects, provided a reformed single-volume space with rear full-width gallery, raised perimeter and a centrally placed bespoke five-piece communion table and benches.[34] The spread of ecumenicism in the mid 1960s led to the ecumenical experiment at Livingston New Town in 1965 where the Church of Scotland and the Scottish Episcopal Church shared St Columba (1965–6), by Graham Law of Law and Dunbar-Naismith, a new modest harled box with bell-tower.[35]

Within Catholic church architecture, the position was more complicated. The power of tradition was strong and remained so until the 1950s, but the gathering force of liturgical and architectural change on the Continent

Metropolitan Cathedral of Christ the King, Liverpool
Frederick Gibberd's competition-winning design of 1960 marked a turning point in the development of Modern church architecture in England and Wales. **RIBA**

would eventually overpower it and burst into Scotland, largely through revolutionary innovations in the work of Gillespie, Kidd & Coia in the later 1950s. Continental Catholic liturgical/architectural innovations focused on the most important act of the liturgy, the celebration of the Eucharist. The community of the church, the people, was the reason for a church's existence, and its design must above all celebrate that role. Internationally speaking, the liturgical movement in Catholic architecture had developed mainly in Germany, and later in France, between the two wars. German church design, through the pioneering work of Schwarz, was in the vanguard, while the debates in France were concerned with appropriateness of the modern idiom in religious worship, and with the use of non-Catholic artists in religious art. The church authorities in Rome also contributed to the debate: in 1925, the Feast of Christ the King was inaugurated by Pius XI, in which the centrality of the altar in the liturgy was emphasised by detaching it from the main body of the church. The Encyclical Mediator Dei, of 1947, a precursor of the Constitution on the Sacred Liturgy (1963) of the Second Vatican Council, focused the liturgical debate still further; and German Catholic theoreticians published, also in 1947, a report on the liturgical ordering of church buildings, which contributed to the findings of the Second Vatican Council.[36]

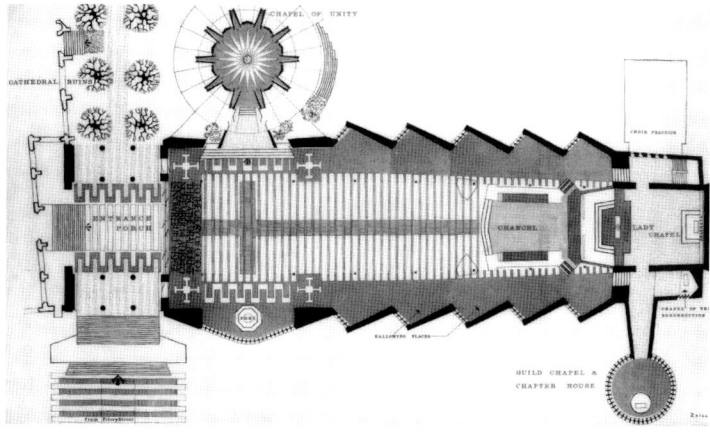

Plan of Coventry Cathedral
This drawing of the cathedral complex shows the new church sitting alongside the remains of the older cathedral. HES DP024932

Across Western Europe, the years between 1947 and 1963 broke the established polarisation between nave and sanctuary in favour of integrated plans. By the mid 1960s, with the official backing of the Second Vatican Council, 'the battle for the single-volume worship space had been won'.[37] As to the formal expression of these changes, a radically different path from Protestant developments was charted by Le Corbusier, who pointed to a more personalised, emotionalistic Modernism of massive yet free-flowing forms, and theatrically lit, shadowy interiors. At his Notre Dame du Haut, Ronchamp (1955), a new agenda of sculptural and poetic form, and individualistic artistic expression, was set out. At Perret's skyscraper-like St Joseph, Le Havre (1951–7), with its near-centralised plan beneath an 84m-high open tower, the effect was more classical, but on an enormous scale. Until the mid 1950s, Catholic church design in Scotland was less affected than in some Continental countries by the architectural implications of this movement for liturgical change; each national church enjoyed effective architectural autonomy in relation to Rome. Among Scottish architects, a significant step towards single-cell eucharistic-community design in a large new project was taken by Basil Spence in a design for the Anglican church: Coventry Cathedral, designed in 1951–4 and built in 1954–62. In a 1956 paper, Spence claimed that 'In the Anglican and Roman Catholic communions, the Altar is the pivot, the spark, the climax, it is the church … Architecture can serve this object: it has done so in the past with some magnificent results.'[38] But many elements of Spence's Coventry project were just as much Traditionalist as overtly Modern in any way. For the Catholic Church in England and Wales it was Frederick Gibberd's exuberantly 'Modern', single-volume Liverpool Cathedral design (1960–7) that marked its architectural turning point. Although pre-Vatican II in date, the cathedral was intended for worship 'in-the-round'. Unlike the West of Scotland's Catholic church building drive, England's peak church building took place in the 1960s, only slowing down in the early 1970s: it was estimated that 600 new Catholic churches were built in England and Wales in the 1960s. Its liturgical reforms, according to Catholic church historian Robert Proctor, developed in stages from the 1960s until the 1970s.[39]

Within Scotland itself, some Catholic alteration schemes pointed to the future – for example, Bishop Walsh's refitting of St Mary's Cathedral, Aberdeen, in the 1950s, with highly simplified fittings and repositioned altar designed to encourage the celebrant to face the congregation in line with Vatican II reform. However, the first consistent expression of these changes in new churches for Scottish Catholicism would come in the work of Gillespie, Kidd & Coia from the mid 1950s.

Coventry Cathedral
Following the destruction of Coventry Cathedral in the Second World War, Basil Spence won the competition to design the new Coventry Cathedral (1951–62)
HES SC1066473

Chapter 3
The Evolution of Gillespie, Kidd & Coia

The general development of Late Modern religious and secular architecture in Scotland was a constant background influence on the Cardross Seminary project. But the most immediate impetus behind the College's design – as well as on Scottish Modern religious architecture in general – stemmed from the firm that was responsible for it, Gillespie, Kidd & Coia. By the late 1950s, through an astute strategy of practice development, the firm had outclassed all other Scottish practices specialising in religious architecture, in its combination of Modern architectural innovativeness with a strong organisational and patronage base.

The firm of Gillespie, Kidd & Coia was established in 1927 when Giacomo Antonio (Jack) Coia (1898–1981) returned to the practice as joint partner with William A Kidd, following the death of John Gaff Gillespie (1870–1926). That partnership was in linear succession to the famous turn-of-the-century firm of Salmon & Son & Gillespie. Kidd himself died six months later in 1928, and Coia then became sole partner. Before that, from 1915, Coia had spent five years as an apprentice with the firm (known, at that time, as Gaff Gillespie & Kidd). During those years he had begun a seven-year course at the Glasgow School of Architecture. There he had acquired a thorough grounding in the Beaux-Arts principles of rationalist, programme-led classical design then ascendant in Glasgow. After obtaining his diploma in 1923, he had worked in the offices of Campbell and Hislop, and A N Paterson, and worked in London for Herbert A Welch and Hollis.

Coia returned home to Glasgow in 1927 at Kidd's request, and for family reasons.[1] Coia's first recorded study trip to his 'native' Italy was in 1923, and its architecture remained a lifelong inspiration.[2] Coia was born in Wolverhampton, England, the eldest of nine children to Italian émigré parents (his father came from a village outside Naples). The family 'continued moving north' and like many other Italian immigrants at the turn of the century, opened a cafe – the Coia cafe was in Glasgow's east end.[3] Italian immigrants

St Bride's Church, East Kilbride, by GKC
St Bride's strikingly Modernist interior also harked back to the firm's grand single-volume churches of the interwar era. **RIBA**

contributed to an emerging heterogeneity within Glasgow's Catholic community, and more recently historians have charted the development of this small community of businessmen (principally in the catering trade) in coastal and inland towns throughout Scotland: John McCaffrey concluded that 'the Italians in particular, with their individualistic business interests, shared little in the educational, economic and political aspirations of the Scoto-Irish in the central belt'.[4] Coia, for example, attended Glasgow's select boys Catholic secondary school, St Aloysius' College, then housed in an 1883–5 Renaissance palazzo type building, designed by the Edinburgh Catholic architect Archibald Macpherson.[5] The school was closely associated with nearby St Aloysius Church, Rose Street, designed and built in 1908–10 by one of the Archdiocese of Glasgow's favoured architects, the Belgian-born C J Menart.

Sixteenth century Italianate in style, the church had a reinforced domed concrete roof, almost bare in contrast with the ornate marble columned nave. According to historian Charles McKean 'it conjures up a vision of Italy for expatriates'.[6] Coia's first attendance at the school was recorded in October 1910, and he left in 1915. He returned to design his school's bronze war memorial in 1948, and his funeral was held at St Aloysius Church in August 1981.[7]

Although, in 1928, Coia's new, or renewed, practice seemed to him 'small and ever diminishing', it was in fact destined to thrive until the 1980s.[8] Over those six decades, Gillespie, Kidd & Coia underwent four main phases of development, of which the third stage coincided with the execution of the Cardross project. In this chapter, as a background to the particular story of Cardross, we trace the evolution of the practice over these four stages. From the mid 1950s the number of building commissions rose sharply, and only especially

Jack Coia beside his bust by sculptor Archibald Dawson (right), 1933
Coia, lead partner of Gillespie, Kidd & Coia from 1928 to 1976, was instrumental in developing the firm's strong relationship with the Scottish Catholic Church.
Jenny Pearson

significant examples of projects can be mentioned. What we see, in the first three developmental stages of the practice (to 1966), is the gradual emergence of a characteristically Modernist philosophy of design individualism, set on a Beaux-Arts foundation of structural and planning logic. This was supported by the longstanding patronage of the Catholic Church. It was through the exploitation of both the centralised and decentralised elements in Catholic church-building organisation that the firm, through a sudden and innovative rupture in the mid/late 1950s, was able to introduce more avant-garde architectural patterns to the Church's building programme. Gillespie, Kidd & Coia, rather than the Church itself, was the chief driving force in the introduction of architecturally innovative plans for Scottish Catholic churches from the late 1950s. And it was also among the leaders in the development of new secular patterns of community design. This development process in Coia's practice depended vitally on the building up of an 'atelier' of enterprising young designers; by the 1960s, Coia was decreasingly involved in active design himself. But it also depended just as much on Coia's skills in organisation and client negotiation. Significantly, it was following Coia's death in 1981, aged 83, that the practice went into a sharp and, in the event, terminal decline. The firm eventually closed down in 1986.

Recent scholarship has examined the extent of the impact, if any, that the Liturgical Movement had on Gillespie, Kidd & Coia's church designs in the 1950s and 1960s, and a monograph on the post-1956 works of the practice was published in 2007.[9] Most importantly, from the mid 1990s onwards, individual design attribution within the firm, particularly for the post-1956 'atelier' projects, was debated on a more public platform.[10] More recently, this tension between the design work of the older Coia, and the younger Isi Metzstein and Andrew MacMillan, has become a subject of interest and debate for architectural historians, chiefly through the analysis of architects' interviews.[11] The interviews carried out by the author in 1996 for the first edition of this book also contributed to that discourse. The design authorship of Cardross Seminary, as we will see, remains relatively undisputed: even Robert W K C Rogerson's biography and homage to Coia, *Jack Coia: His Life and Work* included an appendix authored by Metzstein (the lead architect) on the project design. The implications of these tensions on the historical legacy of the firm will be examined in Chapter 5 and 6, but in this practice overview some reference is made to both atribution recorded at the time of design, and post-practice retrospective attribution. This remains a disputed subject in architectural history.

The Early Years, 1927–45

In 1927, the partnership with Kidd was offered to Coia with a guaranteed weekly salary of £4, but with the death of Kidd, the guarantee became 'more of a fiction than a reality'. The next twelve years of the practice, up to the outbreak of the war, were financially bleak, and Coia was 'forced' to accept the post of Assistant Professor in the School of Architecture in 1928, a position he held until 1938.[12] It was through his early teaching duties that he made contact with several young architects who were to help shape this first phase of his practice. This was the beginning of Coia's quest to turn his office into an 'atelier' in which the creativity of younger designers could be fully exploited. The most important of these early pupils was Thomas Warnett Kennedy, who began studying at the School in 1928 and gained his diploma in 1935, followed by a period of teaching there. Kennedy had been initially introduced to Coia through family connections, becoming his fifth-year apprentice in 1933, but in 1938 he was recorded as 'working as an architect with Gillespie, Kidd & Coia'.[13] Other key students included Alexander Buchanan Campbell (1914–2007) and Robert W K C Rogerson (1917–2007). Campbell was apprenticed to Coia's practice in 1928–30, studied in 1931–7, and subsequently taught at the Art School in the late 1930s, after Coia gave up his teaching post. Rogerson, who was taught by Coia in 1937, never actually worked with the firm, but later in life, as outlined above, he published a biography of his mentor in 1986.[14]

The firm was initially located in 38 Bath Street, but very quickly moved in 1928 to 144 St Vincent Street and remained there for the next eleven years. Although commissions were few, and competition tough from the more established firms, the young architects who passed through Coia's office were attracted by its novel stress on artistic personality. This contrasted strongly with the Beaux-Arts efficiency ethos, pioneered by J J Burnet, which prevailed in most Glasgow offices at that time. Kennedy recalled that when working on the designs for the Empire Exhibition in 1938, 'we slept in our St Vincent Street Office – three nights per week'. Coia's own dashing manner, and his romantic commitment to the ideal of design, proved infectious. On Kennedy's first day in the office, for instance, 'the boss blew in and, planting his elbow on the mantleshelf of the drawing office, raved about the "mother of all the arts – architecture!" Never had I experienced such a torrent of love for design in all its aspects, and my own imagination instantly lit up like a lamp!'[15] The same pattern extended to Coia's teaching. Rogerson related how 'the entry of Jack Coia to the studio meant all stopped and clustered round the board of the fortunate student to be chosen that night. We were fascinated by the repartee, the amount of advice received and above all the enthusiasm generated.'[16] The Beaux-Arts emphasis on structural logic, along with the emphasis on codified precedent, had been reduced by Coia to a subordinate status. He himself asserted, in 1967, that 'I have lived, dreamt, and eaten architecture.'[17]

St Patrick's Church, Greenock, by GKC
Typical of GKC's prewar red-brick churches, St Patrick's (1934–5) had a spacious interior. HES DP231669

In this early phase, apart from commissions for an extension to the Ca d'Oro Building, Union Street, Glasgow (1927), for the Leon Shop, St Vincent Street (1928), and for buildings at the 1938 Glasgow Empire Exhibition, Gillespie, Kidd & Coia developed mainly as a Catholic church practice.[18] This was the time when the patronage basis of the firm's later work was established. The crucial first opportunity came from Campbell's predecessor as Archbishop (1922–43), Donald Mackintosh, in the form of a commission for a new church and presbytery at St Anne's, Whitevale Street, Dennistoun (1931–3).[19] There then followed, in rapid succession, St Patrick's, Greenock (1934–5), St Columbkille's, Rutherglen (1934–40), and St Columba's, Maryhill (1937–8).

These early churches reformulated, and reacted against Glasgow's Pugin & Pugin Gothic tradition of Catholic design. They added a new element of Beaux-Arts planning logic, and abandoned Gothic for a simplified revived Italianate, Romanesque, or Byzantine. The tradition of roomy large, hall-like churches was retained in the form of Latin cross (as at St Anne's) or basilican plans. A further link with the Pugin & Pugin churches was the retention of a hard red external colouring, now in brick rather than sandstone; the latter then being an 'unusual building material in Glasgow'.[20] The move to a simpler round-arched brick style was a general trend within Catholic church architecture in the West in the 1930s–1950s, but Coia added the extra touch of artistic individualism. Coia's Italian-Romanesque style, with elements of Byzantine (mostly in details), resembled the earlier work of Archibald Macpherson, but he combined this with the classicising tendencies evident in, for example, Menart's design for St Aloysius (1908–10), and Reginald Fairlie's triumphal-arch refacing of St Patrick's, Edinburgh (1928–9). Coia's biographer urged readers not to forget 'he was really Italian, albeit a Glasgow Italian'.[21] The principal facade of St Anne's, Dennistoun, was openly classical in disposition, and dominated by round-arched windows and triple doorway. St Patrick's featured a more unconventional triangular facade of red brick with a rich carving of an early Christian character by Archibald Dawson, head of sculpture at Glasgow School of Art. Both St Columbkille's and St Columba's were monumental in scale, employing vast expanses of red brick. The former, in round-arched Romanesque, had an elaborate stone presbytery doorway, and Rutherglen's pre-Reformation priests were commemorated in inscribed tablets set round a relief panel of the Good Shepherd by Jack Mortimer. Inside the broad round-arched interior, were fresco ceilinged side chapels by Walter Pritchard and William Crosbie. The church was opened by Archbishop Mackintosh in 1940. St Columba's, Maryhill, had a massive brick gable cross, set above what was to become a formulaic triple entrance feature – adopted for numerous brick church designs well into the 1950s. The vast interior, with ribbed pointed arch ceiling, had a crucifix by Benno Schotz, and housed the relocated Stations of the Cross by Hugh Adam Crawford from the 1938 Empire Exhibition Catholic pavilion.

In these designs, Coia may also have been influenced by Continental precedents, including the forceful Dutch brick architecture of the preceding decades, or (more relevant to his churches) the brick Romanesque ecclesiastical style of contemporary German architects such as Dominikus Böhm, Schwarz and Steffann. The specialist French magazine *L'Art sacré* (launched in 1936) was reportedly 'always available in Coia's office'.[22] But, unlike these German architects, Coia still remained faithful to a pre-Modern hierarchy of decoration and stateliness; his interwar churches lacked the liturgically led innovativeness of the German works, and the sudden change of direction in Catholic church design in Scotland was introduced by Gillespie, Kidd & Coia only after the mid 1950s.

During the brief partnership of Warnett Kennedy, Continental Modern elements began to become more explicit. The firm's design for St Peter in Chains, Ardrossan (1937–8), with its plain rectangular tower, expressed Kennedy's own interest in 'abstract design', and in recent Swedish architecture.[23] Already, the practice was showing its ability to draw the Church authorities into support of Modern, or semi-Modern architectural innovation. At the opening of St Peter in Chains, in October 1938, the officiating priests praised the austere geometry of the church, congratulating the architects on 'the dignified and simple lines of the new building, with its simplicity and originality of design'.[24] At the Glasgow Empire Exhibition of 1938, organised with typical efficiency by Thomas S Tait, the layout of the buildings which formed the overall exhibition took a generally axial, classical Beaux-Arts form, employing a standard prefabricated unit construction of asbestos sheeting on timber or metal frames. The design of most individual buildings was delegated by Tait to a range of younger architects, working within overall guidelines of flat-roofed plainness and geometrical massing. Coia's practice was awarded the Palace of Industries North, and the Roman Catholic Pavilion. These two designs pointed to some of the postwar differences between

St Peter in Chains, Ardrossan, by GKC
Early Modernist abstract design elements are evident at St Peter in Chains (1937–8). The officiating priests praised 'the dignified and simple lines of the new building'. **HES** SC1500619

'secular' and 'religious' elements in the practice's work – differences which were only reconciled, finally, in the design of Cardross. The Palace of Industries North was a rectangularly massed building of almost classical restraint, employing thin lights of glass in a weighty bowed front. The Catholic Pavilion, which took the form of a chapel, pursued a more assertively 'abstractionist' approach.[25] White, roofless, and with intersecting curved and rectangular forms, it was an early break from the classico-Romanesque church designs of the practice. A campanile-like tower was used and there was a raised area above the sanctuary, presaging the use of a similar feature in the firm's late 1950s and 1960s churches, to allow light into the sanctuary. The building was set on a rubble base, and was prominently decorated with external mural paintings depicting the life and work of the Catholic Church by Hugh Adam Crawford. In 1939, Peter Anson argued that the pavilion 'may mark the beginning of a new epoch in Scottish Church architecture'.[26] The sources for this overtly Modern design were not just Continental. For these were the years when the interpretation of Charles Rennie Mackintosh as a 'pioneer' of Modernism was beginning to take root in Glasgow, especially among students of Kennedy's generation, with the encouragement of Coia. Not only was the overall visual effect of the Pavilion reminiscent of the harled, curved white forms of Mackintosh's domestic works, but there was a more specific reference to the Glasgow School of Art in its screen-like ironwork. The inspiration of Mackintosh was to be one of the most enduring themes in the firm's work, and culminated in the library design for Robinson College, Cambridge (1974–80). The last major commission of this early phase, Knightswood Secondary School, was designed in 1938, but not begun until the early 1950s and opened in 1954. Its main importance was in patronage terms, as a pointer to the centrality of educational buildings – including of course Cardross – in the firm's postwar work. The Knightswood commission, then costed at £150,000, promised some financial security for the practice but, as Coia recalled, 'disaster was only months ahead. The Second World War – and this time Italy was the enemy. I was the son of an enemy alien. My work was stopped, my office closed, and I was back to square one.'[27]

Roman Catholic Pavilion, 1938 Empire Exhibition in Glasgow, by GKC
The forms, finish and ironwork of the Pavillion show clear references to the work of Mackintosh. HES SC461819

The Years of Reorientation, 1945–55

In this transitional phase of the practice, while the bulk of work still comprised new churches, there was a growing move into public commissions for social buildings, such as housing and schools. The foundations were also laid for the definitive form of the Coia 'atelier'. Kennedy moved away to London (and later emigrated to Canada), and a new, younger generation of designers began to arrive, who would fundamentally reshape the nature of the practice in the following decades.

'Frustration and debt were my lot until 1945', recalled Coia, who saw the resumption of the practice after the war as a positive break from the difficulties of the past. During the war years, he occupied himself in study for a degree in town planning, and for a period of time helped the architect Sam Bunton with his repair and replanning work after the Clydebank blitz of 1941. Coia 'opened shop' once again as a private practice in 1945 from the basement of his second home in Hamilton Drive, but with the financial backing of his father, and his brother, Gaetano Coia, he moved to new office premises at 19 Waterloo Street, where the practice remained until 1956.[28]

The co-operative team nature of the practice was beginning to evolve in these transitional years with the arrival of several younger figures, who would later play a linchpin role. In 1945, Isi Metzstein (1928–2012) arrived from school as 'a brilliant refugee boy' to become the firm's new apprentice; he was promoted to assistant in 1953, and a partner in 1966.[29] As an 11-year-old refugee, he had escaped Nazi anti-Semitic persecution in his native Berlin just before the outbreak of the war, boarding the SS *George Washington* as part of the Kindertransport.[30] Coia and Metzstein had family connections, and the latter approached the former, looking for work in 1945.[31] In the early 1950s, another apprentice who was later to be involved in the Cardross project, John Cowell, joined the practice; he was an extremely able draughtsman, and would produce most of the drawings for the seminary. Others who worked for Gillespie, Kidd & Coia for various lengths of time after the war included John Coia, Jack's brother (in the firm during the late 1940s), Kenneth Nugent (1930–2011, employed from 1950 to 1957) and Mieroslaw Lutomski (born 1923, and arrived in 1950 from the Polish army).[32] Lutomski and Nugent both began studying architecture at Glasgow School of Art in 1951, and the former displayed a keen interest in abstraction, illustrating one of his compositions in the School of Architecture Calendar of 1954. Lutomski, who was slightly older than his fellow colleagues, rose to senior assistant in the late 1950s.[33] Alex Macgregor joined the firm in 1953 (leaving in 1963), and Ian Rogers (1927–91) arrived from working in South America, to become an assistant in 1955, leaving in 1963 to join Michael Laird & Partners. Macgregor recalled that Metzstein gave him an important task for his first weekend break after joining the office: he was issued with a list of Mackintosh buildings to visit in Glasgow, and promised a 'test' on Monday morning.[34]

Among the new arrivals of this period, the most important for the future, alongside Metzstein, was Andrew MacMillan (1928–2014). He had come to the firm, at Metzstein's suggestion, from the East Kilbride New Town Development Corporation in 1954; Metzstein had convinced Coia that MacMillan's 'extreme talent' would be 'good for the office'.[35] The two young designers had originally met at Glasgow School of Art, where they both began studying in the mid 1940s; Metzstein had completed his studies in 1953, and MacMillan in 1951. From 1954 onwards, they formed a strong personal and professional friendship, which continued throughout their career together. Staff numbers in this period, according to Nugent, grew to approximately twelve, but although the young individuals who were to change the nature of the practice had arrived, a patriarchal structure, headed by the experienced Coia, was still predominant. Metzstein claimed that in 1945 he entered a 'normal small Scottish office', but by the late 1950s it was in course of fundamental transformation.[36]

The transitional nature of the office structure in this period, which preceded the sharp, innovative break of the later 1950s, was reflected in the hybrid character of its architecture. Postwar austerity hampered projects until the early 1950s, when a number of more elaborate commissions from the Catholic Church were begun. The first churches of the 1950s continued the tradition of Coia's pre-war classically inspired brick designs, but for obvious reasons of cost were less inspiring, although sometimes larger (exploiting steel ties for wider spans), than their predecessors. By the second half of the decade a more rigid geometry and bare aesthetic developed, but despite restrictions the practice continued to commission religious art.

Early 1950s churches included: St Eunan's, Clydebank (1950); St David's, Airdrie (1950); St Kevin's, Coatbridge (1950); St Matthew's, Bishopbriggs (1950) with sculptured entrance panels of St Matthew by Benno Schotz; and St Andrew's, Airdrie (1953). At St

Church of the Holy Family, Port Glasgow, by GKC
Churches such as the Church of the Holy Family (1946, opened 1959) show the transitional nature of GKC's churches in the early 1950s. HES DP108120

Peter and Paul's, Arrochar (1953), the practice made a rare stylistic departure with a modest neo-vernacular harled and slate-roofed church with red stone base and bell-tower entrance. It was set amidst woodland in the small town below the Arrochar hills. However, one early commission, St Laurence's, Greenock (1951–4), was sufficiently lavishly endowed to allow Coia to give full rein to his imagination in church design. It was a replacement for a Pugin & Pugin neo-Gothic church that had been bomb damaged in the 'Greenock Blitz' of May 1941, and most probably benefited from war damage compensation. This massive brick structure, dramatically sited on a steep slope, displayed a more abstract rigid geometry than the earlier churches, and employed the religious form of the triangle throughout, symbolising the Holy Trinity of the Father, Son and Holy Ghost. The vast interior space with ribbed vaulting reminiscent of a ship, culminated in a framed triangular-section sanctuary, and the side aisles, windows and light fittings continued this theme. The boating theme continued with Jack Mortimer's silver sanctuary lamp with a galleon as its central feature. Although the pyramidal massing of St Laurence's was a little reminiscent of Alexander Thomson's St Vincent Street UP Church, the metalwork and other details continued the preoccupation with Mackintosh. St Michael's, Dumbarton (1952–4), seemed to echo the boldly geometrical form of the 1938 Roman Catholic Pavilion. Here, a partially glazed detached tower was introduced, and small diamond and square-shaped windows were punctured into the plain red brick walls, allowing only a little light to the interior.

As outlined in the previous chapter, Gillespie, Kidd & Coia received only a small number of commissions from the Archdiocese of Glasgow in the early 1950s, in comparison with their favoured architect, Thomas Cordiner, but commissions rose again in the second half of the decade. Still hierarchical in overall form, transitional Modernist abstract brick, glazed and timber features were introduced, now influenced by the firm's younger designers. The Church of the Holy Family, Port Glasgow, designed initially in 1946 and opened 1959, had an open brown brick campanile and a timber canopy above the end altar – the latter side lit by full-height abstract coloured glazing. Others included St Maria Goretti, Glasgow (1955), with continuous clerestory; St Joachim's, Carmyle, Glasgow (1956), of grey facing brick and copper roofs; and St Paul's, Shettleston (1957–8), with Coventry Cathedral inspired tower. MacMillan later recalled finishing 'two maybe three' churches which Coia had started but was unable to finish (presumably in the late 1950s).[37] For the most part, the firm's 1950s brick transitional Catholic church designs have been disregarded by architectural historians. Rogerson claimed Coia 'would rather forget them', and Proctor suggested that Coia's 1950s designs had reverted to his own interwar traditional style following Warnett Kennedy's departure.[38]

While these transitional church designs indicated a move away from the pre-war predominance of historical forms and hierarchical decoration, it was in some housing projects that there occurred a more decisive move towards a relatively mainstream international

St Laurence's Church, Greenock, by GKC
Coia's design for St Laurence's (1951–4) employed an abstract rigid geometry. HES SC440079

St Peter's, Cardross

Murray 1st Development, East Kilbride, by GKC, 1952–3
One of two housing developments by GKC for the New Town Corporations.
HES SC1069416

Modernism. In 1951, the firm collaborated with Basil Spence on the Industrial Power Exhibition in the Kelvin Hall (with the Hall of Shipbuilding and Railways as part of the Festival of Britain), with its dramatic interior spaces. A project built for East Kilbride Development Corporation in 1952–3, at Freeland Lane in the Murray 1st Development, was the first of three large housing projects designed by the firm in Scottish and English new towns, and according to Coia, provided the 'first reasonable commission' of this early postwar phase.[39] The three-storey blocks (for which the firm received a Saltire Award in 1953) accommodated 50 flats laid at right angles to each other, with projecting balconies and bold glazed connecting stair-wells. Although still displaying the linear sobriety of Coia's pre-war designs for the Empire Exhibition, they introduced a complexity of design which characterises the next phase of the practice. Finally, this period of the practice was the time when the first design for St Peter's College, Cardross, was initiated, in 1953. This unbuilt design will be discussed more fully in Chapter 4, but even a general comparison between Coia's first design, which segregates the various functions around a spaciously defined courtyard, and the later more complex clustered design by Coia's younger colleagues Metzstein, Cowell and MacMillan, begun in 1959, highlights the startling changes that the practice was to undergo in the years after 1956.

Late Modern Architecture and the Atelier, 1956–69

From the mid 1950s onwards, Gillespie, Kidd & Coia entered its most innovative and prosperous years. Now Coia's concept of grooming an 'atelier' of young designers to produce individualistic and unconventional design solutions collaboratively was realised, and with Metzstein and MacMillan increasingly taking the initiative, the practice moved towards a more intuitively artistic approach, in both formal and socio-architectural terms. This policy would result in some of the most memorable images of Scottish Modern design, but would also have other, arguably less desirable, consequences in practical areas such as user convenience and maintenance.[40]

The relationship with the Catholic Church was at its closest in these years. In 1956, the firm moved to 20 Park Circus, conveniently next door to the Archdiocesan office. The demographic shift in the Catholic population of the urban West was fully underway, and there was a seemingly endless stream of commissions for new churches, within which the firm's bold new design ideas found an increasingly secure place. Building on Archbishop Campbell's confidence in his interwar work, Coia was to play a crucial role in convincing reluctant, often conservative, parish priests, diocesan financial officeholders, and in some instances bishops and archbishops, of the merits of these Modernist designs.[41] Recent research evidences his 'persuading and reassuring' role in the major church projects.[42] While acknowledging Coia's Catholic professional networks, both Metzstein and MacMillan later questioned Coia's personal Catholic faith. MacMillan recalled 'Bishop Ward knew I was an atheist Protestant, he knew Isi was an atheist Jew, and he knew Jack was an atheist – but he knew Jack was a Catholic. He [Coia] kissed his ring.' Similarly Metzstein recounted how 'Desperately he [Coia] went to see the Archbishop and said he was a good Catholic boy – which wasn't true.'[43] This account contradicts that given by Coia's 'friend, student and priest' Kenneth Nugent, who explained during the funeral homily for Jack Coia at St Aloyisius on 18 August 1981: 'His [Coia's] Catholic faith was an integral part of his whole personality … he loved the Church'.[44]

But, such was the pace of Scottish social reconstruction in the mid 1950s, that church commissions now provided only a quarter of the firm's workload. State social building programmes, principally those for new schools and hospitals, gave the practice ample scope to develop their own distinctive contribution to the Late Modern search for community in secular architecture. All these strands of patronage and innovation converged in the Cardross project, which fell right in the centre of this climactic period of the practice.

Over this period, the firm grew to accommodate approximately eighteen staff. New arrivals at 20 Park Circus included Charles MacCallum (1935–2013) who joined as an assistant in 1957, and left in 1967 to work in America; and Gerry Barrett, who joined as an assistant in 1957, but never qualified.[45] Metzstein and MacMillan were promoted to senior assistants, as were Lutomski, Rogers and (later) Cowell. In 1967 Metzstein explained that 'what distinguishes our office is co-operation and freedom to contribute, especially for the five senior assistants'. Coia supported this statement, but underlined his overarching authority, claiming that 'rigid control is needed over quality of staff. I am the judge of what is good and bad. Consultations take place continually.'[46] Contemporary published accounts of the practice have since been repeatedly challenged by Metzstein and MacMillan, chiefly through interviews from the mid 1990s onwards. MacMillan later recalled, for example, that in this very period 'Jack at forty-two had declared himself past it' and Metzstein and MacMillan were left 'to get on with it'.[47] Yet the 1956 profile on Coia in *Architectural Prospect*, penned by architect A Buchanan Campbell, showed a determined professional, lamenting that his busy practice left him 'little time to continue his onetime hobby – cross-country running', but he remained an Honorary Member of the Shettleston Harriers.[48]

As time progressed in the 1960s, Metzstein and MacMillan helped create what the former called a 'teaching office': Metzstein later recalled that he and MacMillan carried out a routine daily supervision of junior staff, visiting 'each drawing table', but although interaction in design was encouraged the practice was 'far from democratic'. Metzstein also recalled the 'crucial role' that Cowell made to the office, and how he 'provided a sensitive interpretation of design', particularly at Cardross and Wadham College, Oxford.[49] The average age of the assistants and senior assistants in this period of the practice, as MacCallum recalled, was thirty, while Coia himself was in his late fifties, and still greatly influenced by Glasgow's late nineteenth and early twentieth century architects and artists. Coia explained in 1967 that 'men like Gillespie, who was a painter and sculptor, were heroes to me', and claimed that his own particular work still displayed a continuity with preceding Glasgow generations of architects: 'it has all the elements of the present. There is no real change in architecture.'[50] This framework of continuity was signficantly different from the concepts of architectural innovation common among the next generation, as represented by Metzstein and his colleagues, who were increasingly given the freedom to shape the structure and work of the practice in this period. Under their influence, the office began to reflect the typical post-1945 move among younger Modernists to reject strict postwar CIAM Functionalism (Congrès International d'Architecture Moderne). In 1965 Metzstein praised Corbusier's postwar work for its 'profound humanism … unconfined by narrow technology'.[51] What linked both generations, however, was the obsessiveness with design instilled by Coia in his younger colleagues, and which continued to pervade the office.[52] As a result of Coia's faith in his two leading designers, Metzstein and MacMillan were made partners of the firm in 1966 – the year Cardross was opened. The period culminated in Jack Coia receiving the prestigious Royal Institute of British Architects (RIBA) Royal Gold Medal in 1969. At the presentation of the medal, architect E Maxwell Fry opened proceedings: 'It is evident in talking to Jack Coia or to his partners Isi Metzstein and Andy MacMillan, that their dedication to art is what moves and directs their lives as architects, and joins them with the tradition of their great city, their own firm stretching back into it, and the qualities that distinguish it, and not just Rennie Mackintosh, rising again to touch their work with true and potent grandeur.'[53]

It was in this environment that the main developments in the firm's religious and secular architecture during this period emerged – the themes which were eventually brought together at Cardross.

St Paul's, Glenrothes, by GKC
St Paul's (1956–7) marked the beginning of a decade and a half of innovation in low budget economical church design. **RIBA**

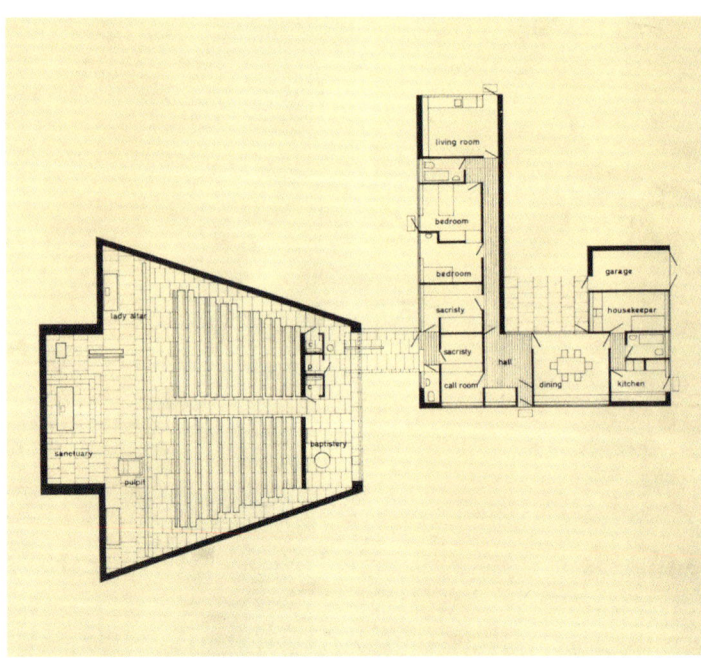

Plan of St Paul's Church
Gillespie, Kidd & Coia Archive, Glasgow School of Art

Church Architecture

Within the religious field, although Coia's interwar type of brick hierarchical church continued to be built in the West into the early 1960s (especially in established parishes), by 1960 a more prominent place was increasingly claimed by a new, free type of design, partaking in the contemporary Continental developments of Late Modern architecture. While the firm pioneered plan-type innovation in the Scottish Catholic Church, liturgical reform (in particular the placing of the altar) was introduced at the request of the client within the gradual post-1965 Vatican II context of the reforming the Scottish Catholic Church. Metzstein repeatedly acknowledged that he prioritised architectural form in his approach to church design, just as Coia had, but for different reasons: in 1965, defending the traditional liturgical arrangements of St Bride's, Coia claimed 'at the end of the day, the church was a place for religious worship and had to feel right for that purpose'.[54] MacMillan professed more interest in liturgy than his fellow partners. In the face of what he saw as clerical conservatism within the Church, he boasted, 'I used to get priests phoning me up, because one priest would say to another, MacMillan knows the liturgy back to front. I made a point of it.'[55] Yet postwar church design reformists such as the NCRG (and later historians of that period) were left frustrated by how little the firm was influenced by that movement. In strict liturgical terms, as Proctor has concluded, St Margaret's, Clydebank (1972), was Gillespie, Kidd & Coia's only church 'actually designed for the new liturgy'.[56] Only a brief overview of the firm's Modernist church architecture can be given here, but Gillespie, Kidd & Coia's significant contribution to twentieth century Scottish church design deserves its own detailed monograph.

With the design of St Paul's Church in Glenrothes, Fife, in 1956–7, Gillespie, Kidd & Coia heralded the beginning of a decade and a half of innovation in low-cost church design. It was Metzstein, MacMillan and, to a lesser extent, Lutomski who were responsible, with Coia's encouragement, for developing this new approach to church design.[57] At St Paul's, an economical design for a New Town extension area (located in the east, rather than in the Glasgow Archdiocese area), the longstanding Scots Catholic tradition of the unitary, hall-like interior was revolutionised, and its external expression was redefined in terms of a poetic formalism. The church was wedge-shaped in plan, focusing the liturgical action upon the altar. The roof was supported by two steel beams spanning the length of the nave. A tall roof projection 'tower', glazed on one side, bathed the altar and smooth interior walls in light. The effect was further heightened by the use of panes of coloured glass, deflecting light off two whitewashed brick screens at the rear of the church, and creating an almost mystical religious space. Externally, the effect of the starkly geometrical form, with its jutting roof tower (grey slated), was accentuated by its construction in painted white common brick. It seated up to 350, and was built at a cost of £14,000 – the firm's interwar St Patrick's, Greenock, by comparison, cost £35,000 and accommodated 500. Being a first generation garden-city concept New Town, Glenrothes prioritised the placing of public buildings in a traditional hierarchical way, allocating them prominent sites (unlike the later Cumbernauld). St Paul's parish turned down a more prominent central site in the town, in favour of a more intimate residential one.[58] In a contemporary press-release MacMillan and Metzstein explained, 'The design of the building is intended not only to embody the relatively modest accommodation in striking form, but also to express the adventurous spirit of the New Town', and its tower would also serve as a 'landmark'.[59]

This pioneering design was conceived more in formal than in liturgical terms. According to Metzstein in 1994, 'it is only by looking back that we can intellectualise'.[60] And, in perhaps the most striking example of the potential for architectural innovation within Catholic decision-making processes, the design was achieved with the active collaboration of Father Piers Grace, the parish priest. He was determined to achieve a bold break with tradition not only in his building but also in his altarpiece, for which MacMillan, continuing the practice's interwar tradition of liberal artistic patronage, engaged the Modern sculptor Benno Schotz. Schotz recalled that traditionalist critics within the Church, on seeing the building under construction, advised Grace 'more than once to have it pulled down and have the design given to someone else'. After Archbishop Gray (of St Andrews and Edinburgh) approved and consecrated the church, Coia phoned Schotz, exclaiming that 'we have broken through with a modern building and a modern cross'.[61] The design has since been attributed to MacMillan.[62] It is interesting to note that the procedure for commissioning a Catholic church differed from that of the Church of Scotland. Father Grace was given a measure of autonomy in choosing his architect, but had to seek the official approval of his archbishop. In the Church of Scotland, however, the selection of architects was dealt with not at parish level but by the governing Church Extension Committee. Arguably, the Catholic patronage system was one of greater extremes, balanced between accentuated conservatism and a potential for sudden and extreme innovation. Where sudden innovation in architecture was combined with massive quantitative pressure for building, the effects would be very visible.

Following a tour of St Paul's organised by Coia in 1961 for the NCRG, James Whyte remarked that Coia lacked any theoretically articulated critique of pre-Vatican II liturgy, but he also praised the 'very honest and practical reasons' that Coia offered as explanations for the church's centralised plan.[63] The British architectural press received St Paul's very positively: in 1959 the *Architects' Journal* argued that it was 'probably the most successful modern church to be built on this side of the English Channel', but the liturgical reformists in the NCRG found the 'theatrical' sanctuary and use of traditional materials problematic.[64] St Paul's modest white forms and slate-roofed tower also evoked the interwar Traditionalist churches of Fairlie and Lindsay. This stylistic tension between modernity and tradition found in some of the firm's innovative church designs proved difficult to reconcile for the more extreme Modernists in the architectural press and the Liturgical Movement.

From the beginning of the 1960s, the practice's new, formal Modern church architecture began a rapid spread across Clydeside, and beyond. Gillespie, Kidd & Coia henceforth enjoyed an effective monopoly of radical Catholic church design: in Coia's own view, none of the other architects of the diocese presented significant competition. In a sign of the inherent power of tradition within church architecture, even in a period of innovation, numerous brick Romanesque-inspired designs still continued to be built by other firms.[65] The bulk of the churches were in the West, with the main client being the Archdiocese of Glasgow, but commissions came from the Diocese of Motherwell, and an occasional one from the Archdiocese of St Andrews and Edinburgh.

At first, up to the mid 1960s, the designs of the firm fell into two broadly basic stylistic categories (although categorisation risks over-simplifying what was a diverse grouping). Perhaps the more innovative, and certainly the more radically centralised in plan, was a category of sculptural, geometrical designs, with dramatic sweeping roofs: some, like St Paul's, were more modest in profile, with elements of theatrical drama. These included St Mary's, Bo'ness (1959–62, demolished); St Joseph's, Faifley (1960–6, demolished); St Martin's, Castlemilk (1959–61); St Benedict's, Drumchapel (1965–70, demolished); and Our Lady of Good Counsel, Dennistoun (1962–6). These bold expressionistic forms were made possible by exploiting Modern techniques such as glued laminated timber construction. Built of load-bearing brick and concrete construction, surfaces were left bare or harled, some with sweeping copper-clad roofs. There was no question of a Beaux-Arts structure-led rationalism. The form was always uncompromisingly given precedence, and later structural problems with some churches may be attributable to that stance. The imaginative work of Le Corbusier, in particular Notre Dame du Haut, Ronchamp, must have been the strongest influence on these highly formal works. The structural virtuosity displayed in the work of Rainer Senn, for example at Our Lady of Lourdes, Pontarlier (1959), also strikingly paralleled these works. And further back was the rich heritage of the Continental avant-garde of the 1910s and 1920s, including Expressionism, Constructivism and the Amsterdam School.

These churches adopted variations of innovative plan-types and seating patterns: dependent first on site, cost and size of congregation. As the 1960s progressed, new liturgical arrangements were introduced, with some changes being made mid-construction. St Mary's, Bo'ness, adopted the same wedge-shaped plan and modest harled profile as St Paul's but was more sculptural in form with a bold linked curved baptistry tower. It was designed by Metzstein and Lutomski. The *Architects' Journal* praised its 'simple, rough, traditionally Scottish interior'.[66] St Martin's, Castlemilk, and the later Our Lady of Good Counsel, Dennistoun, had broader wedge plans, and were designed by MacMillan (assisted by the young architect Derek Mickel).[67] The latter, an inner-city parish church in Glasgow's east end, was designed from 1962 and finally completed in 1966: Robert Proctor noted that the liturgical arrangements were modified during construction when the altar was moved in late 1964.[68] Our Lady of Good Counsel won the 1966

Church of St Mary of the Assumption, Bo'ness, by GKC
The Church of St Mary (1959–62) employed a striking sculptural, geometric design. It was demolished in 1988 and replaced with a new church. **RIBA**

RIBA Bronze Regional Medal, which was presented to the firm at the Glasgow Art Club by Archbishop James Donald Scanlan.[69] The other preferred plan-type for these sculptural forms was the square, with three ranks of seating surrounding the altar: known as u-plan or c-plan seating. St Joseph's, and the two churches of St Benedict's in Drumchapel and Easterhouse adopted this type. The earlier St Joseph's adopted a curved apsidal baptistery and Lady Chapel, and was the first of the firm's churches to depart from a linear plan.[70] The highly formalistic St Benedict's, Drumchapel, had a more centrally placed altar and seating set on the diagonal (adopted earlier at Sacred Heart, Cumbernauld). Again, the placing of the altar was changed during its long design and construction period.[71]

The second main tendency was that of large, load-bearing brick, box-like, rectangular or square-plan churches, plain on the outside, but displaying dramatic interior lighting. The first church to display this tendency, albeit in a somewhat hybrid manner, was St Charles's, Kelvinside (1959–60), with its tall, skeletal tower. This was followed by St Mary of the Angels, Camelon, Falkirk (1960–1), the cathedral-like St Bride's, East Kilbride (1957–64), St Patrick's, Kilsyth (1958–64), and the harled Sacred Heart, Cumbernauld (1961–4). In planning terms, their rectangular plans were still quite close to Coia's interwar basilican layouts, and on the whole were liturgically traditional, and proved more structurally resilient. In their overall architectural form, these rectangular planned churches were comparable to the later work of Schwarz, such as the monumental St Anna, Duren (1956), and the dramatic forms of Holy Cross, Bottrop (1957). Among the smaller churches, St Mary of the Angels employs a simple post and lintel structure strikingly similar to Schwarz's small

Church of the Holy Family, Oberhausen (1958). However, Schwarz's open, plain interiors were very different from the dark, even theatrical treatment of the Gillespie, Kidd & Coia interiors.[72] This quality of theatre and mystery also sharply differentiated the firm's planning innovations from the rationalistic efforts of the NCRG, who questioned what they saw as an excessively personal and intuitive solution to church design, while expressing admiration for its architecture.[73] At St Charles, Kelvinside, Benno Schotz was again commissioned by Coia to design the Stations of the Cross, and large altar cross (Schotz produced a bust of Coia in 1969 for the RIBA).[74] This transitional concrete frame and facing brick church, with its curved-ended sanctuary and stylised fan-vaulted ceiling, has been likened to English neo-Gothic contemporaries, but as historian Gavin Stamp concludes, the firm's brick box features 'stand apart' from English examples, being mainland European in form.[75] The intimate, low-lit timber and brick St Mary of the Angels, Falkirk, was illustrated in architects Robert Maguire and Keith Murray's 1965 *Modern Churches of the World*.[76]

St Bride's, East Kilbride, was Gillespie, Kidd & Coia's most ambitious load-bearing brick type (designed from 1957 and completed in 1964). Linear in plan with a vast single nave, and liturgically traditional, it was envisaged from the outset as a grand statement by both the parish priest and Bishop of Motherwell, J D Scanlan (who became Archbishop of Glasgow in 1964). Scanlan required 'a church of the architectural distinction appropriate to this great venture in town-planning'.[77] The firm wrote in 1965 'The building is conceived as a "Sacred" interior space, whose massive enclosure isolates it from the secular domesticity lapping at the base of its hill site.'[78] The stateliness of

St Benedict's Church, Glasgow, by GKC
The sweeping, curved roof of St Benedict's in Drumchapel (1965–70, demolished 1991) typified GKC's theatrical interiors. **HES** SC358261

St Patrick's Church, Kilsyth, by GKC
The spacious nave of St Patrick's (1958–64) is a powerful example of GKC's brick box churches. **HES** SC1370691

St Margaret's Church, Clydebank, by GKC
The low open ceiling structure created an intimate centrally planned interior (1970–2). **HES** SC446638

St Bride's Church, East Kilbride, by GKC
This cathedral-like church (1963–4), with its red-brick profile and 90ft tall campanile (later demolished owing to structural defects) was always intended to make a grand statement within its New Town setting. Bishop Scanlan wanted 'a church of architectural distinction appropriate to his great venture in town planning'.
HES SC716190

St Bride's red-brick profile and campanile prompted one Scottish critic in 1959 to claim that 'This return to tradition proves the point that tradition need not be a brake on creative ability.'[79] On the other hand, English-based rationalist church architects remained puzzled by the stylistic tensions of Gillespie, Kidd & Coia's church architecture.[80] St Bride's 90ft (27m) campanile was demolished in 1986 because of structural faults. St Patrick's, Kilsyth, similarly adopted a broad rectangular plan, with an unusual side gallery along one flank of the nave. It was entered in the nave flank from a piazza. It was opened by Archbishop of St Andrews and Edinburgh, Joseph Gray, on 17 March 1965, and marked the centenary of the instillation of Kilsyth's first resident priest since the Reformation.[81]

The fortress-like Sacred Heart, Cumbernauld (1961–4), was rendered in coloured harl. Impassive on the outside, it was lit dramatically from the strips of mosaic coloured glass set in rough plaster walls, illustrating the Stations of the Cross, by Sadie McLellan.

By the late 1960s, the distinctions of plan-type disappeared, as the firm's new commissions adopted centralised, non-rectangular layouts, abandoning the polarisation between nave and sanctuary, and, in the smaller churches, setting out to create a more intimate religious experience. By then the Second Vatican Council had taken place, and the existing architectural innovations were reinforced by direct pressure for liturgical change within the Church itself. But the peak of postwar Catholic church building had passed. Ironically, the culmination of Gillespie, Kidd & Coia's post-Second Vatican Council phase, St Margaret's, Clydebank (1970–2), was to be their last major commission from the Catholic Church in the

St Andrew's Church, Livingston
Increasingly GKC's influence was felt in the work of other firms – as seen here in the curved St Andrew's (1968), designed by Alison & Hutchison & Partners.
HES SC1034348

West of Scotland. The modest low-lying St Margaret's set three ranks of stepped seating around the altar, and was dominated by an open 'space frame' grid ceiling structure.

The impact of Gillespie, Kidd & Coia's expressionistic Late Modern churches was widespread throughout Scotland in the 1960s in the specialist field of church design. Further research could, for example, establish the patronage patterns within Scotland's main and smaller denominations, how readily the Modern Movement was adopted by them, and what role the congregation played. Church architecture was, of course, on the periphery of Modern Movement architectural discourse, but a broader historical overview of Gillespie, Kidd & Coia, and other Scottish church architects, particularly in the New Towns, is required. The firm's influence was first felt in the Catholic Church. The low-cost St Paul's, Glenrothes, formula was found at Richard McCarron's Our Lady of Sorrows, South Uist (1964–5), in an even more extreme form (with the parish priest acting as contractor). At St Bride's RC Church, Pitlochry (1968), by James Parr & Partners, its altar rooflight and woodland setting echoed St Paul's. More sweepingly curved forms were seen at Alison & Hutchison & Partners' St Gabriel RC Church, Prestonpans (1965), and St Andrew's RC, Livingston (1968). Yet, the unrealised 1966 design for a new St Mary's Catholic Cathedral in Edinburgh's city centre by T Harley Haddow & Partners (with picturesque perspectives by architect Alexander D Bell), showed no debt to these expressionistic churches: stylistically, the Edinburgh design belonged to the 1950s, and illustrated none of the Late Modern complexity of Gillespie, Kidd & Coia's work.[82]

Brucefield Church of Scotland, Whitburn
Brucefield Church (1964–6) by Rowand Anderson, Kininmonth & Paul, reflected the intensely formal approach of GKC's church designs.
HES SC682250

It might have seemed that, despite the spread of ecumenism, there would be a greater barrier to the emulation of these patterns in the Church of Scotland, with its tradition of Presbyterian clarity and plainness and its concept of the dual-purpose church: for example, Metzstein claimed that Reiach's Kildrum design 'could be converted into a gymnasium'.[83] But even here, in the mid 1960s, the intensely formal approach of the Gillespie, Kidd & Coia churches was reflected, for example, at Brucefield, Whitburn (1964–6), by Thomas Duncan of Rowand Anderson, Kininmonth & Paul, or Craigsbank Parish Church, Edinburgh (1967), by William Leslie of the same practice; and in Cairns & Ford's impassive brick box at Holy Trinity, Wester Hailes (1972). It should be borne in mind that Alexander Thomson's mid nineteenth century churches, with all their emotional power, had been designed for Presbyterian worship. Gillespie, Kidd & Coia's influence soon diminished by the mid-to-late 1960s because church building programmes for the main denominations were, on the whole, complete. In addition, the growing secularisation and liberalisation of Scottish society in the late 1960s and 1970s resulted in further church decline. New church building became rare.

Secular Architecture

The final architectural form of the Cardross Seminary, which took shape from 1959, was closely related to Gillespie, Kidd & Coia's development of a new church architecture, dedicated to the fostering of liturgical intimacy between clergy and people. But the seminary was also a residential and educational complex, to which the rather different values of secular architecture were also applicable. In the late 1950s, it was understood that no lay worshippers would be present here, in what was looked on essentially as a closed, self-contained

Kildrum Primary School, Cumbernauld
This primary school (1960–1, demolished 2004) consisted of low-rise, high-density buildings bordering courtyards. **RIBA**

community. The previous chapter described how secular architecture in Scotland dealt with the Late Modern demands for more complex expression of community, by following two main patterns. Both of these rejected the International Modern preoccupation with rectilinearity and openness. For housing and other background building, there was the so-called low-rise, high-density approach, with its variegated low-height solutions. For more monumental buildings, a more intense, agglomerative pattern was devised.

In their relatively infrequent housing projects, and in their smaller school buildings, the practice followed the low-rise, high-density formula, giving it their own individualistic interpretation. The consistent use of load-bearing construction, along with the innovative plans, linked these solutions to the large load-bearing brick churches of the period. In their pioneering housing project at Cumbernauld New Town, Kildrum (1957–60), low blocks of flats and maisonettes incorporating community facilities were disposed around a landscaped courtyard, and surrounded by rows of two-storey houses. But from around 1960, these remaining elements of segregated rectilinear layouts were abandoned, in favour of the new patterns of continuity and complexity. The carpet-like variant of low-rise, high-density, studded with internal courtyards and secret, dark spaces, was used in a series of smaller schools, including Kildrum Primary School, Cumbernauld (1960–1, demolished from 2004), and Howford Special School, Glasgow (1961–3). Earlier designs by the firm for single-storey courtyard houses at Cumbernauld had been proposed, but turned down by the Development Corporation. An alternative type of continuity, within the low-rise, high-density framework, could be obtained by a kind of linear grouping. This gathered the dense, low shapes into an irregular spine, or, conversely, a hard outer shell running around an

King's Park Secondary School, Glasgow, by GKC
King's Park (1956–62) utilised a multi-level structure to create Metzstein's 'heroic presence' in the community. **HES** SC713493

inner landscaped space: the so-called perimeter plan. Such layouts were applied to single-storey old people's housing at Round Riding Road, Dumbarton (from 1964–7), and to student halls of residence at Hull University (1963–8), with boldly geometric outer façades and complex courtyard groupings.

More directly pertinent to Cardross Seminary's assertive purpose than these low, dense patterns was Gillespie, Kidd & Coia's treatment of the other, more monumental variety of the Late Modern architecture of 'complexity', in which different community activities were combined within large or multi-storeyed structures. From the late 1950s, Gillespie, Kidd & Coia were responsible for the most extended development of this theme in Scottish Late Modern architecture, in a series of buildings which spanned a quarter of a century. Here, in contrast to the individualism of their contemporary church designs, the dominant theme was consistency and restraint. And, in contrast to the open-ended, frame-and-infill concept of megastructure, the firm's complex institutional designs were of a fixed, finite, tailor-made character. Metzstein recalls that 'the load-bearing wall was very important to us. We combined framed and load-bearing structures juxtaposed with each other, as if in a dialogue.' Gillespie, Kidd & Coia's series of large institutional projects began with a group of large secondary schools, some for Catholic denominational education. Reacting against the low-density, hygienic plans which then dominated, with their long corridors and classrooms on one side, they tried to do two things. Internally, the aim, in Metzstein's words, was 'the densification of useable space' through complex 'sectional' planning; and externally, 'to make a school a public building – to give a heroic presence'.[84] At the first two of the series, King's Park Secondary School, Simshill (1956–62), and an extension to Our Lady

Cumbernauld College, by GKC
The building echoes the linear sectional planning of Cardross and the secondary schools. HES SC1021791

and St Francis School (1958–64, in front of an earlier red-brick block of 1954), the firm designed a new type of massively articulated block with central corridor, classrooms on either side, and light thrown deep into the building.

At Our Lady's High School, Cumbernauld (1963–4), the theme was reinforced by putting all accommodation within one block. This was 'a complex, integrated single volume' in which the large communal spaces, including the assembly hall, were situated under the cellular classroom units, and the upper floors were cantilevered out. Externally, the 'statement' made by the looming, linear block of Our Lady's was that of a bold single image (extended 1970). At the Cumbernauld Technical College, possibly reflecting Copcutt's masterpiece next door, the form of a stepped-back A-frame, with infill,

was used. There was 'a little village of smaller structures tucked in under the flank' of the main structure, whose arresting form the architects hoped would convey an image of 'heroic' simplicity.[85] Bellshill Maternity Hospital (1959–62) presented a different form of single-block community, that of an early example of the so-called racetrack plan, of peripheral wards and central services combined in a multi-storey building.

Gillespie, Kidd & Coia's evolution of sectional design led directly to the final realised scheme (of 1959–61) for St Peter's College: the new main college block was an agglomeration of multi-cellular residential units above the large single spaces of refectory and chapels. While it lacked the originality and forcefulness of the open-ended megastructure of Copcutt's contemporary Cumbernauld Town Centre, Cardross took sectional planning to an extreme of precision. Metzstein recalls that 'the megastructure as a form was totally alien to our work. The design for Cardross was so specific that

Bellshill Maternity Hospital, Lanarkshire, by GKC
The maternity hospital (1959–62, demolished in 2003), further developed GKC's concept of creating multilevel planned complexes.. **RIBA**

an infinite, never-ending "flexible" platform – which I believe a megastructure to be – was the antithesis of it.'[86] Whereas international projects such as Cumbernauld Town Centre or the late 1950s works of the French Situationists grouping insisted on flexibility above all else, Gillespie, Kidd & Coia's projects were projected as self-contained, somewhat old-fashioned artistic monuments. Cardross combined Late Modernist ideas of secular community with the expressionistic forms and interior drama of the firm's contemporary church design – a field in which the single grand statement had still remained in vogue. At any rate, by the early 1960s this was, in terms of international architectural theory, a slightly outmoded approach to 'community design'. But, as we will see, the consequences of the architects' design conception of the complex as a self-contained, rather than open-ended community, would not remain just an academic matter. By setting (literally) in concrete a conservative conception of priestly training, the Cardross design would ultimately find itself in conflict with both the values of Vatican II and the realities of declining church membership and secularisation.

By 1966, the date of opening of the extended St Peter's Seminary, Gillespie, Kidd & Coia had established itself as a progressive and professionally acclaimed Modernist practice, receiving British coverage and design awards, and a few international pieces in a variety of architectural journals. Although further accolades were to follow, the practice was about to enter its final phase.

The Final Years, 1970–86

Space does not permit here more than a brief summary of the final decades of the firm's work. The firm's profile was greatly enhanced when Coia received the RIBA gold medal in 1969. As the third Scottish recipient (before him only J J Burnet in 1923 and R R Anderson in 1916) Coia was acutely aware of the perceived 'provincial' status of their west of Scotland practice: 'What does the Gold Medal mean to me? [he concluded] It means, notably, that the provinces are at long last being encouraged … our little nation is finally earning recognition.'[87] Robert Matthew became the fourth Scot to receive the medal the very next year. In those years, the work of Gillespie, Kidd & Coia continued to evolve in response to wider, international architectural trends – notably the first stirrings of Postmodernism. Evoking the work of Mackintosh, they responded to the postmodern demand for a formally richer and more historically rooted architecture, while remaining faithful to the 1960s ideals of complex community solutions and megastructural-type planning seen at Cardross, combined with even earlier Modernist conceptions of the simple or bold artistic statement.

The patronage of the firm gradually shifted towards university commissions in England, partly in response to the decline of construction activity in the previously central areas of its Scottish work. The patronage and organisation of the firm's former Scottish success began to fade away. With Coia's gradual withdrawal from the practice and his final retiral in 1976, his coordinating impetus was lost. His professional contacts with the Catholic Church, which in the past had been essential to the firm's success, had already decreased. The building boom of the 1950s and early 1960s began to slow down at the same time that the post-1966 economic crisis began to undermine the state social programmes which had been the firm's bread-and-butter work. Also, as we will see, relationships with the Church authorities had suffered as a consequence of the time taken to build the St Peter's College extensions, and the maintenance troubles after its completion: symbolically, the practice moved away from Park Circus to Ingram Street in 1976.

On the surface, all remained well. In the 1970s, Gillespie, Kidd & Coia's status grew, and reached its climax in the competition-winning design for Robinson College, Cambridge (1974–80). The firm continued to invest in new young designers, and two new arrivals of the 1970s included Mark Baines (in 1972), and Sandy Wright – both had studied at the Glasgow School of Art, whose school of architecture was renamed the Mackintosh School in 1968. During the commission for Robinson College the staff numbers rose to a maximum of twenty.

The firm's architecture of large community complexes, as refined at Cardross, proved highly suitable to the university-related work of its final period of practice. This phase began with the design of extensions for Wadham College, Oxford (1971 and 1977), on a confined site very different from the wide open spaces of the 1950s and 1960s projects: a forerunner of the typical Postmodernist urban 'intervention'. This work began with new buildings in the college's back quadrangle, including Blackwell's Music Shop (1971–2), and concluded with the design for the library, and an accommodation block for 28 students (completed 1977). The compact design accommodated the library in the northern corner, and the student residence in the south, thus breaking from the single-block educational designs of the previous phase. The library interior, of four floors, formed an intricate network of sunken levels, raised galleries, and connecting stairways. The accommodation block, on the other hand, was built around a small and startling plain courtyard which contrasted with the sculptural outer facade of the complex. Yellow concrete was chosen as a concession to the existing stone-clad Wadham College buildings, but the sculptural outer facade of the complex, in the view of the *Architects' Journal*, still made 'a refreshing, shocking contribution to the gloomy Oxford backstreet in which it stands'.[88] The design for the BOAC Offices, Buchanan Street, Glasgow (1968–70), posed a similar problem of urban context, and provided the firm with an opportunity to design a verticalised infill building in a nineteenth century street.

At Robinson College, the competition-winning plan of 1974 developed the stepped structural patterns of the 1960s education buildings, and the load-bearing perimeter plan of Hull University developed into an urban microcosm, built in local English red brick. A stepped section was used in a similar way to St Peter's, and allowed the lower areas to accommodate the theatre and common rooms; the library, chapel, and teaching areas were also situated in a dense structure, running in parallel, but separated by an internal street. Throughout the Robinson design, a debt to the 'spirit' of Mackintosh

Former BOAC office, Buchanan Street, Glasgow, by GKC
An innovative city centre infill by Gillespie, Kidd & Coia. HES SC843957

was evident: for example, in the lattice windows of the outer walls, and the grid decoration employed in all the main spaces of the interior. In the design for the library, this evocation of Mackintosh reached its climax, and clearly recalled the rectilinear design of the library at the Glasgow School of Art. Although this revival of Mackintosh (part of a world-wide cult of the architect from the early 1970s) was important as a 'national' variant in Scottish Postmodernism, the firm had consistently looked to his work throughout its history. However, the Mackintosh-like personal control during construction, which Metzstein and MacMillan believed essential, did not apply at Robinson College. After the first year of construction, Gillespie, Kidd & Coia experienced seemingly insuperable difficulties in translating this ambitious design vision into a finished building complex, and had to be replaced by another firm as executant architects (with eventual completion in 1981).[89]

In the wake of these troubles, among the senior staff a gradual move began from active practice to university teaching in the 1970s. Metzstein started teaching part-time at the Mackintosh School of Architecture in 1968, and MacMillan was approached in 1973 to become a Professor and the Head of School (as the Glasgow University Chair of Architecture); in 1986 Metzstein became Forbes Professor of Architecture at Edinburgh University (the chair previously occupied by Robert Matthew from 1953). With the completion of Robinson College in 1980, and the death of Coia in 1981, the firm's life as a medium-to-large scale working office was over. In a final gesture to Mackintosh, the practice designed in 1981 a small, whimsically postmodern refectory extension to the Bourdon Building (now demolished) at the Glasgow School of Art, directly opposite 'his' building. Following Metzstein and MacMillan's collaboration in a failed proposed conversion of the Museum of Modern Art, Oxford (1985–6), the firm of Gillespie, Kidd & Coia finally ceased to exist.

By the late 1980s, Gillespie, Kidd & Coia was no longer an architectural practice, but had become something wider and more diffuse: an academic dynasty within Scottish architectural education. Metzstein was head of department at Edinburgh from 1984 to 1987, and remained Forbes Professor until 1991. That year he returned to teach as a visiting tutor at Glasgow's Mackintosh School of Architecture.[90] As the memory of their Cardross and Robinson College troubles faded, Metzstein and MacMillan's combination of past buildings and present teachings (like the work of Mackintosh) were seen as potential inspirations for the ideal of a more humane or enriched Scottish Modern Movement, which was increasingly broadcast by its advocates in opposition to Postmodernism: Metzstein argued that 'the importance of Cardross, and of our work in general, was that it tried to re-define Modern architecture'.[91] But eventually, the influence of the late work of Gillespie, Kidd & Coia would also point in a different (and not entirely positive) direction, when a new and more flamboyant 'iconic modernism' of architectural images emerged around 1995, a movement that, in Scotland, would increasingly hail Gillespie, Kidd & Coia's formalism as a key inspiration for its own image-led 'starchitecture'.

Birth a

nd Death

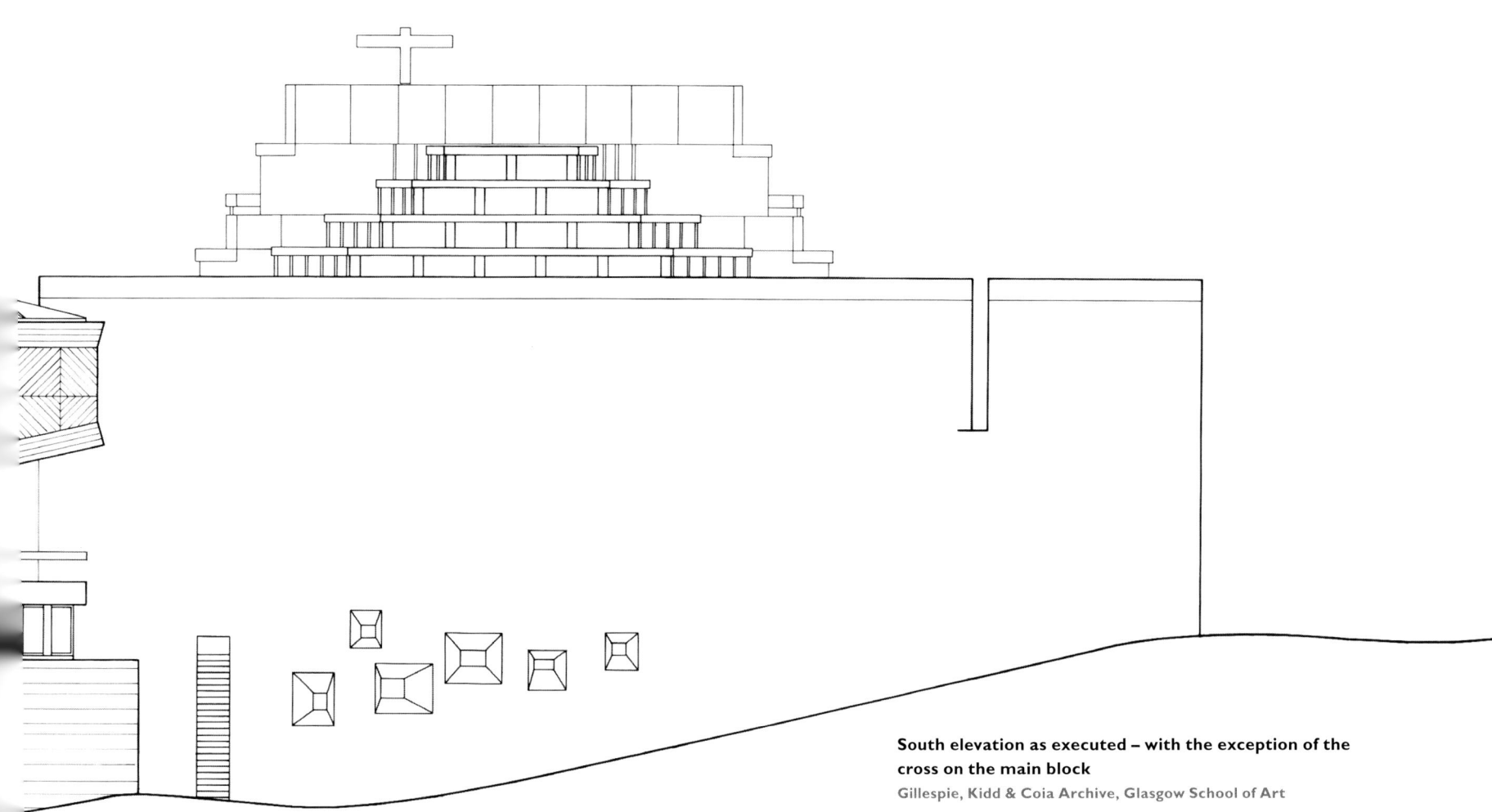

South elevation as executed – with the exception of the cross on the main block
Gillespie, Kidd & Coia Archive, Glasgow School of Art

Chapter 4
Conception and Construction

… a corporate building, where all the occupants make a contribution to the life of a building, and the form … reflects this.
Isi Metzstein, 1993

Ars Longa Vita Brevis, it is said, and we must concur with the sage, for it was six years after the project had begun and long after the time originally estimated for its completion that we finally, on 1st October, 1966, took possession of our new college.
'St Peter's College Magazine', December 1966 [1]

The priests and students of St Peter's College had been waiting since 1946 for a new college building, following the fire at St Peter's, Bearsden, that year (see Introduction). Their patience was eventually rewarded in 1966, with the completion of a structure praised by Archbishop Scanlan, at its inauguration, as 'a unique edifice … of such architectural distinction as to merit the highest praise from the most qualified judges'.[2] Although the diocese authorities began formal discussions with Gillespie, Kidd & Coia on a proposed extension to Kilmahew in 1953, building works did not begin until spring 1961, and the concept of the new St Peter's College, both on the part of the diocese and of the architects, went through various vicissitudes in the years up to and following 1961. This chapter traces the entire story of the development to its completion. The first section considers the motives behind the commission, and the evolution of the initial, unexecuted scheme of 1953–6, considering the reasons why Gillespie, Kidd & Coia's proposal was not proceeded with. The second section focuses on the executed design, devised from 1959, in which the architects and the diocese authorities dramatically changed their approach; this is examined in a detailed description and architectural evaluation. The third section is a brief account of the building process itself. Finally, contrasting with this 'reality', there is the 'image': a summary of the way in which the project was first promoted and reported, especially within the technical and professional press. Overall, the chapter presents a broad picture of the complexities involved in

The extension to St Peter's College under construction, 1964
Construction of the main block, five side chapels, the sanctuary and the corner of the classroom block can all be seen. **Archdiocese of Glasgow**

designing and building a prestigious Modern Movement building, by architects who strove to maintain rigorous control over all areas of design and construction. Since the publication of this book in 1997, Cardross Seminary has been much re-examined and written about through diverse media. These include: the mainstream press and broadcasting; the architectural press; recorded architect interviews; unpublished student theses; film; and several conservation reports and funding applications. The impact of these on current understanding of the original St Peter's will be examined in Chapter 6. The architectural analysis remains, on the whole, based on Metzstein's contemporary texts, some accounts by him in the early 1990s, and his interviews with the author in 1995–6. The revised chapter maintains the distinction between Metzstein's claimed influences and those identified by historians and critics.

As outlined briefly in Chapter 3, the authorship of the executed design for Cardross Seminary was relatively uncomplicated. Contemporary documentary evidence suggests that Metzstein was the lead designer, but with significant input from Cowell and MacMillan.[3] The final project drawings were signed 'Gillespie, Kidd & Coia', but were chiefly drawn by Cowell.[4] The job files or drawings provide no support for the claim, made often in more recent years, that Metzstein designed Cardross in collaboration with only MacMillan. In 2000, Metzstein described how generally both men worked closely together: '…the most important buildings, tended to be designed between us and then we would separate, and one of us or the other would take control, with occasional consultation or involvement'.[5] Absent from the job files covering the final 1959 design is any documentary account of the design brief or process. However, a two-page typed description on the completed project in 1966 (presumably given to the press, see below) stated: 'The college was designed by I Metzstein, J Cowell, and A MacMillan of Gillespie, Kidd & Coia'.[6]

Even a cursory glance at the extensive job files for Cardross Seminary confirms the collaborative nature of project organisation in the firm. Project correspondence from 1959 to the early 1970s was, on the whole, signed on behalf of 'Gillespie, Kidd & Coia', but a reference system for outgoing letters based on the initials of architects, reflected the key roles of Metzstein (IM), Cowell (JC) and MacMillan (AMcM): the last was involved in the early stages when establishing the site, layout and contractors. Metzstein and Charles MacCallum (CC) appear to have dealt with all press and publicity enquiries. An additional nine employees were recorded as contributing to the running of the project. Letters requesting payments from Bishop Ward, and other important financial transactions and negotiations, were sent directly from and to Jack Coia (JAC).

The Commission & First Design (Unexecuted), 1953–6

The events which led to the diocese commissioning a new college are relevant to both the first and second design. The key factors were sheer necessity, and the pride and confidence of the Church in Clydeside, in a context of continuing East–West tensions in Central Scotland.

The future of the old main western seminary, St Peter's College, Bearsden, had been uncertain prior to the fire of 1946. The building was in serious need of repair, and the students were temporarily moved to St Joseph's College, Mill Hill, London, in 1945: in January 1946 the architect Thomas S Cordiner had drawn up abortive plans for alterations. Following the seminary's move to its divided premises at Darleith (in October 1946) and two miles to its south, Kilmahew House (in 1948, a further change necessitated by rapidly rising student numbers), and the diocesan reorganisation, St Peter's was redesignated an inter-diocesan senior seminary in November 1949.[7]

In 1948, in response to the Bearsden fire, and to problems experienced by the Diocese of St Andrews and Edinburgh in obtaining suitable premises for their seminary, Archbishop Campbell entered discussions with Archbishop MacDonald, and the other dioceses, over the formation of a new national senior seminary and male teaching college. Initially, attention focused on St Andrews, site of a previous attempt (in the 1870s) promoted by Lord Bute, which had foundered in the face of local opposition as well as Catholic reluctance to affiliate to a supposedly 'Protestant' university. The hierarchy of Scottish bishops had, in 1945, already purchased a farm outside St Andrews as a possible site, but, in the event, the 1948 proposal focused on the vacant Grand Hotel in the town. This initiative, too, failed as a result of local opposition, and eventually Archbishop Campbell was encouraged by his senior clergy to withdraw from the idea of a joint venture.[8] He now focused his attention on building a new extension at Kilmahew House, and in early 1953 Gillespie, Kidd & Coia were approached to design it. In the same year, MacDonald found suitable premises at Drygrange House, near Melrose, and the notion of a national seminary was abandoned for the time being. From 1958, Drygrange was developed with a series of extensions containing equivalent accommodation to those at Cardross, but in a generally Traditionalist style; the architect was Charles Gray of Reginald Fairlie & Partners.

Before examining the first proposed design for Cardross, the key protagonists in this phase must be identified. We noted above the central role at diocesan level of Archbishop Campbell, and Bishop (previously Monsignor) Ward, responsible as vicar-general for the building of new parish churches. By the mid 1950s Ward was preoccupied with financing the church building programme, but Campbell was under pressure to provide suitable seminary accommodation from Monsignor Charles Treanor, Rector of the existing establishment at Kilmahew.

The key figure of the 1950s at Kilmahew was, however, Father David McRoberts. He is particularly important to this phase of the story for two reasons: firstly, his architectural and artistic interests, which directly involved him in the first design, and secondly, his relationship with the diocesan authorities which contributed to the abandonment of the first design. McRoberts began teaching church history and scripture at St Peter's, Bearsden, in 1943, and became editor of *St Peter's College Magazine* in 1945. But it was his academic

John Cowell, Andy MacMillan and Isi Metzstein, February 1965
The three project architects celebrate – with pints of Guinness– at the 'topping out' ceremony at St Peter's College. **Archdiocese of Glasgow**

achievements outwith the Church, during and after his time at St Peter's, that set him apart from his fellow clergy. Labelled a 'Catholic in a non-Catholic world', McRoberts became a noted medieval historian, and his early involvement in the college magazine led to his editorship of the *Western Catholic Calendar* (1948–74), the *Catholic Directory of Scotland* (1950–74) and *The Innes Review* (1951–78). His intellectual pursuits were eclectic, and among these was a 'strong artistic interest', especially in church furniture and design, which he demonstrated in his 1970 Rhind lectures on the furnishings of Scottish medieval churches.[9] In addition to his involvement in the restoration of the fifteenth century chapel of St Mahew at Kilmahew with Ian G Lindsay in 1953 (discussed in Chapter 2), a range of other projects (including decoration and furnishing at St Andrew's, Greenock, and 1964 decoration work at the Scots College, Rome) reflected his Traditionalist approach, spanning the East–West architectural divide.[10] He was an early member of the Saltire Society, and his conservative stand in relation to architecture was illustrated in his opposition to the proposed demolition, and replacement, of St Andrew's Cathedral, Glasgow, in 1945. He argued, 'Destroy it not, for a blessing is in it.'[11]

McRoberts remained at St Peter's for twenty years, until 1963. He found it a difficult time politically and academically, and later recalled 'the frustrating years I spent trying to coax the members of the staff at Cardross to write articles for the college magazine'. Theologically conservative in his outlook (and later highly critical of Vatican II policies), McRoberts strove to develop an intellectual element in the teaching of priests, and perhaps as a result of this he found himself in confrontation with the authorities of the diocese, particularly Bishop Ward. McRoberts' obituary recalled 'a series of splendid rows' between himself and the

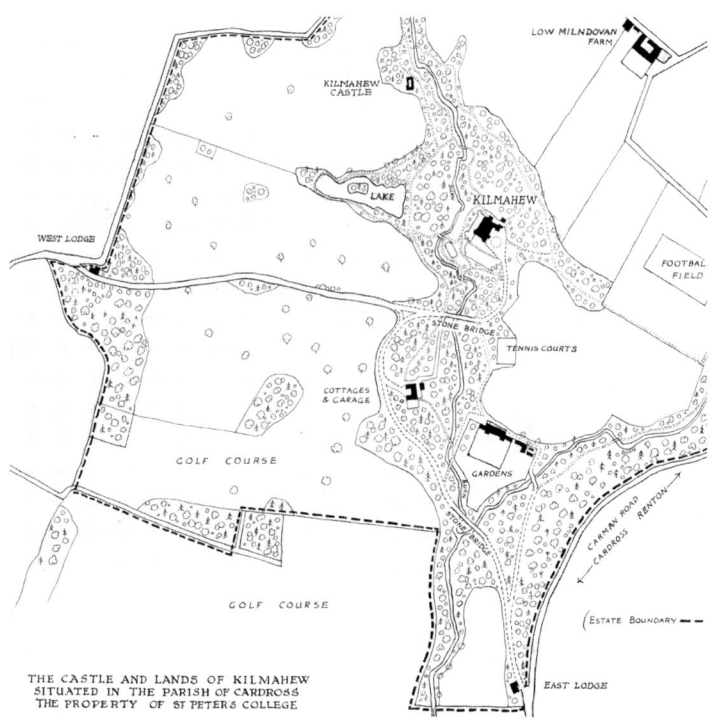

Map of Kilmahew Estate, 1949
The estate boundary indicates the land purchased by the Glasgow Archdiocese in 1948, including the site of the future St Peter's College extension. **Scottish Catholic Archives**

Kilmahew House, designed by J Burnet, 1865–8
The nineteenth century Kilmahew House was to become a key feature in GKC's final design for the extension of St Peter's – incorporating the old within the new. **Archdiocese of Glasgow**

newly appointed Archbishop Campbell, and differences with Ward ('two strong men of radically opposing views'), which led to an inevitable 'coldness' between McRoberts and his diocesan authorities.[12]

Into this arena entered Gillespie, Kidd & Coia, whose professional relations with the Diocese of Glasgow were soon to reach their mid-to-late 1950s high point. According to the extensive job files for the contract in the practice archive, negotiations began with a meeting between Coia, Ward and Campbell in April 1953 and focused on the scale and cost of a 'proposed extension' at Kilmahew, which Coia initially estimated at £250,000. The diocese required accommodation for 115 students; classrooms; library; dining area; chapel; convent block; and swimming pool. The last element was later deleted, and the accommodation reduced to 100. Coia, recognising the complexity of the brief, and the financial rewards the job could bring to his struggling firm, claimed that 'the project is such a large and important one that I feel that several weeks at least should be given to the study of the problem, and would be time well spent'. At this point the diocese introduced McRoberts to the design procedure, and although Gillespie, Kidd & Coia put forward sketch plans after the initial meeting, he was instructed by the Archbishop 'to proceed with them according to the scheme suggested by Father McRoberts'.[13]

McRoberts seems to have co-ordinated small architectural alterations at both Darleith and Kilmahew between 1947 and 1953: for example, in 1951, a scheme of bookcases and tables designed by Cordiner for a new library at Kilmahew. In addition, McRoberts also designed an unexecuted scheme to extend Darleith with a quadrangular block abutting, and at an angle to, the existing house: it was to have had a tower-like diagonal entrance bay not unlike J Steel Maitland's Russell Institute, Paisley (1926–7). Given this track record, the involvement of McRoberts in the Kilmahew project seemed inevitable. His obituary claims that he 'designed a new college on the Cardross site which perfectly harmonised with its setting'. Coia had obviously discussed McRoberts' proposal with him during visits to Kilmahew, and had received from him several copies of a journal

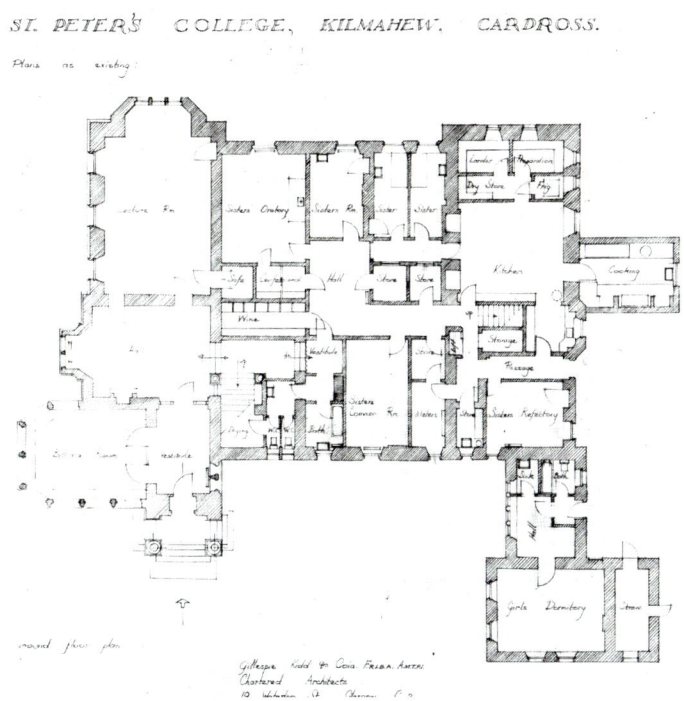

Proposed plans for the ground floor of Kilmahew House by GKC
Coia worked with Father McRoberts on this early scheme for developing Kilmahew House. **Scottish Catholic Archives**

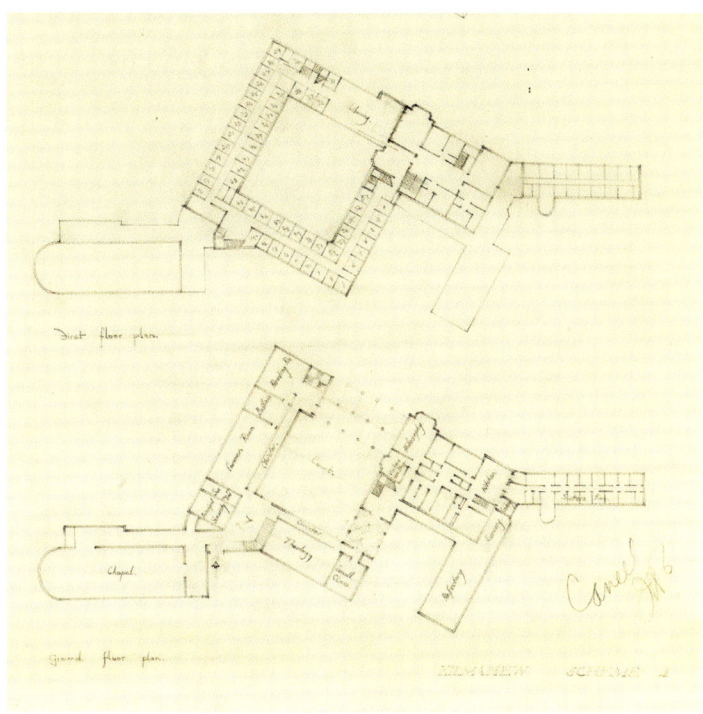

Proposed extension to Kilmahew House by Father McRoberts, 1953
Coia, who worked with McRoberts, appears to have signed the 'Cancel' note on the bottom corner. **Scottish Catholic Archives**

aptly named *The Liturgical Arts*. He told McRoberts that 'I found the books of such interest … that I communicated with the publishers in America and obtained from them what back-numbers they still had.'[14] A former seminarian at Kilmahew, Monsignor Charles Burns, later vividly recalled a visit by Coia to St Peter's around 1955. Burns attended the college from 1951 to 1957, spending his first three years in the 'comfortable, but plain' Darleith House, and his final three years at Kilmahew House. He recalled: 'Kilmahew was a splendid and magnificent house … the first floor was approached by a beautiful staircase, and on the main floor we had two splendid rooms: the drawing room and a dining room. The drawing room had been turned into the chapel, and the original adjacent library had become the sacristy. We had been in the chapel all morning and then went into the dining room for lunch. Coia was welcomed by the rector [Treanor] and joined us for lunch in that beautiful paneled room. After lunch we students returned to the chapel and then to our studies or rooms. Seeing us move from chapel to seminary, he probably thought that was all that we did. I've since thought that the close plan of chapel and dining room on the first floor of Kilmahew House gave Coia his idea of a dining room and chapel being set beside each other in his design.'[15] An account of the new use of the house as a seminary in the June 1949 issue of the *St Peter's College Magazine* corresponds with Burns' later recollections. Then, the ground floor housed offices and the convent accommodation (under care of Sisters of St Joseph of Newark). The three 'essential features of college life' were accommodated on the first floor: the chapel (former drawing room); the refectory (former dining room), and the library. The new library was housed in the original library, but also functioned as a lecture room and chapel sacristy. The second and third floors comprised rooms for staff and students.[16] The author of the article, most probably the editor McRoberts, concluded 'the compact vertical plan of Kilmahew house was not so easily adapted to the requirements of college life as the more rambling, horizontal plan of Darleith'. It was anticipated that the number of theological students would increase to 40, and in 1950 the large ground floor billiard room was converted into a larger main lecture room.[17]

It is difficult to establish the exact chronology of this first design, or the relationship between McRoberts' scheme and Gillespie, Kidd & Coia's design, owing to a lack of documentation, but within McRoberts' papers there exist three unsigned proposals for Kilmahew (presumably drawn by McRoberts) and one sketch-plan, all exploring variants of one basic plan. The key to understanding the relationship between these lies in a letter of October 1955 to Archbishop Campbell, in which Coia explained: 'It will be seen from Father McRoberts' sketches that it was proposed, with the old house as a central feature, to add a sisters' wing to the north, a library and dining room to the north west and a student's block to the south west, with a new chapel adjacent thereto. This means that the old house was an administrative centre and the students' accommodation was built in the form of a three sided square, three storeys in height.' Coia pressed for 'an increase in height of the student accommodation in order to cut down on the ground area it occupies', claiming the site to be a 'fairly congested one'.[18] It would seem, therefore, that Coia and McRoberts worked together, under the direct orders of the diocese. The scheme comprised a range of blocks disposed in a courtyard arrangement around the house, as an administrative core, taking full advantage of the site and views to the north over the steep slope. The idea of a cloister was introduced for the accommodation block; a curved form attached to the convent block was a precedent for the side chapels of the later design. All in all, this abortive design, with its formal layout and cloister, was not unlike the Traditionalism of Peter Whiston's Nunraw Abbey, East Lothian, built from 1952.[19] The subsequent realised design by Coia's younger colleagues was to provide a startlingly different, avant-garde Modern solution to this 'congested' site.

Although Coia continued to work on this first scheme until late 1956, it was shelved and eventually abandoned. The main reason was probably the financial commitments of the diocese in the late 1950s. In an obituary for Monsignor Treanor in 1964, Bishop Ward explained that 'there was nothing he [Treanor] desired more than a college building worthy of its old tradition. With his staff and his students he bore uncomplainingly with the trials of limited accommodation, of separate buildings miles apart. But he readily acknowledged that the building of churches in new housing areas must have priority and that the building of the new college must wait until times were more propitious.'[20] In addition to his oversight role in finance and programming, Ward may have had a second motive for deferring the project. Professional relations between himself and McRoberts apparently worsened in the late 1950s, and he may not have been willing to supervise a project in which the latter was so heavily involved. According to McRoberts' obituaries, his plans were 'discarded [as] the diocesan authorities in Glasgow had their minds set on grander projects'. Monsignor Treanor, rector of St Peter's since 1945, was in ill health, and 'Glasgow was determined that David should not succeed to the vacant rectorship'.[21] Following Treanor's death in January 1963, and the appointment of Rev. Michael J Connolly as rector in March, McRoberts moved to St Charles, Carstairs (as chaplain). By then, his trenchantly conservative views may in any case have become unpalatable to a hierarchy preparing to accommodate encroaching Vatican II ideals.

By the time that the diocese was ready once again to proceed with the Cardross project, the new, atelier-like organisation within Gillespie, Kidd & Coia made a fresh design approach inevitable.

The Second Design (Executed), 1959–67

By late 1959, although the basic brief remained the same, a completely new, much more densely planned design was accepted in principle. Metzstein later recalled: 'Jack Coia's original design was abandoned – it had no unity and no philosophical input.'[22] The new design was developed in a much more informal manner: absent from the job files are any equivalent to the letters and consultations which had preceded the 1953 plan. Metzstein recalled that the initial idea was developed 'in close and exclusive collaboration with the Archbishop – not with anyone else, just the Archbishop himself. No committee, no representatives of the future students – none of the proliferation of present day consultations was brought into play.'[23] It is also likely, however, that Ward was closely involved at an early stage, to discuss the financial management of the project.

In December 1959, Gillespie, Kidd & Coia provided W V Zinn, consultant engineers, with a set of drawings, asking them to advise on 'the feasibility of the structure indicated' and explaining that 'the structure of the

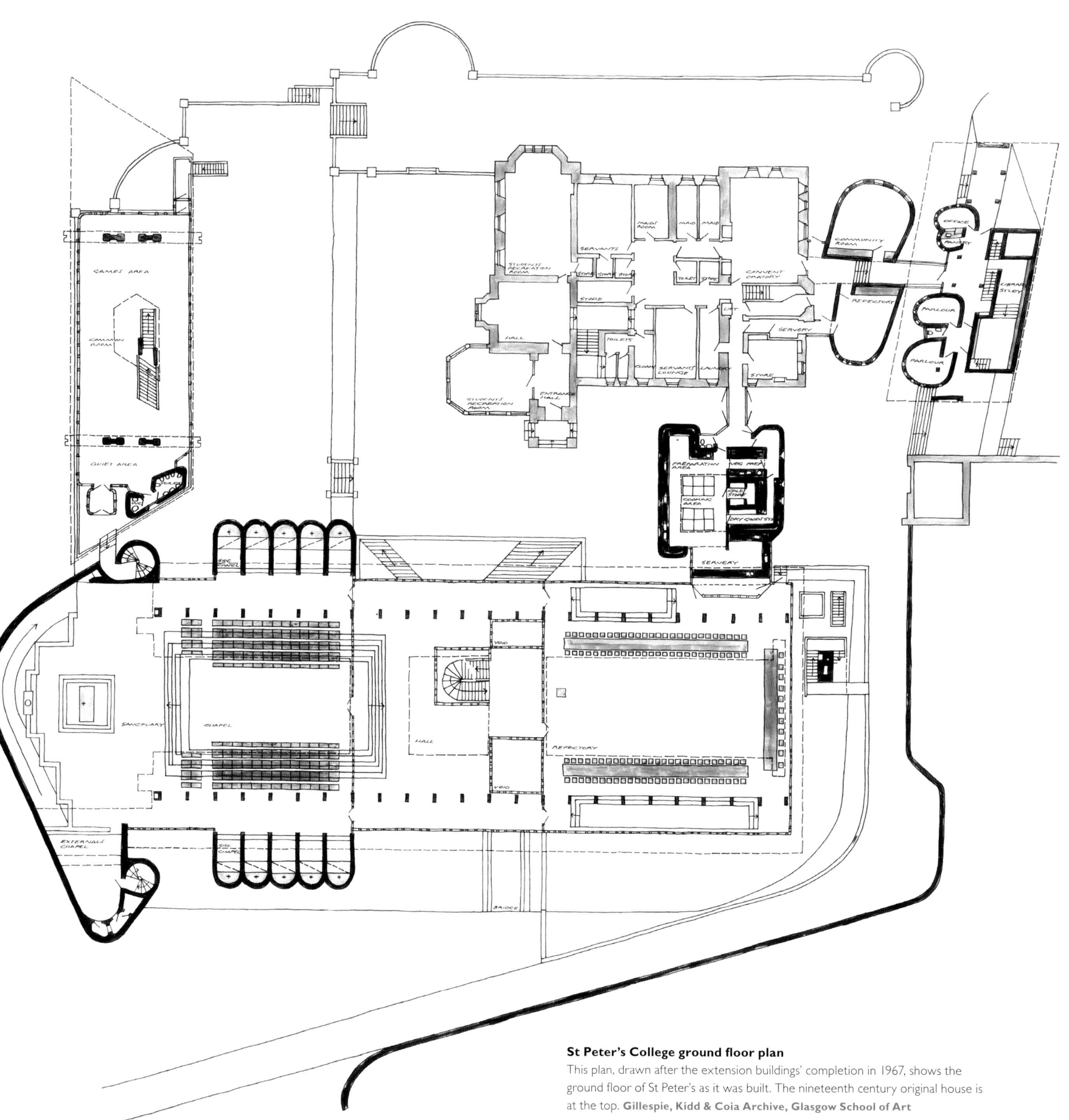

St Peter's College ground floor plan
This plan, drawn after the extension buildings' completion in 1967, shows the ground floor of St Peter's as it was built. The nineteenth century original house is at the top. **Gillespie, Kidd & Coia Archive, Glasgow School of Art**

The original model for Cardross, 1960s
This model shows the full concept of St Peter's College, including the surrounding grounds. **Gillespie, Kidd & Coia Archive, Glasgow School of Art**

basic bedroom floors determines to a large extent the dimensions and organisation of the remainder of the accommodation.'[24] Although the general basis of the design was established at this stage, the earliest surviving full set of detailed drawings is dated December 1961. Within the practice archives, no drawings have yet come to light of the period between June 1959 (when the first drawings were prepared for Zinn) and March 1961, and the set subsequent to that is incomplete. As a result, the following analysis begins with the 1961 designs, and is provisional in some respects. The 1961 design underwent several modifications before its completion, some due to cost considerations, or construction difficulties, but others as a result of 'ongoing' design changes implemented by the architects.[25] The areas of change occurred in the design of the sanctuary block, convent block, kitchen block and classroom block; the basic design of the main block remained relatively unaltered.

The purpose of this section is to outline the 1961 design, to consider the changes which subsequently took place, and provide a description and evaluation of the completed project. First, the general site plan will be discussed, followed by the individual blocks; these are treated in clockwise order, beginning with the existing house and new sections physically attached to it (the convent and kitchen blocks), and passing on to the main block (with its residential and communal areas, and attached sanctuary), and ending with the daringly projecting classroom block. A brief outline of furniture, fittings and decoration, and materials follows. The design chronology is established from the existing drawings (numbering over 500), related job files, and the subsequent recollections of Isi Metzstein. CC plan numbers in endnotes and in image captions refer to the original Cardross drawings in the practice archive, housed in the Glasgow School of Art Archives since 2001. A full list of these original drawings can be found in the St Peter's College: Practice Drawing List Appendix. The orientation used on the plans (and cited in the descriptions below) is slightly simplified by comparison with the actual site orientation: for example 'north' on the plans corresponds to actual north-north-east.

The Site Plan

Metzstein described the location as 'a superb but demanding site'.[26] Kilmahew House was designed by John Burnet the elder (1865–8) for John William Burns. The mansion stood on the level east bank of Kilmahew Burn, just above its confluence with the Wallacetown Burn. The designed landscape for Kilmahew House was carried out for Burns from c1870 onwards (there is no trace of earlier deliberate planting).[27] The landscape was originally composed of several elements. The formal terraces surrounded the house to the south and west: the south had a fountain and the terrace to the west was narrow. These terraces were of made up ground, held within the stone retaining wall. A turning circle sat to the east of the house. To the south, the estate beyond the house and formal terraces consisted of the south approach with south lodge and bridges; the Lower Den; the walled garden in three sections; stable-garage block; the west parklands; and the western approach and lodge. To the north of the mansion was the east parkland with shallow artificial loch with islands, and the steep-sided Upper Den where the ruins of the fifteenth century Kilmahew Castle sat on the west bank of Kilmahew Burn.[28] A network of paths linked these landscape elements amidst the woodlands. In 1895, Cardross Golf Club leased and laid out the farmland south of the west park as a course. The estate was sold in 1919, and when it was purchased by the Archdiocese of Glasgow in 1948, the landscaping appears to have survived relatively intact.

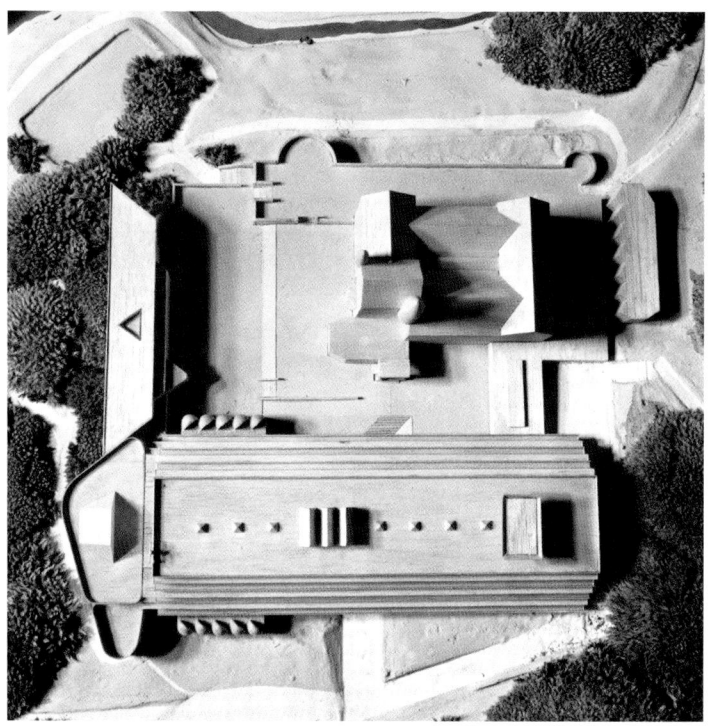

The original model, 1960
Gillespie, Kidd & Coia Archive, Glasgow School of Art

The 1961 drawings comprise plans, sections and elevations of the entire site. It was the level formal terraces and forecourt to the immediate south, west, and east of the original house where the new college extension was to be built. As outlined, these south and west terraces were held within the existing late nineteenth century stone retaining wall, whose retention, intact, was a key element in the design. The north and east end of the expanded site was a natural hill, and an enlargement to the new 'buildable area' was achieved by the erection of a curved concrete retaining wall to the north and east of the site.[29] The limitations of the site, and location of retaining walls, ensured that the basic site plan remained the same from original 1953 conception to completion. The north-east outbuilding of the nineteenth century existing house was to be part demolished, allowing a simple straight link east (which accommodated the kitchen block) towards the main block, and north, towards the convent block.[30] The main block stretched across the entire eastern front of the site, terminating at the sanctuary. To the south-west corner of the main block, the classroom block was connected by an external stair. This block ran at right angles to the main block and, in plan, reached the existing retaining wall which enclosed the western front of the site. The above blocks created the perimeter of the site, and formed a central courtyard. Landscaping was confined to the central courtyard and north-east slope of the site. The courtyard consisted of setted linking paths and replanted trees. Sloping and curved areas of setts were introduced at the north-east front.

The Existing House

The existing house, as outlined above, had been functioning as the college prior to the initiation of the proposed scheme. The house was to be converted to provide 'professorial accommodation' and restored to its 'original residential purpose'.[31] The only deviation from this restoration was the utilisation of the former kitchen as the convent oratory. An executed revision of 1967 provided an innovative remodelling of the space. The existing rectangular space was tapered inwards by creating a false south wall, in which the tabernacle was recessed. In turn, a false west wall cut off another corner, and one window of the room. The altar was centrally placed within this new angled, side-lit space, and ten stalls for the sisters surrounded it to the west. A new partition at the back enclosed the sacristy. There was access to the convent block at the rear.

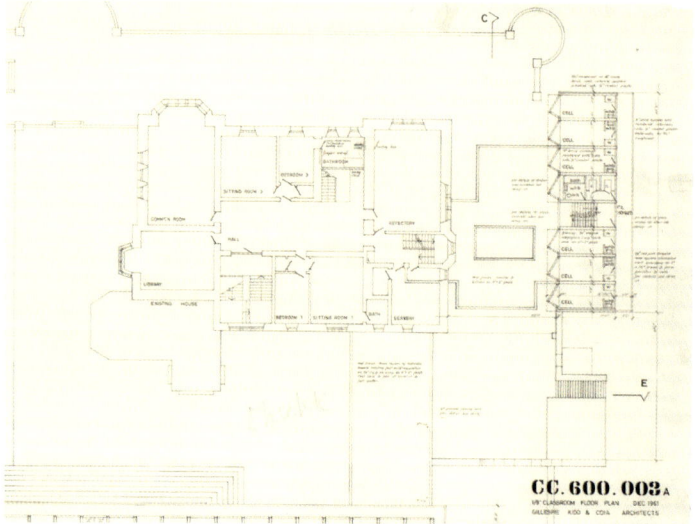

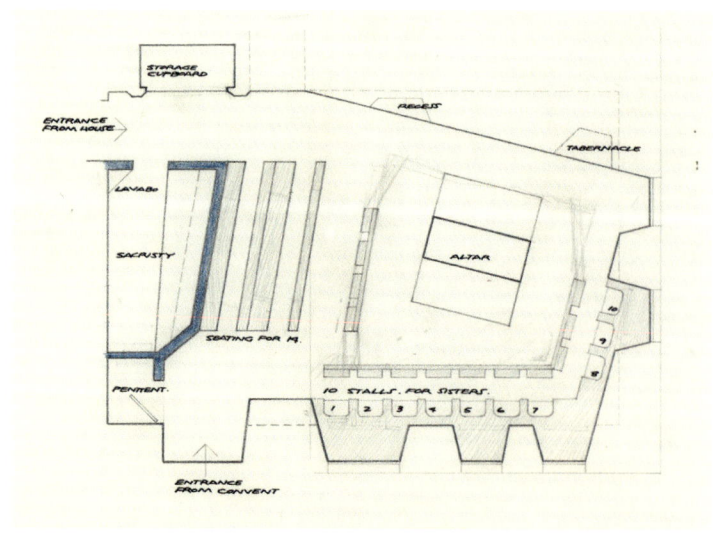

Kilmahew House and driveway
Originally a sweeping path led to Kilmahew House, but as part of the new seminary the house instead formed one side of a courtyard. **Sheena Allan photo archives, with thanks to Michael Wilson**

Drawing of Kilmahew House, December 1961
This first floor plan shows the link from Kilmahew House to the convent block.
CC 600 003A, Gillespie, Kidd & Coia Archive, Glasgow School of Art

Drawing of the convent oratory, February 1967
The plan for the oratory demonstrates an inventive use of Kilmahew House's pre-existing kitchen. **CC 600, Gillespie, Kidd & Coia Archive, Glasgow School of Art**

opposite page
West elevation of St Peter's, December 1961
The compact nature of the site can be seen from this viewpoint behind Kilmahew House. **CC 600 014, Gillespie, Kidd & Coia Archive, Glasgow School of Art**

Revised plan of the convent, August 1963
CC 600 092, Gillespie, Kidd & Coia Archive, Glasgow School of Art

CC.600.014
1/8" WEST ELEVATION DEC. 1961
GILLESPIE KIDD & COIA ARCHITECTS

COMMUNITY ROOM
OFFICE
PANTRY
ORATORY
REFECTORY
PARLOUR 1
WC
LIBRARY STUDY
SERVERY + DIET KITCHEN PANTRY
VEST
PARLOUR 2
LAUNDRY
ENTRY
GROUND FLOOR PLAN
BEDR'M 1
BEDR'M 2
BEDR'M 3
GUEST RM 1
SEWING ROOM
BATH + SHWR
GUEST RM 2
BEDR'M 4
BEDR'M 5
BEDR'M 6
FIRST FLOOR PLAN
CC 600 092
1/8" REVISED CONVENT PLAN AUG. 1963
GILLESPIE KIDD & COIA ARCHITECTS

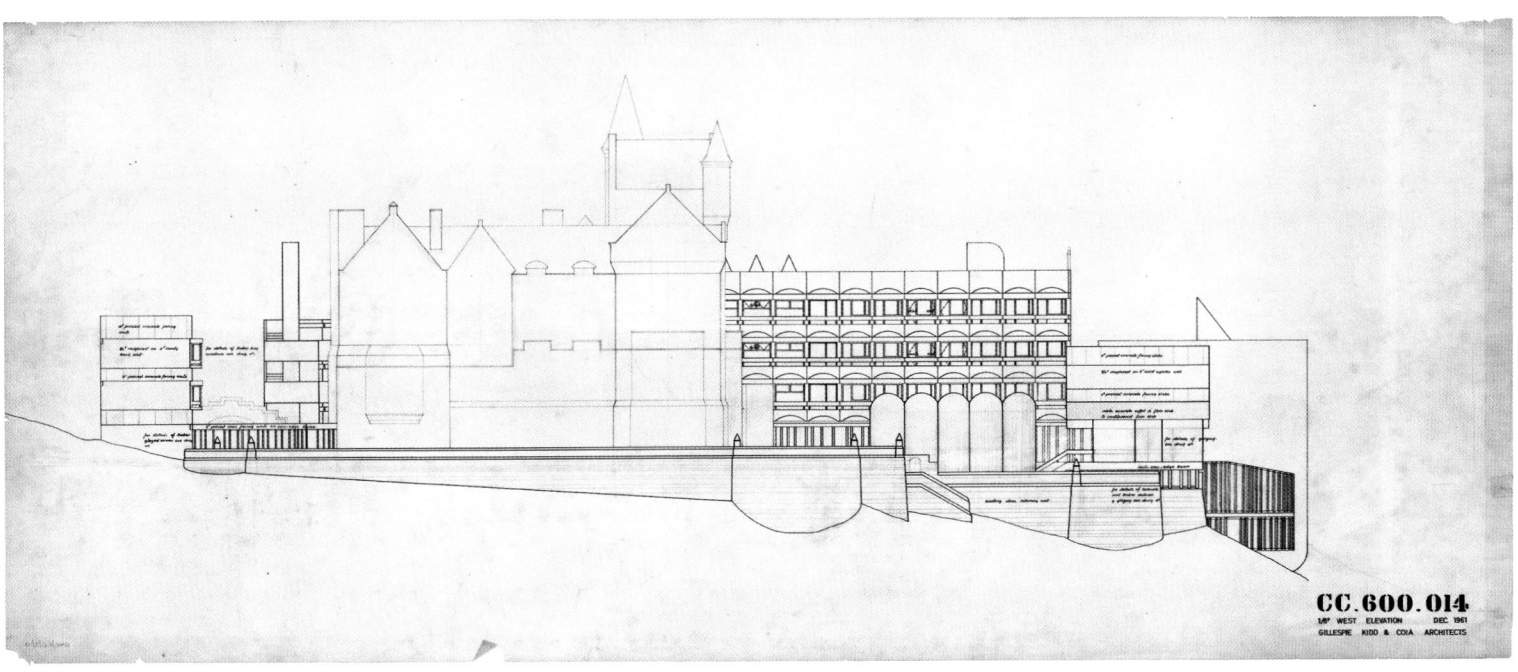

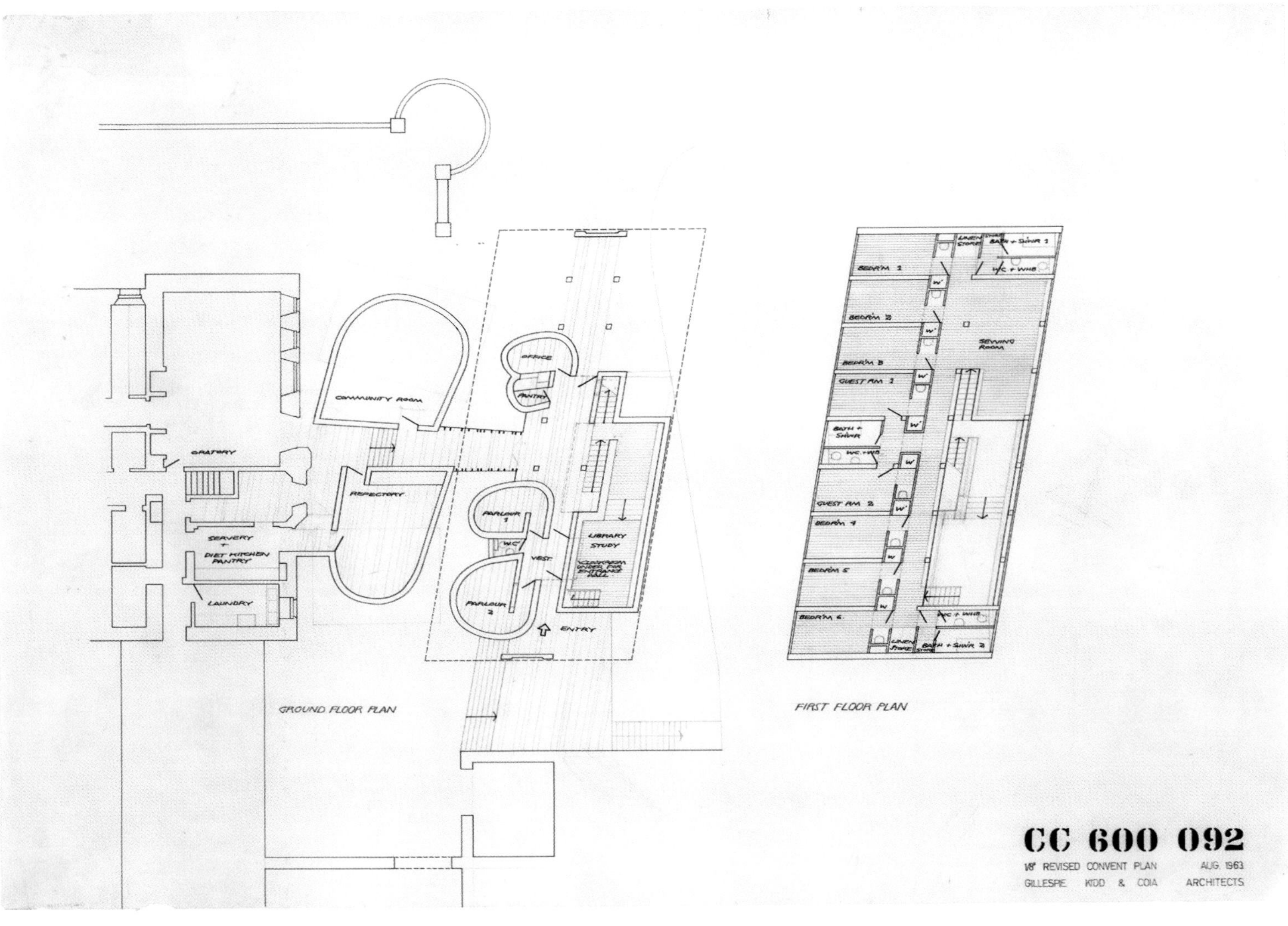

The Convent Block and Kitchen Block

In the 1961 design, the links from the house to the main block and convent blocks were both single-storey, with full-height random mullion glazing.[32] To the north, the link accommodated the convent block community room and refectory, and had a small internal open court. To the east, the link block housed the kitchen and staff dining area.[33] The main convent block consisted of a three-storey block, with the upper two storeys employing projecting angled window bays. The ground-floor plan accommodated the sewing room and parlour. The dimensions of the parallel-placed nuns' cells were expressed externally by the projecting window bays, which were angled to take advantage of the view.[34]

As built, however, the convent block was radically redesigned, in drawings of August 1963.[35] The link now took the form of two load-bearing curved forms, whose roofs, in section, swept dramatically up towards each other. The forms were cut in half by a corridor which linked to the main convent block; the larger space housed the community room, and the smaller housed the refectory. Externally, the link was harled (as were the other convent block ground-floor spaces), while the interior consisted of both white painted walls, and curved varnished wood ceilings. The main block now consisted of a raised reinforced concrete two-storey block, with three load-bearing curved spaces below. These spaces provided an office/pantry, two parlours, and to the north an open, yet sheltered, area to take advantage of the woodland below.

The first floor consisted of the library, reading-room, and sewing areas, with pine-lined wall surfaces and screens. The accommodation on the second floor took the form of six nuns' cells, and two guest suites. The convent was carpeted throughout. The main convent block was now 'subtly' set at an angle to the existing house, 'enlarging the view of the main landscape'; subsequently the projecting window bays of the upper levels (in the 1961 design) were abandoned.[36]

The kitchen block similarly underwent a change in design. This was presumably altered in conjunction with the convent block link, but the internal layout of the kitchen was not confirmed until February 1966.[37]

The link remained single-storeyed but became a load-bearing, harled, semi-curved rectangular block, with a narrow linking corridor to the existing house. In sharp contrast to the previous link block, the space was lit by small irregularly placed windows, and top-lit from the roof. The disposition of these windows was determined by the internal kitchen arrangement. Internally, timber ceilings were employed, and the walls were covered in glazed white tiling.

Community room in the convent block
Gillespie, Kidd & Coia Archive, Glasgow School of Art

opposite
Convent block and refectory, c1966
Gillespie, Kidd & Coia Archive, Glasgow School of Art

The Main Block

Owing to the concentration of initial design effort on the main block, it required the least subsequent development, after the time (1959) that its core concept and means of construction were established. However, the length of the block was reduced somewhat for cost reasons in November 1961, finally measuring 80ft by 184ft (24m by 56m): the detailed changes from the original designs at that date are difficult to establish from the available drawings. Its governing concept, as built, was the sectional principle, of repetitive units layered above and around communal spaces.

In sectional terms, the block was symmetrically arranged.[38] The undercroft of the building – the cloister level – provided access under the block, and through to the internal courtyard. Above the cloister level, 'nestling in the hollowed out interior' were the refectory and chapel levels, which at their centre rise to triple height.[39] The refectory and chapel areas were separated by a centrally placed hall and stair. The chapel had a sunken centre, surrounded by steps. Surmounting, and enclosing, these areas were three cantilevered floors of student accommodation cells which stepped inwards towards each other. The first and second floor had interior and exterior balconies (which led to the in-situ concrete escape stair), while the third floor had an enclosed internal corridor between the two banks of accommodation. Externally, the structure steps back as it rises. The standard dimension of the concrete frame for the main block began with the 8ft (2.5m) wide student cell, and basically determined the form and scale of the entire block. The structure derived from a series of reinforced concrete frames and upper floor cross-walls, placed in situ at 8ft centres, and supported on columns at ground floor. These included deep double cantilevered beams, between which non-structural vaulted ceilings of metal lath and plaster were placed. The specifications for the main block required exposed concrete left unfinished from boarding or other shuttering.

The cloister level created a covered, exposed concrete perimeter walkway below the main block, and provided the initial entrance into the site. A bridge (shown as angled in the 1961 design)[40] crossed over a shallow pool, fed from a natural spring, and led to the open,

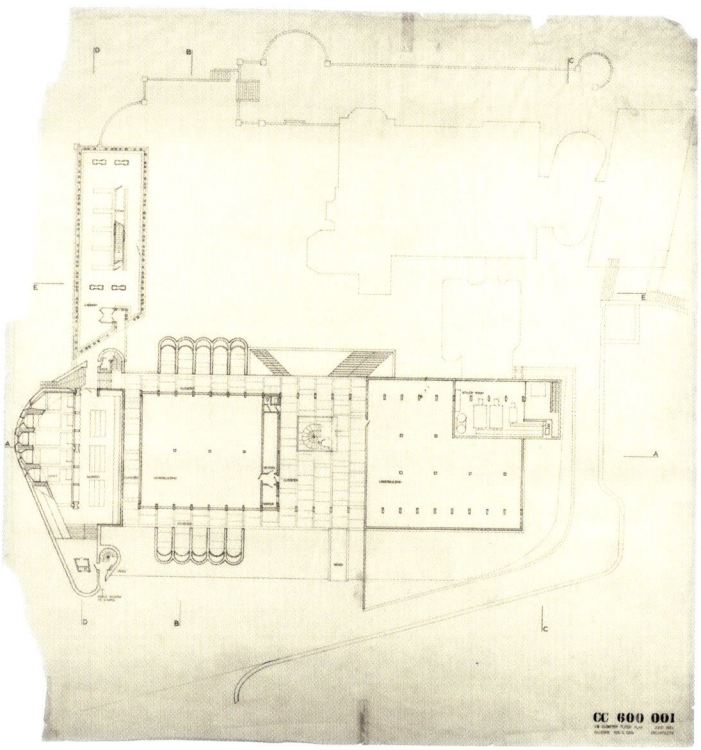

Floor plan of the cloister (lower level in main block), June 1964
CC 600 001, Gillespie, Kidd & Coia Archive, Glasgow School of Art

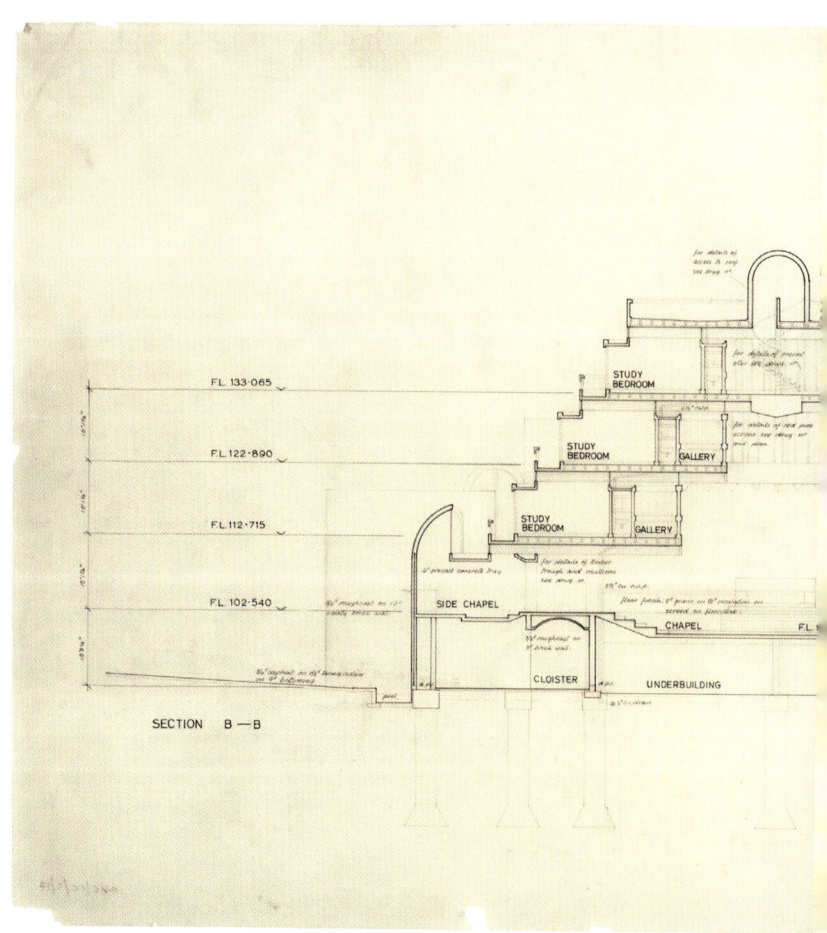

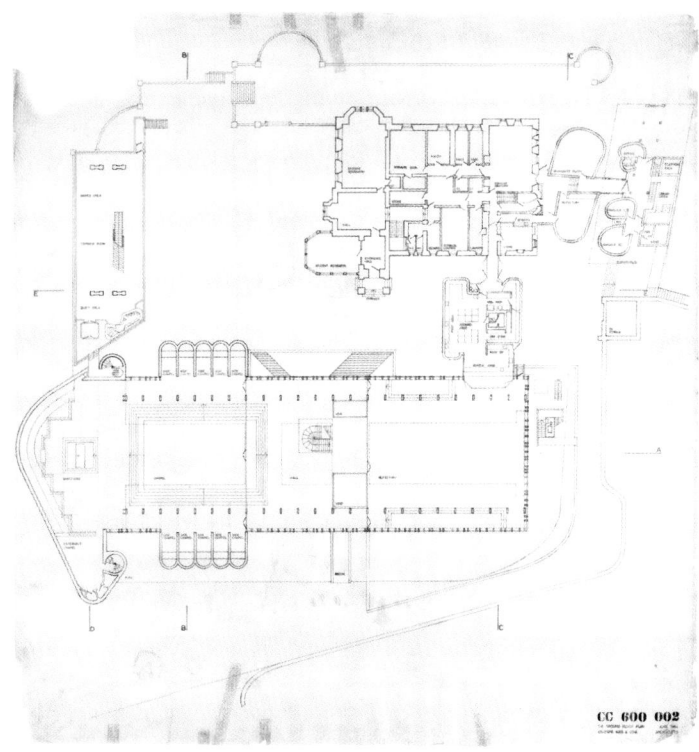

Full ground floor plan, April 1964
CC 600 002, Gillespie, Kidd & Coia Archive, Glasgow School of Art

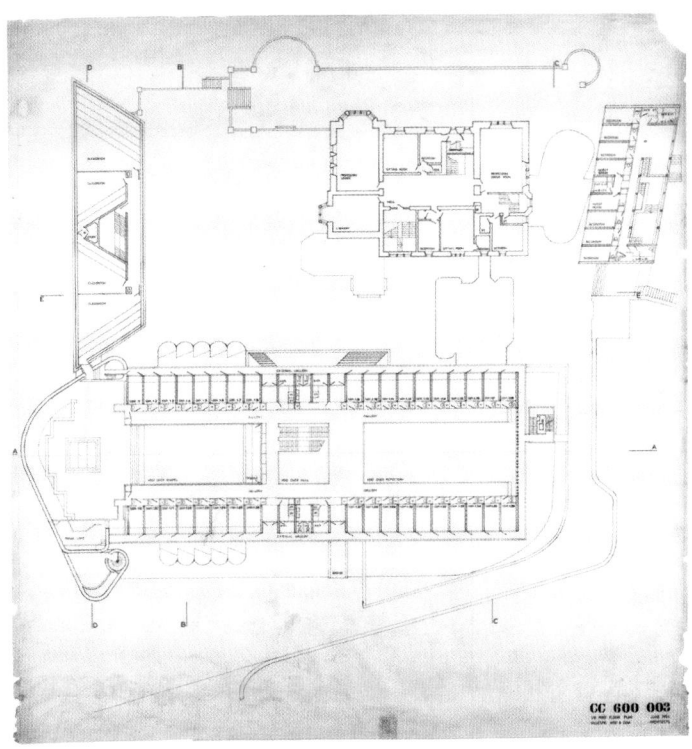

Full first floor plan, June 1964
CC 600 003, Gillespie, Kidd & Coia Archive, Glasgow School of Art

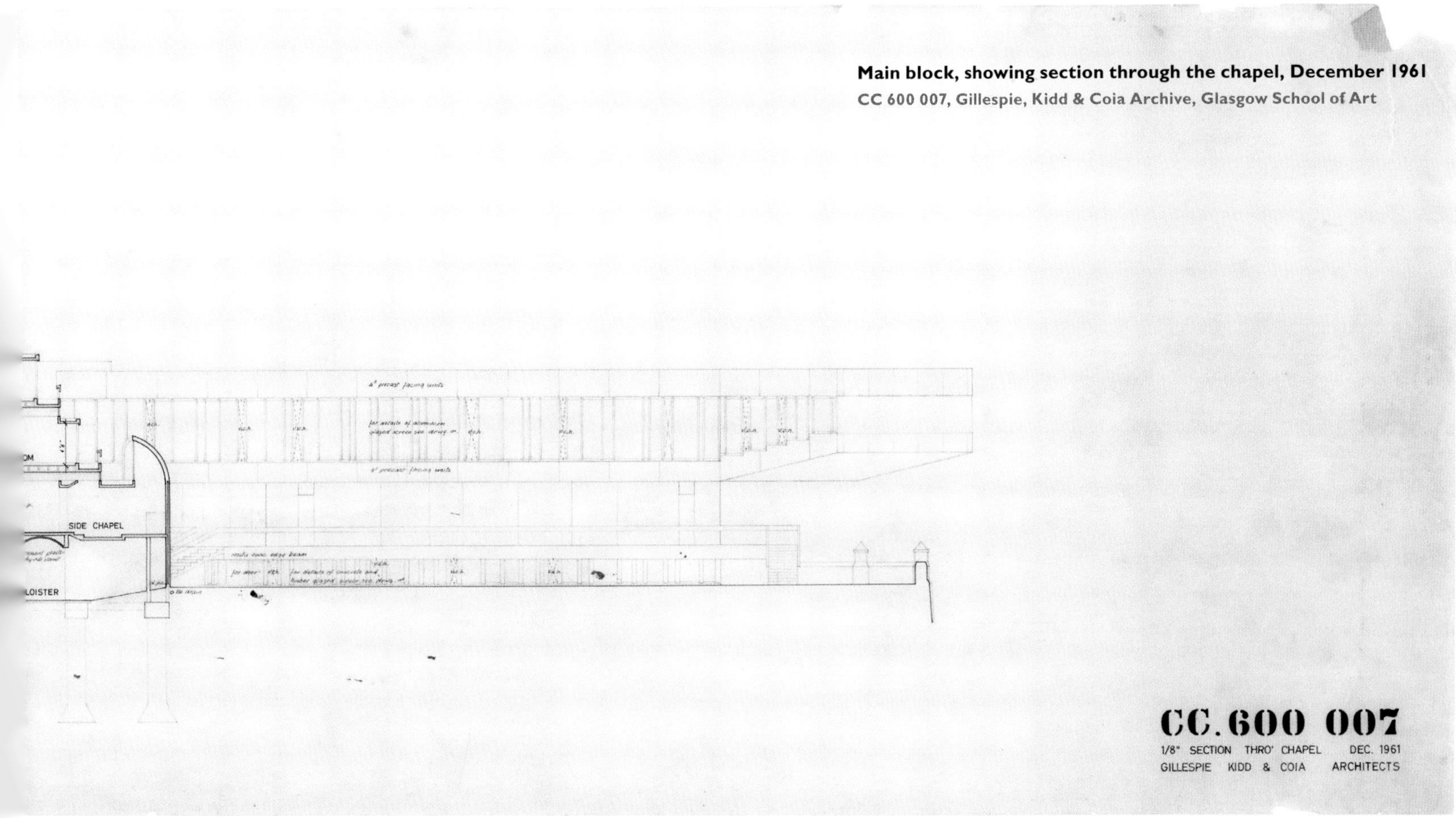

Main block, showing section through the chapel, December 1961
CC 600 007, Gillespie, Kidd & Coia Archive, Glasgow School of Art

yet sheltered, underpass. An enclosed curved stair (in random mullioned glazed units) to the ground floor hall was placed centrally. To the west, two banked flights of steps led up to the central court, one angled towards the existing house, the other towards the classroom block. The vaulted ceilings – painted white – ran the length of the cloister level, indicating an intended circular movement around the perimeter. The lower levels of the five-grouped side chapels were accessed, by the seminary community, on the east and west flanks of the cloister level. These side chapels emerged, visually, out of the shallow pool on the east front.

The ground-floor level accommodated the refectory to the north, and the chapel to the south. The centrally placed hall divided these spaces. The inner space of the refectory, as outlined previously, was formed vertically by the stepped cantilever of two levels of open galleried accommodation; this was also the basic form of the chapel nave area, although the concrete galleries were closed by timber screens. The space terminated at the north in a large stepped gable window. The space was further lit on three sides of the ground floor by random mullioned glazed screens, beyond which, on the east flank, was a shallow pool, embedded in the concrete floor. The underside of the cantilevered-out floors of accommodation had vaulted plaster ceilings (also painted white) which, in contrast to the cloister level, ran the width of the block. A double row of rectangular-section columns was situated under the first cantilevers, on the west and east flanks of the whole block; these, as indicated above, supported the reinforced concrete frame. The ground-floor clear distance between the columns, across the width of the building, was 49ft (15m). The flooring for the entire ground of the main block consisted of a 'patent screed of a dark grey colour' which was laid in large panels. A 'collegiate … three sided table arrangement' placed the two tables of students underneath the 'deep overhang' of the first floor cantilevers, and the high table below the glazed end wall.[41] The link to the kitchen block was placed in the far north-west corner.

To reach the main building, visitors crossed the entrance bridge over the shallow pool, c1968

Gillespie, Kidd & Coia Archive, Glasgow School of Art

St Peter's, Cardross

The hall utilised five bays of the main block; through it rose a centrally placed concrete stair. The random mullioned glazed screens of the refectory were employed throughout the ground floor of the main block, with the exception of the sanctuary. The hall was also top-lit from three rectangular roof lights, and two voids placed to the north of the hall provided light for the cloister level.[42] The partitions which divided the hall from refectory and chapel were of pine and translucent glass.

The accommodation levels were accessed by the central stair in the hall and formed the first, second and third floors. The floors of these three levels did not connect with the south and north walls of the block; they were cantilevered into the created end voids. At the south ends of the first floor of accommodation, two timber 'boxes', with an open view below, protruded into the sanctuary space. These were intended as 'canopies' over the bishop's throne, but also provided a 'discreet view of the sanctuary'.[43] The basic layout of each accommodation level, described above in sectional terms, consisted of identical student 'cells'. The small 8ft wide units provided built-in wardrobes, and a wash-hand basin in a small recess at the entrance.[44] The inner part of the cell was a single vaulted space, lit at one end by a full-width window (with concealed striplighting), and housed a bed, chair and desk. There were load-bearing concrete walls and white painted ceilings.[45] Each row of accommodation had continuous balconies; externally, each cell and balcony front was clad in heavy, exposed aggregate-faced precast units.[46] The red-wood cell window-surrounds were painted dark brown externally.

The ground-floor (chapel) level, comprising a stepped sunken nave 'embedded' in the main block, was flanked on the east and west by five 'brick supporting insitu concrete semi-dome' side chapels. The chapel seating was banked up on each side of the sunken area, and the south bank abutted the 'projection of the great sanctuary'.[47] The internal form of the chapel, as a result of the sanctuary block and side chapels, differed considerably from the refectory.

The glazed north end of the refectory, late 1960s
Gillespie, Kidd & Coia Archive, Glasgow School of Art

The completed main block in use, c1966
Gillespie, Kidd & Coia won a RIBA Bronze Regional Award in 1967 for St Peter's College.
RIBA

St Peter's, Cardross

The Sanctuary Block

The basic external forms of the sanctuary block remained the same throughout the design and construction process, but the internal layout was developed progressively. The 1961 design outlined a load-bearing, deeply curved form terminating at the south end of the main block. It rose from below the cloister level to the height of the first floor. In section a 'processional' ramp led from the ground floor sanctuary to a cloister-level sacristy, and, below that, to a lower crypt level. The sanctuary level was double-height, and top-lit from a wedge-shaped roof light. The 'radiating roof beams' placed below the roof light (drawn in 1961) remained a consistent feature. The small externs chapel, adjacent to the sanctuary and organ loft, with the reinstated organ from St Peter's College, Bearsden, remained unchanged; the 1961 drawings, however, indicate a 'finger' chapel, similar to the side chapels, rising from the externs chapel.[48] The balcony to the lower ramp, in the 1961 design, followed the curved sanctuary wall. The sacristy and crypt level had inserted glazed aluminium units wrapping around the south-west of both levels.

Design changes were made to the sanctuary between January and October 1963, and were only finalised in March 1964.[49] The resultant design introduced a bold stepped profile to the concrete balcony overlooking the sanctuary ramp, and abandoned the three levels of sanctuary – sacristy – crypt.[50] Instead, the lower level became split, with the spacious sacristy situated to the north, and the lower church to the south. At ground level, the large granite altar sat on a stepped platform. The tabernacle sat centrally behind it, on the concrete balcony. Mounted (in 1967) on the rear sanctuary wall was a group of historic carved stones, including a carved pediment and three sculptured crests.[51]

The lower church stepped down the natural fall of the site: the altars were placed in deep recesses of the outer wall, against the exposed concrete north partitioning wall.[52] The aluminium glazed units were replaced by small deeply set (beton-glass) coloured glazed windows, which were set into the altar recesses. The load-bearing walls of the sanctuary block were painted in white, and the reinforced concrete of the sanctuary-floor balcony was exposed and board-marked.[53] The underside of the concrete floor was vaulted in a similar way to the chapel and refectory.

The chapel viewed from the altar platform, late 1960s
Gillespie, Kidd & Coia Archive, Glasgow School of Art

Birth and Death – Chapter 4

92

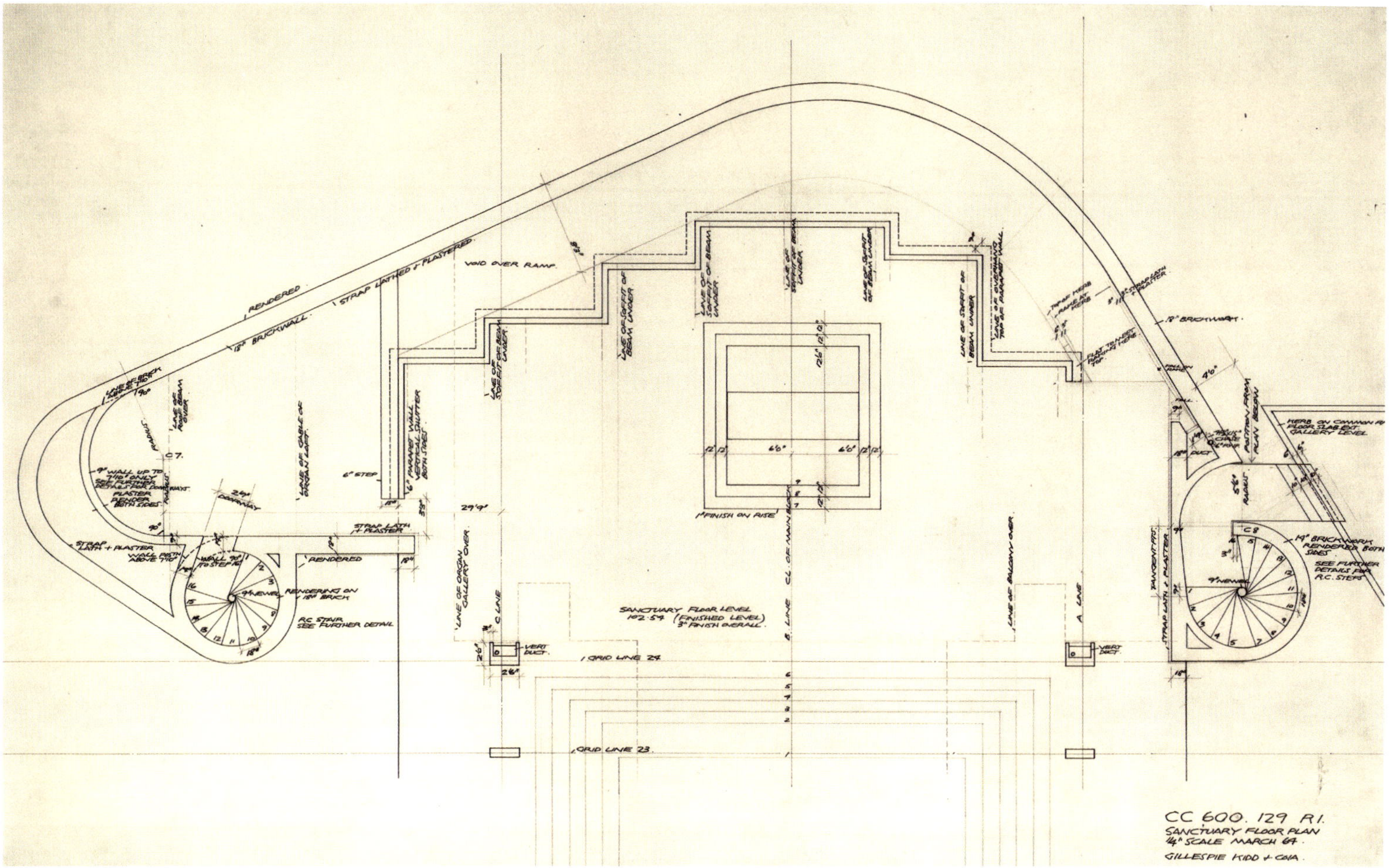

opposite
The chapel and sanctuary with altar, late 1960s
The altar was the kernel of the seminary complex.
Gillespie, Kidd & Coia Archive, Glasgow School of Art

above
Sanctuary floor plan, March 1964
Gillespie, Kidd & Coia Archive, Glasgow School of Art

left
The sanctuary ramp and tabernacle, late 1960s
Gillespie, Kidd & Coia Archive, Glasgow School of Art

The granite altar in the sanctuary

Gillespie, Kidd & Coia Archive, Glasgow School of Art

Chapel, sanctuary and altar, late 1960s
Gillespie, Kidd & Coia Archive, Glasgow School of Art

Steps leading from the crypt to the sacristy and sanctuary ramp
Gillespie, Kidd & Coia Archive, Glasgow School of Art

The load-bearing curved wall of the sanctuary block
Gillespie, Kidd & Coia Archive, Glasgow School of Art

right
Ramp leading from the sanctuary to the crypt
Gillespie, Kidd & Coia Archive, Glasgow School of Art

St Peter's, Cardross

Birth and Death – Chapter 4

The Classroom Block

On the whole, the basic design for the classroom block as indicated on the 1961 drawings was retained, although some changes were made, especially in the choice of materials. As we will see later in this chapter, the complex design did, however, create great problems during construction, as the site was above the poorest ground conditions within the existing retaining wall. The architects revised the structural design and internal layout between 1962 and 1965. The 1961 drawings indicated a three-storey, elongated wedge-shaped block, which accommodated, in descending order, the lecture rooms, the common room, and the library. The executed scheme differed little from this. The complex construction enabled the entire top lecture-room floor to be supported, boldly, on four large 'flat' columns. These columns supported two 4ft (12m) deep beams which, in turn, carried two longitudinal beam-walls spanning 58ft (18m) and cantilevering up to 40ft (12m) at each end of the block. The common room below was 'free from supports' apart from the 'four columns passing through its floor area'.[54] The floor of this level rested on perimeter stub precast columns standing behind the existing stone wall (to preserve its continuity) and reinforced concrete retaining wall.

The lecture-room level (top) consisted of 'two subdivisable spaces' which could, if manipulated, provide four separate rooms, catering for 'the seating needs of different numerical combinations of students'.[55] The rows of seating were stepped at the angled ends of the block, and at each flank of the triangular-shaped stairwell. The roof of the lecture room was of heavy laminated Oregon pine and comprised a double grid of structural and tie trusses, braced by short stalactite posts. The posts had lighting globes attached to them. Originally the entire top floor, which was tapered up at the cantilevered ends, was to be enclosed in random mullioned aluminium glazed screens.[56] The later design adopted, internally and externally, an in-situ concrete surround, which was

The classroom block, c1968
The block housed the lecture hall, common room and library.
Gillespie, Kidd & Coia Archive, Glasgow School of Art

Classroom block lecture theatre
Gillespie, Kidd & Coia Archive, Glasgow School of Art

board-marked with a diagonal herringbone pattern. Light was then provided by a series of roof lights, and a random mullioned glazed screen at the ends of the block. A simpler roof design was proposed in the 1961 classroom block drawings.[57]

The common room level (middle), as indicated above, was a relatively open area, free from supports. Cutting through the space was an angled, two levelled teak stair. The area was fully glazed with a large-paned lower level, and random timber-mullioned recessed level above. The common room's dimensions were established by the height of the two projecting concrete beams; originally this upper level of glazing comprised precast concrete units.[58] The load-bearing harled section at the east end appears to be a later design addition.[59] The common room was also accessible from an external stair to the courtyard. The library level (bottom) was partially sunk below the existing ground level. It was enclosed by random concrete mullioned glazing, and had timber floor, ceiling, windows and wall lining. The library was also accessible externally from the cloister level. At the two lower levels, artificial lighting was provided from exposed fluorescent strips.[60] The main block, in contrast, concealed the artificial strip lighting: for example, under the ledges of the concrete balconies in the sanctuary block.

opposite

Kilmahew House and the classroom block
The Scotch Baronial Kilmahew House dramatically contrasts with the Modern cantilevered classroom block.
Gillespie, Kidd & Coia Archive, Glasgow School of Art

St Peter's, Cardross

The classroom block stairs leading up from the common room
Gillespie, Kidd & Coia Archive, Glasgow School of Art

The stairs from the common room to the lecture room
Gillespie, Kidd & Coia Archive, Glasgow School of Art

Furniture and Fittings

The architects provided detailed specifications for the construction of fittings for the entire complex, and engaged several firms in the process; the main contractor was the Glasgow firm Wylie & Lochhead Ltd.[61] A number of drawings exist of these specifications, and include the refectory and chapel doors, and sacristy fitments.[62] Although readymade furniture was ordered for the complex, from Elders Departmental Furniture Store, Glasgow, and Scandinavian Furnishings, several pieces of specialist furniture were designed by the architects.[63] Detailed drawings survive for the refectory tables, the chapel seating, classroom block seating and writing surfaces, and the convent oratory seating and light-fittings.[64]

The basic form of the furniture appears to have been consistent throughout, with slight variations for each particular function. All the furniture was made of thick, chunky wood, and was simply constructed in the form of intersecting and overlapping planes. The backrests of the chapel seating (made probably by J Grant Ltd) were curved for comfort, as were the planks of the front pews. The convent oratory furniture, and banks of lecture-room seating, followed a similar pattern. The large teak refectory tables, made by T Justice & Sons, Dundee, did not adopt the smooth angles of the chapel seating but employed a more rigid and geometric appearance.[65] These tables were similar, in their design and dimensions, to the hall table at Mackintosh's Windyhill.

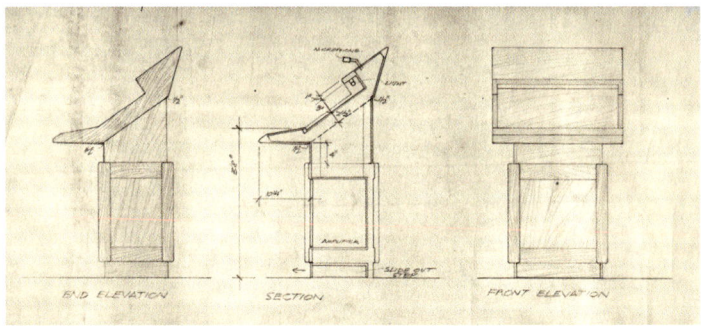

Design drawings for the refectory lectern, designed by GKC
Gillespie, Kidd & Coia Archive, Glasgow School of Art

An Architectural Image of Religious Community

… a plan in which every part would speak to every other part: an association of many small elements – the cells – within large volumes.
Isi Metzstein, 1993[66]

The 'programme' of St Peter's College, the architects claimed, 'lent itself to a very simple solution'. But the building, as executed, was in many ways more elaborate in its architectural conception than any of the firm's previous work. In that respect it was a textbook example of the advanced Modern architecture of the 1960s, which set out to enrich the prewar CIAM Modernist patterns, and called for more individualistic and complex solutions, in both social and visual terms. The design of a seminary, in a 'superb' secluded site, provided Gillespie, Kidd & Coia with very 'specific opportunities' to do just that.[67] The group of new buildings around Kilmahew House interpreted the socio-architectural ideal of community through a highly individual formal response, but remained faithful to the overall Modern concern to create architectural order in the design of new buildings.

The design of the new buildings set out to celebrate, and recast as a Modern 'image', the communal life of the traditional seminary – a pattern, stretching back to the directives of the Council of Trent, which required the trainee priests to be removed from the outside world for their period of spiritual education, and housed in a relatively formal community. The enclosed character of the complex was heightened by the contrast of its hard, intensely designed courtyard spaces with the abrupt, wooded landscape outside.

The structure of the main block set out to accommodate both the formality of the seminary community and the role of the individual student priest within it, in a sense expressing the 'totality' of the life of the student. The aim was to synthesise 'two potentially conflicting principles': the autonomy of the priest (symbolised by the 'cell') and the social and religious structure (symbolised by the chapel and refectory).[68] In a manner inspired by

Trainee priest at the refectory lectern
Gillespie, Kidd & Coia Archive, Glasgow School of Art

St Peter's, Cardross

monastic tradition, the chapel and refectory provided the collective focus of the plan – an eclectic accentuation of the image of community in seclusion. The main block's design 'started with a single cell', and, using concrete frame construction, enveloped the 'kernel' of the whole complex: the chapel.[69]

The formal inter-dependency between the small units and large volumes reflected a concept of ideal religious community: every part 'speaking' to every other part.[70] This relationship between individual and collective functions was central to Late Modern architecture. On the Continent, it was a preoccupation of the 'Forum' group in the Netherlands, as exemplified in Aldo van Eyck's 1960 orphanage at Amsterdam; carried out in a more monumental manner, it also characterised Le Corbusier's Unité d'Habitation, Marseilles (1947–52).[71] The concept of megastructure, as exemplified in Scotland by Cumbernauld Town Centre (1963–7), contained elements of this idea, in its tension between the fixed multi-function frame and the temporary infill. However, as already noted, the idea of 'extensible' megastructure differed considerably from Metzstein and MacMillan's solution at St Peter's. Cardross was an unambiguously finite design: in Metzstein's words, 'It's certainly not a "flexible box" – and that's not accidental.' This may have been a result of the very nature of the seminary, and of course the limitations of the site. However, the formality of the overall concept was offset by informality in the elements: in Metzstein's view, 'close-up the buildings are organic, rich and ad-hoc, but from a distance they are highly classical and cellular – you do not see the village-like organic disorder below'.[72]

In its plan, the new Cardross complex certainly appears rigidly diagrammatic: enclosed, linear and with repeating units. Metzstein later quipped, 'I sometimes can't sleep at night, thinking of all those individual rooms, imprisoned for ever within that giant matrix!' He visualised the main block as a 'linear building of repeating cells' which required closure at one end by 'a gigantic curved wall', and at the other, by a staircase and flue. The existing house, classroom block and convent block set the parameters of this diagram, creating an internal 'collegiate' courtyard. The existing house 'regulated the relationships of the other blocks'.[73] Links, walkways and connecting canopied stairs created a continuous movement throughout the complex. Some links were straight (the cloister circuit), some angled (the canopied link to the classroom block), and others were sinuous (the sanctuary ramp).

The linear movement through the complex reflected the main activities of the seminary. The trainee priest moved from the individual and spiritual enclave of the main block to the communal/educational areas, and out to the internal courtyard. The existing house was the domain of the priests, and the administrative centre for the seminary. It was the first point of contact for any outside visitors, who were guided below the main block, through the cloister level, and up towards the existing house. St Peter's was conceived as a 'nonpublic building', with students not allowed to receive informal visits.[74] The movement of the visitor, under the main block, and through to the internal courtyard – excluded from the enclosed circular stairwell at cloister level – illustrates the layering of movement throughout the seminary. The convent block, although linked loosely to the existing house and (subsequently, through the kitchen link) to the remaining complex, was planned as a 'self contained community'. This autonomy was expressed visually by angling the convent block away from the main complex.

The pursuit of an 'orderly and meaningful sequence' within the seminary related not only to the physical experience of moving around within the building, but also to a more abstract psychological/formal ideal of 'architectural order and discipline'. Metzstein insisted that 'I never use the word "functional"… you have to take account of the psychological effect of the design.' The ordered religious nature of the complex, hierarchically crowned by the chapel, 'invested' the entire main block 'with a church-like character'.[75] The proportions of the main block, and to a lesser extent the convent block, were defined by the width of the individual vaulted cell: the vaulted forms remained the dominant visual measurement throughout. On the lower cloister perimeter walkway the vaults run the length of the block, from the entrance to the sacristy, expressing the length of the chapel above, and indicating the movement along and around the block. On the remaining levels the vaults reflected the breadth of the cantilevered floors, decreasing in size as they rose.

The sanctuary roof light
The stepped roof light of the sanctuary adjoins the main block.
Gillespie, Kidd & Coia Archive, Glasgow School of Art

The sanctuary roof
The roof light viewed from the chapel.
HES SC674775

The movement of the individual in the communal levels of refectory and chapel was a movement below a series of white-painted vaults, and the individual was constantly reminded of the visual dimensions of the single cell above; the projecting vaulted cantilevers also controlled, and framed, the views out to the surrounding site. The rectangular columns, on the cloister and ground-floor levels, emphasised the dimensions of the vaults, supporting at the spring of the vault, and taking on the form of slender planes.

A break from the controlled regularity of the main block was made with the load-bearing sanctuary, which was 'free to sweep in all needed space and formulate itself with an expressive curved wall'.[76] Movement within the sanctuary space itself was, of course, highly formalised, but relief was found in the grand processional movement from lower church to sanctuary, via the perimeter ramp. In perhaps the most dramatic example of the use of controlled lighting in the building, the sanctuary was illuminated by light diffused through the striking gridlike roof structure. Aside from the angled curve of the sanctuary, the main block was generally symmetrical on plan; the symmetry was enhanced by the flanking side chapels, which gave the chapel overtones of a Latin cross-plan.

While the social and psychological ideal of community shaped many physical aspects of the complex, there were also, in parallel to this, elements of the Late Modern concern for pure form, for architecture seen as sculpture. The resulting formal solutions showed evidence of the developing collective personality of the practice, rooted in many ways in the heritage of Mackintosh's architecture, especially the elemental harled shapes of designs such as Hill House. Internally, in features such as the sanctuary roof light and the gridlike door detailing, as well as in some furniture, a general resemblance to Mackintosh was discernible. Cardross's sectional arrangement of small units above large volumes also, in some ways, resembles the corbelled construction method of early Christian beehive cells, such as those on the Garvellachs, Argyllshire, where an early monastery once existed. In these early structures a hollow-section internal cell is formed by corbelling-in the walls and surmounting it with a lintel: but of course there is no reason to believe that this Scottish precedent was in the architects' minds.

The crypt of St Peter's College
Gillespie, Kidd & Coia Archive, Glasgow School of Art

Le Corbusier's Monastery of La Tourette, completed in 1960
Olivier Martin Gambier / Artedia / VIEW

More direct and specific influences, however, stemmed from abroad – especially from some of the chief international pioneers in the postwar rejection of machine-aesthetic smoothness in favour of more a forceful, individualistic variety of Modern architecture. Le Corbusier himself had hailed the rough finishes and irregular shapes of his Unité d'Habitation, Marseille (begun 1947), as a celebration of human nature: 'Faults are human; they are ourselves, our daily lives.'[77]

It was in the choice of materials that St Peter's conformed most closely to this trend. At an early stage in the programme the architects specified that exposed aggregate-faced precast concrete units should be used; in a reference to one of the postwar set-pieces of English social housing design, they asked W V Zinn to provide 'shuttering similar to the exposed concrete work at the Roehampton 11-storey maisonettes for which your firm were the engineers'.[78] As indicated above, exposed concrete was employed in the main block, classroom block and convent block. White painted-harl covered the load-bearing structures of the sanctuary, kitchen block and lower spaces of the convent block. Metzstein later explained that,

internally, 'exposed concrete would have very little presence … you weren't meant to feel you were inside a concrete box'. Externally, however, the presence of concrete was actually very strong. The upper floor of the classroom block, for example, adopted a herringbone pattern of exposed concrete; and the cloister-level walkway was of concrete – an image which strongly contrasted with the traditional covered cloister. The escape stair was boardmarked reinforced concrete, and the lower church featured heavy exposed concrete steps and concrete altars. The sculptural quality of the concrete must have appealed to the architects: Metzstein later claimed that 'we wanted it to look as if it were built by people working on the site, not made in a factory and flown in pieces to the site'.[79]

A visual distinction has to be made between the internal and the external use of materials, if the architects' accounts are to be understood. Internally the exposed concrete was painted in 'broken white', and the 'large areas of pinewood wall panels', such as those in the convent block, were to 'throw out sufficient colour' and 'offset the whiteness'. The extensive use of glazing increased the tonal warmth of the interior, and, at night, concealed artificial lighting was used to provide 'continuity of lighting at all times'. The concern to avoid a spartan concrete environment was also found on the exterior: for example, the aggregate precast panels were selected to 'harmonise with the stone of the existing house'.[80]

Contemporary and later discussion of the possible formal sources of the Cardross design has tended to focus on Le Corbusier's Monastery of La Tourette (1957–60) – an obvious potential influence on a seminary project with overtones of monastic imagery.[81] Aside from the obvious comparisons, such as the secluded site, the collegiate courtyard plan, and the use of exposed concrete, there are several more specific features of La Tourette which the architects drew upon. In final plan the French monastery, although having a separate chapel block, adopted an asymmetrical curved crypt which was positioned on the flank of the chapel. The form of St Peter's sanctuary strongly resembled this. The most striking resemblance was between the interior of that crypt and the lower church of St Peter's, as built. The latter's design, after the changes were made in 1963, adopted a series of bold concrete steps, with exposed concrete altars, and small beton-glass windows which threw a mystical light over the area. The crypt at La Tourette was, by comparison, top-lit, and had layers of brightly painted rough concrete, creating, on the whole, a more visually intense experience. The curved forms of the revised convent block also found a precedent at La Tourette. The first-floor visiting parlours of the monastery were circular harled forms, but whereas those at La Tourette were placed regularly aside each other, those at St Peter's were positioned irregularly.

There were, also, more general evocations of the work of Le Corbusier. The five side chapels, for example, suggested an image of clasping fingers in the anthropomorphic manner pioneered by Corbusier at the Ronchamp chapel (1950–5). The marine overtones of the funnel-like side chapels were also evocative of Corbusier's work, as was the escape stair (which bore a striking resemblance to that of the Millowners' Association Building, Ahmedabad, 1954), and an interesting earlier Continental precedent was Adolf Loos's unexecuted design for the Babylon Hotel, Nice, 1923.[82] Metzstein claimed that external designs only exerted influence in the evolution of the firm's architecture by feeding into its own cumulative traditions, such as the sectional type-plan: he argued that 'each building is built on the foundations laid by the previous one!'[83] Historians attempting to apply scholarly methods in examining the firm's work have sometimes fallen foul of this approach when attempting to identify design influence and parallels, or when placing a project within a broader historical context. The historian Gavin Stamp, who interviewed both Metzstein and MacMillan for the British Library Sound Archive project in 2000, recalled 'getting into trouble with Andy and Isi' when he tried to put their work into a wider context.[84] In turn, historian Robert Proctor cited Stamp's interviews in his own 2006 study of how the direct recollections of architects can end up excessively privileging an 'artistic or authorial concept of the architect's role': analyses of the Metzstein and MacMillan interviews were presented as case studies.[85] Metzstein's retrospective recollection of Cardross Seminary 'as a culmination, a summing up of certain architectural obsessions' is cited by Proctor as an example of the architect acting as his own historian.[86]

Programme and Construction

While the designers' conception of the extended seminary was an amalgam of a religious–social ideal and an architectural image, from 1960 the project began to move firmly into the arena of reality, both from the point of view of those engaged in building it, and from the point of view of the eventual users – the seminary staff and students. The old buildings continued in use throughout the extension work.

It was anticipated in 1960 that the project would start in spring 1961, and would be finished in spring 1963, but in the event works were not completed until spring 1968.[87] The prolongation of the construction of St Peter's College was due to several factors, but it is important to understand, in general, that many of the most prestigious and individualistic Modern Movement architects were particularly concerned to maintain control over all aspects of design, and less preoccupied with a rigid observance of the practical requirements of project management, such as building costs and deadlines, whereas the reverse applied in the case of architecturally mundane or commercially orientated designers.

That contrast was even more marked in the case of Gillespie, Kidd & Coia: throughout all the stages of construction and fitting-out, Metzstein and MacMillan repeatedly intervened with small design developments, and, indeed, were nicknamed 'The Alter Boys' by some of the workforce! At Cardross the difficulty of fully reconciling the artistic and managerial aspects of architecture, in a large and complex project, was highlighted. Contract management within Gillespie, Kidd & Coia was organised very differently from the specialisation and segregation of more commercial offices. According to Metzstein, 'the strength, or some may say the weakness of our office was that we tried to run it on a "hands-on" basis: the guy who was designing the building was also taking the site meeting notes. Yes – we were the "Alter Boys"; but to us it was a question not of altering but developing the design. For example, we always intended to elaborate the roof-light design above the sanctuary, and when the time came to build we did so.' A key inspiration in this respect was Mackintosh: Metzstein declared, 'I sympathise with him – he had problems and was sometimes unpopular with his clients and contractors on site.'[88]

It is the main purpose of this section to provide a brief and factual outline of the construction programme. The sources for this information are the project job files and drawings in the practice archive (housed in the Glasgow School of Art Archives), and the students' own accounts recorded in the *St Peter's College Magazine*. Exploration of the proposed site had been carried out in relation to the 1953 design, but the consultant engineers recommended further investigation.[89] The Kilmahew students recorded the first activity on the new site in March 1960: 'A considerable amount of interest was raised … when a lorry arrived at the house and a collection of machinery was deposited on the front lawn: pipes, ropes, tubes and pulleys … we later learned that for the next few weeks some workmen will be engaged in drilling at certain spots near the present house to test the soil and the rock strata. This is a necessary preliminary to building operations, and thus the new college seems gradually to be becoming something more of a reality.'[90]

The resulting report indicated that 'the poorest ground conditions occur under the lower classroom block'; and in construction the classroom block would duly prove to be the biggest problem for both the architects and the contractors. Negotiations over cost and materials followed the report, and in preparation of construction work, the shrubs and trees surrounding the existing house were cleared by the students (and later re-planted). The quantity surveyors for the project were McLernan & Whyte of Glasgow, and the initial cost for the main contract was originally estimated at £486,010. On St Andrew's Day, 1960, the site was blessed by Archbishop Campbell, and the first sod was cut. The weather conditions were bad, but 'neither howling gale nor driving rain prevented the archbishop from ensuring that the first sod was well and truly turned, the choir meanwhile most aptly singing the antiphon "Jerusalem is deserted, and its walls have been burned down. Come, let us rebuild the walls of Jerusalem. God himself will help us, and we are his servants. Let us arise and build".'[91]

The bad weather, which on several occasions hampered the construction, resulted in postponement of the next stage of work until spring. The building of the massive ferroconcrete retaining wall was begun in April 1961, by the contractors Hunter & Clark, and completed in November that year. As the programme continued, considerations of cost were raised by the diocese in summer 1961, and in July alterations were made to the sanctuary design, in addition to the 'proposed alterations to the student block' in November. The quantity surveyors supplied a new costing of £386,000, but eventually a cost of £434,400 was agreed upon by all parties. For a project of this size, it was decided to proceed using a main contractor rather than separate trades. The diocese were informed by the quantity surveyors and architects that at the proposed cost the 'period of the main contract … will require two and a half years to complete'. Bishop Ward was unhappy with this schedule: 'I feel that this is far too long, and I would hope that it will be possible to knock at least six months off this estimate.' In April 1962, pile driving was begun, much to the interest of the students, and tenders for the main contracts were received.[92]

In June 1962 the firm of James Laidlaw & Sons, Glasgow, accepted the main contract for the project, and agreed to complete it in two years. The consultant engineers had believed Laidlaw to be 'comparatively inexperienced in reinforced concrete', and had urged that 'the contract should not necessarily be awarded to the lowest tenderer'. Perhaps because Laidlaw was already involved with complex reinforced concrete work in Glasgow, including tower blocks, the client chose not to take Zinn's advice. In October 1962, a proposed construction sequence was set out. The main block, classroom (or teaching) block and kitchen block were to be completed in November 1963, and the sanctuary by spring 1964. Owing to the restrictions of the site, and the problems of access for the contractors, it was intended that a tower crane be placed to construct both the main block and classroom block 'in tandem' from a 'railtrack sited across the area of the sanctuary block foundation'. The crane was then to be removed, in mid 1963, after the classroom block had been erected, to allow the 'sanctuary block to proceed'.[93] The erection of the convent block would be the last stage in the sequence. This programme, of course, only related to the structural contract, and did not include the decoration, fitting and furnishing of the complex, or the alteration to the existing house.

Despite the severe winter conditions, the foundations were completed in April 1963; but from that point onwards, the schedule, and order of construction, began to diverge from the original plan. The main block was constructed first, and in late 1963 the further revised sanctuary design, rather than the classroom block, was commenced. To construct the main block, Laidlaw created a 'massive supporting structure' of scaffolding which took the form of a series of huge A-frames with wings on both sides and embraced some 400 tons of tubing: two tower cranes were needed. The main reason for this delay was that the boldly projecting classroom block, whose internal load-bearing structure, according to the architects, had to be rearranged to suit the site conditions. The drawings for this redesign were slow to materialise. The consequences began to unfold in late 1963 and reached crisis point in February 1964: in a letter of 22 February to Coia, Laidlaw's managing director appealed that a squad of fifteen joiners was standing idle for lack of drawings, as 'we have no information at all which will allow us to proceed with fundamentals of the construction'. The architects responded that 'an average force of 45 men has been maintained on the site for the last two and a half months … The present force is fully occupied in the convent

Early stage of construction outside Kilmahew House, June 1961
Archdiocese of Glasgow

The main block A-frame scaffolding, August 1963
Archdiocese of Glasgow

The main block under scaffolding, September 1963
Archdiocese of Glasgow

block and the main block.'[94] By late 1964, construction of the classroom block was at last well underway, and the shells of the main block, classroom block and convent block were complete. Standard fittings and furnishings for the main block, by Wylie & Lochhead, began in early 1964 (continuing until July 1966), those for the Kilmahew House alterations in August 1964, and those for the convent block in late 1964. The main subcontractors for internal infrastructure works were Muirhead & Sons, Grangemouth (laminated timberwork), Andrews Weatherfoil, Slough (central heating) and H M Fulton, Glasgow (electrical work).

On 8 September, 1964, before the 'entire hierarchy of Scotland', Campbell's successor, Archbishop Scanlan, laid the foundation stone on the side wall of the sanctuary, which had not yet received its massive laminated roof beams. The change of archbishops, following Campbell's death in 1963, had relatively little effect on the project, as Bishop Ward, the 'presiding genius at site meetings', continued to supervise it on the diocese's behalf. Yet, an appreciation of Archbishop Campbell, written after his death in 1963, claimed that 'as St Peter's, Bearsden was the memorial of his great predecessor Archbishop Eyre, so St Peter's, Cardross, will be his [Campbell's] memorial and his shrine'.[95] In April 1965, an informal visit of inspection by Scanlan and Ward revealed substantial progress with the classroom block: the scaffolding had just been dismantled, revealing (according to the students) 'a very striking structure of uncompromising severity'. Owing to mounting pressure from Ward for completion, overtime working was introduced by the contractors in April 1965; in December, Gillespie, Kidd & Coia predicted that the classroom block would be 'nearer completion in Spring 1966', but owing to delays in the internal fitting the block was not fully finished until early 1968. The kitchen block was set out internally in early 1966.[96]

The main block, February 1964
Archdiocese of Glasgow

Finally, on 1 October 1966, the students and staff of St Peter's were able to take possession of their 'brand new college', and experienced the inevitable 'teething troubles': 'Doors may break, handles fall off, floors creak and windows jam … the powers that be, in short, had prepared us for anything. This morning, flood waters greeted our arrival in the chapel but there was no Moses to conduct us through.' Later that week, however, the students reported on the first ordination ceremony in the new chapel, when their 'splendid new sanctuary was seen to advantage' in the morning light.[97]

The inauguration ceremony, and solemn opening, for the new college was held on St Andrew's Day 1966. It was attended by the Catholic hierarchy of Scotland and representatives from the Catholic hierarchies of England and Wales, and of Ireland; by representatives from all other religious denominations of Scotland; by the rectors of the other Scottish seminaries, including the Scots College in Rome; by local politicians and representatives from the Catholic societies; and of course by the architects and contractors. Archbishop Scanlan's main role at the ceremony was to celebrate Mass, and give thanks to the various participants in the project. He praised 'the genius of the architects', and declared that 'no architectural conception of such brilliance and quality can be translated into actuality without an immense amount of routine consultation, invigilation, frustration, indignation and perhaps judicious commination'. Bishop Ward, he asserted, was 'utterly beyond praise' for the way in which he had carried out these tasks.[98]

On 21 September 1967, the coffins of Archbishop Eyre (buried in the cemetery at St Peter's, Bearsden) and Archbishop Campbell (buried in Dalbeth Cemetery) were re-interred at St Peter's College (their remains

Interior of main block under construction, c1964
Archdiocese of Glasgow

Convent block under construction, c1964
Archdiocese of Glasgow

were initially received by Ward and rector Canon Connolly at St Mahew's Chapel on the evening of 20 September). Following a 'simple mass' in the new college chapel, they were buried in the crypt below the high altar. In his eulogy, McRoberts recorded 'Archbishop Campbell did not live to see this work complete, but repeatedly he made it known that he wished to be buried in the new college chapel.' McRoberts explained that although both men were 'remote from one another' in history and 'quite different in character … they were both united in their love for this college of St Peter'.[99] He concluded 'Archbishop Eyre's place as founder of St Peter's College is undisputed, but it is no misuse of the term to describe Archbishop Campbell as its second founder. It is indeed fitting that these two men should rest side by side in this place.' Subsequently, after the closure of the college in 1979, Campbell's coffin was moved again to St Andrew's Cathedral, Glasgow.

The last internal finishing works were completed in 1968, and in 1971 complex negotiations regarding the final measurement, and certificate of work, were carried out between architects, main contractor and diocese: the quantity surveyors finally costed the extension project at £609,800, which included £574,575 due to the main contractors.[100]

Press and Promotion

The extension at St Peter's, Cardross, was a prestigious commission for all who were involved, and, because of this, publicity coverage on the project within Scotland and the UK was fairly extensive. The first public display of the design came when a model of the proposed enlarged complex, made in June 1960 by a Mr Farrow of Cumbernauld, was displayed at the Roman Catholic 1960 Vocation Exhibition in the Kelvin Hall, Glasgow. Coverage in the major, English-based architectural journals started with the *Architectural Review*'s 1961 'Preview', in which Gillespie, Kidd & Coia presented their schemes for Cardross and St Bride's, East Kilbride.[101] In August 1962 the practice was approached by the architectural correspondent of the *Financial Times* (which used the same model for illustration) and then in April 1963 by the *Sunday Telegraph*. In early 1963, the project was exhibited at the Exhibition of Church Architecture, in London, by the Central Office

Laying of the foundation stone, September 1964
This high profile ceremony was led by Archbishop Scanlan and witnessed by the 'entire hierarchy of Scotland'. **Archdiocese of Glasgow**

Main block, c1966
Priests on the balcony as the main block nears completion.
Gillespie, Kidd & Coia Archive, Glasgow School of Art

of Information. During construction, journals such as *Concrete Quarterly* sought progress photographs of the works, as did Scottish Television, who were invited by the main contractors, James Laidlaw, to come and film the building in its scaffolding.[102] As construction neared completion, another limited wave of publicity surrounded the project, with the most eventful being the filming of a BBC documentary, *Four Modern Buildings*, in March 1966.[103] It was presented by architect Patrick Nuttgens, who claimed: 'The whole building is an architectural expression of its liturgical function, a house of God where living contemplation and working all combine in a single act of worship.'[104]

After the extended college had been inhabited, press interest continued. *Country Life* proposed an article in July 1967 (titled 'Scottish homage to Le Corbusier'), with *The Herald*, the *Observer*, *The Times* and the *Architect and Building News* all following suit.[105] There was only limited international interest in the project, chiefly in articles in the *Architectural Forum* (New York), and a 1967 article in *Architect and Builder* (South Africa).[106] More generally, in contrast to the prolific journalistic coverage of the project in the last 10–15 years, contemporary accounts in the architectural press were, on the whole, brief and descriptive, although a 1967 article in the relatively obscure journal *Interior Design & Contract Furnishing* was more ambitious and analytical: 'Brutalism, as Banham has said, never really came out of the aesthetic frame reference. Thus a building such as St Peter's College, must be examined in the context of the old architectural tradition, and within that context the building is one of the most superb examples of recent architecture to be seen anywhere in Britain.'[107] It continued 'it is the culmination of their achievement and in Europe only Broek and Bakema's church at Nagele and Sigrud Lewerentz's beautiful brick building in Stockholm are comparable, and of the three St Peter's is the best building.'

In a harbinger of the later sensitivities and antagonisms about 'authorship' associated with Gillespie, Kidd & Coia, an article for the *Concrete Quarterly* came under criticism from the architects, prior to publication in February 1967: 'While we are most anxious not to interfere with free comment and do not in any way deny our debt to Le Corbusier, we are a bit shaken that in our anxiety we have also managed to include elements

The newly completed St Peter's College
Kilmahew House is the central and dominant building in the complex.
Archdiocese of Glasgow

which were neither known to us at the time of the design or, as in the case of Sussex University, designed after St Peter's. It is particularly disturbing to be attributed with eclecticism so wide that it includes elements from unknown and unadmired buildings.'[108] The revised version of the article simply stated 'the architects freely acknowledge their debt to Le Corbusier', and their names were listed, in order, as 'I Metzstein, J Cowell and A MacMillan'.[109] In October 1967 the practice received an RIBA Bronze Regional award for the college, at a ceremony hosted by Scanlan and attended by 150 people: after that, in addition to press coverage, the firm was swamped by requests from university departments of architecture, including Edinburgh and Stirling, to provide tours of the college, and eventually had to decline requests, due to 'pressure of business' in the early 1970s.[110]

The architectural publicity stemming from the design of St Peter's was important not only in its own right, but also for its influence on the course of Gillespie, Kidd & Coia's patronage: it helped open the way to their last major group of commissions, for the English universities. Their relationship with the Church was, by that stage, becoming less central to their work, and also less harmonious – for reasons on which the next chapter will shed some light.

Opening Ceremony at St Peter's, 1966
Inauguration ceremony and solemn opening on St Andrew's Day.
Archdiocese of Glasgow

Chapter 5
The College in Use and in Decline

St Peter's College was a monument to being out of touch ... the church about us was changing, but the liturgical shape of St Peter's, with its multiplicity of altars, was obsolete before it began.
Father John Fitzsimmons, lecturer at St Peter's, Cardross, 1967–80

There was a false monasticism inherent in the design, a modernisation of the monastic concept. But the diocesan clergy were not meant to be monks!
Father James Foley, lecturer at St Peter's, 1965–80[1]

The Second Vatican Council, presided over in its later stages by Pope Paul VI, closed on 8 December 1965. It heralded an unprecedented period of change for the established hierarchy of the Catholic Church, and for the average practising Catholic. Ten months after the Council concluded its tasks (briefly outlined in Chapter 1) the students and staff of St Peter's took possession of their new college: a college which they were to leave for good only fourteen years later. Several factors led to the eventual decision to close the college, in 1980. With the benefit of hindsight, this chapter aims to examine the problems which the college had to overcome, and to assess the reasons for closure. These included extensive changes in curriculum and staff in the aftermath of the Council; decreasing numbers of ordinations in the face of growing secularisation of the Catholic community; financial difficulties on the part of the diocese; and last but not least, the perceived liturgical and practical defects of the new seminary. The chapter concludes with an overview of the history of the abandoned seminary from 1980 to 1994. In this fourteen-year period the seminary buildings gradually deteriorated into a gutted ruin, but from the 1980s, the complex's fate and reputation was affected by the beginning of the re-evaluation of Modern architecture as a potential subject of heritage. This overview

Sanctuary ramp, c1967
The seminary was in active use by 1966, excluding the classroom block.
Gillespie, Kidd & Coia Archive, Glasgow School of Art

St Peter's, Cardross

High Mass at St Peter's College, c1967
Archdiocese of Glasgow

Staff and students of St Peter's, 1968
This photograph was taken during the rectorship of Father Michael Connolly. Front row, left to right, are James Walsh, Joseph Devine, James Quinn, John MacKay, Michael Connolly, James McMahon, James Foley and John Cunningham.
Archdiocese of Glasgow

ends in 1994 when planning consent was granted for the retention of the 1960s seminary buildings in consolidated ruin form as a 'monument', pending future re-use. Yet later that same year, permission to demolish the original Kilmahew House was granted: the original historic core which supplied much of the rationale of the 1960s extension buildings' design was unceremoniously removed. The truncated Cardross Seminary, as we will see in the final chapter, now entered into a new life as a heritage artefact, increasingly divorced from both its own religious and its own architectural history.

Post-Council Reform at St Peter's College

The extent to which the Second Vatican Council would change the Roman Catholic Church, according to many who witnessed this period, could not have been anticipated by the average cleric.[2] Cardross Seminary became a monument to the speed of those changes. There was a radical evolution of ideas as to how it should be used, from the established pre-Council view of a seminary, to the extensive post-Council shifts in curriculum and improvisation within the new building, and, finally, to its redundancy and abandonment. This provides arresting proof that (contrary to some historians' claims of obstruction of reform) the diocesan authorities steadily, and successfully, set about implementing the Council reforms.[3]

The Second Vatican Council was to have a profound effect on the training of priests. It led to the effective abandonment of the principles of isolation shaped by the Council of Trent. Vatican II established an ideal of more integrated training: a combination of the theological, spiritual and pastoral. The training of priests was to become decentralised from Rome, and to take into account the variations of the national arms of the Church, and, ultimately, the requirements of individual parishes. The Council stressed the need for each 'national Church' to have its own 'Programme for Priestly Formation', effectively taking the onus of responsibility away from the Vatican, and the pastoral concerns of each national Church were to be incorporated into all aspects of priestly training. The wider implications of the Council, such as the introduction of the vernacular Mass, the extensive liturgical reforms, and the promotion of ecumenism, were also to bring fundamental change to the training of priests.

Students' common room
Flanking the chessboard: James Ryan (left) and Hugh Kelly (right). In front of column, centre right: Frank Gallagher.
Archdiocese of Glasgow

Seminary visitors in the refectory
Gillespie, Kidd & Coia Archive, Glasgow School of Art

In the West of Scotland, the Archdiocese, and in particular the Cardross Seminary, gradually made efforts to deal with these wide-ranging changes. The initial response at St Peter's to the new aim of integration of trainee priest and parish community came in the first term of 1965. One student related in the college magazine that 'The Aggiornamento [reforms following Vatican II] keeps us busy. External activity is a regular feature in our life now. From Kilmahew we venture forth three times a week …
In the words of the song, The times, they are-a-changing.'[4] But by this stage the new buildings were already well under construction: their governing liturgical conception was not that of 1965, but had already been (figuratively) set in concrete back in 1959. Monsignor James McMahon, Rector of St Peter's from 1972, later explained that 'the changes which were to occur after the Council were not anticipated by our superiors, who were not aware of how they would develop. The existing system of seminary training had served the Church well, and they were products of that system. Obviously they would attempt a well proven formula, so that is why seminaries were remote, and not in the middle of the city.'[5]

It could be argued that the problem of location was not a central concern for this particular seminary. Although Cardross was in the country, it was also a mere 30 minutes from the centre of Glasgow, and 20 minutes from a national airport. The subsequent move to Newlands in 1980 could be viewed as a post-Council, more urban solution, but the later decision of 1985 to establish Chesters College in Bearsden – a leafy suburb of Glasgow – returned the college again to a suburban context. Chesters was an inter-diocesan seminary, but excluded the Archdiocese of St Andrews and Edinburgh, and Diocese of Aberdeen. In that location in 1985, it was no closer to the population (in Vatican II terms) than Cardross in 1966.

Liturgically, too, the Council reforms had implications for seminary life. Father Kenneth Nugent (a former architect, who worked for Gillespie, Kidd & Coia in the 1950s) wrote in 1967 'The chapel is full of atmosphere; one only regrets that the altar is so far back for putting into effect the Constitution on the Sacred Liturgy.'[6] The introduction of concelebration (under which several priests acted together in the administration of the same sacrament, most commonly in the consecration

Students at St Peter's
Trainee priests warm up for a game of football.
Archdiocese of Glasgow

of the Eucharist) eventually made redundant the many side altars, and lower altars in the new chapel. In the opinion of some users, the new building 'was caught in a time-warp, with its proliferation of side-chapels'.[7] The place of private individual prayer, although still part of seminary training, was not central to the post-Council philosophy. Arguably, however, the notion of the secluded trainee priest had become less dominant in practice even in the 1950s: it was claimed by one former lecturer that the building's 'false monasticism' was a result of inadequate consultation of the priests – who were responsible for teaching – by the diocesan hierarchy and the architects. This monastic interpretation of life at St Peter's was accentuated both by the architectural style of the extension, and by the 1966 BBC documentary on the college, which concluded that 'the whole building is an architectural expression of its liturgical function, a house of God where living, contemplation, and working all combine in a single act of worship'.[8] One student, in reaction to viewing the programme, noted that the latter's 'frequent references to our "cells" may have heightened the monastic image of our life created by the style of the building itself'.[9] Nugent, in his 1967 'First Impressions' of the extended seminary, focused on the design directives of the Decree on Priestly Formation, and how these might be introduced at St Peter's through adaptation. Among these were provisions for: studying in small groups; small kitchens for 'light snacks' and socialising; and smaller tables for a 'cafeteria system' in the refectory. The last, he thought, should replace the architect-designed grand monastic refectory tables. He concluded: 'If his [the seminarian's] surroundings are indicative of his vocational attitudes, then this is a building with a challenge.'[10]

Once installed in the new college, and under the diocesan oversight of Archbishop Scanlan (after 1964), the staff and students of St Peter's gradually adapted to the post-Council world. The most significant changes occurred in the late 1960s, when staff changes were implemented by Scanlan, in the hope of both enhancing the theological standing of the seminary, and improving internal relations between teaching staff. Following Monsignor Treanor's death in 1963 and the short acting rectorship of Father McRoberts, a new rector, Father Michael Connolly, was appointed. After Connolly had tried, with limited success, to reconcile the existing staff to the impending reforms and to more academic teaching methods, and to heal personality clashes, Scanlan then undertook a 'monumental purge' of the lecturers, and introduced new men noted for their contemporary approach to theology, such as Father James Foley (in 1965), and Father John Fitzsimmons (in 1967). Scanlan told the historian Dr John Durkan (himself later a visiting lecturer at St Peter's) that 'things were so tense, I just had to sack half of them. Whether it was the right half or not, I am unsure!'[11]

At any rate, from now on Scanlan's desire to formulate a more scholarly, post-Council teaching philosophy prevailed. Fitzsimmons and Foley, under the supervision of Connolly and the 'flexible' remit of Scanlan, devised a new seminary curriculum. Foley recalled that 'each year, in turn, one of the gospels was given prominence – for example, the year of Matthew. In that year, I would teach the concepts of Matthew's church in dogmatic theology, while Fitzsimmons would also focus his teaching, in Biblical Studies, on Matthew. We implemented the Church's revised teaching, based on the liturgical cycle of three years. We took inspiration from church liturgy, and our other courses, such as philosophy, and canon law, to a lesser degree perhaps, emphasised the centrality of Christ. Prior to this, there had been a confused curriculum of liturgical teaching. Alongside all its faults, St Peter's was a happy place to be: we were all grappling with new ideas – they were pioneering and happy times.' On completion of the new library in 1968, the college books (previously stored in the old steading of Kilmahew House) were weeded and catalogued, with the help of a librarian from Glasgow University. Another consequence of the staff changes was the termination of the *St Peter's College Magazine* in 1968. Fitzsimmons claimed that in looking through the previous issues he could see 'no sight of the Second Vatican Council in it … they had been educating the students as if the council wasn't taking place'.[12] In addition to internal changes, the trainee priests and staff of St Peter's avidly attended the celebrated 1968 debates organised by the Scottish Catholic Renewal Movement.

The theological standing of the seminary continued to develop under the office of Scanlan's successor from 1974, Archbishop Thomas Winning. The college, however, lost the 'theological strengths' of Rector Connolly in 1972, through Scanlan's last notable staff change.[13] Scanlan appointed Father James D McMahon to the post, hoping that his strength and decisiveness would help instil greater domestic order into St Peter's and overcome continued factionalism among the staff.

The Crisis of the Priesthood

These reforms in teaching, carried out within the diocese's new 'Programme of Priestly Formation', were constantly dogged by one particular problem beyond the Archdiocese's control: a seemingly inexorable decline in the number of student priests after the peak of 1959–60. Part of a world-wide crisis of the priesthood, this was caused by growing secularisation within the Catholic community and increasing loss of membership from the Church. Ordination rates reached a historically low point in the early 1970s: in March 1972 the Vatican admitted that a total of 13,450 Catholic priests had abandoned the priesthood in the six years between 1964 and 1969, and that the number of priests was falling across the world, but particularly in Europe.[14] By 1972, the enlarged St Peter's College, Cardross, had been officially open for six years, and the building was operating at only around half its residential capacity: the maximum number of resident students at any time was 56. In 1979, the year before closure, the number of students had fallen to just 21.

As indicated above, the building decisions made by Archbishop Campbell and Bishop Ward in 1959 were based on the assumptions of the 1950s. The diocesan authorities reasonably assumed, in the context

Sanctuary block entrance at night, c1966
The seminary buildings were not generally open to the public.
Robert WKC Rogerson

Catholic Church leaders outside St Peter's, c1972
From left to right: the new rector Monsignor James McMahon, Bishop Thomson of Motherwell, Archbishop Scanlan, Auxiliary Bishop Winning and Bishop McGill of Paisley. **Archdiocese of Glasgow**

of rising ordination numbers, that this situation of growth and optimism would continue. The new college would therefore be built to last, would be of 'large and ornate proportions', and would accommodate future growth (for example, in 1949–50 attempts to 'eke out' accommodation by repairing and altering Kilmahew House and its ancillary buildings 'for next year's increased numbers' were underway).[15]

However, there were clear indications of the problems to come. The hierarchy were already aware of some difficulties in recruitment of young Scottish-trained priests, and a Vocations exhibition of 1960, held in the Kelvin Hall, Glasgow, hoped to alleviate this problem in some way. Father McMahon explained in the June 1960 issue of *St Peter's College Magazine*: 'We must appreciate that there is a problem, for the need is not merely universal but local too. We Catholics in the west of Scotland are failing to contribute our share of recruits to the religious orders of men and women, but more seriously we are failing to provide enough secular priests for our own needs.'[16] McMahon continued that 'the first duty of parents [is] to pray for the gift of a priest'. But in the event, those prayers went unanswered: the growing secularisation and liberalisation of Scottish society in the late 1960s and 1970s, and the resulting marked decline in congregations, had a profound effect on the recruitment and role of the priest. The vocation of the priesthood became an unattractive option for the majority of young Catholics in Scotland. As John Cooney noted in 1971: 'Until recently, the priest's position in the church and in society was secure. He was the educated man in the

Catholic community, and their representative in social and cultural affairs. However, the welfare state, the affluent society, the age of leisure, the anonymity of urban life, the decline of religion, and the growth of secularisation, have pushed the priest to the perimeter of society.'[17] McCaffrey had traced the decline in vocations back to the late 1950s, before the impact of Vatican II changes. By the 1970s, he argued, the 'golden age' of parishes served by four or five clergy during the first half on the twentieth century, had ended, and the position had reverted to the 'solitary priest' model of the early-to-mid nineteenth century.[18]

The Crisis of Diocesan Finance

There were also political and financial reasons, specific to the Scottish Catholic Church, which sapped the effectiveness of the Cardross Seminary from the beginning. Although (as already outlined), the financing of the church building programme of the mid and late 1950s took precedence over the new seminary, in the early 1960s Campbell and Ward made concerted efforts to raise funding for the project. Campbell looked to his bishops in Motherwell and Paisley (whose students would, of course, be accommodated at Cardross) for financial support, but Bishop Scanlan refused, on the basis that he had not been privy to the original negotiations for the seminary. The building programme carried on regardless, but relations between Glasgow and Motherwell continued to pose problems. Later in the decade Scanlan himself, now Archbishop of Glasgow, turned to his successor at Motherwell, Bishop Francis Thomson, for financial help. The latter refused, on the same grounds as had Scanlan before him.

After 1974, Thomas Winning inherited, as Archbishop, a financially unhealthy archdiocese from Scanlan. Scanlan's obituary sums up the serious position he left behind: 'During that decade [1964–74] the church suffered a dismal decline. There were many causes but the most obvious is emigration from Glasgow. During those ten years Glasgow lost the equivalent of twenty good healthy parishes. Further, there is no doubt that the morale of the clergy declined in those ten years. Again many causes could be deduced: aftermath of the council, longer wait for parishes, the decay of so many city parishes, for nothing saps the morale more than saying Sunday Mass in a church virtually empty, but I think a major factor was diocesan finance. When he came to Glasgow the diocese had large reserves. When he resigned, without in any way attributing blame to him, the fact was that all the reserves had gone.'[19]

On a national level, the number of Catholics reached a maximum of 15% of the population in the early 1960s, but, as outlined in Chapter 1, the rate of growth was sharply diminishing. While historians and sociologists continue to debate the 'timing, pace and nature of secularisation' within Scotland's Churches, Catholic Church adherence appears to have been initially less weakened than in England and Wales, and major decline was delayed until the 1980s.[20] In 1967 adherence was around 64%, but sociologists have estimate a fall from two-thirds in 1959 to about one-third by 1997.[21] The fastest (estimated) drop in Catholic church attendance was in the five years 1966–71 – between 42,000 and 115,000, according to varying estimates. The number of Catholic marriages between 1975 and 1995 had more than halved from 6,003 to 2,948.[22] In the twenty-first century's first decade, numbers attending Sunday Eucharist were about 33%: back, as John McCaffrey noted, to the levels of the 1830s.

The financing of the expanded St Peter's Seminary may have accounted for a proportion of these financial problems in the 1970s, but the overall system of borrowing from wealthier parishes to fund struggling ones was a more basic source of difficulty. In McHugh's opinion, the appreciation of debt from the 1960s highlighted the 'underlying problem which had confronted successive Vicars-Apostolic and Archbishops', that of 'providing the necessary churches and services from a severely limited capital base'.[23] In 1975, Bishop Thomson of Motherwell inflicted another blow to the financially struggling archdiocese, and to Cardross in particular, when he withdrew his students from St Peter's, and moved them to the eastern seminary of Drygrange, on the grounds that the cost of supporting students at St Peter's was 'crippling' the diocesan finance of Motherwell. Here the additional cost implicit in the post-1953 policy of separate western and eastern seminaries came into the open, and the more ambitious western institution proved to be the more vulnerable: in the words of one former lecturer, 'financially, St Peter's was an albatross around the neck of the diocese'.[24] Only in 1993, with the eventual foundation of a national seminary, Scotus College, Bearsden (a redesignation of Chesters College), was the problem of division and duplication finally and decisively addressed.[25]

The Crisis of Use and Maintenance

In addition to the potential problems of obsolescence in the field of liturgical arrangement, there were other troubles directly connected with the new Cardross building. There was the straightforward problem of scale: the optimistic, expansive size of the complex resulted in practical problems. And there were the problems of the structure's technical performance, which suffered criticisms from the opening of the extensions right up to the date of closure.

The scale of a building intended for 100 students but occupied, at the maximum, by only 56, had serious implications for heating costs. The rise in oil prices in 1974, and the withdrawal of funding from the diocese of Motherwell in 1975, only exacerbated the problem. Size also proved difficult in terms of teaching. Fitzsimmons recalled that the large classrooms were not suitable for intimate group teaching, and an element of 'improvisation' was needed.[26] As time progressed, problems with heating, and with sound insulation, became 'intolerable'; much of the teaching activity was moved to the old Kilmahew House, so that 'students could take refuge, and get some peace and quiet'.[27]

Technical problems, according to those who lived and taught there, were a growing concern. Initial teething troubles were documented by the students in the college magazine, and in the first few days of occupation, one reported that 'doors may break, handles fall off, floors creak and windows jam … This morning flood waters greeted our arrival in the chapel but there was no Moses to conduct us through.'[28] These were followed by more serious and persistent difficulties.[29] Soon after opening, in February 1967, one student related that 'during concelebrated Mass this morning, an ominous crack from one of the beams above the sanctuary served to remind us of the Rector's 'parousia' prophecy. Dreams of depleted staff were banished when nothing more disastrous followed.' Although there were many lesser issues, such as the alleged 'failure' of the chapel seating, the most persistent problems concerned water penetration, in many parts of the complex, and 'woodworm and fungus' in the classroom block.[30] Water penetration in the sanctuary was reported at a peak in the winter of 1967, when a seminarian related that 'a record number of fifty-three leaks in the sanctuary lantern betrayed themselves after very heavy rain. The total for the whole building has not yet been returned.'[31] The ongoing reports on the technical problems encountered by the seminarians stopped, of course, with the termination of the *St Peter's College Magazine* in 1968.

From 1972 onwards, the newly appointed rector, Father McMahon, began a relentless quest (at first, under the overall authority of Ward) to remedy the 'inadequacy' of the building, bombarding the architects with letters of complaint. In April 1973, McMahon went so far as to produce a report, with the help of 'two well-qualified civil engineers', outlining his personal concerns. Water ingress, he told Archbishop Scanlan, was now a problem in most areas of the complex (including the student rooms and the refectory): new areas of penetration included the 'sanctuary lantern' where previous remedial work had had 'little effect'. The refectory and chapel flooring was 'continuing to break up' and no solution had been forthcoming from the architect. McMahon explained that the 'report is so bleak … to rectify the faults will be costly. If, however, they are design faults – as would appear probable – the architects will most likely hold professional indemnity insurance against such an eventuality.'[32] In February 1974 he wrote to John Cowell that the building was no longer 'proof against wind and water', and demanded 'immediate action' from the architects. Despite remedial work by Gillespie, Kidd & Coia in the summer of 1974, in September McMahon reported acerbically to them: 'It may be of interest to you that the roof over the stairway in the classroom block has collapsed.' Reportedly, in November 1974 Gillespie, Kidd & Coia made a 'statement' to the Archdiocese 'disclaiming professional liability' for the building's 'problems'.[33] More repairs were undertaken by the firm in early 1975.

Alongside these exchanges, professional interest in the architectural world continued: a letter by McMahon in December 1973 complained of unannounced visits by architects, problems of water penetration, and timber and cladding deterioration. Father Foley recalled one occasion in the early 1970s when Jack Coia showed a group of 'wide-eyed architectural students around the building while we mopped up the rain water from the floor'.[34] In 1972, film-maker and writer Murray Grigor made his short powerful documentary *Space and Light*, showing 'students in cassocks flitting about the buildings'.[35] Grigor later recalled discussing his ideas with Coia: 'Jack Coia appreciated my Mackintosh film (*Mackintosh*, 1968), but did not want the same biographical approach for his own. "Why don't you just explore the architecture of St Peter's?" he asked, as he shuffled in his carpet slippers along the marble colonnades of the Casa d'Italia, a building which he had recently remodeled, next door to his office in Glasgow's Park Circus.'[36]

In 1979, the decision to abandon Cardross Seminary was taken; the college closed in February 1980, and the students moved to the Glasgow suburban Newlands premises (formerly the Convent of the Franciscan Nuns of the Immaculate Conception), taking some moveable fittings (including, for instance, the library shelving).[37] The declining number of students, the withdrawal of Motherwell diocese from participation, and the stark financial situation of the Archdiocese, all contributed to the closure, alongside the technical problems and (in hindsight) excessive scale of the complex. Yet despite the role of user difficulties in the college's decline, the students and staff, throughout, balanced their practical complaints with admiration for its architectural strengths. In the same way that the students, at the opening, enthused about the 'handsome new chapel' and 'splendid new sanctuary', even after the closure staff could still praise the buildings' 'magical dimensions' and 'brilliance'. In a 1980 album of the move to Newlands, Cardross's last resident students lamented the loss of the popular meeting-space of the main wooden staircase – one of the elements at the centre of the architects' 'community' conception. Father Fitzsimmons recalls: 'Visually, I loved the building. It was brilliant – but utterly useless! I talked to Jack Coia about the problems, and he answered, "God did not create a perfect world!".'[38]

This was an unceremonious departure from Cardross. The 1980 *Catholic Directory of Scotland* simply recorded that 'St Peter's College is to move yet again, this time from Cardross to Merrylee, Glasgow. The present buildings, opened in 1966, are to be sold.'[39] The coffins of Archbishop Eyre and Archbishop Campbell were removed (the historic stone carvings mounted on the sanctuary wall were presumably taken down at the same time). For the Archdiocese of Glasgow, the high profile and costly Cardross Project (in 1972 the 'new college buildings' were valued at £925,000 and Kilmahew House at £60,000) was then apparently consigned to history.[40] Thirteen years later, in 1993, Archbishop Winning, under whose leadership the decision to close Cardross Seminary was taken, claimed 'The opening of our national seminary, Scotus College, ranks amongst the most significant events of this century in the life of the Catholic Church in Scotland.'[41] Scotus College, Bearsden, was housed in a modest nineteenth century classical suburban villa. Winning concluded with a note of caution, 'Time will clearly demonstrate the wisdom of this decision and benefits which will accrue to people and clergy.' Scotus College was not only the first but the last national seminary based in Scotland, as it eventually closed itself in 2009. The main seminary for the training of Scottish Catholic priests then became the Scots College in Rome, Italy, and the nine remaining students of Scotus College were transferred there.

Decline, Vandalism, and Heritage Protection, 1980–94

I am amazed that a building that has never fulfilled the purpose for which it was built, because badly designed and constructed, should even be considered for any award … What the people need from Historic Scotland is not an award but a bulldozer.
Rev. David Brown, 1992

Cardross was never given a chance. The abandonment of so much built capital, let alone an astonishing sophisticated and powerful realization of the ideas which had inspired Glasgow's most celebrated modern firm of architects, really was an avoidable tragedy. The problem, perhaps is not the architecture of Gillespie, Kidd & Coia, but Scotland.
Gavin Stamp, 1994 [42]

Drug rehabilitation centre, mid 1980s
After its closure, the Archdiocese temporarily used the former seminary as a drug rehabilitation unit.
The Herald and Evening Times

After 1980, the abandoned seminary buildings gradually deteriorated into a gutted ruin, but remained, on the whole, as a unified 1960s seminary complex. Throughout these fourteen years, the complex had only one period of active occupation, as a drug rehabilitation centre, but there was a succession of proposals for re-use or conversion. From the late 1980s, its fate and reputation was affected by a new phenomenon in architectural history: modern heritage. In 1992, the derelict St Peter's College buildings were raised to Category A status by Historic Scotland: the entire complex already had government-protected status, by virtue of the Category B listing (in 1971) of the original nineteenth century Kilmahew House, to which the new extension was attached. By the mid 1990s Cardross Seminary was at the forefront of a growing academic and preservationist interest in the postwar architecture of Gillespie, Kidd & Coia. In late 1994 permission was granted to demolish the structurally unsound Kilmahew House. Its demolition removed the original historic core which had supplied much of the rationale of the extension buildings' design. This was the first major setback in what was to become a long campaign to 'save' the former seminary – notably longer than its short life as a functioning seminary. In that same year, planning consent was granted for the retention of the seminary buildings in consolidated ruin form, as a 'monument', pending future re-use. Cardross Seminary now entered its new era as a heritage artifact.

Throughout this period, the Archdiocese of Glasgow retained ownership of the Kilmahew estate and its building, and remained central to its new story.[43] A new grouping now became increasingly involved with the derelict complex, and this included local, regional and national government planning and heritage organisations; voluntary preservation societies; private developers;

Birth and Death – Chapter 5

The former St Peter's College looking north, c1998
Following the demolition of Kilmahew House in 1995, the ruin continued its long-term decline.
Tom Kidd / Alamy Stock Photo

The former St Peter's College looking south, c1998
The footprint of the demolished Kilmahew House can be seen bottom right. The disappearance of the house leaves a wholly misleading impression of the architectural balance of the seminary as originally completed in 1966.
Tom Kidd / Alamy Stock Photo

The ruins St Peter's, 1994
The deteriorating main block, side chapels and sanctuary block.
HES SC713662

planners, academics, architectural critics, and to a lesser extent, contemporary architects. Metzstein was initially reluctant to discuss the vexed question of the condition and future fate of the short-lived and troubled seminary: in 1993 he explained 'Of all the projects I've been involved in, this is the one which is most important to me – a very painful, yet very enjoyable exercise!'[44] But by the mid 1990s, a small group of architects and academics, based mostly at Glasgow's Mackintosh School of Architecture and closely linked in some way or another with Gillespie, Kidd & Coia and each other (to the point that they were later even described by one critic as a 'Holy Family'), began a contemporary reinterpretation of the firm's post-1956 architecture.[45] This revisionist trend was spearheaded by architect Mark Baines, who had worked as an assistant to Gillespie, Kidd & Coia in 1976–9, and began teaching at the Mackintosh School in 1982. MacMillan remained head of school until 1994, and continued as a part-time tutor until 2004. Metzstein continued his role as visiting tutor until 1998.[46] In 1991, architectural historian, conservation campaigner and critic Gavin Stamp also joined the Mackintosh School as lecturer in history. Metzstein, as original lead-designer, remained inextricably linked to the former seminary until his death in 2011. As Cardross Seminary became the focus of increasingly emotive preservationist rhetoric in the mid 1990s (lamenting its loss and misuse), a parallel discourse emerged, setting out to counteract the supposed lack of appreciation of the 'creative inspiration' of Metzstein and MacMillan's architecture, within the historical context of postwar Scottish and British architecture.[47] In turn, this discourse would increasingly elevate Gillespie, Kidd & Coia's post-1956 formalistic architecture into a key inspiration for a fresh generation of 'iconic modernist' designers.

The decision to abandon St Peter's as a seminary, as outlined, took shape in 1979. In that year an application was made to then planning authority, Dumbarton District Council, from the First Hospitality Corporation of America, for change of use of the complex to form a hotel. The company's bid to buy the site was, however, withdrawn, apparently due to its inflexibility for conversion. This did not deter the diocese from moving out, and shortly afterwards, in March 1980, a further application was made, for change of use to a conference centre. This application was also withdrawn. Following these two failed conversion proposals by private parties, the Church authorities decided in 1983 to utilise the empty building as a drug rehabilitation and detoxification centre. This was run by the Social Services section of the diocese, and in a period of five years approximately 1,500 people passed through the programme. Despite this quantitative success, the Archdiocese identified 'deterioration of the building' as the main cause for its closure in 1987.[48] Press reports in the early 1990s recounted 'shock allegations' surrounding the management of the rehabilitation facility, with accounts of 'recovering drug addicts living there in squalor and allegations of financial malpractices involving social security payments'.[49]

During its use as a rehabilitation centre, the diocese first began to think in terms of demolition. Here we encounter for the first time the world of architectural heritage, which was increasingly to become the context for discussion of the buildings' fate. At that stage the extensions were afforded protective status by virtue of the Category B listing of the original Kilmahew House. The diocese submitted a Listed Building Consent application for part demolition in 1983; this was refused by the planning authority the following year – the first of three demolition applications, all unsuccessful in a climate of mounting interest in Modern architecture. In 1989 the Archdiocese was considering re-use as a residential nursing home, but in 1990 an application was made to convert the college building into flats, and in that same year another application for full demolition was made.[50] Both applications were withdrawn.

Preservation and the Works of Gillespie, Kidd & Coia

While these proposals for St Peter's succeeded one another, the world of heritage was witnessing a rapid change in climate towards the revaluation and protection of post-1945 architecture. This was an international phenomenon: the year 1990, for example, saw the foundation of DOCOMOMO (Documentation and Conservation of the Modern Movement), an international federal grouping whose constituent national groups, from 1992, included a Scottish working party. DOCOMOMO Scotland was founded as a voluntary initiative by a small group of professionals with links to heritage and research organisations, and included: Miles Glendinning (then based at RCAHMS); Ranald MacInnes of Historic Scotland; Paul Stirton from the University of Glasgow; and former Scottish Office architect David Whitham. Throughout the twentieth century in Scotland there had been a recurring tension between the aspirations to widen the scope of heritage to embrace more and more of the built environment and cultural landscape, and the practical reality of extending preservation ever further. This issue first came into focus with the growth of industrial archaeology in the mid-to-late 1980s, when Scotland's vanishing traditional nineteenth and twentieth century heavy industries became a heritage concern. 'Recent' preservation only became problematic in Scotland in the early 1990s, however, when the focus shifted to the large postwar ensembles such as peripheral housing schemes, tower blocks and New Towns. DOCOMOMO Scotland focused on compiling new research, but also lobbied for protection of Scotland's most significant postwar buildings and sites. In 1991, founding members of DOCOMOMO Scotland attempted to secure the listing of the internationally significant Cumbernauld Town Centre, but this was vetoed by the then Secretary of State for Scotland Hector Monro.[51] In 1994, a report by DOCOMOMO Scotland highlighted the architectural and historic significance of St Peter's College itself, and of the work of its architects, Gillespie, Kidd & Coia.[52] By the mid 1990s DOCOMOMO refocused on its documentation remit, putting aside lobbying for preservation following a number of unsuccessful attempts to get buildings and sites listed.[53]

In this period, efforts to survey and preserve Scotland's postwar environment were dominated by government-funded initiatives. Unlike almost all other Western European countries, the state heritage system was divided between RCAHMS, undertaking survey, archiving and dissemination, and the much larger Historic Scotland, responsible for listing and, in partnership with local authorities, historic building control. From the mid 1980s, RCAHMS began making new records, and from the 1990s actively collecting archives of Scotland's postwar built environment in response to the increasing academic and heritage interest in that period. A special niche for threat-based recording had been established for RCAHMS under the 1969 Town and Country Planning (Scotland) Act: recording listed buildings prior to demolition, and making that record available to the public, was seen as the final stage in the new conservation development control system. Up until the 1990s only a small number of postwar buildings were listed in Scotland: this statutory remit had no real impact, but by the mid-to-late 1990s it proved effective. This threat-based recording remit, and more specifically the proposed demolition of Kilmahew House, and the convent block in 1993, prompted RCAHMS to carry out an extensive photographic survey in 1994, which ultimately led to the first publication of this book in 1997; in 1980 the drawings for St Peter's College had been copied as part of RCAHMS's survey of private collections initiated by curator Kitty Cruft. Running parallel to this targeted recording was the long-term RCAHMS threat-based survey of large-scale postwar developments and redevelopments, which by the 1990s were becoming obsolete. By the late 1990s RCAHMS had established itself as a leading national resource for the postwar built environment.

Historic Scotland, on the other hand, was tasked with the practical reality of extending protection to include postwar architecture. By the early 1990s Scotland's often controversial postwar heritage was a focus of strong passions and conflicting views.

Since 1980, a decade after the drive behind the national programmes of reconstruction had fallen away, the post-1914 built environment had started to become accepted as potential heritage (an inventory of the immediate interwar period having been pioneered by the Royal Incorporation of Architects in Scotland (RIAS) Scottish Thirties project, which led to Historic Scotland's small-scale listing programme of interwar architecture), but the listing of large postwar ensembles proved a more difficult process owing, mainly, to the traditional evaluative system of listing. Scotland's historic buildings listing had begun in the 1930s (headed by Ian G Lindsay), and from the late 1960s (under the direction of David Walker) developed as one of the widest historic buildings listing programmes in Europe: today it is estimated that one and a half times as many buildings are listed in Scotland as in England.[54] Listing of postwar buildings began tentatively in the late 1980s and early 1990s within a traditional art-historical evaluative system, emphasising especially the work of known architects. As a result, free-standing buildings in single ownership (such as bespoke private houses, churches, schools and administrative buildings), designed by important architects (such as Basil Spence, Morris & Steadman and Peter Womersley), were more easily incorporated into the evaluative system of designation. More generally, Historic Scotland was faced with the problem of how to adapt a system that focused on individual monuments as works of art, and to refocus on an era that insisted on ensemble planning, and it was decided initially to list Modern Movement buildings closest to the traditional evaluative system. The 'group value' of Lindsay's first 1930s lists, which focused on the main streets of Scotland's historic towns and burghs, was increasingly jettisoned as listing developed in the 1990s: ironically, the earlier system was perhaps better-suited for the evaluation of collective postwar environments. South of the border, English Heritage made efforts to tackle these evaluative difficulties by undertaking an ambitious 'thematic study' of postwar architecture in the mid 1990s, including building types such as public housing and schools. Historic Scotland began a 'discussion' on postwar listing a decade later in 2009, in a series of publications.[55] Listing was expanded to include more complex architect-led public works, including new universities, leisure centres, and hospitals. At that stage approximately 200 postwar buildings were listed in Scotland – evaluated under the established system of listing 'but with a rigour on account of their youth'.[56]

Gillespie, Kidd & Coia's architecture was at the forefront of the development of concepts of postwar Scottish heritage, and, as we will see, historical research, contemporary architectural critiques and advocacy of protection went hand-in-hand. The advance of heritage across the firm's oeuvre started tentatively, and was not always smooth. Whereas, in 1986, a restoration grant to prevent demolition of the campanile at St Bride's, East Kilbride, had been refused, in 1987 (the year after the publication of Rogerson's book on Coia), the first listing of one of the firm's postwar works – St Paul's, Glenrothes – was implemented.[57] And in August 1992, the same year that architect Mark Baines delivered the first ever public lecture on the firm's work (other than by the architects themselves) at DOCOMOMO Scotland's founding conference in Glasgow, the St Peter's College buildings were raised to Category A status. The Cardross extension, and the firm's Our Lady and St Francis School, Glasgow (listed in 1989), were the first entirely postwar buildings to be listed at Category A. However, the listing of St Paul's, Glenrothes, in 1987 was followed only four years later by the sudden and highly controversial demolition of the firm's St Benedict's, Drumchapel, Glasgow, just prior to its planned listing in 1991.[58] Its demolition was lambasted by Gavin Stamp as 'wicked [and] precipitate'.[59] The fate of the church first came to Stamp's attention during a tour of Glasgow in Autumn 1990: 'The Thirties Society was deeply impressed [he reported in the *Architects' Journal*]; after a depressing diet of second-rate *moderne* and grim tower blocks of the 1960s nearby, St Benedict's was real architecture worth coming all the way to see … After all, the postwar architecture of Scotland is scarcely inspiring: only the Roman Catholic churches of Gillespie, Kidd & Coia stand out as imaginative, experimental designs of European stature.'[60] The demolition of St Benedict's acted as an impetus for the listing of a number of Gillespie, Kidd & Coia church buildings (St Charles', Kelvinside was listed in 1992), and in September 1994, another fourteen postwar Gillespie, Kidd & Coia churches were listed by Historic Scotland, bringing the total of the firm's listed churches to twenty-one (including both pre-war and postwar). Ranald MacInnes and John Hume (Chief Inspector of Historic Buildings from 1993, and an enthusiast for religious architecture) were instrumental in these listings. MacInnes, in his capacity as a historic buildings inspector, remained directly involved with Cardross Seminary from the late 1980s onwards.

St Benedict's Church, Drumchapel, Glasgow, by GKC, 1965–7
Listing of this church was in planning prior to its swift demolition.
Gillespie, Kidd & Coia archive, Glasgow School of Art

Demolition of St Benedict's, 1991
The demolition of St Benedict's spurred on a wave of new listings of Gillespie, Kidd & Coia churches. HES SC440354

Diane Watters and Miles Glendinning of RCAHMS at Cardross, 1994
Author Diane Watters and architectural historian Miles Glendinning at the ruined Cardross Seminary prior to the demolition of Kilmahew House. HES SC713638

It was hardly surprising that the work of Gillespie, Kidd & Coia was given a privileged position in postwar listing, as their church designs were so strongly dominated by aesthetic rather than social or technical concerns.[61] Despite their Modern Movement innovations in plan-type and formalistic innovations, the churches remained stately monuments, rooted in a traditional local religious culture with traditional clients – especially in the West of Scotland. Coia's insistence on incorporating 'religious art' only increased the heritage art-value of the churches. In general, church architecture stood out as an anomaly within a postwar welfare state structure, and was on the periphery of Modern Movement architectural discourse. Despite seismic liturgical changes, as listed buildings churches differed little from their nineteenth century counterparts. On the whole, Modern Movement conservation issues of re-use and material authenticity proved relatively unproblematic for postwar church restorations, in contrast to the complexities facing listed housing schemes or tower blocks. Yet, as we will see, as a hybrid religious–secular complex, the former St Peter's Seminary was not exempt from the complexities of Modern Movement conservation.

It was the technical failings of Gillespie, Kidd & Coia's listed churches (arguably also a concern in the case of low-cost postwar churches designed by other architects) that potentially posed the greatest financial problem for their continued use. An ongoing series of press articles from the mid 1990s highlighted the troubled 'award-winning Catholic buildings plagued by structural faults', beginning with the unlisted St Benedict's, Drumchapel, and followed by the listed St Benedict's, Easterhouse, in 1996.[62] Although the Cardross complex, as a ruin, was largely exempt from these ongoing problems of technical performance, its poor performance-record when in use continued to come under criticism in the 1990s. However, in its new role as a heritage artifact, considerations of the original functional failures were increasingly deemed irrelevant.

Cardross Re-evaluated

In this next phase in its life, the master narrative of the ruined St Peter's Seminary was strikingly unlike the history of its original commission, design and use, and was instead shaped by a powerful tragic discourse focused on its abandonment and its supposedly unappreciated architectural beauty. The foundations of what was later described as the 'myth' of Cardross Seminary, and the broader 'cult' of Gillespie, Kidd & Coia, were formed in this period.[63]

The growth in historical and preservationist interest in postwar Gillespie, Kidd & Coia buildings inevitably began to spark a public debate about Cardross: an 1989 article reported 'a sorry sight', and lamented 'another name has been added to the roll call of Scotland's threatened architectural heritage'.[64] In 1990, the former seminary buildings were added to the Scottish Civic Trust's 'Buildings at Risk Register'. Following the 1991 St Benedict's demolition, press-debate (led chiefly by Gavin Stamp) shifted to focus on Cardross. A flurry of press coverage in the lead up to the Walker Group report in March 1992 repeated the preservationist themes first applied to St Benedict's. In a lengthy 1992 article by Lucy Musgrave in *Scotland on Sunday* the

The continuing ruination of the former St Peter's
HES SC713655

Archdiocese's 'dubious track record of care for its modern buildings', evidenced by its withdrawal of site security in May 1991, was attributed to Archbishop Winning having 'little love for St Peter's College, contrary to his predecessors'.[65] She concluded: 'Gillespie, Kidd & Coia is perhaps Scotland's most important postwar architectural practice thanks to the two prodigies [Metzstein and MacMillan] who designed these incredible buildings … now famous for their brilliance.' Responding to the Walker Group's report, the *Scotsman* described the buildings as having once been the 'jewel in the crown of modern Scottish church architecture'.[66]

At that point, Musgrave reported that Historic Scotland was considering 'upgrading its status'. Amidst increased press coverage, concerns had indeed emerged over the effectiveness of statutory protection of the 1960s buildings within the pre-existing Category B listing of Kilmahew House. At some point prior to September 1992, the 1960s linking kitchen block had been part demolished and the physical link between the listed historic house and the Gillespie, Kidd & Coia extension was severed. It was argued that this could be interpreted as a removal of the legal protection of listing from the 1960s buildings, and could potentially allow the Archdiocese to disregard a repairs notice 'recently' served by Dumbarton District Council. A technical adjustment to upgrade the existing listing to Category A was implemented in September 1992.[67]

The upgrading proved relatively uncontroversial and was particularly welcomed by the architectural heritage community. Ian Fernie, director of the planning authority, admitted 'It is an unusual building to become A-listed … [but] it is one of the finest modern buildings of its day.'[68] Through the letters page of *The Herald*, support and objections were voiced; Gavin Stamp claimed the A-listing 'fully justified'.[69] An early example of the heightened heritage campaigning rhetoric which was later to typify debates surrounding the former seminary, came in a letter of support from chairman of DOCOMOMO International, architect Hubert-Jan Henket, based in the Netherlands. He had recently visited the seminary 'with DOCOMOMO friends and colleagues': 'I was amazed and appalled to see this famous religious complex, which belongs among the world's top buildings of architectural importance of the second half of the twentieth century, in a terrible state of destruction and dereliction … Although Glasgow witnessed a phenomenal building boom after the Second World War, only a few buildings are important for their outstanding beauty and atmosphere. Therefore it is only wise to save St Peter's seminary in Cardross by bringing it back to its original state.'[70]

The local authority anticipated the upgrading would be 'likely to come as a shock to the Roman Catholic Church'.[71] The Archdiocese made no official announcement, but issued a 'pledge' to maintain the estate. Dissent came indirectly from one priest based at the Archdiocese offices in Glasgow, whose views, according to Historic Scotland, could serve 'as an indication of the church's attitude to its newly-imposed statutory responsibility'.[72] In a lengthy letter to *The Herald* entitled 'Rainwater at the high altar' (following on from its report on the upgrading), Rev. David Brown, based at St Andrew's RC Cathedral House, Glasgow, objected vigorously: he was 'amazed and angered … that a building that has never fulfilled the purpose for which it was built, because badly designed and constructed, should even be considered for any award. As one who lived there from 1969 to 1975, who has developed osteoarthritis as a result of its damp living conditions, I can testify that the design and building work merit censure rather than award. And I am angry that a body like Historic Scotland should effectively impose a massive financial obligation on the RC community of Glasgow to maintain a building it neither needs nor wants.' Brown questioned the morality of public monies, if forthcoming, being spent on an empty building: he asked 'Can anyone seriously imagine regular busloads of the public wishing to visit it anyway?'[73]

The focus of Brown's deep-felt 'anger' was the technical performance of the 1960s extensions: 'I admit to having had a little chuckle when I read the obligation to make the building wind and watertight. This is clear proof that those responsible for A-listing know little of the building, for no matter how much money is available for repairs this can never be achieved. Never since the day the college was opened, could it ever have been described as wind and watertight. On rainy days it was impossible to use the high altar, as water would drip or pour on to it from all directions. As college sacristan for two years, my duties involved standing by the side of the church with a portable altar for assembly on dry ground before the start of mass. Indeed, it is just possible that if the building had been a wind and watertight structure in the first place, St Peter's College, Cardross, may still be alive today.' In reply, Stamp accepted that the original functional failings were 'correct', but concluded 'these had little to do with the closing and abandonment of the seminary'.[74] In the early 1990s national and local press highlighted these technical and functional failings: the *Scotsman* talked of saving the 'holey seminary' noted for 'roof leaks'.[75] This ongoing debate was not resolved, but by the late 1990s, as Chapter 6 uncovers, the question of original functional and technical failure of the seminary was no longer relevant to the ruined monument, or the campaign to rescue it.

In August 1993, Metzstein himself spoke briefly and somewhat reluctantly about the fate of the college buildings: 'I can certainly say that if they try to pull it down, I'll have the last laugh: the building would be almost as difficult to demolish as it was to build!' In his opinion, the complex might be suitable for conversion in some circumstances; but equally, he would 'rather enjoy the idea of everything being stripped away except the concrete itself – a purely romantic conception of the building as a beautiful ruin!'[76] He was then taking part in an architectural dialogue with Mark Baines on Cardross during a series of seminars organised by the Royal Fine Art Commission for Scotland. Academic interest in the work of the practice had developed further in the early 1990s. As outlined above, Metzstein and MacMillan were then both based at the Mackintosh School, and the extensive practice archive was housed in its basement. Here the previous decade's transformation of Gillespie, Kidd & Coia and its key personnel from an active practice into a university-based academic dynasty began to encourage cross-fertilisation between the teaching of present-day architecture and the pursuit of heritage – in the manner already seen in the case of Mackintosh. When Baines was joined by Stamp in 1991 (latterly as professor, and leaving in 2003), within their own disciplines they developed a hybrid contemporary/heritage interest in the former firm's work. In his 1992 talk at the DOCOMOMO Scotland conference Baines described how his first 'task' was to contextualise the firm's 'post-Coia' postwar work within a UK framework, and stressed that following the firm's short listing for Robinson College, Cambridge, in 1974 'whatever the media perception, the real driving forces within the practice, alongside many other talented individuals, were in fact Andy MacMillan and Isi Metzstein'.[77] Baines adopted an increasingly didactic approach to the firm's work in his role as architectural teacher, and his later work analysed the buildings as if he was examining them newly completed. In this early overview a note of architectural rhetoric was already evident: he listed Metzstein and MacMillan's architectural 'principles' as the 'regulation of light'; the 'educational section'; the 'load-bearing wall'; and the complex relationship of 'old into the new'. Metzstein, in an uncharacteristic endorsement of architectural critics in 1996, claimed 'Mark Baines is sympathetic and knowledgeable about our work.'[78]

Stamp's academic work was not, unlike that of Baines, especially focused on Gillespie, Kidd & Coia, but as a highly influential preservation campaigner, his writing on the fate of St Peter's College in this period helped define its 'heritage reception' for over fifteen years, and encouraged the escalation in its perceived significance from a relatively regional and national commission (when new) to a heroic international masterpiece (under the new interpretation). Within this period, the re-evaluation trend culminated in the 1994 publication of the first *Mac Journal* of the Mackintosh School of Architecture, devoted to the work of Gillespie, Kidd & Coia (and marked MacMillan's retirement from the school). MacMillan's successor, Charles MacCallum, was also a former Gillespie, Kidd & Coia employee. Alongside Baines, Stamp and MacCallum, a host of historians and architects contributed essays to the volume. English architect Colin St John Wilson recalled first meeting the 'new blood' of Metzstein and MacMillan at Cambridge in the mid 1960s: 'We are all familiar with the refrain 'Andy and Isi' as if it were a single name', he concluded. On Cardross Seminary, architect Patrick Hodgkinson explained 'I have written about St Peter's in the present tense from the visit I made twenty-five years ago [before] the organised vandalism which caused its death mask.'[79]

Through the *Mac Journal* a new body of laudatory writing devoted to Metzstein and MacMillan's legacy emerged to challenge the much-attacked 1980s hagiography of Jack Coia (see below). The first exhibition of the practice's work, Themes & Variations (designed by Baines), was held in February 1996.

Proposals and Debates

In spite of growing academic and heritage interest in the building, St Peter's Seminary remained in a ruinous state. Local press, concerned for safety, reported that prior to 1991 'Men with dogs patrolled the grounds' but since then, 'the owners had withdrawn security'.[80] The local authority, perhaps in anticipation of the list upgrading, issued an emergency repairs notice (to be carried out in 72 days) on the Archdiocese in late July 1992.[81] The Archdiocese responded with a 'pledge' to maintain the estate. On behalf of the Church Tom Connelly explained that fencing recently erected around the seminary buildings at the cost of £20,000 'had been vandalized within days': 'We are looking after the college, and neighbouring Kilmahew House but there is only so much that we can do if this vandalism continues.'[82] The local police, Connelly explained, were 'keeping an eye' on the site, and he asked for the local community 'to play its part'. The Archdiocese was granted an extension to the emergency repairs order.[83]

Faced with a building deteriorating fast from neglect and vandalism, the diocesan authorities then appointed the Walker Group to draw up plans for marketing and restoration in March 1992. Architect John Miller admitted 'It will be a hard slog to identify a use for the building and there are clearly no short term solutions.'[84] The group estimated that it would take at least £5 million to restore it. Later that year the Archdiocese reported that 'with the recession continuing things had fallen through' with several interested parties.[85] In view of the Archdiocese's continuing financial difficulties, no work was carried out.[86]

The potential for new housing development in the grounds of the Kilmahew estate was being discussed as early as 1992, but the area was protected from development as a designated planning Green Belt. Two further planning applications made by the Archdiocese in partnership with the developers Classical House in late 1993 proposed that the college buildings and site should be developed jointly. Classical House was a recognised specialist in historic building re-use, and director Douglas Loan (and later John Sheridan) retained a development interest in the site up to 2007.[87] The Archdiocese explained in October 1993 that this 'ambitious but practical' property development formed part of a five-year strategy aimed at wiping out the Church's massive overdrafts of £12.7m.[88] With regard to the college, the first scheme proposed the conversion of the main block into six domestic units (described as townhouses, and anticipated to sell for £250,000 each) and the demolition of the convent block, and 60 new houses in the grounds. The second scheme proposed the retention of the seminary buildings in consolidated ruin form, as a 'monument', pending future re-use, and 24 new houses in the grounds.[89] The new houses, designed by Davis Duncan Partnership, were planned for the site of the walled garden and stable block. The 'secured ruin' option had first been discussed with the local authority in August 1993, and the developers were trying to establish at the time of application if Historic Scotland's Historic Buildings Council's grant-aid could be awarded for a listed ruin.[90] Grant-aid would be available for stabilisation only with the 'firm assurance' it was part of a restoration plan.[91] The application specified that if either of the schemes was approved a programme of forest maintenance would be carried out with a fund of £50,000 and sum of £75,000 would also be gifted for a new Visitors Centre.[92]

In this instance, local amenity societies and heritage societies both objected, but for different reasons. Opinion was divided in the Cardross Community Council, chaired by the local minister Rev. Andrew Scobie, but it finally withdrew support based on the lack of detailed plans for the ruin. It was not opposed to residential development.[93] A number of local residents were still objecting to the listing upgrade of 1992, for example Michael Wilson told a local reporter: 'The Coia buildings should be blasted to the heavens. They're like a submarine pen. I wouldn't live there for £5 never mind £250,000' (by contrast Wilson was vocal in the fight to save Kilmahew House, see below).[94] National heritage bodies came together in a site visit to the former seminary buildings to consider the 1993 proposals, arranged by John Gerrard of the Scottish Civic Trust on 11 January 1994. Attending alongside Historic Scotland and representatives from the local planning authorities were the developer Douglas Loan; Paul Stirton of DOCOMOMO Scotland; Gavin Stamp as chairman of the London-based Twentieth Century Society; and Rev. Kenneth Nugent of the Catholic Heritage Commission. Letters of objection and support were made to the council, and Stamp's letter supporting the 'mothballing' second scheme was characteristically compelling and emotive.[95] He stressed that while the Twentieth Century Society did 'not normally comment on cases concerning twentieth century buildings in Scotland … we do so in this case because of the national significance of the work of Gillespie, Kidd & Coia and the supreme importance of the seminary buildings at Cardross. We have no doubt whatever that St Peter's College at Cardross is one of the very finest modern buildings in Scotland and was, both as a formal conception and as an executed building, a brilliant architectural achievement of European significance.'[96] He continued his attacks on the Archdiocese, which in his view had 'impeded any sensible proposals for the continued use of the seminary buildings' due to their 'unrealistic expectations of financial return'. The first proposed scheme, he argued, 'represents an unacceptable and damaging mutilation of the original architectural conception' and opposed demolition of Kilmahew as an 'essential part of the Gillespie, Kidd & Coia conception of St Peter's'. But, he concluded, retention must lead to 'eventual restoration' – if the Archdiocese could not be 'compelled' to repair the buildings, the site should, in the society's opinion, be 'transferred to a more responsible owner'. Just as the Catholic Church representative who objected to the listing upgrading in 1992 had anticipated that the financial burden of the building would inevitably fall on the public purse, Stamp similarly lamented: 'it is intolerable that public money as well as private will now have to be spent on their restoration'.

In anticipation of planning refusal, developer Douglas Loan gloomily warned that the seminary and site 'may lie dormant forever' if the plans were not approved, and he correctly anticipated 'In six months time there

Kilmahew House
The fire damaged shell of the listed Kilmahew House before permission was given for its demolition in 1994. HES SC674772

is not going to be another magic solution and it could reach the stage where the problems are unsolvable.'[97] The Archdiocese's official newspaper *Flourish* voiced its frustration: '… it is beginning to look as if nothing will ever satisfy the authorities short of complete restoration of an unwanted, impractical building in a remote corner of Dunbartonshire, whatever the cost'.[98] Amidst threats of appeal, but with strong local and national backing, the planning applications were finally refused by both district and regional planning committees, on the advice of their planning departments in May 1994.[99]

In early May 1994 Dumbarton District Council approved the second consolidated-ruin ('mothballing') proposal for the seminary extensions (one part of the 1993 application).[100] At that point the Scottish Historic Building Trust (SHBT) had entered the debate with a provisional idea that it might take over the ruined complex in the short term, restore it, and then 'sell it-on'. Its chair John Clare estimated that refurbishment work could cost £3 million and the costs could be met by grant giving bodies (such as Dunbartonshire Enterprise), and stressed 'the original architect, Isi Metzstein, would be consulted on any alteration work.'[101]

All parties regrouped once again and in August 1994, at what was probably the first of many 'workshops' devoted to discussing the future use of the former St Peter's College buildings, several solutions to 'encompass the whole of Kilmahew Estate' were proposed (the 1993 application had offered funds for the future maintenance of a proposed new public park on ground to the north of Kilmahew House).[102] The 1994 Market Assessment Report, compiled for Dunbartonshire Enterprises to examine potential re-use, proposed that a 'St Peter's Project Champion' be identified to find a new use for the buildings, and concluded, among other things, that a broader 'art works' cultural theme for the whole site was a strong option: 'the architectural merit of St Peter's [it argued] may not in itself be sufficient as the focus for any cultural tourism-based redevelopment.'[103] The consolidated ruin proposal, despite approval in 1994, was not implemented, but significantly a precedent for the concept of a ruin, set within an 'art works' landscape, had been established. It would take a further 20 years for that to become a reality, as we will see in the final chapter.

The drive for conservation suffered a major setback that same year when Kilmahew House, already structurally unsound from a fire of 1990, was again gutted by fire in May 1994.[104] The historic building, which had housed St Peter's Seminary from 1948 to 1966, had supplied much of the rationale of the extension buildings' design, and functioned as the seminary's administrative centre, now, perversely, became a threat to the Gillespie, Kidd & Coia buildings. In June, the Archdiocese's surveyors warned of 'risks to the "A" listed buildings to the north and to the Kitchen block to the east' if urgent action was not taken to demolish Kilmahew before it collapsed.[105] The Secretary of State for Scotland Hector Monro corresponded with Historic Scotland in late 1993 to relay strong local objections to the demolition of the Victorian house, and in particular those of local history researcher Michael Wilson.[106] Despite an independent structural report in the following September, which concluded 'the building could be saved but it will depend wholly on the practicality of clearing the inside safely and on the cost of reinstating the roof, floors and internal fabric', permission to demolish the house was given by Dumbarton District Council in November 1994.[107] It was, according to Historic Scotland, in 'a desperate condition … and subject to the most extreme vandalism'.[108] Gavin Stamp lamented the loss of 'Burnet's innocent Victorian house'.[109]

Directly linked to these failed proposals was a series of press articles on the fate of the former St Peter's by Stamp in *The Herald* and *Independent*. An intense debate in *The Herald* regarding the architectural authorship of Cardross, and other Gillespie, Kidd & Coia buildings, followed in late 1994. With this debate a number of key themes began to shape the new discourse for the abandoned seminary buildings: a discourse which was increasing separated from the historical reality of St Peter's College, and from its original story as set out in the previous chapters of this book. Key themes now emerged: the neglect of St Peter's by an un-thinking and philistine client; the misfortune of its unappreciated heroic architects (seen solely as Metzstein and MacMillan); and the way in which its architecture could, in turn, inspire a contemporary rebirth of Scottish Modern architecture. Almost perversely, in view of Monsignor McMahon's earlier efforts against water ingress, Stamp now claimed publicly that neglect by the Archdiocese was indirectly responsible for the ruined state of the seminary: in the 1994 article he wrote of 'obscene, sacrilegious vandalism', while admitting that the Archdiocese had been 'saddled with huge maintenance bills', and he later described the 'malicious abandonment' of St Peter's by the Archdiocese.[110] According to Stamp it was 'a secret masterpiece, a building quietly spoken of as the finest example of modern architecture in Scotland … along with Thomson's St Vincent Street Church and Mackintosh's School of Art, it is one of the truly great monuments of Scottish architecture.' He concluded that its 'poignant condition somehow symbolized the sad state of Scottish architecture'.[111]

This new, polemical climate concerning the reception of Cardross culminated in a heated debate between Stamp, Jacqueline Coia (Jack Coia's daughter) and Rogerson

(Coia's biographer) over design-authorship, which took place in the letters page of *The Herald* between October and December 1994.[112] At the core of this debate was an attempt by Coia and Rogerson to challenge Stamp's attribution of the design of St Peter's to Metzstein and MacMillan alone. In an increasingly heated exchange, Stamp accused Rogerson of hagiographic admiration of Jack Coia, and Jacqueline Coia of 'filial obsession' in suggesting her father was in any way responsible for the design alongside the 'real architects' of Cardross, while Rogerson countered that Stamp 'should be more careful to check his facts before putting pen to paper'. The latter, in turn, retorted that he had 'spoken to several architects who worked in the office between those years [1950–66] who had direct knowledge of the way designs were made' – including of course his colleague Charles MacCallum in the Mackintosh School of Architecture. Once again, Glasgow School of Art and its supposedly once-unacknowledged 'genius' designer Mackintosh supplied a poignant parallel case – although, surprisingly, no reference to the other named architect of St Peter's College, John Cowell, was made in all this debate. Metzstein and MacMillan, at least among the architectural and preservation elites, were now firmly recognised as the sole design-architects of St Peter's. Throughout this period the regional and local press (and the locals), talked of the 'Coia buildings', and it was always identified as Jack Coia's design.[113] With the listing upgrading in 1992, national coverage began to make some reference to Isi Metzstein. A new myth was emerging, shaped around one of Modernism's most powerful themes – that of the tragic, betrayed and unappreciated artist (in this case GKC and its two 'leading designers'). The ruined Cardross Seminary was, as the following chapter will show, at the forefront of this myth-making.

Chapter 6
Salvaging St Peter's

Once a modernist phalanstery ... St Peter's is now a chapel perilously hidden in an enchanted forest, a Piranesian ruin, and the wreck of scheme after scheme for redevelopment. But ruination is a process of entropy, not a steady state: if nothing happens St Peter's will soon melt away, reduced by theft, arson, rhododendrons and rain.
Edward Hollis, architect, 2011

Now, nearly 50 years on from the day it opened, we witness the first steps in a new and radical form of regeneration; one that accepts loss and ruination as part of the site history and sets out a mission to imaginatively re-use a great late modernist structure and in so doing, reflect the same social dynamism and ambition with which it was conceived.
Angus Farquhar, Creative Director, NVA, 2013 [2]

This final chapter will trace the protracted, but ultimately successful, battle to salvage the ruined remnants of St Peter's College and Kilmahew estate. This is an extraordinary story, which saw the transformation of the derelict complex, reputedly a millstone round the neck of its owners the Archdiocese of Glasgow and valued at £250,000 in 1997, through a multi-million pound public-funded part-restoration project, begun in 2015. At the end of this period, spanning just over twenty years, a new 'viable' use was finally found for Cardross Seminary – as an international cultural centre.[3] Between 18 and 27 March 2016, a public art event, Hinterland, was staged by its new owners, the public arts charity NVA. The event, which attracted 7,500 people, officially opened the former seminary buildings to the general public: a free preview night was attended by 600 locals.

The previous chapters examined the 'real' history and context of St Peter's College: its commission, design, reception, use and initial decline. This chapter, by contrast, is not an orthodox architectural historical account of a building. Instead, it recounts a protracted series of events which included planning proposals, inquiries, cultural events, heated preservation debates, funding applications and numerous reports – with a local, regional and national press involved in recounting every development. Throughout this more recent

Kilmahew estate
Clearing the woodland and cutting back the rhododendron. **NVA**

story, the decaying ruin of the seminary itself was the tangible backdrop to events: it sat patiently awaiting its fate. As an unoccupied ruin it had, by the mid 1990s, become a piece of heritage – a modern monument of dereliction – and as a result it would take on a new value separate from its original purpose and meaning. The key heritage principle of re-use enabled the St Peter's preservation campaigners to focus solely on what it might now become, and to disregard judgement on its past performance as a teaching college.

In 2004, one journalist ironically reported that 'St Peter's refuses to go away'.[4] This new story, at first glance, appears to be an uninterrupted series of false starts, bureaucracy and preservation squabbles leading to a final solution, but its narrative can be divided into three phases. The first two distinct periods examine the development of two separate failed planning applications: 'Re-viewing Cardross' covers a period 1995–2002, and 'Heritage Squabbles and Stalemate', provides an account of the most vigorous era of preservation campaigning from 2003 to 2008. Finally, the most recent phase, 'Cardross Consolidated', examines 2009 to the present day, and focuses solely on NVA's successful and still ongoing project.

At the heart of the former seminary's second history is a modern-day 'mythic tragedy', a new story peddled by professionals, enthusiasts and the press from the mid 1990s onwards: that of a 1960s building of unique beauty and international significance, designed by heroic but unappreciated architects, misused and abandoned by a philistine Catholic client, and left at the mercy of an uncaring society. In parallel with this myth-making process, alternative and more nuanced narratives were also at first available, from 1970s students at the college as well as local

St Peter's with Kilmahew House, c1990
The former seminary before the demolition of Kilmahew House.
Guthrie Aerial Photography Archive, Glasgow School of Art

St Peter's without Kilmahew House, 1998
By the late 1990s, with Kilmahew House demolished and the 1966 complex thus 'decapitated', there was still no definite plan for the future of the remaining A-listed college buildings. **HES** SC674777

Cardross residents, both of which contradicted the views of preservationists. Increasingly dominant was the 'heroic myth' which precipitated mounting calls to save St Peter's for the nation – expressed in similar language to that of the anti-modern campaigns to save Victorian architectural buildings in the face of postwar reconstruction in the 1960s and 1970s. A media campaign to save the complex, fed into by an array of architects, historians, artists and journalists, was fuelled both, on the one hand, by fears of threat and loss, and on the other, by a late-Romantic love of ruins and decay. Like the majority of conservation campaigners in Britain since Pugin and Morris in the nineteenth century, they also required a bogeyman as a focus for their attacks. Gavin Stamp first proposed the Archdiocese of Glasgow as villains in the early 1990s, but by the middle of the next decade, Historic Scotland was being targeted as responsible for the 'neglect' of the ruins. The architectural advocates of a new, image-led 'Iconic Modernism' that started to dominate contemporary architecture from the mid 1990s led a shift in professional and public perceptions of the building, from a subject of regional (Clydeside) and national architectural interest when new in the 1960s, to the object of international attention as an 'iconic' ruin of the new millennium.

Throughout this new, preservation-orientated story, the key protagonists remained the owners (the Archdiocese until 2011), the local authority (in 1996 the regional and district authorities were replaced by the single unitary authority of Argyll and Bute Council), Historic Scotland and voluntary amenity societies. During the three phases of this story, new influential groups entered, and exited, the rescue debate. The developer Classical House, for example, finally withdrew after fourteen years of involvement in 2007, and in turn Manchester-based Urban Splash withdrew quickly following the impact of the 2008 global economic crisis. The London-based, preservationist Twentieth Century Society and the specialist conservation architects Avanti (spurred on by the London-based architectural press) dominated the second phase of the rescue programme and campaign. But, on home ground, it was the activities of the newly formed St Peter's Buildings Preservation Trust

St Peter's following NVA's clearing and cleaning work, 2016
Another decade and a half on and St Peter's is in a state of stabilised ruination. Half of the sanctuary roof has collapsed, the classroom block is entirely open to the elements. **Courtesy of Reigart Contracts**

St Peter's, 2016
Nature has reclaimed the footprint of the old Kilmahew House.
Courtesy of Reigart Contracts

(SPBPT) which played the chief role in elevating the ruinous condition of Cardross Seminary into a national and international issue.

The new, devolved Scottish Parliament of 1999 had no immediate impact on the rescue movement, despite culture and development being a devolved matter. But by 2003 the Government, through its conservation agency, Historic Scotland, was becoming more engaged, especially during the 'political fallout' of the 2004 application. In the final, post-2009 phase of the ruin's story, the Scottish Government became directly involved with support and funding, through its Architecture Policy Unit (formed in 2001). By 2011, grant-giving bodies, and in particular the Heritage Lottery Fund (HLF, established in 1994) and Creative Scotland (formed in 2010), became central to the future development of the former seminary. Although initially relegated to the periphery, the arts sector, and in particular artists Toby Paterson, Dan Dubovitz and filmmaker Murray Grigor, came increasingly to the fore. Finally, the Scottish arts charity NVA was to prove crucial to the eventual solution. The local Cardross community, for many years overlooked amidst the never-ending national preservation squabbles, were by 2011 harnessed to both support community engagement and crucially validate public funding for the final solution. Some institutional representatives, such as Ken Crilley (Archdiocese) and Ranald MacInnes (Historic Scotland), maintained involvement throughout the whole period, but new protagonists, most notably architect and writer Penny Lewis, and artist Angus Farquhar of NVA, joined the ongoing saga. Metzstein claimed retrospectively of the firm's architecture that 'each building is built on the foundations laid by the previous one!'[5] The long campaign to rescue the former seminary in this period was similarly built upon the ideas and achievements of predecessors: examining that final solution, with the benefit of hindsight, it would appear that nothing was in fact new.

There is no evidence of direct involvement of the surviving architects Metzstein and MacMillan (Cowell having died in 1993) in the preservation campaign archives. Both men were omnipresent in newspaper articles, particularly after 2007, and when asked made comments on planned proposals to reporters. Penny Lewis, the lead campaigner following Stamp's return to London, and co-founder of SPBPT, met Metzstein in 1999 in her capacity as the *Scotsman*'s architectural correspondent. She developed a close professional relationship with him, and she later explained 'He didn't talk about St Peter's, he wasn't particularly interested in what was going to happen to it, but it was a source of frustration for him.'[6] Almost all of the architects and academics who were involved with Cardross during this period held interviews or discussions with Metzstein, and to a lesser extent MacMillan, and some discovered that any views at variance to Metzstein's own might lead to disharmony (see also Chapter 4).[7] The architects had a direct input into the 2007–8 Gillespie, Kidd & Coia exhibition, in collaboration with its curator, Mark Baines. The broader impact of the writings and preservation activities of Gillespie, Kidd & Coia's circle of admirers, who were described as 'The Holy Family' by one unsympathetic commentator, will be examined later, within the context of the firm's legacy.[8] This more recent heritage narrative became, as we will see, increasingly divorced from the reality and the vicissitudes of the original commission. Repackaged as both a set-piece of modern architectural heritage and a harbinger of 'contemporary iconic design', the historical significance of Cardross as an expression of the general confidence of postwar Catholicism in the West of Scotland, and of the attempt to reflect that confidence through a social-architectural image of community, was increasingly disappearing from site.

The phased chronological developments relating to the ruin were played out within the broader architectural, conservationist, and to a lesser extent, political contexts of the late 1990s and the new millennium, and, in turn, impacted on its more recent reception. The Archdiocese donated the St Peter's site to NVA in 2011 (full legal ownership by the latter is expected in spring 2017), and the development of the Catholic Church was no longer relevant to its story as a ruin. Despite this, some preservation campaigners and critics referenced the emerging abuse scandals within the Church, and the general public loss of confidence in it as an institution, to further highlight the alleged earlier 'neglect' of the complex.[9] Far more central to the ongoing campaign to save the former seminary was the broader retrospective re-evaluation of Gillespie, Kidd & Coia. From the mid 1990s this took two main forms: firstly, the architect-led re-evaluation of their late works as an inspiration for new 'iconic' architecture; and secondly, a preservation-led re-evaluation spurred on by threats of loss and demolition of listed church buildings. The culmination of this 'cult' of Gillespie, Kidd & Coia among contemporary architects was the 2007 exhibition and publication, *Gillespie, Kidd & Coia, Architecture, 1956–1987*, held at the national Scottish architecture centre, the Lighthouse in Glasgow. Writing that same year in an article in the *Scotsman*, Stamp called Metzstein and MacMillan 'God's architects'.[10] From 1999 onwards a number of postwar listed Gillespie, Kidd & Coia churches, all with ongoing technical problems, were repaired and restored with substantial public funding. The culmination of Gillespie, Kidd & Coia's heritage legacy was, as we will see, the granting of over £7.45 million local and national public funding from 2010 onwards for the part-restoration of the Cardross ruin.[11]

Re-viewing Cardross, 1995–2002

The cruelly vandalised Cardross should be stripped of its dilapidated facings so that its structure may stand overlooking the Clyde as an archaeological monument.
Gordon Benson, architect, 1996 [12]

Throughout almost the entire period covered by this chapter the core problem of the ruined seminary complex and Kilmahew estate remained the same: what was to be done with a heritage-protected modern ruin of increasingly international reputation (but of limited financial or development value), set within a locally significant landscape designated and protected as Green Belt, and owned by a regional institution already financially burdened by the cost of the original failed project, and unable and unwilling to act? The predicament seemed most immediate and urgent to local commentators, such as Cardross councillor Ronald Kinloch, who argued in 2000 that 'now the area is so derelict and so regularly frequented by undesirables [that] it has become almost a "no go" part of the village'.[13] The key issues remained: Could a viable re-use for the gutted former seminary and estate be found? Who might be willing to pursue that re-use? What would be the fabric and cultural cost of a new use to the ruin and estate? And, finally, and most importantly, who would pay for it? This dilemma was eventually – albeit partially – resolved in 2016. At no point in this twenty-year period, unlike its phase of initial decline, was demolition a considered option.

This first stage of the ruin saga witnessed one failed planning application of 1998, amidst a growing realisation of the scale and economic challenges of rescue. It contrasted with the period prior to 1995, which in planning terms followed a fairly typical pattern of reports and applications succeeding each other. But, from 1997 onwards, a more nuanced understanding of the complexities of the local planning and national heritage issues, and the financial burden facing the owners, emerged. An impasse continued during the last years of the leadership of Cardinal Winning until his sudden death in 2001: he was accused by preservationists as having 'little love for St Peter's College'.[14] Media and academic interest in the ruins continued to grow, however, and the first monograph devoted to its history was published in 1997 (the first edition of this book).[15] Also indirectly relevant to the fate of the ruined St Peter's was the financial life-line thrown to some of the firm's listed churches by publicly funded HLF grants from 1999 onwards.

The Abortive Proposal, 1997–2000

A single outline planning application in 1998 by the Archdiocese, with developers Classical House, dominated the debate but, as we will see, was finally refused after a public local inquiry in January 2000. As a precursor to the new application, negotiations between the owners, developers and local authority began in 1997 after an appeal against the refusal of a previous planning application for new housing was dismissed in March 1996 – an outcome attacked by Ronald Kinloch as 'a tragedy for the village'.[16] Despite numerous planning applications only two elements had been approved in 1994: the demolition of Kilmahew House on health and safety grounds; and the consolidated-ruin proposal. The demolition of the house in 1995 removed the original historic core which had supplied much of the design rationale of the 1960s extension buildings (while, ironically, now allowing them to be re-envisioned as an autonomous 'icon'), and with the 1996 appeal dismissal the latter element was also shelved. 'What now for St Peter's?' the *Helensburgh Advertiser* asked in 1996.[17]

In preparation for the next application, a series of meetings attended by the local authority, Historic Scotland and developers Classical House, were hosted by the Archdiocese offices. The chief outcome was the preparation of a maintenance masterplan by architects Page and Park and landscape architects Ian White Associates. In 1997 it was estimated that restoring the seminary complex would cost £7–10 million (almost double the estimated cost of £5 million in the 1992 Walker Report).[18] In preparation of the masterplan, architect David Page examined four options for new housing in the estate grounds. He established the design and financial implications of each scheme, and the profit each could potentially yield for maintenance works on the ruin and the estate landscape. These included options for 39 new houses in the walled garden; two further options of 30 and 21 houses; and a final option of no housing. The servicing of plots for housing would, he argued, be very costly. Page concluded that while the 39-house option would break even (by covering professional costs and the land value, estimated at £430,000 by the Archdiocese), the 21-house option was 'aesthetically very acceptable'.[19] Regardless of the level of development, however, substantial additional funds, in the form of large grants, would be needed if any repair and landscape work was to be carried out. Faced with such a bleak financial breakdown, Page urged the group to find a way of relieving 'the Archdiocese of the burden of St Peter's', and set up a buildings preservation trust to raise funds to buy the estate from the Archdiocese. He concluded that the ruin had 'major problems', but work could, however, start on the estate landscape: in 1998 Ian White Associates duly produced a Statement on Landscape Management.

It was during these discussions that Historic Scotland began to address the potential conflict with its regulation of the ruin, posed by the realities of the financial implications of restoration. The policy on architectural ruins followed by Historic Scotland and its predecessors had been influenced on the one hand by the Ruskin –

Morris – SPAB 'anti-scrape' tradition of opposition to restoration and reconstruction, and on the other hand by the split between two protection arms of the organisation: the so-called Ancient Monuments branch, with its stringent preservation of uninhabited, mostly medieval ruins (such as the ruined Kilmahew Castle, north of St Peter's, which was designated a 'scheduled monument' in 1992); and the Historic Buildings officials, whose power rested on the broader but far less interventive framework of 'listing'. Here, ruins enjoyed no special sacrosanctity, and there was a presumption in favour of buildings in full use. The former seminary fell into the second of these categories, despite being upgraded to category A when already a ruin (a rare, but not unparalleled decision). In 1997, Historic Scotland chief inspector John Hume stressed that the St Peter's extension should 'not be kept as a ruin', but that repairing the vandalised Victorian south lodge (demolished in 2013) and estate architecture should be the 'first priority'.[20] Historic Scotland's approach changed, however, as the financial and practical realities of rescue and re-use of the complex emerged. Following the 2008 Avanti conservation assessment, the agency accepted that a consolidated ruin was a valid, but not preferred conservation option. When NVA's part-consolidated ruin/part-restoration proposal was first mooted in 2008, however, Historic Scotland finally accepted this as a pragmatic solution.[21]

Page and Park's study of 1997 highlighted the financial limitations of any enabling development (where profit from new housing sales funds restoration) on the Kilmahew estate. At this point the Archdiocese, according to Classical House, was keen 'to rid itself' of the site and buildings, and there was still 'no clear interest by an end user at present despite reports and advertising'.[22] As outlined previously, the cost to the Archdiocese of the original extension alone was, by 1971, estimated at almost £700,000, and in 1972 the whole seminary complex was estimated for insurance purposes at £985,000. Yet by 1997, the buildings and estate together were valued at just £250,000.[23] The Archdiocese wanted to recover the land value and developer and architect costs to date (at least), and so another application was put forward.

The August 1998 outline planning application for 33 new dwellings, in a ribbon development alongside the listed south lodge area of the estate, was markedly similar to those of 1993. It was still an enabling development, although less financially ambitious, at a total cost of £1.44m. As before, it included the formation of a country park but it now specified that there would be funds for repair to make safe the ruin, which would be handed over to a newly formed trust in which the council would be a principal member. An overall development dowry of £100,000–150,000 was proposed. The transfer of lands and funds would be the subject of a separate legal agreement.[24] It was primarily a Green Belt planning issue for the local authority (now Argyll and Bute Council), and as it was contrary to the existing development plan, the Scottish Executive was to be consulted. Historic Scotland was consulted on the basis that the new development might affect the setting of the A-listed building and the scheduled Kilmahew Castle.

Unlike the 1993 application, local and national opinion was clearly divided in this instance. The local authority fully supported the application, and the applicant had worked 'in partnership' with Argyll and Bute Council and the local community in its preparation, but the proposal was still eventually refused at a public inquiry in 2000.[25] The failed 1998 proposal was significant to the future development for several reasons: it reflected growing frustration at a local planning and community level to find a solution for the problematic site; increased press coverage; undermined the credibility of enabling development as a future option; shifted focus to the practicalities and costs of maintaining the ruin; and in turn repositioned Historic Scotland's role as central to future decision-making. Supporters promoted the community benefits of the proposal, through the maintenance of estate grounds and scaling down of development. Ken Crilley, Director of Development for the Archdiocese, stressed 'This is not a money spinner for the Catholic Church.'[26] He protested in 1999 that 'the archdiocese have spent considerable sums to protect and maintain the estate and buildings to date, but feel that without a permanent presence on site their efforts

The former altar and sanctuary, 2002
Dubowitz's *Wastelands* photography captures leftover fragments of the building's active years and documents its new status as a ruin. **Dan Dubowitz**

St Peter's, Cardross

are fruitless and the financial reality is that the Church can no longer afford to upgrade and maintain the Estate.'[27] As a safeguard, he guaranteed that no further development would follow.[28]

The ever-pragmatic Rev. A J Scobie of Cardross Community Council (CCC) stated 'Although the building can never be used for anything again, we are keen to see it made safe and are keen to encourage the idea of a country park with access for local people.'[29] The CCC argued that limited residential development would be beneficial for the local community, and provided a detailed historical study by local Michael Wilson on the working population of the Kilmahew estate before the war, which concluded that its total resident population had been in excess of 80, and that the proposal 'would in effect restore a situation essentially equivalent to that previously obtaining'.[30] Objections to Green Belt development came from amenity societies (the Scottish Civic Trust and the Architectural Heritage Society of Scotland), and the local press reported a 'Village divided over plan'.[31] There was concern that that development dowry of £100,000 was insufficient, and this was further supported by objections from the environmental group Clydebelt. Its spokesman Gordon Doughty estimated that 'at the most it will pay for a few weeks work a year'.[32] Cardross Golf Club and local residents objected because 'the new houses near to the golf club's fourth green could be at risk from bombardment of miss-hit shots'.[33] The club also argued that there was no real demand for new housing in Cardross: whereas in 1996 there was a housing of shortfall of 58 homes, there was now a surplus of 2,000.[34]

Historic Scotland's position, as consultee, was a little more complicated, but in summary its interests lay in the impact of the new development on the listed building, St Peter's, and scheduled monument Kilmahew Castle. Owing to its proximity and 'national' status, the chief concern was with the former, and in December 1999 Historic Scotland formally withheld its support from the proposed enabling development, owing to concerns that it was only a 'temporary' and financially ill-defined solution for the listed building stabilisation.[35] Following this decision, in December 1999, a public inquiry was held at Geilston Hall, Cardross, in January 2000.[36] On

the recommendation of Deputy Chief Reporter James McCulloch that it was contrary to Green Belt policy, the proposal was turned down in August of that year by the Scottish Executive. McCulloch had concluded that the enabling financial package was insufficient to 'deal with any requirement arising from the re-use of the seminary', as it would mostly be absorbed by the cost of the new houses.[37] In reporting the news *The Herald*'s headline proclaimed: 'Church loses lengthy battle over architecturally-important buildings … designed by celebrated Glasgow architect Jack Coia.'[38] At this stage, the general local and national press still firmly identified Coia, rather than Metzstein and MacMillian (or Cowell), as the architect of St Peter's.

The Heritage Legacy and Re-evaluation of Gillespie, Kidd & Coia

As we saw, the bolstering of Gillespie, Kidd & Coia's legacy by the heritage sector was founded on a traditional evaluative listing system which favoured named architects and public buildings. The practical implications of the listing of Gillespie, Kidd & Coia's churches emerged in the early-to-mid 1990s just as the 1994 planning proposal for the ruined Cardross was being refused. Within this period, Historic Scotland and Heritage Lottery grants for repair and restoration of churches 'plagued by structural faults' were awarded to Sacred Heart, Cumbernauld, St Benedict's, Easterhouse, Glasgow, and St Patrick's, Kilsyth.[39] The listed St Benedict's, in the diocese of Motherwell, was suffering structural problems when an application to demolish it was made in 1996, but refused. At that point Bishop Joseph Devine launched a £3m appeal to secure cash for repairs to churches in his diocese, but East Kilbride-based architects DTA carried out a feasibility study for St Benedict's which revealed 'over the last two decades, there have been a number of technical problems relative to water penetration, heat loss, and structural stability', and estimated that it would cost £1.25 million to fix.[40] The church spokesman, Monsignor Tom Connelly, told *The Herald* 'Some of the fancy architecture was more suited to the continent,

The former refectory
Dan Dubowitz

St Peter's, Cardross

Photograph from Dubowitz's *Wastelands* publication
Dan Dubowitz

where there is a higher level of sunshine … but parishioners at St Benedict's had raised thousands of pounds over the years to pay for repairs of their church.'[41] In November 1999, St Benedict's received a £1.6 million restoration grant from the HLF. In the late 1990s Sacred Heart, Cumbernauld, was similarly awarded repair and restoration grants: the work was carried out by architects Page and Park in 1996–7.[42] The restoration and repair of St Patrick's, Kilsyth, begun in concept in 1992, and completed 2001, was the key Gillespie, Kidd & Coia listed building project in the period: an eight-year project, led by Brooke Miller Partnership in close collaboration with Historic Scotland. Architect Neil Gillespie reviewed the project for the *Architects' Journal* in 2001, praising its 'great sensitivity to the original design' but recognising the challenge (particularly in the roof) of 'rectifying the technical problems' associated with the 'dark side of the firm's reputation'. The total cost of £1.4 million was met by the HLF, Historic Scotland and the Archdiocese.[43] Subsequent HLF-funded Gillespie, Kidd & Coia restoration projects included a £1.1 million grant towards a £2 million project to restore St Bride's, East Kilbride, in 2014, and a more modest £25,000 for the conversion of St Martin's, Castlemilk, that same year: generous repair grants were also forthcoming from Historic Scotland.[44]

The developing heritage context also had implications for the future of the ruined seminary. Some historians began to argue that Gillespie, Kidd & Coia's prominent position in the listing of postwar architecture was leading to an unbalanced understanding of Scottish Modernism. In 2002, for example, Miles Glendinning argued that the veneration of Gillespie, Kidd & Coia, together with the traditional art historical values of Historic Scotland listing, with its emphasis on individual monuments and private-practice architects, tended to undermine the more important role of collective public offices such as the New Town architects' departments, or private practices rooted in the public sector, like Robert Matthew Johnson-Marshall (RMJM).[45] He cited the near-exclusion of Cumbernauld New Town from 'heritage' protection as an example of this imbalance: instead of being thrown a conservation life-line, he argued, this 'most internationally influential piece of Scottish modern urbanism' was awarded the notorious media-generated Carbuncle Award in 2001 (and compared to Kabul). This imbalance, Glendinning argued, also chimed in with the branded approach of contemporary 'iconic' architecture, whose designers referenced the ruined Cardross 'masterpiece', as a 'tragic legend' in their campaigns of image-led commodification.[46]

Postmodernists' earlier rejection of Modernist functionalism had led in turn to the contemporary dominance of the individualistic architect-personality. This tendency was only amplified under Iconic Modernism. At the Mackintosh School of Architecture, the predominance of the Gillespie, Kidd & Coia legacy continued after the retirals from teaching of Metzstein in 1998 and MacMillan in 2004. Within Scottish architectural writing on Gillespie, Kidd & Coia claims were increasingly made that the designs of Metzstein and MacMillan were of

The former classroom block lecture hall
Dan Dubowitz

unique 'international standing within the Modern Movement'.⁴⁷

In 1996, an exhibition, Themes & Variations, curated by Baines was hosted at the Architectural Association in London, accompanied by a lecture from Metzstein, and introduced by London-based Scottish architect Gordon Benson, who hailed the firm as one of the few 1960s British practices who were 'searching for a reasoned advance from the pre-war modern movement … against the costume-parade that has stood for architecture for 25 years'.⁴⁸ London critics and historians, however, were more sceptical: responding in the *Architects' Journal* Alan Powers argued that Cardross's 'potential as an epic ruin is diminished by the sketchy nature of the solid looking construction, a problem that makes some other buildings [by the firm] less satisfying on close acquaintance'.⁴⁹

In the early 2000s, the theme of the 'authorship' of the complex resurfaced with renewed force. Throughout the 1990s, in the West of Scotland at least, both local and regional press had still identified Coia as the figurehead of the practice, and the seminary ruin was known locally as 'the Coia building' (see Chapter 4). In a 2000 article, Gavin Stamp argued, on the basis of interviews with Metzstein and MacMillan, that they were the true chief designers of the firm from the mid 1950s onwards, and were indeed equal in standing to the 'greats' of Scottish architecture, such as Alexander Thomson, J J Burnet and Mackintosh – a category to which Jack Coia, according to Stamp, clearly did not 'belong'.⁵⁰ In May 2001, Metzstein and MacMillan gifted the majority of the Gillespie, Kidd & Coia archive to Glasgow School of Art. A 'cult' of Gillespie, Kidd & Coia now began to emerge in parallel with the strengthening 'myth' surrounding St Peter's. The 2002 winter issue of *Prospect*, Scotland's leading architectural journal (which later became a vehicle for the campaign to rescue the former seminary), featured a front cover of both architects. In the associated interview 'MacMillan and Metzstein, in their own words', they were asked 'How do you account for the "cult" of Gillespie, Kidd & Coia?' Both architects attributed it to their avoidance of 'utilitarian, non-heroic projects', and (more puzzlingly) to the fact that 'we travelled up and down to London quite a bit'.⁵¹

Heritage Squabbles and Stalemate, 2003–8

As a contemporary ruin it is more moving than it would be fully restored, or stabilised. How to incorporate these views in any discussion about its future is open to question. But as a starting point, it is worth admitting that for many, St Peter's appeal lies not so much in its architecture, as its marvellous decay
Richard J Williams, 2006⁵²

In this second phase of the former seminary's new history as a 'heritage object', the contrast between the dormant ruin, and the vigorous campaign to save it, was at its most striking: in 2004 journalist Caroline Ednie argued that 'St Peter's refuses to go away, both physically and as a presence in the consciousness of the country's creative community'.⁵³ In that year, yet another planning application was put forward, again proposing a residential enabling development, but now with proposed works of consolidation and part-restoration.

Cardross Culture and Early Campaigning

In the wake of the 2000 planning refusal, there was a lull in the preservation debate, but into this vacuum a new image-led contemporary artwork interest in the ruined St Peter's emerged. In response to news that the developers Classical House and the Archdiocese (under the direction of Archbishop Mario Conti from 2002) were once again formulating another enabling development, a small but influential group of campaigners came together to form a single pressure group to campaign for the restoration and re-use of the ruined complex.⁵⁴ The Cardross Regeneration Trust (later renamed the St Peter's Building Preservation Trust, SPBPT) was formally constituted in January 2004. Central to this movement was architect and writer Penny Lewis, the editor of *Prospect* magazine (2003–8). Lewis used the journal as a vehicle to raise awareness of the fate of the former St Peter's, and the work of Gillespie, Kidd & Coia in general.⁵⁵ In 2006, she argued that 'I don't accept the argument that the seminary is better as a ruin than a working building. The trust is concerned that the building will not survive another year of ice and vandalism. I don't want to be melodramatic about it but this may be the last chance to save St Peter's as a usable building.'⁵⁶

Former student room
Dan Dubowitz

MacMillan and Metzstein, *Prospect*, winter 2002
Retrospectives of Metzstein and MacMillan's work increasingly became a focus of the Scottish architectural press. **Courtesy of Prospect / Urban Realm**

John Deffenbaugh, *The Herald*, February 2004
SPBPT member John Deffenbaugh highlighted the plight of the seminary.
The Herald and Evening Times

Arguably the most important contribution by Lewis to the campaign, however, was the way in which she brokered a new link with contemporary artists, sensing that Cardross's dramatic ruination could provide an ideal context for contemporary installation-based art. While students and artists had already shown an interest in the ruined seminary, such as student Helen McCrorie's 2002 video installation *Sanctuary*, Lewis systematically pursued the theme in *Prospect*.[57] In doing so she broadened the ruin's appeal significantly beyond the narrow bounds of architectural historians. Lewis adapted the Stamp discourse of the tragically misused and abandoned architectural masterpiece into a new narrative of an 'iconic' ruin as the locus for contemporary artistic pilgrimage, and for efforts to uncover more abstract values of 'hidden beauty and meaning'. In 2003, the first of two *Prospect* front covers to feature the ruined seminary, entitled 'Dereliction of Duty – what is to be done with Cardross?' illustrated new photography of the ruin by artist and architect Dan Dubowitz, as part of a broader project to interpret 'wastelands' in Scotland, England and Italy.[58] For Dubowitz the ruin had value as a discarded and uncontrolled space: 'There it sits, abandoned, unloved, unpreserved, unprotected, sitting in the idyllic landscape in exactly the same way as a ruined castle or a stately home or an abbey might … Nothing remains but the core, the mass of the structure. It has become a piece of archaeology quite quickly.' Lewis encouraged artistic responses to promote and foster debate on the cultural significance of the ruin, for example, suggesting that Dubowitz's

SPBPT members *Prospect*, March 2006
John Deffenbaugh, centre, and Penny Lewis, right, were prominent members of SPBPT. **Courtesy of Prospect/Urban Realm**

Cardross, *Architects' Journal*, September 2006
In a ten page feature, the *Architects' Journal* documented the relentless deterioration of the seminary. **Architects' Journal**

images of a failing concrete structure could be read as a 'metaphor for the scandals in the Catholic Church and the broader crisis of belief in traditional religions'.[59] In reality, however, the abuse scandals in the early 1980s focused not on Cardross but on St Andrew's College, Drygrange, in the Borders.[60] The 2003 Cardross-themed *Prospect* issue also contrasted the Catholic Church's supposed lack of enthusiasm for the Cardross extension with the 'rave reviews in the architectural press'. The reverse had actually been the case: contemporary articles had been short and factual, whereas Archbishop Scanlan, at the 1966 inauguration, had glowingly praised 'the genius of the architects' in devising an 'architectural conception of such brilliance and quality'.[61] Nevertheless, the inevitable conflation with contemporary 'iconic' architecture soon followed,

and in 2003, Lewis pronounced Cardross Seminary 'one of Scotland's truly iconic pieces of architecture', and in 2005, *Prospect* announced that the ruined annexe had been voted by its readers as Scotland's 'top modern building'.[62]

Further new installation art works focusing on the former seminary were picked up by an eager press. These included Toby Paterson's April 2003 'New Facade' exhibition at Glasgow's Centre for Contemporary Arts. Paterson's interest was in the original built commission and its decay, and the work consisted of a wall painting, a new large concrete wall and a series of paintings on perspex.[63] However, the filmmaker and writer Murray Grigor proved the most adept at harnessing contemporary art to the Cardross preservation campaign. In April 2003, he first began considering returning to the ruined St Peter's, and over the following year he was instrumental in the creation of *A Film for Cardross: Resurrection Cycle* – a collaboration with opera singer Lesley Boyd and artist Dan Dubowitz, including a short film of an installation set in the ruin, accompanied by Boyd's singing at the altar.[64] The final artwork in this cycle was an online 3D virtual restoration of Cardross Seminary by Stephen Colmer of Soulis Technologies in late 2003.[65] Conservation architect James Simpson welcomed this approach, arguing that the complex 'was such a lousy piece of building as to be, to all extents and purposes, incapable of satisfactory repair and restoration. Now that you have done this [virtual restoration], the sooner the physical remains are removed the better!'[66]

During 2003, these artistic efforts cumulatively created a new and glamorous reputation for the ruined remnants of the seminary, with Dubowitz describing it as a 'cult' site, and *Scotsman* journalist Jim Gilchrist writing that it was 'regarded by many as an icon of postwar Scottish architecture'.[67] During this period, in parallel with the dominant arts-led narrative, it should also be noted that the building became a focus for some of the leading graffiti artists in the UK – all on an informal word of mouth basis.[68] And by the end of the year, Dubowitz and Lewis had co-founded (with architectural student John Deffenbaugh) the Cardross Regeneration Trust to 'champion' the cause of the ruin.[69] Deffenbaugh represented a new generation of Cardross enthusiasts, whose interpretation was profoundly conditioned by contemporary-art romanticism: he had first encountered 'surreal photographs' of the ruin in the early 1990s when still at high school.[70] The Cardross Regeneration Trust initially said it had no 'predetermined right or wrong solutions' in mind, but in the adversarial preservation debate surrounding the 2004 stabilisation proposal, it eventually adopted a strong stance in favour of full restoration.[71] Deffenbaugh recounted the Trust's first meeting in Glasgow's Babbity Bowster bar: 'It was a very lively event and the agenda went out of the window quite early on. Really, the whole thing turned into a bit of a free for all, but I think that was what was needed – everyone talking very passionately about the College and what should happen to it.'[72]

Stalled Proposal 2004–6

… one must ask if the time has not come to put it [Cardross] out of its stained and ruined misery. Better that than another three decades of wrangling and recrimination.
Mike Russell, *The Herald*, 2004 [73]

Alongside these new and fervently artistic initiatives, the more pragmatic narrative of planning proposals continued in 2004. A new and contentious application was submitted in July, with Classical House and the Archdiocese as the joint applicants: Ken Crilley explained in that month that 'We are going to have one last go at this.'[74] The application, a re-run of the 1998 proposal, had three inter-dependent parts: an enabling development of 28 houses; the stabilisation of the former seminary buildings; and the creation of a community park, together with restoration of two listed bridges within the estate, all at a total cost of £600,000. Unlike the failed 1997 application, the works to the ruin now required listed building consent. From 2002, Argyll and Bute Council was actively exploring ways to support future plans for the site; the application identified a general housing area on lower ground south-east of the former seminary, including the walled garden area and the Lower Den.[75] Historic Scotland was again consulted on the basis that the new development might affect the setting of the A-listed building and the scheduled Kilmahew Castle. This time round, the focus of public debate and opposition had decisively shifted to the proposed works on the ruin. By June 2005, Historic Scotland advised Argyll and Bute Council against granting listed building consent, and formally rejected the application in 2006, although it was only formally withdrawn by the Archdiocese in August 2013.[76]

In 2004, the applicant's team included Keppie Planning, ARM Architects, and the structural engineers Clyde Design Partnership who compiled the report on the proposed stabilisation works.[77] The listed building consent stabilisation involved the removal of all debris from the ruin.[78] In the main block, excluding the reinstated single bay, the roof, vaulted ceilings, suspended floors and finishes were to be removed to 'completely expose' the in-situ and pre-cast concrete structure, and it would be repaired if necessary. The 'vertical' slice would reinstate one complete roof bay and one complete floor bay at each level, and provide waterproofing. Numerous subsidiary structures were to be demolished, and after completion the Archdiocese would gift the stabilised ruin to a newly formed trust. In November 2003, Classical House had approached Historic Scotland to consider taking the ruin 'into care', but Historic Scotland questioned the 'viability' of such a move, and refused the offer, just as the local authority had previously.[79] The cost of the proposed works was estimated at £430,000 – just as previously stated by the Archdiocese in 1997.[80]

Although the community-impact angle of the proposal was emphatically stressed, with the *Catholic Observer* reporting on 'Community renovation plans for former seminary', in this case local opinion remained divided. Cardross Community Council was in favour of 'modest development' to generate finance, and journalist Jim Gilchrist of the *Scotsman* recalled a chat with one local: '"Best thing to do now is to knock it down", grumbles a shopkeeper in Cardross, while giving directions to the former seminary. "The junkies use it and the vandals have made a mess of it. It's a real eyesore".'[81] Architectural conservation societies, by contrast, lined up unambiguously in defence of the complex. The SPBPT and the London-based Twentieth Century Society both used the time-honoured language of urgency and threat, and argued: 'It's hard to tell how much time is left', and the structure was 'twelve months away from being beyond saving'.[82] The significance of the building grew with every successive press release, and the SPBPT eventually hailed it as Scotland's most 'important cultural icon'.[83] The narrative of the supposedly neglected and abandoned masterpiece did not include any acknowledgment of original functional and technical problems, and only an occasional journalist attempted an alternative approach. In 2003, when Jim Gilchrist suggested to Andy MacMillan that Cardross's 'merits were in form rather than function, MacMillan retorted 'Rubbish … Basically, they didnae clean the gutters and if you don't clean the gutters in the middle of a wood, you get water ingress. Any excuse to get rid of it …'[84] Other pro-restoration campaigners conceded that there might have been building faults, but argued that they were nothing to do with the architects: Nick Barley (then editor of *The List*), argued that 'if the building was flawed, it seems to have been at a level of engineering and construction rather than design, with concrete pouring techniques that were just too ambitious for the West Coast climate'.[85] Lewis similarly attributed problems to 'a construction industry struggling to deal with new techniques' and, in 2007, Stamp insisted that the building was 'superbly constructed and fitted out with timber joinery of high quality'.[86]

Alongside the work of the Cardross Regeneration Trust/SPBPT, the London-based Twentieth Century Society assumed an increasingly high-profile role in the case, despite the convention that the London-based 'period' societies (such as the Georgian and the Victorian societies) should not operate in Scotland. The lead roles in the Twentieth Century Society's involvement now passed to Cordula Zeidler and Patrick Duerden, with Gavin Stamp stepping back from the campaign, lamenting, 'Oh dear, Cardross … it has all been so depressing.'[87] The Twentieth Century Society's influence was further strengthened with the arrival in 2005 from English Heritage of a new chief inspector at Historic Scotland, Malcolm Cooper. Previously based in Manchester, Cooper had experience of working with the society, as he also had with the Manchester-based developers Urban Splash, who would develop a scheme for the ruin in 2008.

The conservationist objections focused on three main inter-connected issues with the proposed stabilisation works: that the stripping-back proposal not only was not geared to any specific future use and was too costly to be covered by a mere £430,000, but would in fact accelerate the structure's deterioration.[88] The Twentieth Century Society argued that 'exposing the concrete frame to the elements could be disastrous' and make any future restoration a practical 'impossibility'.[89] The hypothetical character of the proposal was accentuated by the lack of any market interest for re-use, including in 2003 (in consultation with Scottish Enterprise Dunbartonshire) and in 2005, when Historic Scotland also came to the conclusion that there was 'no market interest in the seminary complex'.[90]

These concerns led directly to the SPBPT publicly withdrawing its support for the application in early

Metzstein and MacMillan, 2008
Metzstein and MacMillan with their honorary degrees from Glasgow University (on behalf of Glasgow School of Art), awarded in 2008. **McAteer Photograph**

October 2004.⁹¹ In the ensuing acrimony, the SPBPT was effectively barred from talking directly with the Archdiocese, and communications were channelled through John Sheridan of Classical House, who held several meetings with Lewis and Deffenbaugh. According to the SPBPT, Classical House showed 'no desire to collaborate' and the proposed works were on 'a take it or leave it basis'.⁹² But behind the scenes, the SPBPT was energetically pursuing future funding with the HLF, and in consultation with a number of 'eminent' architects, engineers and surveyors.⁹³ By the end of 2003, Deffenbaugh admitted 'It would seem that Cardross is beginning to take over my life.'⁹⁴ Lewis and the SPBPT 'blamed the archdiocese and its agents' as 'the people who should be held responsible for the current state of St Peter's and the planning impasse. Had the archdiocese shown the slightest willingness to work with us or to employ an architect with relevant expertise we might still be supporting their application.'⁹⁵ Mike Russell (later to become the SNP's Minister for Culture), writing for the *Scotsman*, despaired at the 'wrangling and recrimination' surrounding the ruined seminary.⁹⁶ By June 2005, Historic Scotland, increasingly under pressure from conservationist lobbying, advised Argyll and Bute Council against granting listed building consent. Both organisations commissioned reports from surveyors Montagu Evans and estate agents Ryden, which concluded that the enabling development would not yield sufficient funds to carry out work required, and that the original costing of £430,000 was not 'robust'.⁹⁷ The SPBPT's own report estimated that a cost of £1.2 million (in 2005) would only cover repairing the perimeter fence, reinstating areas of damaged sanctuary roof structure, providing weather protection, and the installation of security lighting.⁹⁸ Two years later, Avanti Architects' conservation assessment estimated that the works proposed in the 2004 application would cost £2.88 million.

In the spirit of traditional British conservation campaigning (with its requirement for an identifiable bogeyman and publicity stunts) the SPBPT now re-focused its campaigning against Historic Scotland. In late January 2006, the trust repaired and padlocked the south entrance fence and posted the key to the agency's headquarters in Edinburgh. It was promptly posted back, with an accompanying letter from Cooper explaining that while HS was strongly committed to the conservation of the remaining buildings at St Peter's, they were 'not in our ownership, and we are unable to take responsibility for the fence or the building'.⁹⁹ This event was reported in the *Sunday Herald* and the *Observer*, and the Twentieth Century Society hailed it as 'a heroic act, but also one that should shame those who have a statutory duty to protect historic buildings'.¹⁰⁰ All this time, the ruin was suffering further vandalism and deterioration: by July 2005, a section of the sanctuary roof had collapsed, and vandals had seriously damaged a major portion of the convent building; Zeidler lamented that 'this act of vandalism is desecrating in every sense'.¹⁰¹ In September 2006, the *Architects' Journal* reported that an SPBPT banner hung on the main block earlier that year, reading 'Occupier Wanted: Scotland's

Best Building Seeks New Owner', itself had been defaced: someone had sprayed a red line through 'Best' and replaced it with 'Worst'.[102]

In March 2006 Historic Scotland formally refused listed building consent on the grounds that the proposal was inconsistent with planning guidance note NPPG 18, and that the enabling development would not yield enough income to pay for proper consolidation.[103] The agency anticipated 'political fallout' from its decision: senior inspector Ranald MacInnes warned that 'further, sustained decay of this extremely important, Category A-listed building would result in very strong protests from the heritage lobby in Scotland, who see Historic Scotland, and ultimately, the Scottish Ministers, as the last line of defence against cultural loss of this magnitude'.[104] In April that year, a spokesman for the Archdiocese wrote that it had been ' "led a merry dance" for years now by the planning authority and Historic Scotland, and we are simply not prepared to listen any further'.[105] In the climate of greater departmental accountability and ministerial accessibility under devolution, the campaigners were increasingly able to appeal direct to culture ministers, whether Labour (Patricia Ferguson) or SNP (Mike Russell, Linda Fabiani and Fiona Hyslop).

The Lighthouse Exhibition and the Mythologising of St Peter's

These preservationist activities formed part of a wider campaign to promote the 'international' status of Cardross, Metzstein and MacMillan, and Gillespie, Kidd & Coia. This trend culminated in the 2007 Lighthouse exhibition and publication *Gillespie, Kidd & Coia, Architecture, 1956–1987*. The next part of this chapter attempts to disentangle the three key strands of this trend: the claims of the significance of St Peter's; the attempts to win round local opinion; and the architect-led 'cult' of Gillespie, Kidd & Coia as designers.

In the first area, the identification of Cardross by *Prospect* as Scotland's 'top modern building' and architect Richard Murphy's slightly earlier (2003) claim that it was 'the most important postwar building' set the tone for future press reporting.[106] For many, it was now taken as read that the building had always commanded the most

Exhibition: Gillespie, Kidd & Coia: Architecture 1956–1987
The 2007 Lighthouse exhibition celebrated the firm's post-1956 works.
Andrew Lee

exalted architectural standing – in contradiction to the reality of the coverage of the newly completed extension in the 1960s.[107] In anticipation of the *Prospect* issue devoted to St Peter's in March 2006, Tim Abrahams told the *Sunday Herald*, 'They have one of the greatest architectural assets in Scotland on their hands and it is being left to rot.'[108] The SPBPT, he claimed, had had to deal with 'an aging archdiocese, which … sees its own waning influence in the ruins of St Peter's'.[109] Undaunted by these 'obstacles', the SPBPT successfully nominated Cardross for inclusion in the World Monument Fund's 100 most endangered sites in June 2007. It was now 'one of the world's most endangered buildings', Lewis claimed.[110]

In the second area, local opinion was also shifting. Some, such as Rev. Scobie of Cardross Community Council, saw the SPBPT as an unwelcome interloper, attacking them for 'interfering in something that is a local problem when they have no local presence. It is a crazy dream to think it could be restored. It will cost millions just to make it safe, let alone do anything else with it.'[111] *Scotsman* journalist Gilchrist returned in 2007 to test local opinion on the ongoing saga. His account identified a shift towards favouring its restoration, but opposition remained. One local was happy for it to be demolished, but wished to remain nameless 'because some of my friends are all for it'.[112]

The third area, that of elite architectural discourse, was far removed from the practical concerns of local politicians and residents, and was concerned largely to argue for the 'international' status of the seminary extension, and of Metzstein and MacMillan. In 2005, for example, Mark Baines argued that 'There can be little doubt that the architecture of Gillespie, Kidd & Coia can be considered to be of international standing. The thematic nature of their work targeted universal themes … Their significance has so far received little or no mention in the annals of architectural histories and with some buildings already destroyed and others endangered they may soon pass into the realms of mythology.'[113] These 'universal themes' were purely architectural: 'plan and promenade; the articulated section; integrated structure; light; and the inhabited wall'.[114] These 'themes' were not substantiated by specific historical documentary evidence (see Chapter 4), but Metzstein later alluded to them in a 1996 interview, albeit also stressing that 'when we were designing we did not have a formula – just a feeling'.[115] In a 2004 Twentieth Century Society newsletter, Patrick Duerden described the seminary extension as an 'internationally significant work' which occupied 'a central position in the history of Scottish architecture in the latter half of the twentieth century' and following a Twentieth Century Society tour the following year, delegates attended a 'dinner with Isi Metzstein, Andy MacMillan and Mark Baines'.[116] One architectural commentator claimed the firm's church designs 'put Scottish architecture in a European league' while another argued 'Surely Rem Koolhaas was aware of this great architectural monument [the ruined St Peter's] when he designed his Bordeaux House.'[117] In 2004 Metzstein and MacMillan received the Scottish Design Awards lifetime achievement award for contribution to architecture and architectural education.[118]

Underlying this new interpretation was an understanding that the firm's work could no longer be confined within the 'limited' world of Scottish architecture – thus avoiding potentially uncomfortable comparisons with far more prominent postwar Scottish architects such as Robert Matthew and Basil Spence, who were also attracting significant scholarly research and publication in the late 1990s and the first decade of the new millennium.[119] In 1996, Metzstein protested, 'I don't want to be … regionalised. I believe in regional architecture, but … I don't want to be seen as having a kind of limited vision.'[120] Even international precedents, such as the work of Le Corbusier, at times no longer seemed enough. For example, the Twentieth Century Society's Duerden argued that 'St Peter's College acknowledges no precedent in its arrangement of the facilities of the seminary. This most remarkable building is comparable in some respects to the work of Le Corbusier at La Tourette, but is also a departure in that La Tourette was essentially a modelling of a traditional arrangement of spaces, in contemporary garb.'[121] An especially contentious aspect of contextualisation was the relationship of GKC's work to the patronage of the Church. Here, from 2004, historian Robert Proctor made a new and significant intervention, in a series of publications culminating in the 2014 book, *Building the Modern Church: Roman Catholic Church Architecture in Britain*.[122]

In a 2006 article on the problems posed by oral testimony within architectural history, Proctor also touched on a more general issue within scholarship of Gillespie, Kidd & Coia: the role of Metzstein and MacMillan in controlling the narrative of their own history.[123] Using them as his main case study, Proctor argued that their personal accounts, conveyed in historical interviews, were sometimes contradictory, and often set out to undermine the lead-designer status previously widely ascribed to Jack Coia (whom they, according to Proctor, often cast as a 'fool'), and to 'reascribe the author function from Coia to themselves'.[124] Proctor cited other cases, such as that of Ralph Erskine, in which architects used interviews to control the narrative of their own practices. In support of this argument, Gavin Stamp argued that 'in my experience, *all* Modern architects try to control and rewrite their own history'.[125] In a mid 1990s interview, Metzstein even went so far as to demand that published work on the practice should 'have nothing in the text which implies that Jack Coia designed St Peter's, or any other building post-1950'.[126] In contrast to the debates about Coia's role, Cowell's prominent role in the commission was forgotten.

All of this, however, had little effect on the wider public discourse of St Peter's, within which, from 2007 onwards, both Metzstein and MacMillan were generally identified as the complex's designers, a narrative which found media champions in the likes of Kirsty Wark, George Wylie and Murray Grigor.[127] Also playing an increasingly prominent role was the head of the Government's Architectural Policy Unit since 2002, architect Ian Gilzean, who had had previously worked for the Scottish Arts Council (1994–99) on its Capital Arts Programme funded by the National Lottery Fund. Gilzean, as we will see in the final part of this story, was instrumental in supporting, through government grants, early NVA interest in the ruined seminary.[128]

The major retrospective exhibition *Gillespie, Kidd & Coia, Architecture, 1956–87*, curated by Mark Baines, was held at the Lighthouse, Glasgow, from November 2007 to February 2008. The accompanying image-based catalogue was edited by Johnny Rodger with contributions from Baines, and architects Gordon Benson and Colin St John Wilson. Initiated in 2006, the exhibition (including two commissioned films directed by Metzstein's son, Saul) and book formed part of a larger programme which included the cataloguing of the practice archive gifted to Glasgow School of Art (GSA) in 2001, and an outreach programme. The project was chiefly funded by a Heritage Lottery Fund grant of £342,000.[129] It was a partnership project run by the Lighthouse, with the GSA as its 'cornerstone'.[130]

The core of the catalogue was a list of 22 key projects, including St Peter's Seminary, with original architectural drawings and completed project photographs, and a brief summary of the building function. The buildings were analysed as if they were newly completed, with historical contextual information in a short introductory chapter summarising the practice's development.[131] The exhibition received extensive, but not always positive, coverage in the mainstream and specialist press.[132] At the launch, catalogue contributor Benson claimed 'Andy and Isi are like Sherpas who can discern what's really happening in society and interpret it: an architect like that can move like a radar across the page, picking up, like no-one else can, what's in front of him, behind, him, and on each side of him', and journalist Iain Gale conclude that Metzstein and MacMillan were 'arguably the greatest living architects in Scotland today'.[133]

With its emphasis above all on the celebration of Metzstein and MacMillan, its most immediate effect on the Cardross saga was to further strengthen the attribution of the seminary's design solely to Metzstein and MacMillan – as evidenced, for example, in an exhibition review by Gavin Stamp, simply entitled 'God's architects', in the *Scotsman*.[134] John Allan, who would become lead architect for the 2007–8 conservation assessment for Cardross, concluded that the exhibition was 'likely to increase current interest in the building and entrench its position in the national architectural canon still further'.[135] Even Rodger's relatively detached introductory historical essay returned to the theme of Coia vis-à-vis Metzstein and MacMillan, arguing

The main block, 2011
St Peter's seen shrouded by trees and set behind a locked gate and high steel fence.
HES DP106842

that by 1952 (aged 54) 'Jack Coia's [lack of] personal ability to adapt to environmental circumstances and show vision in his design work, and in his patience and determination to see through the full arduous, complicated business of designing and constructing a building' had been 'exposed' by Metzstein and MacMillan.[136]

This view began to provoke criticism from some historians. Lewis reported in *Prospect* that the reception of the exhibition had been mixed, and in the same issue Glendinning criticised it as a 'hagiographic' project whose praise of the architects as 'prophets, seers and visionaries' had prevented a historically contextualised examination of Gillespie, Kidd & Coia as a practice deeply rooted in the Catholic culture of the West of Scotland.[137] He concluded that the 'Holy Family' (his term for the circle of 'admirers' who had shaped the exhibition) had 'emptied out the real Gillespie, Kidd & Coia, rooted in the real Glasgow, and put in its place a faceless "brand" made up of generalised images and rhetorical slogans that could apply interchangeably to any signature architect anywhere.'[138] Some journalists also questioned the density of architectural rhetoric in the exhibition: Susan Mansfield in the *Scotsman* related that 'at the door, you are offered a glossary of architectural terms and once you are in you realise why you need it … I found myself back with the glossary looking up "articulated section" and "inhabited wall!"' She concluded 'The exhibition is a celebration. This approach has the effect of alienating those who find GKC's work difficult. If you don't find these buildings ground-breaking and beautiful, it implies, why are you here at all?'[139]

The Avanti Conservation Assessment, 2008 – Towards a New Vision

As we will see, it was only once the defenders of St Peter's set out to broaden the appeal of the seminary complex beyond the discourse of architectural 'masterpiece', and also to incorporate the history and values of the nineteenth century landscape, and the potential for new public art, that a new future for the complex really became practicable. In particular, a 2008 conservation assessment report by Avanti Architects brought into sharper focus the practical and funding problems facing the ruins. Historic Scotland, which funded the report at a cost of £90,000, had been under increasing pressure from Cardross campaigners from 2004 onwards to commission an architect-led conservation plan, using a shortlist of London-based practices supplied by the Twentieth Century Society.[140] In June 2006, Historic Scotland formally approached the Archdiocese to begin the process of commissioning a report which would 'identify necessary repairs to the seminary complex', categorised according to urgency. The commissioning of Avanti for this report in January 2007 ushered in a decade of involvement by the practice with the ruined seminary.[141] Allan, a recognised specialist in the study and conservation of English twentieth century architecture, assembled a chiefly London-based professional team, although in Edinburgh Addyman Archaeology produced a detailed assessment report of the pre-1966 buildings. The SPBPT contended that Scotland had so far had only 'limited experience of conserving modern buildings', but that 'now is clearly the time to learn'.[142]

The report, St Peter's Seminary Conservation Assessment, which was funded by Historic Scotland, was over 300 pages in length, but its main recommendations were concentrated in Section 4 (condition analysis); Section 5 (options definition), and Sections 6–9 (schedules of works based on the identified options).[143] The condition analysis concluded that the in-situ reinforced concrete structures of the main, convent and classroom blocks were generally in sound condition but with some localised damage.[144] Of the main block it reported that the precast concrete was generally sound, but the gallery handrail was failing and that substantial parts of the roofs were missing (with the sanctuary roof in a 'perilous' state).[145] The CRL 'Condition Assessment' concluded that 'considering the age, environment of exposure, i.e. aggressive coastal marine, and the obvious neglect, the structural "hardware" elements appeared generally to be in reasonable condition'.[146]

The St Peter's Seminary Conservation Assessment, 2007
This detailed report totalled over 300 pages and presented three options, along with costs, for the future of St Peter's. **Avanti Architects**

Architects' model of NVA's plans for St Peter's College, 2014
NORD Architecture, courtesy of NVA

avanti architects

ST PETER'S SEMINARY
Cardross

CONSERVATION ASSESSMENT
Volume 1 (of 2)

Main Report

OCTOBER 2007

STATUS: FINAL DRAFT FOR COMMENT: LIMITED ISSUE

The Urban Splash 2008 scheme, by Hoskins Architects
This architects' drawing shows the sanctuary and chapel as a swimming pool and health spa. **Hoskins Architects**

Urban Splash proposal, 2008
Urban Splash proposed a cube-like residential block on the former site of Kilmahew House, restoring the original architectural balance of the truncated complex. **Hoskins Architects**

The report established six potential options.[147] Option 1, The Consolidated Exhibit (estimated at £4.08 million), would secure and conserve viable fabric, including repair of vaults, but would not preclude future full restoration. Option 2, The Holding Option (£2.73m), would stabilise and secure the ruin on a temporary basis. Option 3, The Restoration Option (£11.36m), would entail full re-use. The fourth option, The Stabilized Structure (£2.88m), was the same as that proposed in the 2004 planning application. Option 5, the Do Nothing Option, was a continuation of the situation which had developed over the previous 30 years. Finally Option 6, Demolition (£1.66m), was branded 'inadmissible'. The creation of a country park was also estimated for, at a cost of £1.6 million. The report only provided a proposed schedule of works for options 1–3 (and the country park) on the basis that these were the only appropriate ones for the future of a ruin of this level of significance.[148] The 'symbolic' significance of the Modernist ruin was foregrounded as unique in heritage terms.[149]

In its reaction to the findings in November 2007, the SPBPT had to confront the unwelcome news of the unexpectedly high costs of full restoration, and its membership soon began to break up.[150] In 2008, developers Classical House also withdrew after fourteen challenging years of involvement with the site.[151] All the interested parties were now faced with three conservation-appropriate options, all with a substantial price tag, and Historic Scotland remained under pressure to find a solution.[152]

Events now began to overtake the findings of the conservation report. One plan for re-use and

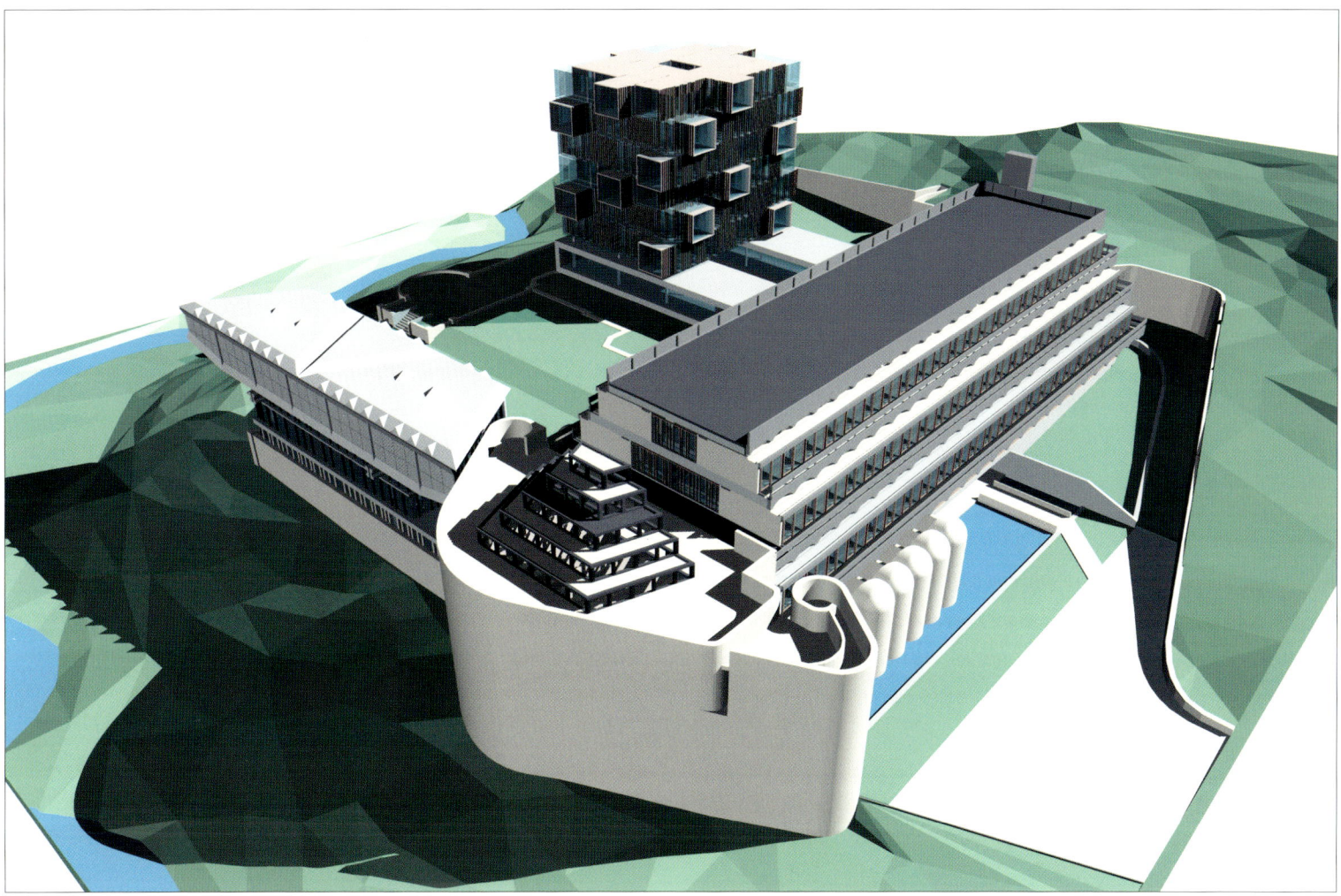

Bird's eye view of the Urban Splash redevelopment scheme
The recession of the late 2000s brought these dramatic restoration plans to a halt. **Hoskins Architects**

restoration, first mooted in 2005, was formalised during 2008 (by Manchester-based developers Urban Splash) but came to nothing, while another plan for public-art focused re-use, by arts-charity NVA, also emerged in 2008. John Bute (the 7th Marquess of Bute, whose ancestors had been one of modern Scotland's leading Catholic families) also became interested in financially backing the scheme, and argued that 'it's an incredible building and it's great the original architects are still around to consult'.[153]

Urban Splash, headed by multi-millionaire Tom Bloxham, had first expressed an interest to Historic Scotland in 2005.[154] Inspired by the final draft of the Avanti report, their preliminary plan was to sympathetically restore the seminary and convert it into residential apartments (just as Classical House's 1992 proposal had) and build some contemporary villas in the grounds.[155] At that point Urban Splash had reportedly made a significant cash offer to the Archdiocese.[156] For a brief period Urban Splash considered converting the main block to a hotel (an idea originally considered in 1979), but Metzstein opposed the hotel idea, declaring that he 'would like it made into a music centre for young musicians, who could live there in residence and have concerts …'[157] By late 2008, the scheme had morphed (now under the design direction of Urban Splash's consultant architect, Gareth Hoskins) to accommodate a health and sports centre in the main block with residential buildings in the grounds. With grant-aid of £55,000 from Historic Scotland, the developer investigated a private–public scheme (estimated at £18 million) in late 2008, in close consultation with Metzstein and MacMillan: the latter gave the Hoskins scheme his approval 'They are the most sensitive of all the proposals we have seen for the building, considering its original use.'[158] NVA worked with Urban Splash on the public art element of the proposal for two years, but by late 2009, Urban Splash had withdrawn its interest, owing to the 2007–8 global financial crisis, and because there was no commitment of public funding.[159] The proposal had involved much radical intervention in the fabric and privitisation of the space, all within a highly commercial framework. In retrospect, Farquhar recalled that 'NVA were very uncomfortable with the invasive nature of the proposed scheme and how it would destroy the architectural integrity of the building complex.'[160]

Throughout this debate the previous assumption that the Church was ultimately responsible for the fate of St Peter's was replaced by a new narrative, in which the Government was increasingly identified as having the chief moral and financial responsibility to save the ruin. Nick Barley, by then director of the Lighthouse, argued that 'this masterpiece should be preserved for the Scottish people'.[161]

From early 2008 onwards, artist Angus Farquhar of the Scottish public arts charity NVA began speaking independently to the Archdiocese and other interested parties (including John Allan) about the possibility of NVA getting directly involved in finding a less costly solution for the ruined seminary – a part-ruin / part-restoration plan under which the ruin and the landscape would be transformed into a public art venue, more or less on the model of Avanti's Consolidated Exhibit option. NVA was established in Glasgow in 1992 (its name being an acronym of a Latin slogan meaning 'involved in public affairs'). Led by creative director Farquhar, its collective artistic approach was intended to facilitate new permanent and temporary works, and encourage audience participation. Unlike all the previous proposals, NVA's scheme was to be a public venture, mainly funded by public grants and private charitable donations. Farquhar asserted ambitiously that 'we are now ready to grasp the mantle of bringing St Peter's Seminary and woodlands back to its local community and the nation'.[162] The first practical step in what was to become an eight-year long NVA partnership project (to date), came in early 2009 when it was awarded a Scottish Arts Council grant to explore the potential for temporary and permanent art works on the site.

Cardross Consolidated, 2009–16

Regarded as one of Europe's greatest modernist buildings … this major investment will see key elements restored while others will be consolidated to allow the public safe access to large scale events and performances as well as to smaller community activities.
Heritage Lottery Fund Scotland, March 2016[163]

This final phase of our story, rather than being dominated, as previously, by planning applications, was now defined by a succession of successful NVA bids for funding grants, and by ever-shifting phased plans based on that funding. The sole planning application, during this period, in January 2013, attracted no debate or controversy and passed by almost unnoticed. NVA proposed a completely new alternative strategy, that of a publicly funded scheme of cultural and local benefit, as against the previous proposals' concept of a costly private venture which would limit public access. New funding from 2010 onwards – won in competition against other heritage and arts projects – was augmented by private sponsorship. The passionate and determined Farquhar, like Gavin Stamp and Penny Lewis before him, was soon identified by the media as the new saviour of St Peter's, and like his predecessors he was a skilled media operator. To date (May 2016) the project has received £7.45 million from public grant-giving bodies, and £2.67 million in private donations – with a current aim to raise a further £1 million.[164]

By contrast with previous developments, this proved to be a settled period where all the interested parties worked together. These included the Archdiocese, Historic Scotland, Argyll and Bute Council, the local residents, and – more importantly for NVA and the future of the ruin – the main public grant-giving bodies, Creative Scotland and the HLF. NVA also received direct ongoing financial support from the Scottish Government through its Architecture and Places unit (headed by Ian Gilzean). Crucially, these interested parties no longer included the Gillespie, Kidd & Coia survivors: Metzstein died in

2012, followed by MacMillan in 2014.[165] In the wake of their departure, Cardross was changing context again, and becoming yet more de-contextualised, shifting from an object of claims of timeless architectural genius to an anonymised abstract artistic installation.

NVA's proposal was developed from 2008, including detailed plans after the group secured ownership in March 2011. After Archbishop Philip Tartaglia succeeded Archbishop Conti in 2012, the site was gifted to NVA in 2013, following which their project secured its first major funding grant. Relying on public funding inevitably slowed and complicated the planning process, but NVA proved highly adept both at obtaining public grants and at changing course when funding fell short. This section will provide an overview of the chronology and practical aspects of NVA's plan, and of the works carried out to date – including a provisional assessment of its reception, and of the intellectual debates staged by NVA as an integral part of their project plan. It will conclude with a brief overview of NVA's first major public art event staged in the ruins: 'Hinterland'. The last section of the book will provide a contemporary image-led essay by Farquhar on the vision behind NVA's scheme and its future plans.

The Evolving NVA Plan, 2009–14

It's not an attempt to fully recreate or bring the whole building back to its original state. It would be economically impossible to do that. It will sit in part in its ruined state; there will be parts addressed from a conservation point of view and parts brought back into use as wind and water tight spaces. So the core buildings will have a mix of reinstated, consolidated and untouched elements and equally, across the whole site, there's that same balance going on.

Rolf Roscher, ERZ landscape architects, 2015[166]

NVA's proposals for the built and landscape fabric were developed over a five-year period, and fell into three main successive plans, with Plan 1 of 2009 beginning on a modest scale, Plan 2 of 2011 becoming more ambitious, and the final Plan 3 of 2013 retrenching to a more pragmatic and less-costly solution. Despite these vicissitudes, however, the overall artistic and intellectual vision remained the same. The core aim was to establish cultural, educational and research programmes based on the site of the ruin and its estate, exploiting that site itself as one of the main subjects of the programmes. Exploring public art, and exploiting it as mechanism for community and wider engagement, was *the* underlying principle of the proposal. An international research network, Invisible College, was to be formed. On a more practical level, the site was to be open to all.

The first plan of 2009 was not presented in any great detail but was based on a version of the Avanti report's Consolidated Exhibit: the Avanti report estimated a cost of £4.08 million for that option, but initially NVA were looking to secure £3.5 million to consolidate the main block and allow a phased repair of the classroom block and the landscape.[167] The original NVA concept was not focused solely on the ruined seminary buildings, but on the estate as a whole, with its ruins and landscape – a highly significant shift in focus from the previous intense focus on Modernist architectural genius. Plan 2 was supported by two separate £100,000 grants from Creative Scotland in May 2010 (to produce an art commissioning plan) and March 2011 (to develop a masterplan). As fully developed, Plan 2 was at one point costed at £17.4 million, but was finally established at £11.5 million.[168] At this point NVA formed a design group, consisting of London-based visual arts consultant Gerrie van Noord and Rolf Roscher of Glasgow-based landscape architects ERZ. Later the group was expanded to include Brian McGinlay of NORD Architecture (who had offices in Glasgow), and John Allan of Avanti. The collaborative nature of the contemporary project in some ways recalled the original atelier-like organisation of design on the seminary. Farquhar, as creative director, proved to be the recognised public face of the project, which now had a new branded title reflecting its embrace of the estate landscape: 'Kilmahew/St Peter's'.[169]

The November 2011 masterplan, led by Rolf Roscher, proposed a scheme combining consolidation and rebuilding. The main block was still to be stabilised, but now an element of restoration and conversion was proposed: the kitchen block was to be demolished to secure emergency access. Landscape rehabilitation, public access and transportation were central to the plan: for example 'a dense block of birch trees' was planned to 'echo the original spatial arrangement' of the demolished

Birth and Death – Chapter 6

Bird's eye view of seminary complex, NVA masterplan, 2011
This drawing illustrates the vision for the seminary – part restoration, part ruin, making the buildings an integrated feature of the landscape.
ERZ Landscape Architects, courtesy of NVA

Exploded axonometric of St Peter's College from the NVA masterplan
This overview shows the proposed plans and uses for each element of Gillespie, Kidd & Coia's former seminary buildings.
ERZ Landscape Architects, courtesy of NVA

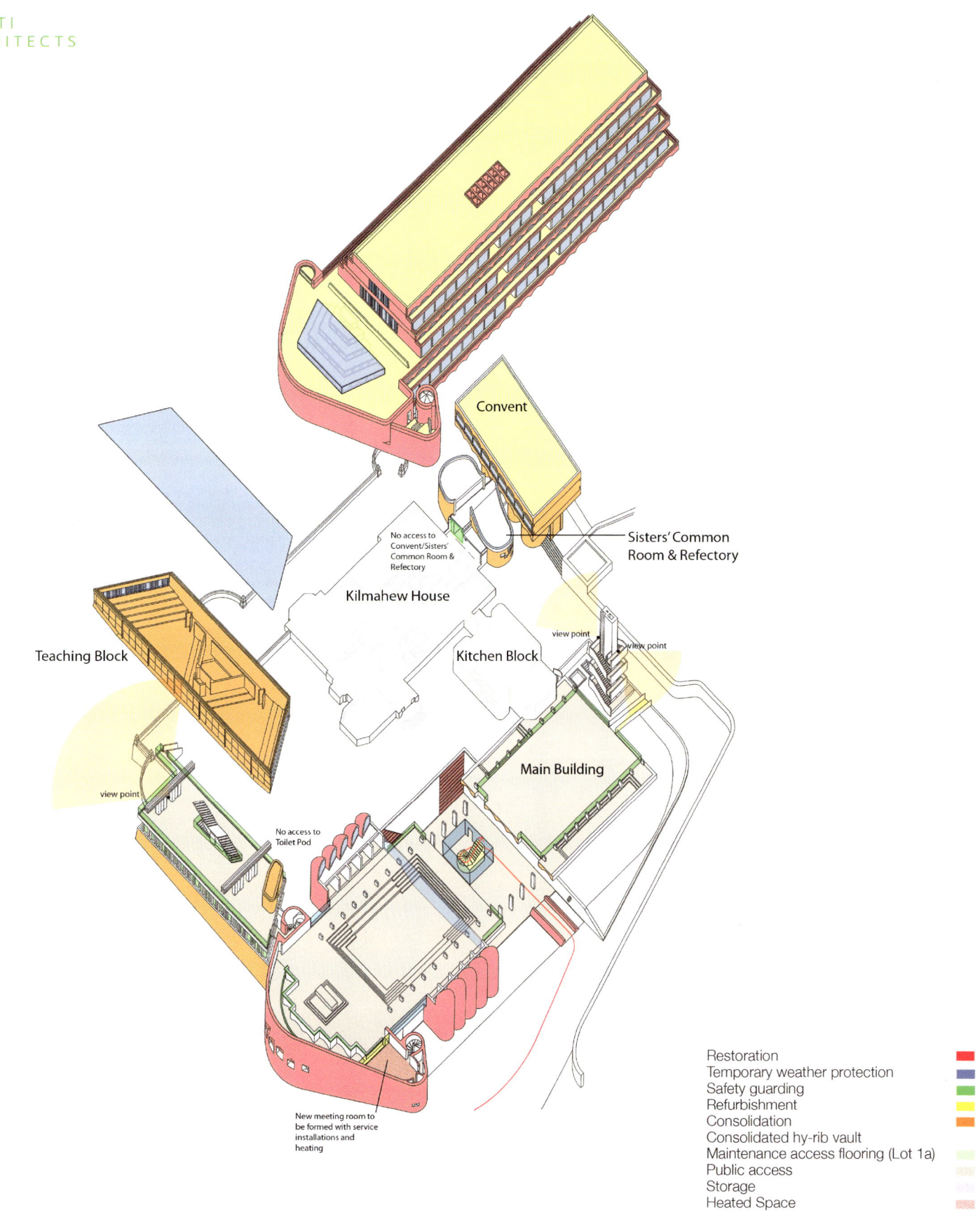

Kilmahew House, and to form 'a discrete space' for 'quiet, personal discovery'. The wider landscape was to include 'creative interventions', woodland cabins and camping facilities.[170]

Ultimately, the part-restored buildings were to accommodate a range of uses: performance and exhibition space (main block); teaching, exhibition, interpretation and library space (classroom block): office/work space for NVA (convent accommodation block, refectory and common room); and two houses for staff in the walled garden complex. The repair and part-restoration aimed to make good original damaged fabric, and replace if no longer fit for purpose. The building was to have a new roof and the sanctuary roof was to be rebuilt in replica. In addressing the issue of the technical failures of the original GKC design, the architects (Avanti) proposed selective replacement of defective design detail, all to be done 'with discretion'. Staged funding arrangements dictated that works should be carried out in a complex series of chronological phases, with 'each phase being complete in itself'.[171] Their report explained that 'the current project scope is not expected to achieve the complete restitution of the entire seminary complex but rather that certain elements may need to be consolidated in a "holding operation" until such time as resources permit further work'.[172]

Funding was immediately sought for the first phase of work, the cost was estimated at £6.75 million: the joint-funders were anticipated as the HLF, Creative Scotland, Historic Scotland, and Argyll and Bute Council. A repair grant application for £5.5 million was made to Historic Scotland, but at that point the amount exceeded Historic Scotland's full national funding allocation for two years: instead NVA was awarded a maximum grant of £500,000 in 2012.[173] The Scottish Government continued to support the scheme and invited NVA to organise the 2010 Scottish contribution to the 12th Architectural Biennale in Venice with a grant of £70,000. Fiona Hyslop, who succeeded Linda Fabiani as culture minister in 2009, was promoted to cabinet secretary in 2011. The first approach to the HLF's Scottish office for major funding, in 2012, proved initially unsuccessful, and NVA immediately began re-structuring its proposals. In the third and final plan established in 2013, the proposal was significantly cut back to focus on the part-restoration of the former seminary main block.[174] This refectory would be a kept as consolidated ruin open to the elements, and the chapel and sanctuary would be fully restored (with a replica roof) to create a 600-capacity venue. The methods and scope of repair and restoration were the same as those set out in the 2011 masterplan, including concrete repair works to the main structural carcase, restoration of external cladding, and repairs to the rendered vaulted ceilings. The teaching, convent and kitchen blocks were merely to be stabilised, and the innovative landscaping scheme would, in the short term, be restricted to the area surrounding the seminary ruins and walled garden, including a new single-storey pavilion building adjacent to the walled garden.[175] An access plan included restoration of three nineteenth century estate bridges, and the formation of a car park and a network of paths in the walled garden.

After a period of consultation with Historic Scotland, Argyll and Bute formally approved listed building consent for these works in June 2013, and Historic Scotland also fell into line behind the part-consolidated ruin approach in the face of the practical and financial barriers to full restoration. In 2009, chief inspector Malcolm Cooper had argued that long-term consolidation was contrary to HS's listed building policy, but by 2011, Ranald MacInnes had come out in favour of consolidation, arguing that 'once you have decided, as a society, as a culture, that this thing needs saving, this thing needs preserving in some form or another, then you work out practically how to do that'.[176] This revised and scaled back plan was estimated to cost between £7.5 and £8.5 million, and now gained HLF support, with a first phased grant awarded in December 2013. Farquhar hailed this as 'a pivotal moment … The seminary is held in high regard throughout the world. It has now been given the chance of a second life after 25 years of decline.'[177] In early 2014 the project received a development award of £100,000 from Creative Scotland, and £25,000 from Argyll and Bute Council to carry out an Audience Development Strategy.[178] In 2016 the final grants from the HLF of £3.85 million and £400,000 from Creative Scotland were awarded, as was £650,000 from the Cosla/Scottish Government Regeneration

Capital Grant Fund. In November 2014 the design team was appointed, comprising Avanti Architects, ERZ Landscape Architects (continuing John Allan and Rolf Roscher's involvement respectively) and NORD Architecture (Brian McGinlay).

The Rebuilt Cardross

A building that was an undoubted failure, [and] hated by its owner, has become not just a poignant ruin, but a compelling architectural monument … Like ruined temples and abbeys, Cardross – despite its stylistic modernity – is a relic of a lost civilisation.
Gavin Stamp, 2015 [179]

An integral part of NVA's proposal focused on visitors' individual engagement with the ruin and landscape: in 2011, they estimated some 30,000 people would visit each year. This expansive engagement vision encouraged a new wave of interest in the ruin from the Scottish and UK cultural elite, and stimulated a succession of artistic, philosophical and architectural-theoretical initiatives and ideas from 2008 onwards, all engaging with the ruin and landscape. Perhaps the most significant of these was the 'To Have and to Hold' debate curated by NVA as part of the 12th Venice Architectural Biennale in November 2010, and accompanied by Murray Grigor's 'wordless portrait' film *Space and Light Revisited*. The 2009 film, a painstaking shot-by-shot recreation of an original 1972 film by cinematographer Seamus McGarvey, had premiered at the Royal Scottish Academy of Music and Drama in September of that year.[180] The Venice debate was recorded and commemorated in a multi-authored publication of 2011, *To Have and to Hold: Future of A Contested Landscape*. Edited by Gerrie van Noord, it incorporated quotations from the discussion alongside rhetorical questions. In NVA-backed initiatives such as this, the process continued of shifting Cardross away from discourses of tragic loss, and of the genius of architect-creators, towards an artistic approach that was more inclusive – as well as international in scope. Ian Gilzean recalled later that one of the aims of the 2010 Venice debate was to 'shift it [the ruin] into an international context'.[181]

Two of the key themes repeatedly raised in these debates and publications were the meaning and nature of ruination, and the emphasis on open-ended process and public engagement, especially in NVA's own work. Despite the initial pressure within the architectural world for full restoration, Ian Gilzean now urged pragmatism: 'we must accept that the functional aspect has gone'. Among architects committed to the Gillespie, Kidd & Coia legacy, an enthusiasm for the 'ruin' solution was also now growing: John Allan eagerly anticipated that St Peter's would be 'perhaps the first truly authentic modern ruin', while Ed Hollis argued that 'a lot of the mythologizing of St Peter's over time is actually deeply romantic. I think we are allowed to be romantic about modernism, because its tale is so tragic'.[182] The romantic ruin idea appealed even more to the mainstream media: Rowan Moore of the *Guardian* wrote 'There is no place like it, on these islands, for the mutual battery of multiple forces, for the thumping, pummelling and attrition of creation and destruction, the incessant beating of weather, vandals and arson against rocks of obstinate architecture. It is like watching medieval knights club each other to death yet standing. It is a mud-wrestle of culture and nature. Only the scorched, rusticated carcass of John Vanburgh's Seaton Delaval Hall in Northumberland can come close.'[183]

In engagement terms, the 'five centuries' of history on the site, from 'medieval to modern' were to be a vital support, shifting the focus away from academic history or architectural hagiography in favour of a broader, more democratic 'human history of the site'.[184] Individuals' experiences and memories, and the reception of the buildings and site, were all to be to be examined, a process which, Farquhar anticipated, would in turn influence the decision-making process, in 'a reflection of its long narrative of abandonment and dereliction'.[185] Much emphasis was placed on the creative process in part-restoring the ruin, and on its open-ended nature – given that each phase was self-contained in itself.[186] Farquhar correctly anticipated that NVA's focus on learning through process might prove complicated to implement in practice, explaining 'Many public-funded solutions want outcomes with such sparkling clarity that some of the more open-ended approaches can seem vague rather than the best way to the right answer.'[187]

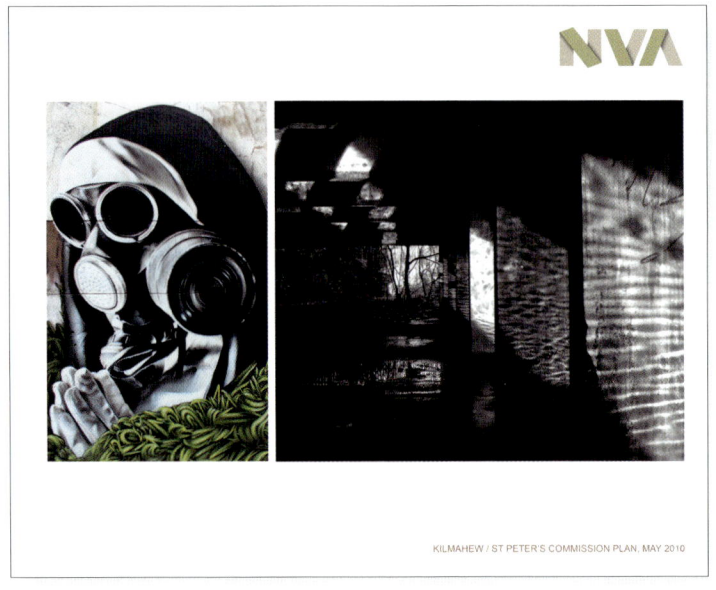

NVA's Commission Plan, May 2010
This plan proposed to 'set the building within the wider landscape as a total artwork and make it the fundamental starting source and starting points for all future interventions'. NVA

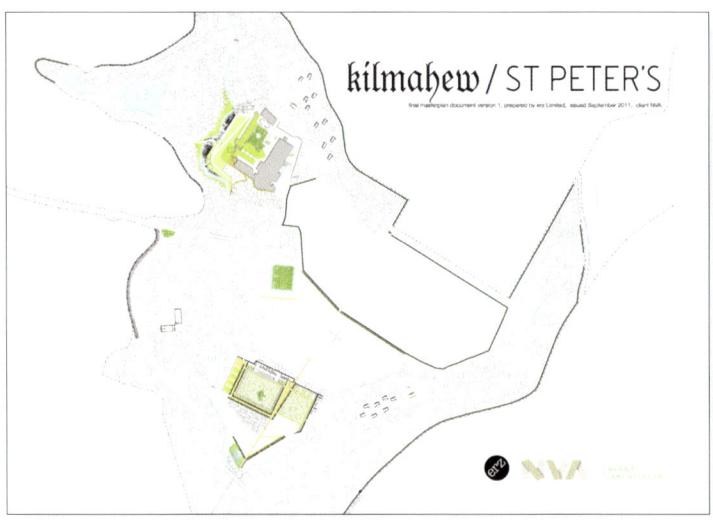

Kilmahew/St Peter's masterplan, November 2011
NVA worked with Avanti Architects to produce a masterplan which focused at first on the seminary buildings, walled garden and woodland cabins.
ERZ Landscape Architects, courtesy of NVA

Ian Gilzean later recalled that some funders, particularly the HLF, initially had 'difficulty in grasping some of NVA's more radical ideas'.[188]

The Invisible College, an academic research network and 'future field station', was established following an initial £100,000 AHRC grant in 2011, and ran for an initial three years with well attended site activities including growing schemes, archaeological digs, physical archiving and debate. A soundscape was commissioned from geographer Michael Gallagher.[189] By contrast to the architectural elitism of much of the previous advocacy, there was now a strong emphasis on the embedding of the project in the local Cardross community – an essential for HLF and other public funding support – and local opinion fell into line behind the plans of NVA and its funding partners.[190] NVA, unlike almost all its predecessors, actively engaged the community through workshops, talks and events.[191] In April 2009, resident Catriona Macauley argued that 'it will be an amazing place if we can have the woodlands back, and restore the special atmosphere and simply unique qualities of the location'.[192] The local press garnered support, reported funding news and attracted volunteers – the last being an important element of NVA's plan.[193] By summer 2010, clearance work on the woodlands was being planned and volunteers called for, but site security remained a problem. In August 2013, a serious accident left a teenager in hospital, and Farquhar warned local residents not to go on the site of the ruins.[194] Despite the general support from the local community, publicity also demanded an element of contention and controversy, and in a 2015 article for the *Guardian*, Farquhar remarked that 'I could find 10 people today within 10 square miles who would willingly put a bomb under it.'[195]

The Hinterland Effect

Now we can embark on the task of making St Peter's a permanent inspirational venue for creativity, learning and debate. It will surely be the outstanding heritage rescue project of our time.
John Allan, Avanti Architects, 2016[196]

Hinterland[197] was the first in a series of planned NVA public art interventions, set in the ruined St Peter's. Staged on the evenings of 18–27 March 2016, this event attracted a sell-out audience of 7,500: a free preview night was attended by 600 locals. *Hinterland* not only marked the official opening of the former seminary site and its immediate landscape to the general public, but

The Invisible College leaflet for Lighthouse event, 2012
The Invisible College is a research hub, inspired by Kilmahew/St Peter's, bringing together the local community, artists, activists and academics. **NVA**

Hinterland leaflet, 2016
In this booklet NVA outlined the *Hinterland* Manifesto and their aims for the future of Kilmahew/St Peter's. **NVA**

was also part-funded by the Scottish Government as the official opening event of its year of Architecture, Design and Innovation, and of the 2016 Festival of Architecture. In anticipation of this event, and to complete the first part of the multi-phased project, work began on clearing and environmentally cleaning the site in June 2015: specialist contractors Reigart undertook asbestos removal, cleared debris and stabilised 80 vaulted ceilings.

Hinterland was a collective work under the creative direction of Angus Farquhar and visual director James Johnson. The light design was by Philip Supple, projection mapping by Novak creative studio, with bespoke instillations by Glasgow sound/art/performance collective 85A. The music was composed by Rory Boyle and performed by the trumpeter Bede Williams and the St Salvator's Chapel Choir of St Andrew's University. The large creative and project teams were augmented by 70 volunteers. The project's overall aims and ethos were summed up in a 'manifesto' authored by Farquhar, which explained that 'Hinterland is an abandoned inland area not far from the sea or a major river. It is a place without people, the definition of a backwater … our *Hinterland*, by contrast, will be established as a place to walk, talk, grow, eat, think and debate; taking part in re-discovering the rich history of the landscape and the people who lived there.'[198] The built remains, interpreted through a lens both of modernity and classical antiquity, were central to NVA's vision of place: Farquhar argued that 'the Agora was established in Ancient Greece as the public engine for constructive human activity; it was both the forum for debate as well as the physical setting where relevant topics were discussed: business, politics, current events, or the nature of the universe and the divine. Hinterland aims to re-invoke the spirit of the Agora.'[199] In its visual approach, the project 'draws on industrial heritage, ruination, graffiti, and … the birth of modernism, referring back to Malevich and supremacism, and we're creating one really bold, coloured moment where we bathe the building in colour in homage. Much of the rest is very monochrome.'[200] Farquhar emphatically distanced the project from commercial son-et-lumière events: 'Our work has seriousness, purpose, and intent. It is not a light show, we are public art with light as one of our mediums.'[201]

Hinterland had an almost uniformly positive reception, with extensive coverage in Scottish and UK newspapers, illustrated by striking images of

Birth and Death – Chapter 6

three above
Classroom block, convent and the external wall of the crypt, May 2016
HES DP237808, DP237846, DP238653

right
The main block, May 2016
HES DP237830

Angus Farquhar, director of NVA, 2015
NVA, which took ownership of St Peter's College from the Archdiocese in 2011, held *Hinterland*, their first public art show on the site, in March 2016.
Robert Perry

the ruin, bathed in light. The new dominant Cardross discourse of open-ended modernity was much to the fore: journalist Joyce McMillan, for example, identified *Hinterland* as 'our twenty-first century response' to the ruined seminary, and described it 'more like a starting point than a conclusion … like the packed introductory paragraph of a conversation that could go on for decades – a conversation about structure, water and light, about faith and the crumbling of faith'.[202] Allan Radcliffe of *The Times* praised NVA's amazing atmospherics: 'In their hands the revered building has become an ornate canvas to which we, the audience, further project our own associations and contemplations.'[203] Some reviews in the architectural press still referenced the traditional narrative of the abandoned work of architectural genius: for example, Elizabeth Hopkirk of *Building Design* rejected NVA's more extreme cultural-philosophical positions and argued that 'fortunately Metzstein and MacMillan's architecture is too thrilling to be sidelined and redemption can be found just walking through the building, its decaying concrete caressed by roving lights and audience hands'.[204] And one writer in the magazine *Urban Realm* concluded that 'Whilst seminary architects Andy MacMillan and Isi Metzstein sadly couldn't be at the [*Hinterland*] launch they will surely have been looking down on the celebrations, no doubt satisfied that this architectural space, so unlike any other in the UK, is in safe hands.'[205]

But overall, by 2016, a new, more neutral narrative of the romantic ruin was now firmly in the ascendant. the *Guardian* argued that 'Hinterland's alchemy of light and sound helps us detect the invisible beauty that lurks amid the ruination.'[206] Archaeologist J Alexander Durnan argued that 'Had it remained in use as it was designed, or been turned into a hotel, or flats, it would still be considered a modernist masterpiece – but not much else. The period of abandonment is what has defined this modernist relic, and is why it developed such a cult (and now more mainstream) following.'[207]

What had not changed since the Metzstein and MacMillan days was the language associated with Cardross, with positive and negative terminology such as 'legendary', 'infamous' and 'mythical' used throughout *Hinterland*.[208] The claims of the building's international significance were further accentuated, with the NVA project adding a new overlay of artistic glamour. At the *Hinterland* launch, for example, Scottish Culture Minister Fiona Hyslop proclaimed that 'St Peter's is a building of world significance which continues to inspire,' and Rolf Roscher added that 'St Peter's seminary and its associated landscape may reasonably be regarded as Scotland's most significant lost cultural landmark.'[209] The local *Helensburgh Advertiser* reported that 'St Peter's/Kilmahew' had been identified as one of the world's top 15 'breathtaking building projects' of 2015 by CNN News – alongside iconic architectural projects in New York, Abu Dhabi, Shanghai and Mexico City.[210]

The gulf between this narrative and the regional or even local architectural status of the Cardross extension buildings when newly completed, half a century previously, is so extreme that it might be more accurate to talk of today's complex as an essentially new artistic project, constructed around a postwar architectural skeleton – a project with very different aims from those of the original church clients and architectural designers, balancing a globalised language of 'iconic status' with a very practical focus on local community engagement and regeneration. Ever aware of local impact, the head of HLF Scotland, Lucy Casot, concluded 'Its transformed estate will become a natural haven for the local community to explore and enjoy, and be proud of.'[211] And the *Helensburgh Advertiser* reported a 'Hinterland effect' which had Helensburgh town centre 'buzzing', and boosted trade by 15%. The visitors were 'blown away by its skeletal beauty', the newspaper reported.[212]

With funding secure, the next phase of the works is programmed to begin in spring 2017. John Allan predicted, 'Now we can embark on the task of making St Peter's a permanent inspirational venue for creativity, learning and debate. It will surely be *the* outstanding heritage rescue project of our time.'[213] Many an ambitious and grand statement has been made during the long (nearly 70 years) history of St Peter's Seminary and its ruin at Cardross. Farquhar recently said that 'there is no other architectural story quite like it in the history of the twentieth century'.[214] Perhaps, with its transformation into a permanent art installation, a secure long-term future is at last in prospect for St Peter's. Whether that stability will enhance or undermine its status as a cult-object of tragic drama remains to be seen.

Conclusion

This book provides a detailed historical account and analysis of the St Peter's College extension project: a story spanning over 60 years which divides neatly into two – the story of its design and use, and the story of its decline and salvage. The book concludes with a brief evaluation of these two narratives. Evaluating the contemporary 'success' or 'failure' of the original commission is a multi-faceted, but relatively straightforward task. Evaluating its status as a ruin, or as a derelict heritage artifact of the past, and its transformation from a 'real object' into a discourse, is less easy. An evaluation of the results of its current conversion into a permanent art installation is, of course, outwith the scope of this publication.

Was Cardross a success or a failure, as a work of Catholic patronage and of Modern architecture? The answers are complicated and, some might argue, ultimately inconclusive. St Peter's position in the context of postwar Scottish Catholicism seems very clear, seen from today's point of view. It was an anachronism – a built embodiment of ideals which, even as construction proceeded, were turned upside down by Vatican II. And its viability was then further undermined by the mounting economic and social difficulties of the Church in the following years. But that is very much the judgement of hindsight. If these changes, largely unforeseen at the time, had not taken place; if the 1960s had seen continuing Church expansion in Scotland, as in some other countries (such as Poland), then the large and ambitious seminary would have been far more economically viable, and the design and maintenance problems of its new extension could have been more easily corrected.

To evaluate the architectural success or failure of the seminary extension's design is a more difficult matter. Traditionally, the success of a work of architecture has been judged by whether it adequately combines the three criteria first devised by Vitruvius: beauty, practical usefulness and constructional stability. The Cardross design was widely praised for its imaginative beauty, in both the straightforwardly visual sense and also in the sense of providing a sophisticated social-architectural image of community. But at the same time there were the prolonged troubles of maintenance and use – some of them made worse by factors such as the underoccupation of the building and the failure to heat it properly.

This apparent polarisation of image and use at Cardross stemmed, ultimately, from the fact that twentieth century Modern architecture had reshaped the traditional Vitruvian concepts of architecture in a way which prevented any kind of easy judgement of practical success. The nineteenth century's architectural styles had balanced visual and practical criteria, within formulae which were based on well established historical precedents: there was relatively limited scope for variation. But Modern architecture broke away from these codes and towards more fluid recipes, which tended much more to extremes. There was Functionalism, with its concentration on method or social provision, at times to the exclusion of appearance. And there was a new, intensely artistic kind of architecture, driven by individualistic intuition. In Metzstein's words, 'Modern architecture is very eclectic: there is nothing that is not allowed in Modern architecture – as long as the *spirit* is Modern'.[1]

On the whole, Scottish mid twentieth century architecture was a fairly restrained, consensual matter, and Scottish Modern design emphasised social and contextual work, rather than individualism. The designers of Gillespie, Kidd & Coia belonged to a minority who tried to pursue the Modern Movement's ideals chiefly within a framework of aesthetic creativity. For example, in the 1970s, Metzstein declared that '"high" architecture … is art, social art, that enhances life', and denounced 'the sterile limitation of man's spirit … manifest in Ministry design guides and system building'. In 1996, he stressed that, in the firm's 1960s work, 'we did not have a formula – just a feeling'.[2] But, by the 1990s, these arguments over the definition of Modern architecture became less relevant, following Postmodernists' complete rejection of one side of the Modern equation (the collective or anonymous conception of Functionalism). The individualistic ideal of the architect as a personality now became prominent. A new generation of Scots architects placed much more emphasis on the artist–architect, and on the creation of 'form' in its own right, and by the mid-to-late 1990s, a new, image-led 'Iconic Modernism' started to dominate contemporary architecture. Thus, from the perspective of the present day's image-led architecture, the ideals embodied in the Cardross design arguably seem very comprehensible: the question of 'failure' need not arise.

What values, then, has the St Peter's complex accrued during its life as a heritage artefact? Since 1992, when the ruined seminary extensions were raised to Category A (a rare, but not unparalleled decision by Historic Scotland), it has had a fixed status as an architectural and historical monument. Since the late 1980s, the buildings of the 1950s and 1960s have no longer been seen as a contemporary matter, but instead as something of the past. But by comparison with previous advances of the frontiers of heritage, there have been difficulties in assimilating Modern architecture, because of the specialised, precisely tailored building solutions that it sometimes created. It could be argued that Gillespie, Kidd & Coia's tailormade approach to design might have exacerbated the rapidity of obsolescence of the Cardross complex, and that an 'open-ended', megastructure-type design might have fared better: Metzstein noted that 'a megastructure could be converted: the difficulty with Cardross is that it is, and has proven to be, difficult to convert'.[3]

Crucially, as a modern monument of dereliction, the truncated Cardross complex was able to take on a new value separate from its original purpose and meaning. The central heritage principle of re-use enabled the St Peter's preservation campaigners to focus solely on what it might now become, and to disregard judgement on its past performance as a former teaching college: some conservationists took this to an extreme, blaming the state of the ruins on the culpable neglect of a work of art, while omitting to mention the earlier difficulties of the project.[4] As a ruin it was also largely exempt from the criticism of ongoing problems of technical performance targeted at in-use Modernist heritage: considerations of its original functional failures could here, again, be deemed irrelevant. As such, the complex could then qualify, for example, for inclusion in a list of the world's '100 most endangered sites', issued in June 2007 by the World Monument Fund.

Ironically, in the pursuit to save St Peter's, preservationists adopted similar language to that of the anti-modern campaigns to save Victorian architectural buildings in the face of postwar reconstruction in the 1960s and 1970s. In a campaign fuelled, on the one hand, by fears of threat and loss and, on the other, by a late-Romantic love of ruins and decay, a powerful 'myth' emerged. This new story (proselytised by professionals, enthusiasts and the press from the mid 1990s onwards) was that of a 1960s building of unique beauty and international significance, designed by heroic but unappreciated architects (with the design now attributed solely to Metzstein and MacMillan), misused and abandoned by a philistine Catholic client, and left at the mercy of an uncaring society.

While this myth spurred mounting calls from preservationists to 'save' St Peter's for the nation, alongside it a broader, architect-led re-evaluation of Gillespie, Kidd & Coia's late works also began to coalesce, acclaiming their designs as a potential inspiration for the new 'iconic' architecture of the 1990s onwards. Among younger Scottish architects the reputation of Gillespie, Kidd & Coia has continued to soar. Taken as a whole, the general 'cult' of Gillespie, Kidd & Coia shifted and expanded professional and public perceptions of the ruined buildings, from a subject of chiefly regional (Clydeside) and Scottish architectural interest when new in the 1960s, to the object of international attention as an 'iconic' ruin of the new millennium. In the course of this repackaging of the truncated remains of the seminary as both a set-piece of modern architectural heritage and a harbinger of contemporary iconic design, the historical significance of Cardross as an expression of the general confidence of postwar Catholicism in the West of Scotland and of the attempt to reflect that confidence through a social-architectural image of community, has increasingly disappeared from view.

Overall, then, we can straightforwardly conclude that the Cardross Seminary complex originally began its life as a bold but controversial set-piece of twentieth century Modern architecture and Catholicism in Scotland, but that, whatever the building's vicissitudes in the past or future, it now has gained the additional, immutable status of an architectural and historical monument. Perhaps, with its transformation into a permanent art installation, a secure long-term future is at last in prospect for St Peter's. Whether that stability will enhance or undermine its status as a cult-object of mythical tragic drama remains to be seen.

Main block following NVA's clearing and cleaning work, May 2016
HES DP237823

The Sanctuary
Architect's digital render of the proposed renovation, 2016
McGinlay Bell

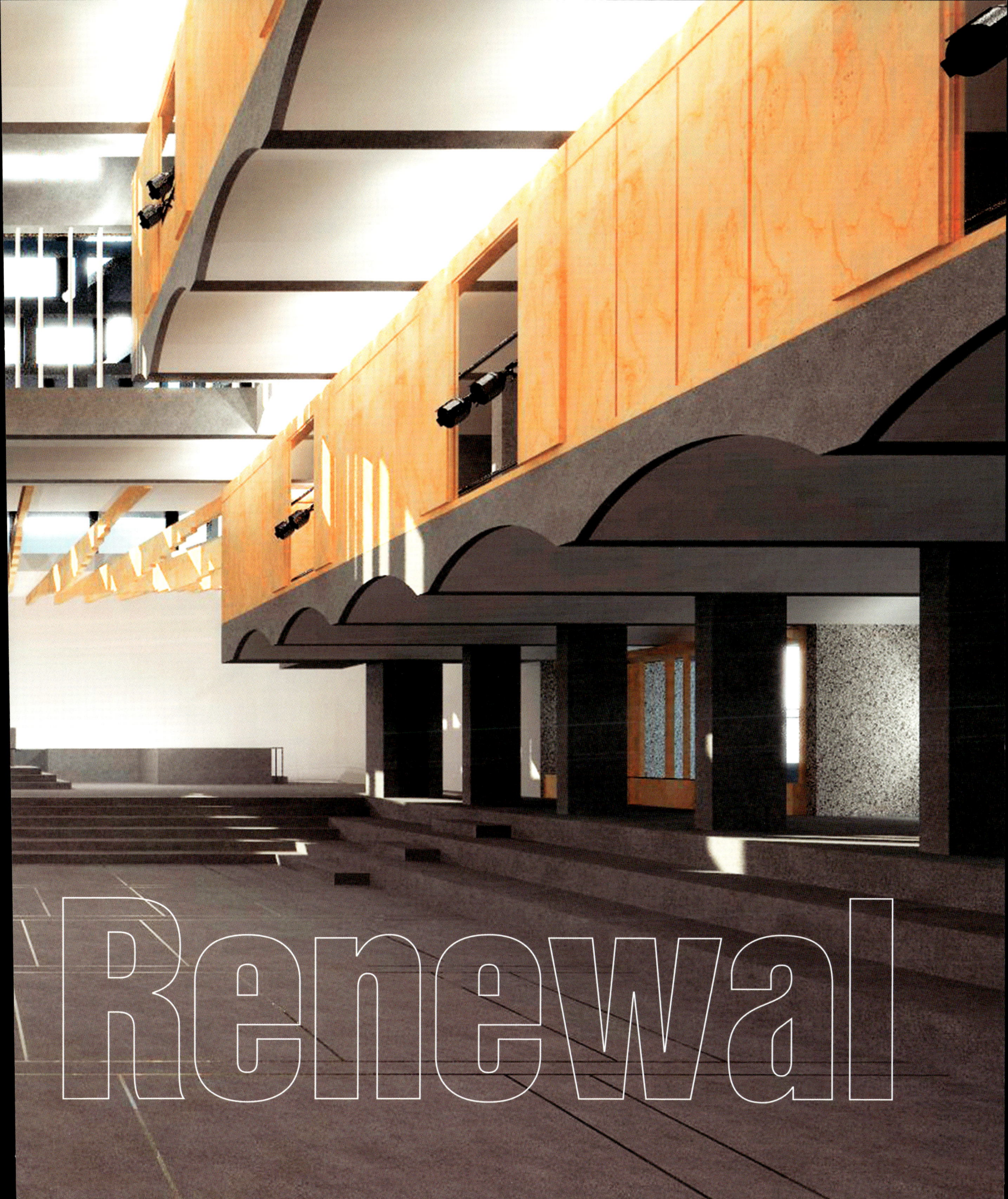
Renewal

The Future of St Peter's

By Angus Farquhar, NVA 2016

Why on earth would anyone spend eight years trying to rescue this wreck of a building?

In the mid 1980s I was in an industrial band called Test Dept. We were five scrawny lads living in London – all of us drummers – who liked playing tight rhythms on all manner of found objects. We used lead piping, hammer handles and sledge hammers fashioned into drumsticks which we rained down on a variety of metal foraged from the countless scrapyards that pockmarked the Thames. Every few weeks an old rag and bone man with a horse and cart came by the basement we rehearsed in to drop off large petrol tanks. We had no electricity and played by candlelight, the soundwaves always sending plaster showering down from the ceiling. It was a near Dickensian scene of doom and squalor.

Looking for instruments and places to play, we explored the wastegrounds that littered London's hinterland – former power stations, abandoned factories.

You could wander for days through remnant sites full of the fractured memories and the lost purpose of heavy industry. But for us they were places of creativity. Being the posh boy in the group I was shunted off in my grandfather's 1930s pinstripe suit to charm and cajole property developers and middle managers into allowing us to stage epic concerts in abandoned arches, old factories and empty railway stations. And we were not alone. In the dust and shadows whole tribes of musicians, film makers and artists conjured new realities out of crumbling concrete and twisted steel.

After Test Dept, I set up NVA, an independent arts company (the letters stand for nacionale vita-activa, meaning 'the right to influence public affairs'). The fascination with making art in special locations, rather than theatres, galleries and concert halls, never left me. At NVA, we created the walk-through performance 'The Storr', on the Isle of Skye, inviting some 6,500 people to interact with the presence of the landscape over the course of 42 nights. Following the illegal invasion of Iraq, we founded the Hidden Gardens, a sanctuary garden built out of wasteland at the back of the Tramway arts centre in Glasgow. And we took The Speed of Light, a physical celebration of collective running, from Edinburgh and Salford to Yokohama and the rehabilitated industrial landscapes of the Ruhr.

After two decades, however, I was looking for a new direction, for a plan that moved NVA away from large scale but transitory live performance, and focused again on permanence. And then one snowy January morning eight years ago, it popped into my head: St Peter's.

I knew that there was an abandoned building, somewhere outside Glasgow, where young priests had been trained in the 1960s. Braving the winter cold, I set off with a hardy group of colleagues to visit it. Parking in a rutted layby just beyond the small village of Cardross on the Firth of Clyde, we walked into the densest forest of rhododendron you can imagine. We soon lost all sense of direction. We found an old castle keep and the remnants of a walled garden, but no sign of the legendary ruin.

Undefeated, a week later I tried again with my NVA co-director Ellen. This time we spotted a huge harled wall rising up through mist. Slipping through a broken fence we entered one of the most imposing structures I have ever witnessed. Huge half burnt beams hung precariously overhead, wooden sections of roof covering peeled away into space, dark underground crypts were mounded with detritus. Hundreds of floating plaster vaults, curved like repeating waves, had been smashed, leaving plaster and mesh hanging down in strands. Every surface was covered in graffiti, varying from highly original artworks to standard tagging and disturbing references to infamous mass killers and torturers. Crunching underfoot was 25 years of accumulated dirt, glass and shards of unidentifiable metal, as well as thousands of windblown asbestos fragments. The place brought to mind the moments after a bombing. When leaving I turned to Ellen and asked her if we should take it on. A nod of the head and that was that. The course of our lives changed from that moment.

This development represents a new form of cultural regeneration. People like us do not get to own places like this. Yet, as has been detailed rigorously in Diane Watters' history, a number of conventional schemes to adapt St Peter's have come and gone over the last twenty years. These have varied from the banal (brick built estate in the walled garden) to the grandiose (seminary converted to luxury apartments surrounding a new block of flats rising from the foundations of the demolished baronial house). Each was inappropriate as a response to the complex topography and unique history of Kilmahew and paid scant regard to the architectural value of the former college. In the early days we were treated as poor cousins in the matrix of profit driven proposals, with developers seeking informal partnerships with us (and our charitable aims …) as a way of making planning gain. It was a matter of biding our time and keeping our hand in the game.

We continued to quietly build support from local to governmental level for a public solution. With the combined impact of the recession and the accelerating deterioration of the building we eventually became seen as the last chance for its survival. Our radical yet practical premise was that St Peter's had currency in its broken state. There was value in the ruination and we would seek to incorporate rather than eradicate the effects of time on the structure. The gradual deterioration had been partly caused by the West of Scotland weather and rapid plant colonisation; but it was also accelerated by successive waves of hardcore vandalism and intentional arson. The balance between our plans for the seminary as a shared crucible for creativity versus its attraction as a graveyard for wanton destruction was not easily calibrated.

From 2009 onwards the core vision for the future of St Peter's was established through discussions between Rolf Roscher of the landscape architecture studio ERZ, the eminent art historian and editor Gerrie van Noord and myself. Key ideas and themes emerged including seeing the building as an integrated artwork and a form of experience; positioning the site as a subject for creativity and learning; embracing conflict and maintaining a sense of the unknown; promoting the public as active protagonists in the scheme and valuing each incremental intervention in itself, not as a step to a 'complete' solution. St Peter's was also positioned within its wider setting as a 'productive landscape'.

This inherently experimental and at times antagonistic approach, aiming to maintain a palpable sense of 'otherness', was not an easy sell with multiple funders. We were attempting to raise £8 million pounds during a recession. There was initially a degree of skepticism shown by our main institutional partners. Many grand schemes to save this highly challenging building had come and gone and it remained a seemingly unresolvable national problem. If it had not been for some enlightened private patronage at the start, it is unlikely that we would have been able to progress.

Trust gradually came as we worked through every issue raised, taking on sage advisors and responding stoically to constructive criticism. We established a strong and stable creative team with John Allan and Fiona Lamb of Avanti Architects, Brian McGinlay from NORD (now McGinlay Bell Architects) and Rolf Roscher who also led the masterplanning. There was a sense of guarded optimism that the site had a future once more.

In 2010 NVA was commissioned by the Public Art Fund of the National Lottery, through the Scottish Arts Council, to develop our discussions into an aesthetic strategy for St Peter's – 'an extraordinary place that demands an extraordinary response'. Our plan stated that the underlying premise is to explore if public spaces can advance social change. Can the experience of a landscape be so profound, other or different that it changes people's lives and inspires them to change society?

The aim was to build on multiple imaginative manifestations rather than attempting to return it to the functions of the past. There was no intention to resuscitate the ruined seminary purely through a 'degenerative' or a 're-generative' process in which it would draw its meaning from either an evolving process of decay or a commitment to renewal leading back to its pristine 1966 condition. Our aspiration was, and remains, to pursue a 'generative' third approach which reaches beyond traditional conservation solutions. This sees the evolving landscape and its structures as an inspiration for practical artistic production and learning, involving the public in that evolution. With the diverse support we had gathered, by 2014 we were ready to take the first steps that would make our plans for St Peter's come to life.

NVA is the latest in a long line of groups and individuals to be drawn by the siren call of St Peter's. Kilmahew's wider landscape has been changed repeatedly by human activity ranging from an early Christian monastic retreat, the building of a late medieval castle keep, to the establishment of a nineteenth century baronial mansion house set in a fully crafted Victorian designed landscape. This estate included semi-ancient woodland, roads, bridges, paths, lodges, stables and a large kitchen garden with glasshouses. Now it exists only as a fragmentary and partially erased storehouse of past lives – and the pyramidal social structure it once sustained.

Our work is yet another layer in its multi-faceted story. Although the plan we are undertaking follows in a tradition of engaged arts practice, there is a difference in where this will be taking place. The seminary complex and historical grounds of Kilmahew offer a rich palimpsest through which to recover past meanings while reaching for new language to describe current conditions. In Cardross the juxtaposition of a radical twentieth century building within a bucolic Victorian landscape provides a sense of uncertainty that demands an interaction. The perceptible culture clash is exciting and thought provoking. The dilapidated Modernist structure has now been stripped back so far that only the essence of the original building survives, yet it is still full of personality.

Our cultural programme has the potential to be presented in any location on the estate, indoor or out. However, the primary spaces will include the partial restoration of the chapel into an enclosed, heated and technically equipped event and performance space. There will also be a largely un-structured internal/external exhibition area in the consolidated refectory, and an exhibition, teaching space and reading room in the former sacristy and crypt. Other selected areas will be left safe and usable though unrestored – to further illustrate and embrace the building's history of neglect and informal use while offering artists less mediated spaces to respond to.

We will gradually rehabilitate the wider estate to reveal the complex changes it has experienced – while avoiding over-interpretation. At the heart of this approach is The Invisible College – a research network led by Hayden Lorimer and Ed Hollis that connects academics, educationalists, contemporary artists, architects, local people and wider communities of interest. It uses the woodlands and the partially ruined form of St Peter's as a centre for informal learning and a locus for debate and new thinking.

A significant proportion of the capital investment focuses on venue infrastructure and on making the site safe, secure and practically useable. The next initiative by The Invisible College will include the introduction of experimental viewing structures to enable people to quantify risk and understand the process of the site's transition from total ruination. This makes the most of St Peter's return to being a building site, opening the doors at moments when hoardings would normally exclude access. We believe that the site preparation and build have relevance and provide public interest at all stages of its evolution, rather than at an imagined perfect end point. This is not just about artists interrogating large abstract ideas, but leads on to offering useful ways to get involved on a daily level, from walking, running, observing, archiving, making, growing and cooking, through to thinking and discussing.

At NVA, we primarily commission art that has a social function. We question whether art can be useful in pointing the way to alternative ways of thinking and doing. We believe that the time is right to be asking this as we examine our role as a small, progressively minded country in a complex world. To ask what the nature of community identity is in twenty-first century Scotland. We aim to honour the historical, social and political values embedded in these buildings and their setting while unlocking the potential for the complex to expand into the present.

Throughout the liminal period of the seminary's decline, the lively and illegal use of the buildings has demonstrated the strange hold ruins have over the human psyche, whether through our response to ancient castles or the destroyed car factories of Detroit. While the site became increasingly dangerous due to the build-up of high levels of asbestos and toxic waste, it still offered an unmediated outlet for the often darker sides of the creative mind. The buildings have been practically documented in hundreds of graffiti images, films, videos and artworks. Its informal adoption by an entire generation of artists, architects, musicians and urban explorers is testament to unfettered inventiveness and the need for autonomous creative spaces in which to play and expand consciousness. It is in this spirit that the new design seeks to maintain the rawness that has been forced onto the building. We will not attempt to hide the dilapidation and will actively allow bold new spatial geometries created by recent collapse to stand without additional adornment or restoration. Ironically the free nature of the design, its relationship to archisculpture or Corbusier's positioning of architecture as a 'walkthrough' experience, has increased as more of the original building has disappeared. Such tensions and contradictions between past intent, present loss and future direction are part of its inherent qualities.

The photographs that follow, chosen by NVA lead designer James Johnson and myself, capture the spirit of Kilmahew/St Peter's over the last decade. Even within this short period of time you can witness powerful shifts, as the full force of a series of tough Scottish winters hit the building, alongside significant fires and vandalism. The transition to a cleaned and partially consolidated structure, the removal of rhododendron and the production of Hinterland, signify the first bold steps in its next stage of evolution. For all the material flaws I love the ambition and dynamism of the original design. Reality may not have borne out the hopefulness with which it was conceived; but one of the continued challenges of art is to point the way towards as yet uncharted possibilities.

Landscape

Kilmahew woods have been around for a long time. They are formed by two steep sided gorges that knit together to become the Auchinfroe burn, which runs down to Cardross village and the Firth of Clyde. The sharp sides of Wallacetown glen and Kilmahew saw this area passed over for timber extraction when many other woodlands in the area were decimated over the last millennia. There are plenty of self-seeding oaks remaining that speak of the days before extensive management and cosmetic planting.

The main path along the western banks of Kilmahew burn dates back to medieval times. A minor droving route linked Carman hill with the old Stoneymollan 'coffin road' to Balloch and Loch Lomond. But most of what we see was established in the mid nineteenth century. Due to the dramatic topography, the first estate was laid out around the baronial mansion in a relatively discreet fashion, adding signature trees here and there, some of which now have girths in excess of 4 metres. Laurel and Ponticum were added as wind breaks and border decoration and lines of graceful European limes delineated old farming enclosures and the route from Kilmahew estate to the nearby Kilmahew Castle.

The walled gardens with grand heated glasshouses and orchards were active for just over a century, being managed by only four gardeners over that period. All manner of exotic and Mediterranean fruits were grown in Victorian times and later the needs of 60 seminarians were met through careful stewardship.

Today, all the efforts of the last two centuries have faded and we are left with a broken but surviving landscape. When we first arrived the rhododendron was so thick on the ground that it was impossible to read or understand the original layout of the estate. Much of the historic local plant material had been eradicated through acidification of the soil and a losing battle for light in the undercroft. It was clear from the state of many trees that unless we intervened on a drastic level the integrity of the woodland would be irreversibly damaged over the next 25 years.

Bold moves come at a price, even when driven ecologically for the right reasons. In clearing thousands of rhododendron bushes the woods were allowed to breathe again for the first time in 50 years, but I mourned the mystery of enclosure, not knowing what was round any corner, struggling to figure out where you were. Over the years we will re-introduce barriers and foils again and play with that sense of restriction and openness.

Almost nothing that is left 'works'. You could describe it as a landscape of absence, full of fading reminders of former glories and centuries of domestic life. Gates and fencing have been pulled back into the earth and incorporated into the bodies of trees, bottle dumps spill down sharp inclines. By comparison when I visited the grounds of Culzean Castle on the Ayshire coast, with its perfectly preserved Orangery and Gazebos, I found it bland and somehow trapped by the past – as if you knew what to expect at every stage. Culzean is a living museum expressing how the super-rich created perfect fantasy worlds to entertain themselves. The loss and fracture seen at Kilmahew, on the other hand, is honest. It only faintly echoes the days of private ownership and the model that has dominated so much of Scotland's rural life. The landscape is now porous where once it was gated. Having to enter it through cracks makes it no less compelling – perhaps even more.

Walled gardens

Neil Davidson

Footbridge in Kilmahew grounds
Alaisdair Smith

Renewal

Kilmahew burn
One of two small rivers on the estate feeding Kilmahew Lake
Neil Davidson

The Ruin

It took time to figure out what I was looking at when first wandering round the main seminary block. The level of destruction was so complete in places that it was impossible to read how interiors were framed, levels connected or screening demarcated different spaces. In the teaching block and crypt the piles of detritus were overwhelming, so that entry was not possible on some floors. I couldn't think of it as a working building. It was disconnected from the grainy images of young students in black cassocks scurrying to mass, cleaning floors or relaxing in glass-sided rooms.

Gradually I put a timeline in place starting with two young architects, who, like many before them, were unafraid to quote from buildings they liked and other architects that they admired. Who introduced subtle historical and geographical references into the designs in a way that was true to themselves and their passions. One of Andy MacMillan's family members recalled visiting as a small child and being given a bottle of ginger by kind nuns at the back of the mansion house. Playing in the woods, she remembers the image of her dad standing on the driveway in the distance, his arms waving up and down as he remonstrated with the site foreman. It must have been a battle to ensure that the more experimental edges in the plans weren't rubbed out through a protracted and difficult construction period.

When I first visited, half of the floating glulam beams that radiate out from the curvilinear wall behind the main altar were still intact. On a good day with the sun high in the sky, sharp geometric shadows and shapes were cast onto the floor and walls of the sanctuary and chapel. It came to life as a vast Constructivist sculpture or Suprematist installation. Suddenly the artistry of the original plans came to the fore and a charge of discovery ran through me. Witnessing the main spaces transformed by light and shadow confirmed reports from former priests and students whose celebration of Mass was sometimes enhanced profoundly by the setting. Early on our creative team decided that the restoration of the laminated timber beams, roof and original ziggurat roof light would be a priority.

I began to build a picture of how the components of the design functioned together. Kilmahew House was the destroyed nineteenth century centrepiece and nodal point around which the new buildings were composed and choreographed. The stone structures and the retaining walls allowed the site to sit up like a raised garden above and within the mature woodland estate. The main block was formed by a series of stepped floors elevated on fine piers. Cantilevered above the refectory and the chapel, the simple study bedrooms punctuated the outer walls en masse like a honeycomb, generating the large internal voids of

The teaching block
Angus Farquhar

the refectory and sanctuary. Floating staircases, cast in-situ out of concrete, linked the progression of floors together. Isi Metzstein described his design as being 'against dogma', creating a dizzying array of non-standard spaces.

Against the dominant central plan axis of the chapel and refectory there were a series of informal spatial sequences. Ten side chapels clasped the outside of the chapel like the fingers of Christ, also referencing agri-industrial and military silos. The huge curved flanks of the load-bearing apse wall gave shape to a rising ramp that dramatically linked the sacristy to the sanctuary floor. The external wall was rough harled in the style of an old baronial castle with little light penetration except through small irregular windows that punch through to the crypt. The careful control of daylight echoed Mackintosh. Fragments of red, green and orange window glass represented the only use of colour throughout.

Undressed, fair faced timber board marked concrete walls; glass and wooden framing were used in combination to create different rhythms throughout, dominated internally by the wave-like repetition of multiple barrel roofed vaults. To some seminarians this reflected a neo-medieval austerity; to others the severity of a war-time bunker. The buildings were organised around the movement and procession of the student priest throughout the day with open cloisters continuing the traditions of monastic retreat. A shallow moat recalled historic defences refracted through Japanese minimalism. Diverted spring water ran between levels down a monumental iron chain that would not have looked out of place in the Clyde shipyards.

The destroyed sanctuary roof light and the main block (when seen in section) echo the ziggurats of ancient Mesopotamia, referenced as one of the earliest 'social' architectures. The teaching block was by contrast a leap into the future; a spaceship flight deck, drawing on the bold cantilevers of Lloyd Wright to arc over the foundation walls of the demolished Victorian house, allowing panoramic views down to the canopy, gorge and river below.

All pieces of a complex puzzle, but for me it was by visiting the Couvent Sainte-Marie de La Tourette that the overall design finally fell into place. Le Corbusier's Dominican Priory, completed seven years before St Peter's College, rises at the head of a valley set in open countryside near Lyon. Key elements from the brutalist canon were transposed to re-appear at St Peter's. As through a kaleidoscope, forms were fractured and reconfigured in key parts of the Scottish building. There was no pastiche, rather a direct homage to the ideological father of Modernism and one of his greatest designs.

All of these elements cohered into the design of St Peter's and as a result it was free of restraint. Even if now it exists as a post-functional sculpture, it has life and energy and a story to tell.

The sanctuary and broken altar
NORD Architecture

Teaching block and staircase
NORD Architecture

Main block and central staircase
NORD Architecture

Teaching block staircase
NORD Architecture

The main block looking towards teaching block
McAteer Photograph

The sanctuary block spiral stair
NORD Architecture

Main block
McAteer Photograph

The Altar

The deconstructivist architect Bernard Tschumi stated that there is 'no space without event'. If architecture is the dramatic frame for activities then St Peter's is a powerful expression of ritualised physical form. At the heart of the ruined seminary is a brutally smashed altar, jackhammered into huge chunks at the behest of the Archbishop of Glasgow in 2015 to ensure no profane acts continued to take place on the last consecrated element within the seminary (the rest of the building being deconsecrated after its closure). According to the code of Canon Law, deconsecration of a church does not include the altar which remains associated with sacredness. An altar, whether fixed or movable, must be reserved for divine worship alone, to the absolute exclusion of any secular use. An immovable altar loses consecration if the top or table, even for a moment of time, is separated from the base. James Johnson, NVA's lead designer, happened to be there at the time of the altar's destruction, and managed to save the smaller tabernacle altar. In St Peter's we see both the idealised framing of religious life and the reality of how that has played out.

The tension between the traditions of the oldest religious organisation in the western world seen in such a contemporary setting is not without irony. In 1910 Pope Pius X introduced the 'Oath Against Modernism' which he defined as heresy. It was last sworn voluntarily by seminarians and priests at St Peter's in 1968. Before its withdrawal from general use following the Second Vatican Council they would intone:

I firmly hold, then, and shall hold to my dying breath the belief of the Fathers in the charism of truth, which certainly is, was, and always will be in the succession of the episcopacy from the apostles. The purpose of this is, then, not that dogma may be tailored according to what seems better and more suited to the culture of each age; rather, that the absolute and immutable truth preached by the apostles from the beginning may never be believed to be different, may never be understood in any other way.

The altar and sanctuary
James Perry

next spread
The smashed altar
James Johnson

The Clean Up

Following detailed surveys we found that every surface of the seminary complex was coated with fine asbestos dust. After 30 years of fabric disintegration, hazardous materials had been wind-blown around the interior and exterior of the buildings. Something had to be done. We worked in close partnership with Reigart contractors to tackle the immediate problems. After months of painstaking clearance, severe winter conditions led to a number of vaults collapsing down into the refectory and chapel, showing just how fragile the superstructure had become. In response, Reigart used Permaseal – a spray foam for roof insulation – as an innovative solution, creating a new bonding layer over the surviving vaults which allowed 80 to be saved from destruction.

I was worried whether the site clearance would 'ruin the ruin'. What if the powerfully desolate character which had attracted so many people to visit and make work there over the last two decades was erased? What if, in becoming safe, it would also become bland? But week by week the original lines of the building were re-revealed, showing the experimental and sculptural qualities of the design to startling effect. As it was cleared of debris a new clarity and lightness pervaded the different spaces.

In particular the loss of a number of vaults opened up a clean void from chapel floor to roof encompassing three tiers of the inwardly stepped study-bedrooms. All that is left is the original reinforced concrete frame within which they sat. The vertical splitting amplifies the American artist–architect Gordon Matta-Clark's provocation that there can be 'completion through removal'. That in the release from function and through violent disintegration, a new use has appeared spontaneously. Rather than restore the full chapel, we will use this open structure, which by random collapses has created a startling new light channel, casting fresh shadow lines and shapes to the sunken floor below.

Main block stairway
NORD Architecture

next spread
The 'cells' and side chapel
HES DP238662

Main block stairs
HES DP237841

Windows to the crypt
HES DP237856

Chain by the main entrance pool
Colin McLean

Main block, first floor
HES DP238665

The cloisters
HES DP237825

Graffiti

The architect and designer Buckminster Fuller stated that, 'all human progress is made in the outlaw area' – and St Peter's has long been a mecca for graffiti artists. Less mediated places where formal uses have receded and there is no sense of ownership release the imagination. There are no arbiters of taste here, except where a new generation directly critique the work of well-known graffiti artists who are thought to have sold out by taking commercial commissions. Alongside highly original interventions, the walls have also attracted shadowy haters and baiters, referencing acts of violence and sexual transgression through crude commentary left in the darkened recesses.

What the years of image-making and tagging have done is to pierce the grandiosity of the design. The idea of this building as a 'machine for living in' has failed and the graffiti is its epitaph. At its best, the International Style which influenced St Peter's promoted the philosophy of a radical architecture with universal application – which rejected the faux-nationalist gestures of Nazism. Yet the aesthetic was also appropriated by dictators from the far right and left, as the state-aggrandising style of choice. Such a paradox is useful in undercutting my utopian tendencies when talking about what remains.

If I am drawn to anyone as a precursor to NVA's choices, it is to the Brazilian architect Lina Bo Bardi and her description of a 'Humble Architecture'. Our ownership is born out of the failure of the building and standard forms of regeneration. In three centuries a landscape has gone from being privatised, to institutional, to abandoned, to public once again. We are recycling on a vast scale with many original features kept visible and so retaining their personality. This does not imply that every new intervention will be delicate. The building was designed as an attack on the senses and if we lose this visceral quality we will also have failed in our task.

By the altar on the south wall of the sanctuary
Gill Pendleton

Trainee priests' rooms, main block
McAteer Photograph, left, and Elaine Graham, right

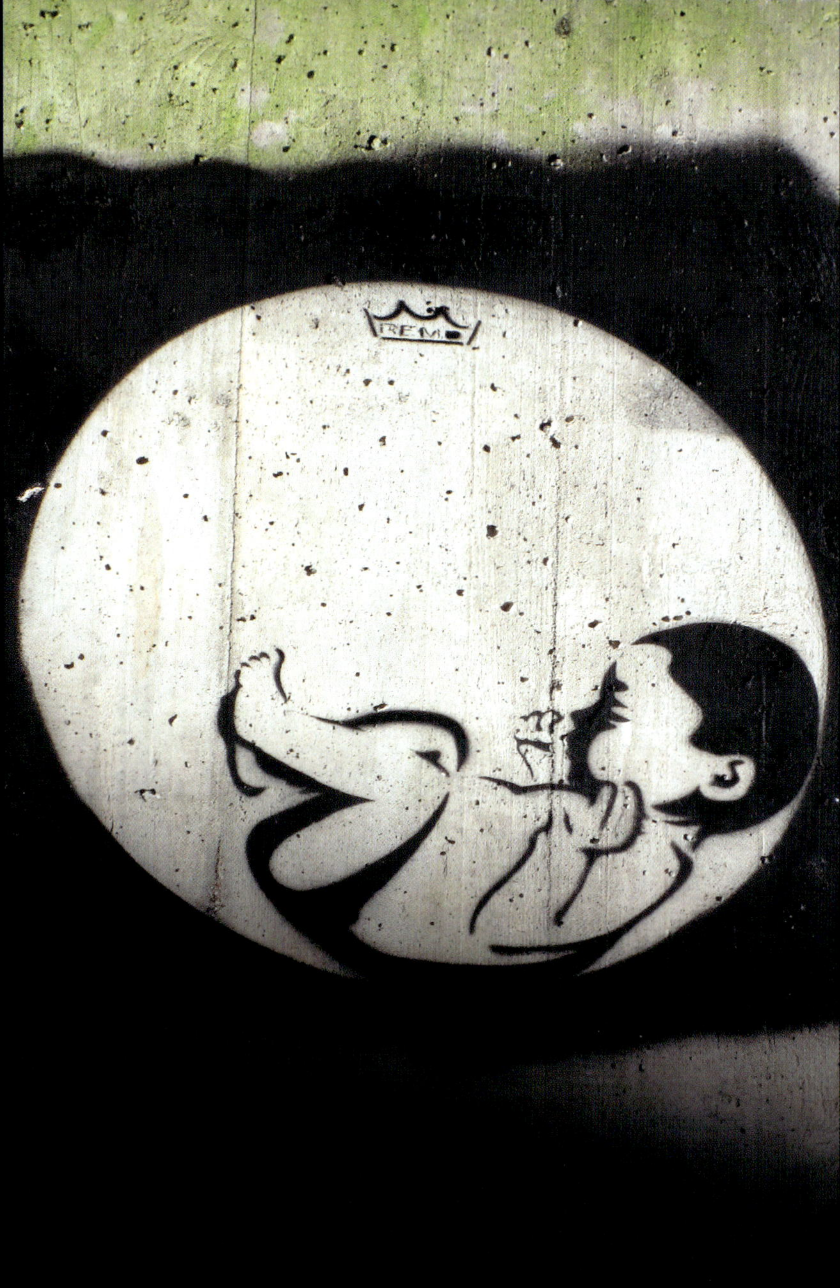

In the kitchen block
Tom Paterson

Retaining wall, near main block stair tower
James Johnson

Hinterland

Our Hinterland production launched the Festival of Architecture in March 2016. This was the long awaited moment to change the state of St Peter's, to re-introduce it publicly as a creative catalyst: to play the building as an instrument. Following the site clearance it no longer conformed to the romantic view of a standard ruin. We had intervened and it was ready to begin a different life. If we imagine the new building as a state of mind, then Hinterland was its first real statement of intent. I wanted to mark this threshold by using the dated form of a manifesto, to establish that we were dealing with more than bricks and mortar, to question again whether the ideas that led to the building's formation had currency.

The postwar years that gave birth to St Peter's, that saw the establishment of the United Nations and the European Union, free education and healthcare along with public funding for the arts, represent a pinnacle in democratic achievement. The idea was that rather than just accepting the world as it was, you could jointly build a better one. As we appear to teeter on the precipice of a new dark age, such dreams now seem fragile and distant. But they remain utterly vital.

St Peter's had originally been conceived to promote critical study on the nature of the divine. Patterns of movement around the building were paramount in confirming a sense of ritual within daily life.

Hinterland adapted the narrative of a walk to open up the material layers of the building and how you experience them. From the gorge floor and woods you entered through a sally port (a thin slit in the side of the external apse wall). From the sacristy you turned into the stepped crypt replete with floating altars that were surplus to requirements from the day they were built. By travelling through it you instinctively began to uncover the architectural narrative.

A curved ramp took you upwards onto the sanctuary floor, with the tabernacle intact beside the smashed main altar. A reversal through the sanctuary linked to the open cloister and spiral steps to the upper ground floor of the teaching block, now a belvedere with views back out through the woods to the night sky above. The shift in elevation from 'below to above' was literally and metaphorically borne out by the design.

The building had been liberated from its former passage into an informal and secular pilgrimage. An early thought was to re-saturate the walls with sound, to echo acoustically its recent past with composer Rory Boyle's haunting setting of ancient and modern choral music. Projections expressed the character of entropy, the slow disease of ceaseless disintegration. In contrast we also elucidated the sharply symmetrical lines of the original plans and paid a centennial homage to the pioneering Russian abstract artist Kazimir Malevich and the birth of Modernism, referencing his famous Black Square as well as the coloured geometric planes of his later works.

The lighting amplified the rhythm of the built structure, articulating repeated wave patterns, modulating the presence of the internal and external spaces and form. The expanding and contracting of depth and height released and emphasised the sheer poetry of the design. St Peter's was freed from the shackles of time.

The teaching block
McAteer Photograph

St Peter's, Cardross

Main block during *Hinterland*
Danny Lawson / PA Images

next spread
Main block
Murdo MacLeod

left
Main block with side chapels and teaching block. Each visitor to *Hinterland* **walked with a glowing light stick.**
Alaisdair Smith

right
Teaching block
McAteer Photograph

Main block with light projection
Alaisdair Smith

The exterior wall and windows of the convent
Alaisdair Smith

Individual candlelit Mass altars
McAteer Photograph

Renewal

Hinterland Manifesto March 2016

The teaching block
NORD Architecture

Freedom of thought and the capacity to empathise with difference is central to life beyond mere survival. It follows that our society is not static but something we can influence and evolve collectively.

We can determine our own political, social and cultural reality. Sharing our values through public art enables us to confirm our humanity, exchange ideas and engage our past, present and potential futures.

While art has the capacity to entertain, it also exists to provoke, contest and search for new realities. Locating creativity within democratic processes defines a progressive political system.

The Agora was established in Ancient Greece as the public engine for constructive human activity, it was both the forum for debate as well as the physical setting where relevant topics were discussed: business, politics, current events, or the nature of the universe and the divine.

Hinterland aims to re-invoke the spirit of The Agora.

Our shared human experience is at breaking point. There is widespread failure in our political and economic systems. Internationally we are unable to find peaceful means to resolve disputes or tackle major environmental issues. Mass displacement through war and social breakdown in many countries has never been more acute and we live with the magnitude of this every day.

In Scotland our recent faltering steps towards resolving disagreements around our future trajectory stand as a testament to the potential for non-violent change. The extension of this debate from the national to global, the ability to accept what you do not necessarily agree with, is of essential value.

End Notes

Chapter 1

1. J F McCaffrey, 'Roman Catholics in Scotland: Nineteenth and Twentieth Centuries', in C Maclean and K Veitch (eds), *Scottish Life and Society: Religion*, 2006, pp 173–4. McCaffrey died in 2002, and his chapter was published posthumously

2. McCaffrey, 'Roman Catholics in Scotland', p 593

3. McCaffrey, 'Roman Catholics in Scotland', p 178

4. McCaffrey, 'Roman Catholics in Scotland', p 170. For the complex relations between native, immigrant and 'convert' Catholics in nineteenth century Scotland see S K Kehoe, *Creating a Scottish Catholic Church: Catholicism, Gender and Ethnicity in Nineteenth-Century Scotland*, 2010. Recent studies have also challenged the established accounts of a poor and insular Scottish urban Catholic community, providing a more nuanced and complex story where Catholics participated in aspects of Scottish society in the twentieth century. See M J Mitchell (ed), *New Perspectives on the Irish in Scotland*, 2008; B Aspinwall, 'Catholic Realities and Pastoral Strategies: Another Look at the Historiography of Scottish Catholicism, 1878–1920', *Innes Review*, 59, spring 2008, pp 77–112. For broader overviews see: I Maver, 'The Catholic Community', in T M Devine and R J Findlay (eds), *Scotland in the Twentieth Century*, 1996, pp 269–84; T M Devine, *The Scottish Nation, 1700–2000*, 1999, pp 486–500; and G Walker, 'The Religious Factor', in T M Devine and J Wormald (eds), *The Oxford Handbook of Modern Scottish History*, 2012, pp 585–601

5. McCaffrey, 'Roman Catholics in Scotland', pp 172–3

6. See J O Hagan and R A David, 'Forging the Compact of Church and State in the Development of Catholic Education in Late Nineteenth-century Scotland', *Innes Review*, 58, spring 2007, pp 72–94; A Bain, 'The Significance of the Bonnybridge School Case of 1922–1929 for Catholic Education in Scotland', *Innes Review*, 62, May 2011, pp 70–81; G Vaughan, 'Papists Looking after the Education of our Protestant Children! Catholics and Protestants on Western Scottish School Boards, 1872–1918', *Innes Review*, 63, May 2012, pp 30–47; and N Carlin, *Holy Cross Academy, Edinburgh: The Life and Times of a Catholic School, 1906–1969*, 2009

7. McCaffrey, 'Roman Catholics in Scotland', pp 179–80

8. T M Devine (ed), *St Mary's Hamilton*, 1995, pp 118–19; also T M Devine (ed), *Irish Immigrants and Scottish Society in the Nineteenth and Twentieth Centuries*, 1990

9. J Cunningham, 'Church Administration and Organisation', in D McRoberts (ed), *Modern Scottish Catholicism*, 1979, pp 73–91

10. J Darragh, 'The Catholic Population of Scotland', in McRoberts, *Modern Scottish Catholicism*, p 223; C Brown, 'Religion and Secularism', in T Dickson and J H Treble (eds), *People and Society in Scotland*, vol. 3, 1992, p 61

11. Output of Catholic and Protestant building 1945–61: 'Style in Church Building', *The Herald*, 6 April 1961. Nineteenth century background: B Aspinwall, 'The Formation of the Catholic Community in the West of Scotland', *Innes Review*, 33, 1982, pp 44–57

12. C G Brown, *Religion and Society in Twentieth-Century Britain*, 2006, pp 2, 26. For the specifics of church building in England and Wales post-1955 see R Proctor, *Building the Modern Church: Architecture in Britain, 1955 to 1975*, 2014, and M P Hornsby-Smith, *Catholics in England, 1950–2000*, 1999

13. G Walker, 'The Religious Factor', in Devine and Wormald, *The Oxford Handbook of Modern Scottish History*, pp 585–601

14. M Glendinning and D M Watters, 'Cumbernauld New Town: Reception & Heritage Legacy', *Architecktura & Urbanizmus, Journal of Architectural and Town-planning Theory*, 46, 2012, p 286

15. R Boyle and P Lynch (eds), *Out of the Ghetto? The Catholic Community in Modern Scotland*, 1998, p 1; Brown, *Religion and Society in Modern Scotland*, p 54–5. Brown illustrates this trend using data from 1984 when 8.6% of the population of Edinburgh were Catholics, but for surrounding Lothians it was 11.6%. He also highlighted that in the West of Scotland in 1984 the density of Catholics was higher in Motherwell and Monklands (35.9%) and Dunbartonshire (33.5%) than in the city of Glasgow

16. Obituary of Right Reverend James Ward, *Catholic Directory of Scotland* (hereafter CDS), 1974, pp 376–80

17. Ward obituary

18. Obituary of Most Reverend James Donald Scanlan, CDS, 1977, pp 370–8

19. On Vatican II in general, see Richard P O'Brien, *Catholicism*, vol 2, 1980

20. K Nugent, 'Churches and Liturgy', in J Macaulay and C Hermansen (eds), *Mac Journal One: Gillespie, Kidd & Coia*, 1994, pp 26–31

21. Letter from Dr John McCaffrey, 1996. Several years later McCaffrey explained that 'Conclusions drawn in the 1970s and 80s as to the affects [of Vatican II] on Scottish Catholics keep changing.' McCaffrey, 'Roman Catholics in Scotland', p 185

22. J Cooney, *Scotland and the Papacy*, 1982, pp 96–7; Interview with Dr John Durkan, 25 August 1995; see also A Ross, 'Development of the Catholic Community', in McRoberts, *Modern Scottish Catholicism*, pp 44, 50–1; T Gallagher, *Glasgow, The Uneasy Peace*, 1987, pp 263, 284; J Cumming and P Burns (eds), *The Church Now*, 1980, p 62; S McGinty, *This Turbulent Priest: The Life of Cardinal Winning*, 2003; V Belton, *Cardinal Thomas Winning: An Authorised Biography*, 2000

23. Cooney, *Scotland and the Papacy*, p 98

24. McCaffrey, 'Roman Catholics in Scotland', p 185

25. *St Peter's College Magazine*, December 1963, p 47

Chapter 2

1. *RIAS Quarterly*, 38, 1932

2. P F Anson, 'Modern Catholic Architecture in Scotland', *The Catholic Directory*, 1939, p 366. See D M Watters, 'Twentieth Century', *The World of Worship: An Exhibition to Celebrate the Millenium in Scotland*, 1999, exhibition booklet, pp 40–8

3. For Celtic revival in the nineteenth and early twentieth century monuments see A MacKechnie, 'Carn air a' Mohonadh: Gaeldom's Monuments – Cairns, Crosses and Celticism', *Journal of the Scottish Society for Art History*, 13, 2008–9, pp 22–13

4. 'Reginald Francis Joseph Fairlie, 1883–1952', Dictionary of Scottish Architects, www.scottisharchitects.org.uk; P Nuttgens, *Reginald Fairlie, 1883–1952: A Scottish Architect*, 1959

5. Fairlie reportedly lamented the 1930s abandonment of stone and the adoption of the red brick round-arched style 'spawned by Westminster Cathedral' for Catholic church buildings: 'he observed diffidently "It seems to be what they want"', cited in 'Reginald Francis Joseph Fairlie, 1883–1952', Dictionary of Scottish Architects, www.Scottisharchitects.org.uk

6. Nuttgens, *Reginald Fairlie*

7. A Ross, 'Development of the Catholic Community', in McRoberts, *Modern Scottish Catholicism*, p 47; see also *Catholic Directory*, 1939, p 381. Works by P F Anson include: *The Catholic Church in Modern Scotland*, 1937, and *Underground Catholicism in Scotland*, 1970

8. See P F Anson, 'Catholic Church-Building in Scotland', *Innes Review*, autumn 1954. Scott-Moncrieff published an architectural overview *Catholic Edinburgh* in 1957. Rev. J Dalrymple claimed 'he was the sort of person who, I suspect, does not exist in England. All his life he was mixed up in the politics, art, literature and religion of Scotland.' Obituary of George Scott-Moncrieff, *The Tablet*, 7 September, 1974, p 22

9. McCaffrey, 'Roman Catholics in Scotland', p 185

10. Obituary of Father D McRoberts, *Innes Review*, 30, 1979, pp 3–15. See D M Watters and M Glendinning, *Little Houses: The National Trust for Scotland's Improvement Scheme for Small Historic Homes*, 2006, pp 12–22

11. See 'Profile, Leslie Graham MacDougall', *Architectural Prospect*, autumn 1956

12. J F Mathew had completed Lorimer's historicist crow-step gabled central towered St Margaret's Church, Knightswood, Glasgow (1928), following Lorimer's death

13. Anson, 'Modern Catholic Architecture in Scotland', p 367

14. See C Fenton and D Walker 'The Modern Church', L Campbell, M Glendinning and J Thomas (eds), *Basil Spence, Buildings & Projects*, 2012, p 104; Ultimately a relatively plain church was designed and built by H S Goodhart-Rendel (1959–60), John Gifford, *Dumfries and Galloway, Buildings of Scotland*, 1996, p 567

15. Colin McWilliam claimed that Easthouses made attempt to break 'the bondage of the symmetrical convention in church design', C McWilliam 'Eleven New Churches in Edinburgh', *Edinburgh Architectural Association Year Book*, 1961, pp 81–93

16. See Fenton and Walker, 'The Modern Church', pp 104–17

17. McWilliam, 'Eleven New Churches in Edinburgh', pp 81–93

18. McCaffrey, 'Roman Catholics in Scotland', p 172

19. See J Sanders, 'Pugin & Pugin and the Diocese of Glasgow', *Architectural Heritage*, 8, 1997, pp 89–107

20. 'Giacomo Coia, Royal Gold Medal Address', *Building*, 27 June 1969. Other references quote Coia as saying 'red sandstone'. Cited in J Rodger (ed), *Gillespie, Kidd & Coia: Architecture 1956–1987*, 2007, p 11

21. Robert Lorimer, *Country Life*, 17 August 1918, cited in Gifford, *Dumfries and Galloway*, p 332

22. See Proctor, *Building the Modern Church*, pp 19–21

23. Pre-Modern Movement Scottish church architecture of the 1950s has not attracted detailed academic study yet, but in his pan-British overview of 1955–75, Robert Proctor highlights some design similarities between Catholic architecture in Scotland and England, but chiefly focuses on Gillespie, Kidd & Coia's Modernist work; see Proctor, *Building the Modern Church*; for Cordiner see p 84

24. I G Lindsay, *The Scottish Parish Kirk*, 1960, pp 88–9; see also 'Influences of Changing Forms of Worship on Building Design', *The Herald*, 4 December 1953, p 3

25. See F Bardgett, 'Missions and Missionaries: Home', in Maclean and Veitch, *Scottish Life and Society: Religion*, pp 505–6

26. Peter Whiston, 'Postwar Church Architecture', *Architectural Prospect*, November 1956, p 22. See also 'Peter Whiston', obituary, the *Scotsman*, 18 February 1999, p2

27. *RIAS Quarterly*, 97, 1954

28. J L Paterson, 'Image for a City', *Prospect*, 8, 1957

29. P Walker, *Clergy Review*, December 1981, pp 437–44

30. A Wheeler, 'Minds Meeting' lecture, Royal Fine Art Commission for Scotland, 15 August 1995. D M Watters, 'St Columba's Glenrothes: A Postwar Laboratory for Reformed Worship', *Architectural Heritage*, 12, 2001, pp 66–87

31. *The Herald*, 6 April 1961, p 6; interview with Professor Whyte, 15 October 1995. NCRG ideas: see for instance Hammond, *Liturgy and Architecture*; and Hammond, *Towards a Church Architecture*, especially the contributions by C Davis and P Hammond

32. For NCRG see R Jeffrey (ed), *The Twentieth Century Church: Twentieth Century Architecture vol 3*, 1998; R Macguire and K Murray, *Modern Churches*, 1965

33. For similar English contemporary types see, for example, Holy Family, Southhampton, England, by Liam McCormick (1966), which utilised similar materials and forms to the earlier Kildrum Parish Church, illustrated in Proctor, *Building the Modern Church*, pp 83–4

34. See M Glendinning and D M Watters, 'Cumbernauld', in R Close, J Gifford and F A Walker (eds), *Buildings of Scotland: Lanarkshire and Renfrewshire*, 2016, pp 232–59

35. See E M Wills, *Livingston: The Making of a Scottish New Town*, 1996, pp 78–80

36. Hammond, *Towards a Church Architecture*, pp 245–7

37. P F Smith, *Third Millennium Churches*, 1972, p 78, cited in P D Walker, 'Church Architecture', *The Clergy Review*, December 1981, p 440

38. B Spence, *The Builder*, 22 June 1956

39. Proctor, *Building the Modern Church*, pp 1–3; for Liverpool Cathedral, see pp 55–6, 152–6

Chapter 3

1. 'Jack Antonio Coia', Dictionary of Scottish Architects, www.scottisharchitects.org.uk. For Coia's life and work see also: R W K C Rogerson, *Jack Coia: His Life and Work*, 1986, and G Stamp, 'Coia, Giacomo Antonio [Jack], 1898–1901', Dictionary of National Biography, 2004, pp 437–8

2. According to Rogerson, the original sketches and measured drawings from this trip hung for a period in the corridor of the School of Architecture at the Glasgow School of Art, and were 'lost' at the time of publication, Rogerson, *Jack Coia*, p 5. Stamp records that Coia made a study trip in 1924, Stamp, 'Coia, Giacomo Antonio [Jack]', p 437

3. Stamp, 'Coia, Giacomo Antonio [Jack]', p 437

4. McCaffrey, 'Roman Catholics in Scotland', p 179. See also T Colpi, 'The Italian Community in Scotland: Senza un Campanile?, *Innes Review*, 44, 1993, pp 153–67 and *The Italian Factor: The Italian Community in Great Britain*, 1991

5. The school was originally founded in 1859 by the Jesuits as the Collegiate Catholic School in a house in Charlotte Street in the east end. It was relocated to Hill Street in 1866. See J McCabe, *The History of St Aloysius' College*, 2000, pp 17–34, 59–64

6. C Mackean, D Walker and F Walker, *Central Glasgow: An Illustrated Architectural Guide*, 1989, p 147

7. See 'Funeral Homily for Jack Coia, 18 August 1981, preached at St Aloysius, Glasgow, by Kenneth Nugent, S. J.' in Rogerson, *Jack Coia*, pp 122–3. The College War Memorial was funded by the Old Aloysian Association: Rector J Brady praised Coia's 'exquisite design for the Memorial Shrine', cited in an undated illustrated booklet produced to commemorate its funding and design. Information kindly provided by Susannah O'Rourke, St Aloysius College, 18 March 2016

8. *Building*, 27 June 1969, p 26

9. See R Proctor, 'Churches for a Changing Liturgy: Gillespie, Kidd & Coia and the Second Vatican Council', *Architectural History*, 48, 2005, pp 359–72; R Proctor, 'The Architect's Intention: Interpreting Postwar Modernism through the Architect Interview', *Journal of Design History*, 19 (4), 2006, pp 296–307; Proctor, *Building the Modern Church*; J Rodger (ed), *Gillespie, Kidd & Coia: Architecture 1956–1987*, 2007; G Stamp, 'The Myth of Gillespie, Kidd & Coia', *Architectural Heritage*, 11, 2000, pp 68–79

10. J Macaulay and C Hermansen (eds), *Mac Journal One: Gillespie, Kidd & Coia*, 1994

11. Stamp, 'The Myth of Gillespie, Kidd & Coia', pp 68–79; Proctor, 'The Architect's Intention', pp 296–307 and Rodger, *Gillespie, Kidd & Coia: Architecture*, pp 20–2

12. *Building*, 27 June 1969, p 26

13. Glasgow School of Architecture calendar records, 1938; letter from Warnett Kennedy, to M Glendinning, 7 November 1995

14. Rogerson, *Jack Coia*

15. Letter from Warnett Kennedy, to M Glendinning, 7 November 1995

16. Rogerson, *Jack Coia*, p 106

17. Interview with A Buchanan Campbell, 1993; letter from Warnett Kennedy to M Glendinning, 7 November 1995; N Thomson, 'Building a New Scotland', *Scottish Field*, September 1967, p 49

18. See N Baxter, 'Early Coia Buildings' in Macaulay and Hermansen, *Mac Journal One: Gillespie, Kidd & Coia*, pp 15–19

19. Interview with A Buchanan Campbell (who gained his first practical experience working on this commission for Coia), 1993

20. Stamp, 'Coia, Giacomo Antonio [Jack]', p 438

21. Rogerson, *Jack Coia*, p 104

22. Proctor, *Building the Modern Church*, p 51

23. Letter from Warnett Kennedy to M Glendinning, 7 November 1995

24. A Ross, 'The Development of the Scottish Catholic Community', in McRoberts, *Modern Scottish Catholicism*, p 47

25. 'Abstractionist', letter from Warnett Kennedy to M Glendinning, 7 November 1995

26. Anson, 'Modern Catholic Architecture in Scotland', p 367

27. *Building*, 27 June 1969, p 26

28. Ibid

29. Rogerson, *Jack Coia*, p 36

30. 'Isi Israel Metzstein, 1928–2012', Dictionary of Scottish Architects, www.scottisharchitects.org.uk

31. 'Suffering Little Children', *Scotland on Sunday Spectrum*, 10 December 1995, p 4

32. Author interview with Charles MacCallum, 6 December 1995

33. Ibid

34. Author interview with A Macgregor, 22 August 1995

35. Author interview with I Metzstein, 18 January 1996

36. Ibid

37. A MacMillan interview with J Rodger, November 2003, cited in Rodger, *Gillespie, Kidd & Coia: Architecture*, p 25, fn 19

38. Rogerson, *Jack Coia*, p 37; Proctor, *Building the Modern Church*, p 49

39. *Building*, 27 June 1969, p 26

40. Author interview with C MacCallum, 6 December 1995

41. 'Confidence', Professor David Walker, 1999, cited in Stamp, 'The Myth of Gillespie, Kidd & Coia', p 71. Walker detailed 'He [Coia] certainly had the confidence of Archbishop Donald Mackintosh and particularly Donald Campbell, but I think there were a few tiffs with James Donald Scanlan probably because by that time the defects of his churches were more apparent. His relationship with Winning was bad, which of course ended his church practice.'

42. Proctor has quoted office correspondence from and to Coia of the late 1950s and early 1960s to illustrate his mediating role, particularly when initial designs were presented to the clients. At a crucial stage in the design of St Bride's, East Kilbride, in the mid-to-late 1950s, Coia wrote to the secretary of the Motherwell Diocese finance board 'I have been thinking over Monsignor Roger's ideas for the Church in the style he suggests, and while it would give an interesting effect it would be rather a ticklish problem to design a Church in the style he suggests. I think that it would be much better for me to come through and spend an hour with His Lordship and discuss the whole situation again', letter to Rev. C Craigen, 5 July 1954 cited in Proctor, 'Churches for a Changing Liturgy', p 321, fn 66. For St Partick's, Kilsyth see Proctor, *Building the Modern Church*, p 5

43. A MacMillan interview with J Roger, November/December 2003, cited in Rodger, *Gillespie, Kidd & Coia: Architecture*, p 25, fn 39. I Metzstein interview with Gavin Stamp, 24 July 2000, British Library Sound Archive, C467/55/01, cited in Rodger, *Gillespie, Kidd & Coia: Architecture* p 25, fn 39

44. K Nuggent, cited in Rogerson, *Jack Coia*, p 122

45. According to MacCallum, Barrett 'was very well read and extremely argumentative', author interview with C MacCallum, 6 December 1995

46. *Scottish Field*, September 1967, p 49

47. A MacMillan interview with J Rodger, November 2003, cited in Rodger, *Gillespie, Kidd & Coia: Architecture*, p 25, fn 19. MacMillan's dates would suggest that Coia believed himself 'past-it' in 1940

48. Campbell was a former employee of Coia's, A B Campbell, 'Profile, Jack Coia, F.R.I.B.A', *Architectural Prospect*, 1, February 1956, p 25

49. Author interview with I Metzstein, 18 January 1996

50. *Scottish Field*, September 1967, p 49

51. Metzstein paper, in Gillespie, Kidd & Coia Archive; author interview with C MacCallum, 6 December 1995

52. Author interview with C MacCallum, 6 December 1995

53. E Maxwell Fry, 'Jack Coia: Royal Gold Medalist 1969', *RIBA Journal*, July 1969, p 281

54. Cited in Proctor, *Building the Modern Church*, p 180

55. A MacMillan, interview with J Rodger, November 2003, cited in Rodger, *Gillespie, Kidd & Coia: Architecture*, p 25, fn 35

56. Proctor, 'Churches for a Changing Liturgy', p 316

57. C MacCallum claimed that 'the symbiotic relationship between Isi and Andy did not include Lutomsky … he was a self-contained man, and was not qualified', author interview with C MacCallum, 6 December 1995

58. Proctor also details that Reginald Fairlie was commissioned (before 1955) for a sketch design in the central site. Fairlie died in 1952 and it would most probably be Reginald Fairlie & Partners, Proctor, *Building the Modern Church*, p 286

59. Press release, undated, Glasgow School of Art Archives, GKC/CG/1/8, cited in Proctor, *Building the Modern Church*, p 286 and pp 49–51

60 Interview with I Metzstein, 12 October 1994; interview with Professor James Whyte, 15 October 1995

61 B Schotz, *Bronze in my Blood,* 1981, p 211

62 Stamp concludes that it was MacMillan who 'probably took the leading role in the design of the Glenrothes church', Stamp, 'The Myth of Gillespie, Kidd & Coia', p 70. He cites Charles MacCallum's recollection of 1994: 'I remember, too, how Father Grace, the parish priest, later described to me [MacCallum] the moment of creation, with Jack on his knees in the old presbytery, sketching out the concept before his very eyes, on the back of a newspaper. Nothing could have convinced him the truth was otherwise, and people need their dreams', C MacCallum, 'Gillespie, Kidd & Coia: The History of the Firm', in Macaulay and Hermansen, *Mac Journal One: Gillespie, Kidd & Coia*, p 14

63 Author interview with Professor James Whyte, 15 October 1995

64 *Architects' Journal*, 5 February 1959, pp 231–8, cited in Proctor, *Building the Modern Church*, p 51; Hammond, *Liturgy and Architecture*, p 105, cited p 179

65 'Competition': author interview with Fr K Nugent, 10 October 1995

66 'Two Churches', *Architects' Journal*, 31 October 1962, pp 103–12

67 Ibid

68 Proctor, *Building the Modern Church*, p 200

69 Rogerson, *Jack Coia*, p 89

70 Proctor reports that when Metzstein was asked in 1965 by J M Richards (editor of *Architectural Review*) to give material on St Bride's for publication, he instead gave St Joseph's because it was 'of a more advanced liturgical from', letter from I Metzstein to J M Richards 23 June 1965, GSA, GKC/CEK/1/7, cited in Proctor, *Building the Modern Church*, p 180. See also Proctor, 'Churches for a Changing Liturgy', pp 359–72

71 Proctor, *Building the Modern Church*, p 200

72 R Schwarz, *The Church Incarnate,* 1959 (English edition)

73 Author interview with James Whyte, 15 October 1995

74 A plaster bust of Coia is held at the Scottish National Portrait Gallery, Stamp, 'Coia, Giacomo Antonio [Jack]', p 438

75 Proctor, *Building the Modern Church*, p 79, and Stamp, 'The Myth of Gillespie, Kidd & Coia', p 72

76 R Maguire and K Murray, *Modern Churches of the World*, London, 1965, pp 144–5

77 'Solemn Opening, St Bride's Church, East Kilbride', 1964, cited in Proctor, *Building the Modern Church*, p 288

78 Gillespie, Kidd & Coia, 'St Bride's Church & Presbytery – East Kilbride', typescript, 24 July 1965, correspondence files, Gillespie, Kidd & Coia Archive

79 A M Doak, 'Building in Prospect', *Architectural Prospect*, summer 1959, p 12

80 Proctor, *Building the Modern Church*, pp 170–9

81 See www.saintpatrickskilsyth.org.uk

82 For St Mary's scheme see Proctor, *Building the Modern Church*, pp 292–5

83 I Metzstein, 'Minds Meeting' lecture, 15 August 1995, Royal Fine Art Commission for Scotland

84 Author interview with I Metzstein, 26 August 1996; I Metzstein, lecture (with A MacMillan) for Twentieth Century Society, Glasgow, 24 September 1994

85 I Metzstein, lecture, 24 September 1994

86 Author interview with I Metzstein, 26 August 1996

87 'Jack Coia: Royal Gold Medalist 1969', *RIBA Journal*, July 1969, p 282

88 *Architects' Journal,* 5 October 1977, pp 620–1

89 For a detailed historical account see O Saumarez Smith, 'Robinson College, Cambridge, and the Twilight of Collegiate Modenism, 1974–81', *Architectural History*, 55, 2012, pp 369–402

90 Information from Catherine Stevenson, Mackintosh School of Architecture, 12 April 2016

91 Author interview with I Metzstein, 26 August 1996

Chapter 4

1. I Metzstein, 'Minds Meeting' discussion, August 1993, Royal Fine Art Commission for Scotland; *St Peter's College Magazine,* December 1966, p 117
2. *St Peter's College Magazine* (hereafter *SPCM*), December 1966, p 121
3. Metzstein claimed in retrospect that he was 'partner in charge' and that Cowell was 'job architect', author interview, 8 March 1995
4. Author interview with I Metzstein, 18 January 1996
5. Metzstein interviewed by G Stamp, 24 July 2000, British Library Sound Archive, F8457, cited in Proctor, 'The Architect's Intention', p 297
6. 'St Peter's College at Cardross', typescript, 5 April 1966
7. The original St Peter's College in Partickhill, Glasgow, was opened in 1874 by Archbishop Charles Eyre. See K Wenell, 'St Peter's College and the Desacralization of Space', *Literature and Theology*, 21, 2007, pp 259–75
8. M Turnbull, *Cardinal Gordon Joseph Gray,* 1994, p 51
9. *Scottish Catholic Directory,* 1980, pp 377–89; J Darragh, 'The Catholic Population of Scotland', in McRoberts, *Modern Scottish Catholicism*, p 223
10. St Mahew's was one of several properties neighbouring Kilmahew estate purchased by John William Burns in the 1870s, Avanti Architects Limited 'Conservation Assessment, Volume 1, St Peter's Seminary, October 2007', 2007, p 286
11. James Darragh, obituary of D McRoberts, *Innes Review,* 30, 1979, pp 2–15
12. Darragh, obituary of McRoberts; Darragh, 'The Catholic Population'
13. Gillespie, Kidd & Coia Archive, Cardross correspondence file (hereafter CCF), letter from GKC, 15 April 1953; CCF, letter from the Archdiocese to GKC, 22 April 1953
14. D McRoberts papers, Scottish Catholic Archives; Darragh, 'The Catholic Population'; CCF, letter from J Coia to McRoberts, 29 May 1953
15. Author interview with Monsignor Charles Burns, 16 March 2016. Burns was ordained in 1957, and 'sent' to the Scots College in Rome. In 1961–2 he was the University of Glasgow Ross Scholar at the Vatican Archives, and from 1962 to 1997 he was the archivist of the Vatican Secret Archive
16. 'Kilmahew', *SPCM*, June 1949, p 9
17. Accommodation remained limited in 1949 and a number of students were 'lodged' in the nearby garage-stable block, Kilmahew, *SPCM*, June 1949, pp 9–10
18. McRoberts papers; CCF, letter from J Coia to Archdiocese, October 1955
19. See 'Nunraw Abbey', in J Hogg (ed), *The Scottish Border Abbeys vol 1*, 1986, pp 39–48
20. Darragh, 'The Catholic Population'; Darragh, obituary of McRoberts
21. Darragh, 'The Catholic Population'; Darragh, obituary of McRoberts
22. Author interview with I Metzstein, 14 March 1995
23. 'Minds Meeting', August 1993, discussion between I Metzstein and M Baines
24. CCF, letter GKC to Zinn, 4 December 1949
25. Interview with I Metzstein, 12 October 1994
26. I Metzstein, 'The Architecture of St Peter's College, Cardross', in Rogerson, Jack Coia, pp 110–14 (hereafter: Metzstein, 'Cardross')
27. This account is based on the 1998 site visit assessment notes by landscape historian Christopher Dingwall, included in a letter from Christopher Dingwall, Garden History Society, to Argyle and Bute Council, 16 October 1998, in Historic Environment Scotland files, SH/19, part 2. See also Avanti Architects, 'Conservation Assessment, Volume 1, St Peter's Seminary, October 2007', 2007, pp 43–53
28. Dingwall recorded in 1998 'Apart from one very old Sycamore just to the north of the ruin, there is no trace of earlier planting … nor any sign of earlier deliberate planting on the banks of Kilmahew Burn', 1998 assessment, letter from Christopher Dingwall, Garden History Society, to Argyle and Bute Council, 16 October 1998, in Historic Environment Scotland files, SH/19, part 2
29. CCF, letter from GKC, 7 June 1960; plan KS133/ KS134; Metzstein, 'Cardross'
30. Detailed in drawing CC600004A
31. GKC practice archive, typed description of building by I Metzstein, 5 April 1966 (hereafter: Metzstein, description); Metzstein, 'Cardross'
32. Detailed in drawings CC600009/014
33. Detailed in drawing CC600002A
34. Detailed in drawing CC600002A-4A
35. Detailed in drawing CC600092
36. Metzstein, 'Cardross'. Detailed in drawings CC600098/100/101
37. Detailed in drawing CC600293-111
38. Detailed in drawings CC600007/8/9
39. Metzstein, description
40. Detailed in drawing CC600.001(December 1961 version)
41. Metzstein, 'Cardross'
42. Roof lights detailed in drawing CC600010
43. Interview with I Metzstein, 25 April 1996
44. Detailed in drawing CC600009
45. Metzstein, 'Cardross'
46. Detailed in drawing CC600180
47. Metzstein, 'Cardross' and description
48. Metzstein, 'Cardross'. Detailed in drawing CC60012
49. Detailed in drawings CC6000105/110/111/125
50. Detailed in drawing CC600129
51. These stones commemorated the re-internment of Archbishop Eyre and Archbishop Campbell
52. Detailed in drawing CC600129R1
53. CCF, draft press release from Moore Todd Associates, Glasgow: letter to GKC, 29 December 1966
54. Metzstein, description
55. Metzstein, 'Cardross'
56. Detailed in drawings C600007/013
57. Detailed in drawing CC600011
58. Detailed in drawing CC600007
59. Information from Isi Metzstein, 1996
60. Detailed in drawing CC600310
61. CCF, letter from GKC to Wylie & Lochhead, 9 March 1965
62. Detailed in drawing C600
63. See for instance CCF, letter from Elders to GKC, 31 August 1965
64. Detailed in drawings CC600296 (refectory tables), CC600288/ 88A/89 (chapel seating)
65. CCF, letter from T Justice to GKC, 1 March 1966
66. Metzstein, 'Minds Meeting', 1993
67. Metzstein, 'Cardross'
68. Metzstein, 'Minds Meeting', 1993
69. Metzsetin,' The Architecture of St Peter's College, *SPCM*, December 1966, p 132
70. Metzstein, 'Minds Meeting', 1993
71. P Serenyi, 'Le Corbusier, Fourier and the Monastery of Ena', *Art Bulletin,* December 1967
72. Metzstein, 'Minds Meeting', 1993; author interview with I Metzstein, 26 August 1996
73. Metzstein, 'Minds Meeting', 1993
74. Metzstein, 'Minds Meeting', 1993
75. Metzstein, 'Cardross', and author interview, 1995
76. Metzstein, 'Cardross'
77. Le Corbusier, *Oeuvre Complète,* 5, 1946–52, p 191, cited in C Jencks, *Le Corbusier and the Tragic View of Architecture,* 1973, p 42
78. CCF, letter from GKC to Zinn, 22 February 1961
79. Metzstein, 'Minds Meeting', 1993
80. CCF, draft press release from Moore Todd; Metzstein, 'Minds Meeting', 1993; Metzstein, 'Cardross'
81. P Hodgkinson, 'St Peter's Seminary, Cardross', in Macaulay and Hermansen, *Mac Journal One: Gillespie, Kidd & Coia*, pp 42–3

82 T van Doesburg, *On European Architecture,* Nijmegen, 1986, pp 92–3

83 Metzstein, 'Minds Meeting', 1993

84 Stamp, 'The Myth of Gillespie, Kidd & Coia', p 72

85 Proctor, 'The Architect's Intention', pp 295–307

86 Metzstein interview with G Stamp, 24 July, 2000, British Library Sound Archive, F8457, cited in Proctor, 'The Architect's Intention', p 302

87 CCF, letter from GKC to Michael Person of *Architectural Review,* 27 August 1960

88 *SPCM,* December 1964, p 115; 'Alter Boys': interview with Father J Fitzsimmons, 29 May 1996; interview with I Metzstein, 26 August 1996

89 CCF, letter from Zinn to GKC, 17 February 1960

90 *SPCM,* June 1960, p 260

91 CCF, letter from GKC to McLernan & Whyte, 7 June 1960; letter from McLernan & Whyte to GKC, 27 November 1961; *SPCM,* 24 (95), p 266

92 *SPCM,* 25 (97); CCF, letter from GKC to Zinn, 26 July 1961; letter from GKC to McLernan & Whyte, 14 November 1961; letter from McLernan & Whyte to GKC, 17 October 1961; letter from McLernan & Whyte to Ward, 29 November 1961; letter from Ward to GKC, 29 November 1961; *SPCM,* June 1962

93 CCF, letter from I Metzstein to J McSparran & McCormick, 11 May 1972

94 *SPCM,* June 1963, p 35; GKC practice archive, drawings CC600105/110/111, dated October 1963; CCF, letter from J Laidlaw to Scottish Television, 23 September 1963; letter from I Metzstein to McSparran & McCormick, 11 May 1972; letter from J Laidlaw to GKC, 10 September 1963 and 27 February 1964; letter from J Laidlaw to Coia, 27 February 1964; letter from GKC to Ward, 20 February 1964

95 'An Appreciation', c1963, cited in *The Bulletin, St Margaret's, St Joseph's, St Finnan's and Cille Chorill,* gaeldom.com/bulletin (accessed 31 March 2016)

96 CCF, letter from Laidlaw to GKC, 22 October 1964; *SPCM,* December 1966 and June 1965, p 32; letter from Laidlaw to GKC, 9 April 1965; letter from GKC to *Concrete Quarterly,* 22 December 1965

97 *SPCM,* December 1963, p 143

98 *SPCM,* December 1966

99 'The Re-internment of Archbishop Eyre and Campbell', *SPCM,* 1967, p 51

100 CCF, letter from Ward to GKC, 22 June 1971

101 'Seminary, Cardross, near Glasgow', *Architectural Review,* January 1962, pp 18–19

102 *SPCM,* December 1961; CCF, letter from GKC to *Architectural Review,* 27 July 1960; letter from H Brookaman to GKC, 21 August 1962; letter from GKC to T M P Bendixon, 26 April 1963; letter from GKC to Central Office of Information, 11 February 1963; letter from Laidlaw to Scottish Television, 23 September 1963. Progress was also recorded in the *Architects' Journal,* 6 May 1964

103 *SPCM,* June 1967

104 Cited in Wenell, 'St Peter's College and the Desacralization of Space', pp 259–75. See also: *Architect & Building News,* 22 November 1967, pp 864–5; 20/27 November 1967, pp 1012–3; and 3 January 1968, pp 40–1

105 M Webb, 'Scottish Homage to Le Corbusier', *Country Life,* 27 July 1967; 'St Peter's College, Cardross', *Architects' Journal,* 1 May 1968

106 'St Peter's College, Cardross; Architects: Gillespie, Kidd & Coia', *Architect and Builder* (South Africa), September 1967, pp 22–6

107 'St Peter's College, Cardross, nr. Glasgow; Architects: Gillespie, Kidd & Coia', *Interior Design & Contract Furnishing,* August 1967, pp 22–6

108 CCF, letter from GKC to *Concrete Quarterly,* 7 February 1967

109 'Scottish Seminary: St Peter's College, Cardross', *Concrete Quarterly,* 72, Jan–Mar, 1967, pp 16–23

110 'RIBA Architecture Awards 1967. Scotland: St Peter's College, Cardross', *RIBA Journal,* p 182; *SPCM,* December 1967; CCF, letter from GKC to Mr Berry, Leeds Polytechnic, 6 April 1971

Chapter 5

1. Interviews with Father John Fitzsimmons, 29 May 1996, and Father James Foley, 30 May 1996
2. Interview with Father Fitzsimmons
3. Cooney, *Scotland and the Papacy*, pp 96–7
4. *SPCM*, December 1965, p 66
5. Interview with Monsignor McMahon, 29 May 1996
6. K Nugent, 'Living At Cardross: First Impressions', *Clergy Review*, March 1967, p 210
7. Interview with Father Fitzsimmons
8. *Cardross Seminary, Glasgow, Four Modern Buildings*, BBC, Episode 4, 1966, www.bbc.co.uk
9. Interview with Father Foley; *SPCM*, 26 May 1966, p 105
10. Nugent, 'Living At Cardross', pp 209, 211–12
11. Interview with John Durkan, 25 August 1995
12. Interviews with Father Foley and Father Fitzsimmons
13. Interview with Father Foley
14. *The Herald*, 30 March 1972, p 11
15. Letter from Dr J McCaffrey; *SPCM*, 'Kilmahew', June 1949, p 9–10
16. *SPCM*, June 1960, pp 237–42
17. *The Herald*, 30 September 1971, p 10
18. McCaffrey 'Roman Catholics in Scotland', p 188
19. Obituary of the Most Reverend James Donald Scanlan, former Archbishop of Glasgow, *CDS*, 1977, pp 370–8
20. G Walker, 'The Religious Factor', in Devine and Wormald, *The Oxford Handbook of Modern Scottish History*, p 593. For the Catholic Church in England and Wales see C G Brown, *Religion and Society in Twentieth-Century Britain*, 2006, pp 2, 26
21. McCaffrey, 'Roman Catholics in Scotland', p 187
22. C G Brown, *Religion and Society in Modern Scotland*, 1997, p 54
23. Dr Mary McHugh, 'The Development of The Catholic Community in the Western Province', 1990 (thesis, Strathclyde University), p 210
24. Interview with Father Donaldson (lecturer at St Peter's, Cardross, 1972–80), 28 May 1996
25. Fr M Regan (ed), *Scotus College: The National Seminary in Scotland, Official Handbook* (to commemorate the solemn opening of Scotus College, 4 October, 1993), 1993
26. Interview with Father Fitzsimmons
27. Interviews with Monsignor McMahon and Father Fitzsimmons
28. *SPCM*, recorded 5 October 1966, cited in Wenell, 'St Peter's College and the Desacralization of Space', p 270
29. *SPCM*, December 1966
30. *SPCM*, June 1967, p 21; CCF, letter 4 November 1972, GKC to Ward; letter from Cowell, 7 April 1973
31. *SPCM*, December 1967, recorded 9 November 1967, cited in Wenell, 'St Peter's College and the Desacralization of Space', p 272
32. Letter from J McMahon to Archbishop Scanlan (with brief report attached), 7 April 1973. This was copied to the Bishop of Motherwell and Paisley, Bishop Ward, Bishop Winning, and Gillespie, Kidd & Coia
33. Cited in the site chronology of the 2007 Avanti report, Avanti Architects, 'Conservation Assessment, Volume 1, St Peter's Seminary, October 2007', 2007, p 290. The chronology is chiefly based on published sources (much of the data post-1953 taken from the first edition of this book) but some primary sources were consulted and not referenced. The 'statement' may survive in the practice job files now held at the Glasgow School of Art Archives
34. Interview with Monsignor McMahon; CCF, letter from Cowell, 7 April 1973; see letter of 16 February 1974; letter from GKC, 3 July 1974; letters from McMahon to GKC, 25 September 1974 and 21 December 1973; interview with Father Foley
35. J Gilchrist, 'Temple to Ruined Dreams', *Scotsman*, 18 April 2003, pp 8–9. Cinematography was by Mark Littlewood, camera work by Tony Cridlin, and it was edited by Patrick Higson. The score was composed by Frank Spedding and conducted by Marcus Dodds
36. M Grigor, *Space and Light Revisited*, 2009, p 3. See also P Lewis, 'Televisionary', *Prospect*, January/February 2001, pp 33–5. Cardross Seminary was also one of 28 projects featured in P Willis, *New Architecture in Scotland*, 1977, pp 56–7
37. The formal opening of St Peter's College, Newlands took place on 18 March 1980
38. *SPCM*, December 1966, 5 February 1967 and 12 February 1967; interviews with Father Foley and Father Fitzsimmons
39. Cited in Wenell, 'St Peter's College and the Desacralization of Space', pp 259–75
40. Estimate based on insurance replacement costs, letter from McLellan & Whyte to Gillespie, Kidd & Coia, 23 May 1972
41. Cited in Regan, *Scotus College*, p 5
42. Letter from Rev David Brown, St Andrew's Cathedral House, 90 Dunlop Street, Glasgow, *The Herald*, 28 September 1992; G Stamp, 'Postscript', in Macaulay and Hermansen, *Mac Journal One: Gillespie, Kidd & Coia*, p 23
43. Cardross Golf Club finally purchased the former estate east parkland in 1987, which it had leased from the late nineteenth century
44. Metzstein, 'Minds Meeting', 1993
45. M Glendinning 'Icons', *Prospect*, Issue 129, winter 2007, p 47
46. Information from Catherine Stevenson, Mackintosh School of Architecture, 12 April 2016
47. 'Dedication', in Macaulay and Hermansen, *Mac Journal One: Gillespie, Kidd & Coia*
48. Correspondence with Annette Moran, Archdiocese of Glasgow, 1996
49. 'Community Unites in Bid to Save St Peter's: Luxury Homes Plan for Crumbling College', *Helensburgh Advertiser*, cutting, author files, undated, probably 2003; I Fernie, 'Historic Scotland Issues A-list Protection for Derelict Seminary', *The Herald*, 14 September 1992
50. Historic Scotland 'note for file' by J Hume, 24 April 1989, HGG/A/SH/19, part 1
51. See Glendinning and Watters, 'Cumbernauld New Town: Reception and Heritage Legacy'
52. D M Watters, *St Peter's College, Cardross: Report for DOCOMOMO Scottish National Group*, 1994
53. See G Glendinning, 'Modern Heritage', Prospect, November/December 2002, pp 30–1
54. See M Glendinning, The Conservation Movement: A History of Architectural Preservation: Antiquity to Modernity, 2013, pp 285–7; D M Watters, 'Recording our Recent Past: RCAHMS Postwar Sites and Monuments Archives, 1945–80', *Architectural Heritage Society of Scotland Magazine*, spring 2010; D M Watters, 'Recording our Recent Past: Scotland's Survey and Preservation Initiatives for Postwar Sites and Monuments, 1985–2012', *DOCOMOMO International Specialist Committee for Education and Technology Newsletter*, spring 2012
55. J Gillon and D McDowell, *Edinburgh's Postwar Listed Buildings*, 2011. See also Historic Scotland, *Scotland: Building for Future Essays on the Architecture of the Postwar Era*, 2009; D McDowell, *Glasgow's Postwar Listed Buildings*, 2012
56. Historic Scotland, *Scotland: Building for Future Essays on the Architecture of the Postwar Era*, 2009, p 102
57. The case officer was Aonghus Mackechnie of Historic Scotland
58. A list description was drafted by A Mackechnie; see '60 Drumchapel Road, St Benedict's Church, Presbytery and Hall', typescript note, undated, author research files
59. Stamp, 'The Myth of Gillespie, Kidd & Coia', p 79, fn 15. Stamp records his lead role in the press debate: *The Herald*, 19, 23, 26 and 29 March, 3 April 1991; *Independent*, 27 March 1991, p 17; *Building Design*, 29 March, 5 and 12 April 1991, p 12 and *Private Eye*, 29 March 1991, p 9
60. G Stamp, 'Astragal', *Architects' Journal*, 1990, pp 6–7
61. Historic Scotland, *Scotland: Building for Future Essays on the Architecture of the Postwar Era*, p 99
62. 'Listed Church Faces Demolition', *The Herald*, 23 April 1996; 'Gillespie, Kidd & Coia Church Threatened with Demolition', *Architects' Journal*, 2 May 1996, p 11. The application for demolition was withdrawn in October 1997

63 D M Watters, 'Cardross Seminary: Modernity, Decay and Ruin', *DOCOMOMO-US National News*, Fall 2007, pp 3–15; D M Watters and J Deffenbaugh, 'Debate', *Prospect*, 129, winter 2007, pp 43–5

64 *Art Work*, April/May 1989, p 6

65 L Musgrave, 'Praying for a Miracle to Redeem St Peter's', *Scotland on Sunday*, 3 February 1992

66 *Scotsman*, 27 March 1992

67 Letter from Historic Scotland to Sir Hector Monro, Minister of State in the Scottish Office, 15 September 1992, HES files, HGG/A/SH19, part 1

68 'St Peter's College Top Listing', *Helensburgh Advertiser*, 4 September 1992; Fernie, 'Historic Scotland Issues A-list Protection for Derelict Seminary'

69 G Stamp, 'A Listing Fully Justified', *The Herald*, 20 September 1992

70 H J Henket, 'Dereliction of St Peter's', *The Herald*, 23 September 1992

71 Fernie, 'Historic Scotland Issues A-list Protection for Derelict Seminary'

72 HS note on file by J Hume, 30 September 1992, HES files, HGG/A/SH19, part 1

73 Letter from Rev. David Brown, St Andrew's Cathedral House, 90 Dunlop Street, Glasgow, *The Herald*, 28 September 1992

74 Stamp, 'A Listing Fully Justified'

75 'Scheme to Save Holey Seminary', *Scotsman*, 27 March 1992

76 Metzstein, 'Minds Meeting', 1993

77 M Baines, 'Post-Coia Coia: The Postwar Architecture of Gillespie, Kidd & Coia', typescript of lecture from video recording, DOCOMOMO files, 1992. M Baines, 'Post-Coia Coia: The Postwar Work of Gillespie, Kidd & Coia', in M Glendinning (ed), *Rebuilding Scotland: The Postwar Vision 1945–75*, 1997, pp 129–36

78 Metzstein interview with author, 26 August 1996

79 Macaulay and Hermansen, *Mac Journal One: Gillespie, Kidd & Coia*, pp 9, 45

80 M Cullen, 'History in the Wrecking! How Buildings Worth Millions have Drifted to Rack and Ruin', *Helensburgh Advertiser*, 27 March 1992

81 Fernie, 'Historic Scotland Issues A-list protection for Derelict Seminary'

82 T Connelly, cited in D Steele, 'Church's Pledge on College', *The Herald*, 16 September 1992

83 L Cochrane, 'Catholic Church Told to Protect St Peter's', Lennox Herald, 11 September 1992

84 Cullen, 'History in the Wrecking!'

85 Ibid

86 *Scotsman*, 27 March 1992

87 'Church asks developers to work a miracle', *The Herald*, 25 June 1993

88 'Property plan to clear Church debt, *The Herald*, 29 October 1993

89 Dumbarton District Council Planning Department, planning application, 22 October 1993

90 Letter from Dumbarton District Council to Classical House, 11 August 1993; note on file, November 1993 and 25 January 1994, HES files, HGG/A/SH19, part 1

91 Note on file, 25 January 1994; The Historic Scotland note on file also recorded 'The Historic Buildings Council fairly recently opined that it would not be within their statutory power to recommend grant solely for the purpose of consolidation (or stabilising) a building. They regard themselves as being in the business of repairing buildings.' Letter from Historic Scotland to Classical House, 3 February 1994, HES files, HGG/A/SH19, part 1

92 L Kinney, 'Church Unveils Plans to Transform Site of St Peter's College', *Dumbarton Reporter*, 3 November 1993

93 'Plan to Transform Site of St Peter's College', *Helensburgh Advertiser*, 5 November 1993; H Reilly, 'Villagers Unhappy with College Plans', *Lennox Herald*, 5 December 1994; 'No Housing Development at College', *Helensburgh Advertiser*, 29 April 1994

94 Reilly, 'Villagers Unhappy with College Plans'

95 The AHSS was also represented, see E Crawford, 'St Peter's College, Cardross Dumbarton', *Architectural Heritage Society of Scotland Newsletter*, spring 1994, pp 40–3

96 Letter from G Stamp, chairman (in Glasgow) of The Twentieth Century Society, to Dumbarton District Council, 14 January 1994

97 K Esson,'What the Future Could Hold for the Crumbling Remains of St Peter's', *Dumbarton Reporter*, 1 April 1994

98 Editorial, *Flourish*, May 1994, cited in 'Church Set for College Appeal', *The Herald*, 30 April 1994

99 'Report Slams Plans for St Peter's College', *Lennox Herald*, 1 April 1994

100 'Not a Prayer for St Peter's', *Helensburgh Advertiser*, 1 May 1994

101 L Cochrane, 'Charity Could Step in and Take Over Derelict College', *Lennox Herald*, 22 April 1994; 'Report Slams Plans for St Peter's College', *Lennox Herald*, 1 April 1994

102 Letter from EDAW planning consultancy, to R MacInnes, Historic Scotland, 26 August 1994; letter from D W Loan, Classical House, to Dunbartonshire District Council, 10 October 1994, HES files, HGG/A/SH19, part 1

103 'St Peter's College, Cardross, Market Assessment' prepared for Dunbartonshire Enterprises by EDAW, 30 September 1994, p 9, HES files, HGG/A/SH19, part 1; 'Former St Peter's College, Cardross Feasibility Study' by Classical House, February 1994

104 'Malicious blaze at college' *Dumbarton Reporter*, 25 May 1994

105 'Condition Survey Report on Kilmahew House, St Peter's Seminary, Cardross, Dumbarton, For the Archdiocese of Glasgow,' by McClain Collier & Partners, Glasgow, 28 June 1994, HES files, HGG/A/SH19, part 1

106 Monro had reportedly been approached 'by a Mr Wilson in the British Midland lounge shortly before boarding the flight to London' about the fate of the Kilmahew House. Richard Wilson was the son of Michael Wilson of Cardross. A flurry of inter-departmental correspondence ensued, and one civil servant amusingly noted 'Oh how I wish Mr Wilson's parents lived next to the Gourock Ropeworks and their son could command the Secretary of State to do something to preserve *that* building.' Correspondence, 20 December 1993 to 21 January 1994; note on file, J Reynolds to J Hume and R MacInnes, HES files, HGG/A/SH19, part 1

107 'St Peter's College, Cardross, Kilmahew House, Structural Report', by J C Turner, Senior Engineer, Scottish Office, 23 September 1994, HES files, HGG/A/SH19, part 1; 'Fire-ravaged Kilmahew House to be demolished', *Lennox Herald*, 2 September 1994

108 R Machines to J Hume, 1 November 1994, and letter from J Reynolds, Historic Scotland, to Dumbarton District Council, 4 November 1994, HES files, HGG/A/SH19, part 1

109 G Stamp: *Independent*, 21 December 1994, p 22

110 Ibid; see also G Stamp, *The Herald*, 29 October 1994; G Stamp, 'Postscript' in J Macaulay and C Hermansen (eds), *Mac Journal One: Gillespie, Kidd & Coia*, 1994, p 52

111 G Stamp, *Independent*, 21 December 1994, p 22

112 Authorship debate: *The Herald* letters, 2, 12, 14 November 1994, 2, 9, 19 December 1994

113 For example, M Wilson cited in Reilly, 'Villagers Unhappy with College Plans'

Chapter 6

1. E Hollis, 'Anxious Care and Unsightly Aids', in E Hollis and G van Noord (eds), *To Have and to Hold: Future of A Contested Landscape*, 2011, p 54
2. A Farquhar, quoted in 'Lottery Cash to save St Peter's Seminary in Cardross', BBC News online 5 December 2013, www.bbc.co.uk/news/uk-scotland-glasgow-west
3. K Crilley, *The Lennox Herald*, 28 January 2000, p 5
4. C Ednie, 'A Modern Tragedy', *The Herald Magazine*, 7 February 2004
5. Metzstein, 'Minds Meeting', 1993
6. P Lewis, author interview, 23 March 2016
7. Stamp, 'The Myth of Gillespie, Kidd & Coia', p 72; Proctor, 'The Architect's Intention', p 302
8. Glendinning, 'Icons', p 47
9. P Lewis and D Dubowitz (photography),'Animated Space', *Prospect*, Jan/Feb, 2003, p 27; T Abrahams, 'Keeping the Faith', *Prospect*, March 2016, p 27
10. G Stamp, 'God's Architects', *Scotsman*, 27 October 2007
11. Figures provided by NVA, 3 June 2016
12. G Benson, cited in P Hodgkinson and C Melhuish, 'Upholders of the Modern', review of lecture and exhibition, *Building Design*, 3 May 1996
13. R Kinloch,'Plans backed by Council, *Helensburgh Advertiser*. 27 January, 2000
14. Musgrave, 'Praying for a Miracle to Redeem St Peter's'
15. Fiona Holland, 'Last Rites for St Peter's?', May 1997, news cutting, author's files; Rory Murphy, 'A Dream in Ruins', *Helensburgh Advertiser*, 22 May 1997; K Nugent, 'In Praise and Remembrance', *Prospect*, June 1997, p 35; P Wilson, 'A Little Movement', *Manifesto*, 1997, pp 13–17
16. R Kinloch, '"Tragedy" for Cardross', *Helensburgh Advertiser*, 13 June 1996
17. 'What now for St Peter's?' *Helensburgh Advertiser*, 6 June 1996
18. Notes on meeting of 9 September 1997, attached to letter from K Crilley, Archdiocese of Glasgow, to Argyll and Bute Council, HES Files, HGG/A/SH/19, part 1
19. Ibid
20. J Hume, notes on meeting of 9 September 1997, attached to letter from K Crilley, Archdiocese of Glasgow, to Argyll and Bute Council, HES Files, HGG/A/SH/19, part 1
21. Ranald MacInnes later recalled that Historic Scotland's support of the consolidated ruin option was a 'big step forward, but it chimed with other international projects', and was generally accepted by heritage professional by 2012, correspondence with author, 3 June 2016
22. D Loan, notes on meeting of 18 August 1997, attached to letter from Archdiocese of Glasgow to Argyll and Bute Council, 20 August 1997, HES Files, HGG/A/SH/19, part 1
23. Ibid
24. Letter from Argyll and Bute Council to Historic Scotland, 23 September 1998, HES files, GG/A/SH/19, part 2
25. K Crilley, cited in Argyll and Bute Council, 'Minute of the Formal Planning Hearing of the Helensburgh and Lomond Committee' held at Gielston Hall, Cardross, 24 March 1999, HES files, HGG/A/SH/19, part 2
26. K Crilley, cited in A McNair, 'Planners Approve Bid to Save St Peter's College', *Lennox Herald*, 16 April 1999
27. K Crilley, cited in Argyll and Bute Council, 'Minute of the Formal Planning Hearing of the Helensburgh and Lomond Committee'
28. K Crilley, cited in McNair 'Planners Approve Bid to Save St Peter's College'
29. K Bell, 'Development Deal could Safeguard Historic College', *Helensburgh Advertiser*, 10 September 1998
30. Michael Wilson typescript report, incorporated in 'Statement of Case' by A J Scobie, Chair of Cardross Community Council, December 1999, HES files, HGG/A/SH/19, part 2. In a statement of historical fact, Wilson wrote: 'On the estate there were in total twenty-eight buildings, twelve inhabited by people and a total resident population of forty-five. To this can be added further staff who came in daily and frequent guests, since in the original Kilmahew House five of the ten bedrooms were for guests. Subsequently when St Peter's College was built and completed in 1965, Kilmahew House, the new College buildings and the two lodges were all in use. There was close contact between the College and the local community and I was myself a frequent visitor. At that time there was a resident teaching staff of twelve with up to five extra mural lecturers, together with five sisters, four maids, and up to fifty students, and large families in the two lodges. That made a total resident population in excess of eighty.'
31. A Eleftheriades, 'Village Divided over Plan', *Helensburgh Advertiser*, 8 April 1999; 'These housing plans fly in the face of logic', letter from Flora and Alistair Leckie, Cardross, to *Helensburgh Advertiser*, 22 April 1999
32. Eleftheriades, 'Village Divided over Plan'
33. A McNair 'Controversial New Plan to Save St Peter's College', *Lennox Herald*, 5 March 1999; G L Hearn Planning, '"Cardross Kilmahew Estate" Town & Country Planning (Scotland) Act 1997, Called in Application Statement of Case on behalf of Cardross Golf Club', 27 October 1999, HES files, HGG/A/SH/19, part 2
34. Mr Cockburn, cited in 'St Peter's College Enquiry', *Lennox Herald*, 28 January 2000
35. J Souness, 'Historic Buildings Inspectorate Statement of Case', 21 October 1999; letter from Scottish Executive to Historic Scotland, 1 September 1999, 'Note of the Pre-Inquiry Meeting held on 28 September 1999; A Mackechnie, note on file, 20 and 21 October 1999, all HES files, HGG/A/SH/19, part 2
36. A McLeod, senior planning officer, Argyll and Bute Council, quoted in 'Housing Plan for Village Hit by U-turn', *Helensburgh Advertiser*, 11 November 1999
37. 'Plans Backed by Council', *Helensburgh Advertiser*, 27 January, 2000; 'Church Loses Lengthy Battle over Architecturally-important Buildings', *The Herald*, 2 October 2000
38. 'Church Loses Lengthy Battle over Architecturally-important Buildings', *The Herald*, 2 October 2000
39. 'Latest in Series of 1960s Award-winning Catholic Buildings Plagued by Structural Faults', *The Herald*, 23 April 1996, p 4
40. D Toner, DTA, cited in 'Latest in Series of 1960s Award-winning Catholic Buildings Plagued by Structural Faults'; 'Another Listed Gillespie, Kidd & Coia Church Looks Set to be Demolished after a Feasibility Study Said it Would Cost £1.25 Million to Repair', *Architects' Journal*, 2 May 1996
41. 'Latest in Series of 1960s Award-winning Catholic Buildings Plagued by Structural Faults', *The Herald*, 23 April 1996, p 4
42. Sacred Heart received a phase 2 HLF Scotland grant of £112,500 on 28 September 1999
43. N Gillespie, 'Act of Faith', *Architects' Journal*, 12 April 2001. To help prioritise future Historic Scotland grant funding applications for Gillespie, Kidd & Coia listed buildings, and assess the broader heritage impact of these projects, Ranald MacInnes compiled a detailed review paper in 2002, which categorised the listed buildings into five groups. See R MacInnes, 'Setting Priorities for Gillespie, Kidd & Coia Buildings Priority List', 12 April 2002.
44. 'St Bride's East Kilbride: Report on Repair Programmes and Fundraising', June 2015; 'Funding Boost for Stallan – Brand Refurb of Scottish Church', *Building Design*, 7 October 2014
45. M Glendinning, 'Modern Heritage', *Prospect*, 2002, pp 30–2
46. Ibid
47. M Baines, 'Themes and Variations: The Postwar Designs of Gillespie, Kidd & Coia', *The Twentieth Century Society Newsletter*, winter 2004/5, pp 4–5
48. Cited in P Hodgkinson and C Melhuish, 'Upholders of the Modern', *Building Design*, 3 May, 1996. Metzstein, when asked about contemporary architectural awards in an interview of 2002, voiced scepticism and singled out Benson & Forsyth's Museum of Scotland which 'did not receive the recognition it deserved', A Forrest, 'MacMillan and Metzstein, In their Own Words', *Prospect*, 88, November/December 2002, pp 19–21
49. Alan Powers, 'Retrospective with a Didactic Approach', *Architects' Journal*, 16 May 1996, p 70
50. Stamp, 'The Myth of Gillespie, Kidd & Coia', pp 68–79, quotes, pp 68, 77
51. Forrest, 'MacMillan and Metzstein, In their Own Words'
52. R J Williams 'The Modernist Ruin' *Prospect*, March 2006, p 30
53. C Ednie 'A modern tragedy' *The Herald Magazine*, 7 February 2004
54. Letter from Classical House to Buildings at Risk Register, 29 January 2003, HES files, HGG/A/SH/19, part 3
55. *Prospect* started as the *Quarterly of the Incorporation of Architects in Scotland* in 1922, and adopted the new name in 1956 (the first new issue included a profile of Jack Coia; see Chapter 3). In 1978–85 it was co-edited by Mark Baines, who recalled that they 'always desperately looking for good buildings to put in but there weren't that many around'. In 1999 it moved publisher to the Carnyx group, and from 2009 it changed name again to *Urban Realm*; see A Chambers, 'Retrospective', *Prospect* , June 2004, pp 35–6
56. P Lewis, 'Prospectus', *Prospect*, March 2006, p 3
57. M Wade, 'Artistic Talent is Caught in Bowie's Web: The Best Work of Scottish Students Goes on Display to the World in Singer's Showcase of Modern Art', *Scotsman*, 29 March 2002
58. P Lewis and D Dubowitz, 'Animated Space', *Prospect*, Jan/Feb, 2003, pp 22–9; D Dubowitz, *Wastelands, The Presence of Absence: Three Sanctuaries, Cardross, Gorton, Sam Gimignano*, 2003
59. P Lewis, cited in P Lewis and D Dubowitz, 'Animated Space', p 27
60. 'Drunken Parties at the Seminary', *Daily Mail*, 1 March 2013. For a brief history of the seminary see *Drygrange: Twenty-five years*, 1978

61	*SPCM*, December 1966		89	Letter from C Zeidler, Twentieth Century Society, London, to Argyll and Bute Council, 15 September; letter from A Wilkinson, SAVE Britain's Heritage, London, to Argyll and Bute Council, 26 August 2004, HES files, HGG/A/SH/19
62	Deffenbaugh, 'Cardross', p 4			
63	E Harrison, 'Toby Paterson: New Facade, Architectural Studies', *Metro*, 15 April 2003; J Gilchrist, 'Temple to Ruined Dreams', *Scotsman*, 18 April 2003, pp 8–9; Paterson's artwork based on St Peter's was illustrated in 'A Seminal Moment', *Prospect*, 121, 2006, pp 16–17		90	Letter from Scottish Enterprise Dunbartonshire to Classical House, 6 October 2003; R MacInnes, 'St Peter's Seminary, Kilmahew, Cardross', 'Report on file', May 2006, HES files, HGG/A/SH/19, part 4
64	P Wilson, 'A Song at Twilight', *Building Design*, 25 June 2004; 'Cardross', *Prospect*, July 2004, p 4		91	Letter from SPBPT to Archbishop Conti, 8 October 2004
			92	Letter from SPBPT to Archbishop Conti, 22 September 2004
65	S Lyall, 'Devine Intervention', *Architects' Journal*, 18/25 December 2003, pp 46–7; letter from M McDonell, Soulis Technologies Ltd to R Emerson, Historic Scotland, 23 October 2003, HES files, HGG/A/SH/10, part 3; S Swain, 'Virtual Visions – But Could they Become Reality?', *Dumbarton & Vale of Leven Reporter*, 19 May 2004, pp 10–11; letter from F McAveety, MSP, Minister of Tourism, Culture & Sport, to Soulis Technologies Ltd, November 2003, HES files, HGG/A/SH/10		93	Letter from SPBPT to Archbishop Conti, 22 September 2004; following withdrawal, SPBPT set up a design team to look at alternatives to proposed treatment by Clyde Design Partnership, 'St Peter's Seminary Trust Object to Proposals to Stabilise College', *Prospect*, December 2004, p 4
			94	Letter from J Deffenbaugh to author, 23 December 2003
			95	Letter from P Lewis, *The Herald*, 29 November 2004; P Lewis, interview with author, 23 March 2016. In 2006 Abrahams stated 'it has been an excruciating two years for the trust'. T Abrahams, 'Keeping the Faith', *Prospect*, 121, 2006
66	Correspondence from James Simpson to Martin McDonell, 19 December 2003, author's copy			
67	Z Blackler, 'Modern Ruin Proposal for Derelict Cardross', 2003 journal cutting, author's files; Gilchrist, 'Temple to Ruined Dreams'		96	Russell, 'Even Dear Architectural Friends must Pass On'
			97	'Assessment of Development Appraisal for Outline Planning Consent for Development at Kilmahew Estate, Cardross, Report for Argyll & Bute Council', by Ryden, November 2005, HES files, HGG/A/SH/10, part 3
68	Author correspondence with A Farquhar, 9 June 2016			
69	Letter from J Deffenbaugh to author, 17 October 2003			
70	Deffenbaugh, 'Cardross', p 4; J Deffenbaugh, 'OK GO! Scotland's Youth Centre: The Regeneration of St Peter's College, Cardross', BA Architecture (Honours) Thesis Project, University of Dundee, 2003		98	Letter from G Murray, SPBPT, to K Crilley, 19 July 2005, HES files, HGG/A/SH/10, part 3
			99	Letter from M Cooper to J Deffenbaugh, 8 February 2006, HES files, HGG/A/SH/19, part 3; *Prospect*, 121, March 2006, p 5
71	Letter from J Deffenbaugh to author, 20 January 2004			
72	Letter from J Deffenbaugh to author, 10 February 2004		100	Johnston, 'Campaign Aims to Force Repair of "Best Building"'; *Observer*, 29 January 2006; *Prospect*, 121, March 2006; letter from C Zeidler to M Cooper, Historic Scotland, 12 December 2005, HES files, HGG/A/SH/19, part 3
73	M Russell, 'Even dear architectural friends must pass on' *The Herald*, 4 December 2004			
74	Listed building consent application lodged 5 July 2004 and Historic Scotland consulted formally on 12 August 2004; S Swain, 'New Hope for Future of St Peter's College, Cardross', *Helensburgh Advertiser*, 8 July 2004, p 8		101	Letter from G Murray to K Crilley, 19 July 2005; letter from C Zeidler to M Cooper, Historic Scotland, 12 December 2005; letter from SPBTP to HS, 23 March 2006, HES files, HGG/A/SH/19, part 3
75	Keppie Planning, 'Kilmahew Estate, Cardross, Supporting Planning Statement', June 2004, p 31; In 2002 the Argyll and Bute Structure Plan had a general clause inserted to enable development on Green Belt if supported a building recognised in the Buildings at Risk Register, and in 2003 the estate was identified as a Potential Development Area in the Consultative Draft Local Plan, but as a result of local objections the Kilmahew estate was deleted as a PDA. In the Argyll and Bute Local Plan of 2009, Kilmahew was identified as an Area for Action and remained as such in the 2015 plan, then considered a local 'potential regeneration/redevelopment' area, information received from Mark Lodge, Argyll and Bute Council, 19 May 2016; Swain, 'New Hope for Future of St Peter's College'		102	A Mead and C Sullivan (photographer), 'Cardross', *Architects' Journal*, 224, September 2006, pp 27–41
			103	Letter from Historic Scotland to Argyll and Bute Council, 14 March 2006; MacInnes, 'St Peter's Seminary, Kilmahew, Cardross'
			104	MacInnes, 'St Peter's Seminary, Kilmahew, Cardross'
			105	Ibid; letter from Archdiocese of Glasgow to Historic Scotland and Argyll and Bute Council, 26 April 2006, HES files, HGG/A/SH/19, part 4
76	The listed building applications were withdrawn from Argyll and Bute's legacy list of applications because they were out-of-date (on 13 August 2013), and also superseded by a new application form NVA, information from Angus Gilmore, Argyll and Bute Council, 16 May 2016; letter from SPBPT to J Allan, Avanti Architects, November 2007		106	'St Peter's Top of List', *Prospect,* November 2005; R Murphy, *Sunday Herald*, 27 July 2003, cited in Keppie Planning, 'Kilmahew Estate, Cardross, Supporting Planning Statement', June 2004, p 27
77	CDP, 'St Peter's College, Cardross, Proposed Consolidation and Reinstatement Works', October 2003; 'Saving Cardross', *Prospect*, June 2003, p 5		107	Johnston, 'Campaign Aims to Force Repair of "Best Building"'
			108	Ibid
78	Keppie Planning, 'Kilmahew Estate, Cardross, Supporting Planning Statement', June 2004, p 24–26		109	Abrahams, 'Keeping the Faith'
			110	Letter from SPBPT to J Allan, Avanti Architects, November 2007; letter from Jonathon Foyle, WMF Britain, to Historic Scotland, 27 September 2007; letter from Historic Scotland to WMF Britain, 5 October 2007, HES files, HGG/A/SH/19, part 4; 'College on Endangered List', *Dunoon Observer*, 22 October 2007
79	Letter from G Munro, Historic Scotland, to J Sheriden, 16 February 2004, included in Keppie Planning, 'Kilmahew Estate, Cardross, Supporting Planning Statement', June 2004, Appendix 7			
80	Notes on meeting of 9 September 1997, attached to letter from K Crilley, Archdiocese of Glasgow, to Argyll and Bute Council, HES Files, HGG/A/SH/19, part 1		111	'College on Endangered List', *Dunoon Observer*, 22 October 2007
			112	Gilchrist, 'Out of The Ruins?'
81	D Nicholson, 'Community Renovation Plans for Former Seminary', *Catholic Observer*, 9 July 2004; Gilchrist, 'Temple to Ruined Dreams'		113	M Baines, 'Themes and Variations: The Postwar Designs of Gillespie, Kidd & Coia', *The Twentieth Century Society Newsletter*, winter 2004/5, pp 4–5
82	C Zeidler and Patrick Duerden, 'What Future for St Peter's College?', *Twentieth Century Society, Newsletter*, winter 2004/5; J Johnston, 'Campaign Aims to Force Repair of "Best Building"', *Sunday Herald*, 12 February 2006, p 18		114	M Baines, 'Themes & Variations', in Rodger, *Gillespie, Kidd & Coia, Architecture, 1956–1987*, pp 48–69
			115	I Metzstein, author interview, 26 August 1996
83	Letter from A Wilkinson, SAVE Britain's Heritage, London, to Argyll and Bute Council, 26 August 2004; letter from C Zeidler, Twentieth Century Society, to Argyll and Bute Council, 15 September 2004, HES files, HGG/A/SH/19, part 3; letter from SPBPT, Edinburgh, to Archbishop Conti, 22 September 2004		116	Zeidler and Duerden, 'What Future for St Peter's College?', p 20; C Zeidler and P Duerden, 'Gillespie, Kidd & Coia in Context: Post War Architecture in and around Glasgow, The Twentieth Century Society, 22–24 April 2005', tour brochure, 2005. Walking tour by Clive Fenton
84	Gilchrist, 'Temple to Ruined Dreams'		117	Mead and Sullivan, 'Cardross'; N Barley, 'Cardross Seminary', *Urban Realm*, 20 December 2004
85	N Barley, 'Cardross Seminary', 20 December 2004, urbanrealm.com			
86	P Lewis, 'Why Save St Peter's?', *Prospect*, 121, 2006, pp 18–23; Stamp, 'God's Architects'		118	P Lewis, *Prospect*, June 2004, p 15
87	Correspondence from G Stamp to C Strang, 28 August 2004, HES files, HGG/A/SH/19, part 3		119	M Glendinning, R MacInnes and A Mackechnie, *History of Scottish Architecture*, 1996, pp 485–7; M Glendinning, 'Robert Matthew', *Prospect*, June 2004, pp 28–9; P Long and J Thomas (eds), *Basil Spence: Architect*, 2007; L Campbell, M Glendinning and J Thomas (eds), *Basil Spence: Buildings and Projects*, 2012; M Glendinning, *Modern Architect: The Life and Times of Robert Matthew*, 2008
88	Letter from C Zeidler, Twentieth Century Society, London, to Argyll and Bute Council, 15 September, HES files, HGG/A/SH/19			

Chapter 6 continued

120 I Metzstein, interview with Robert Proctor, 3 November 2004, in Proctor, 'The Architect's Intention', p 302

121 Cited in Zeidler and Duerden, 'What Future for St Peter's College?'

122 Proctor, *Building the Modern Church*

123 Proctor, 'The Architect's Intention', pp 296–307

124 Ibid, p 299

125 Correspondence from G Stamp to M Glendinning, 5 November 2007; Ranald MacInnes also recalled 'Andy MacMillan commented to me once that "[Norman] Foster controls every word that is written about him"', author correspondence, 3 June 2016

126 I Metzstein, interview with author, 26 August 1996

127 Wilson, 'A Song at Twilight'

128 Lewis, 'Why Save St Peter's?'

129 'St Peter's Architect Celebrated', *The List*, 2 October 2006

130 N Barley, cited in Rodger, *Gillespie, Kidd & Coia: Architecture*

131 This approach partly resulted from an acrimonious restructuring of the authorship team in 2006, removing almost all historians or non-GSA participants. See also A MacMillan, L McDermott, 'Architects of Misfortune?', *Big Issue*, 1–7 November 2007

132 C Coyle, 'Design Archives', *Homes & Interiors Scotland*, October 2007; Colin St John Wilson, 'The Holy Alliance', *Architects' Journal*, 25 October 2007, pp 53–4; 'Concrete propositions', *Metro*, 2 November 2007, p 31

133 G Benson, cited in Glendinning, 'Icons'; I Gale, 'Enlightenment at the Altar of Modernism', *Scotland on Sunday*, 18 November 2007

134 Stamp, 'God's Architects'

135 Avanti Architects, 'St Peter's Seminary, Conservation Assessment', final draft, October 2007, p 14

136 J Rodger, 'Towards the MacMillan and Metzstein Years', in Rodger, *Gillespie, Kidd & Coia: Architecture*, pp 11, 21

137 M Glendinning 'Icons', *Prospect*, Issue 129, 2007, p 47. Lewis reported that one sole 'architectural heretic' had written in the visitor book that Gillespie, Kidd & Coia 'were a gross failure given that most of their buildings were obsolete and decrepit', cited in P Lewis, *Prospect*, Issue 129, p 1

138 Glendinning, 'Icons'

139 S Mansfield, 'Misinterpreted Blueprints', *Scotsman*, 16 November 2007, pp 6–7

140 Letter from C Zeidler, Twentieth Century Society, to R MacInnes, 17 August 2004; in 2005 Gordon Murray urged the Archdiocese to carry out a 'comprehensive feasibility study', letter from G Murray to K Crilley, 19 July 2005; the report was originally estimated at £30,000 but further grant funding was sought to meet the costs, note on file, October 2006 and 11 February 2010, all HES files, HGG/A/SH/19, part 3 and 4

141 Letter from R MacInnes to K Crilley, 6 June 2006, HES files, HGG/A/SH/19 (loose file)

142 Lewis, 'Why Save St Peter's?', p 19; P Lewis, author interview, 23 March 2016

143 Avanti Architects, 'St Peter's Seminary, Conservation Assessment', October 2007

144 Ibid, pp 16–18

145 Ibid, pp 17, 103

146 Ibid, pp 143, 132–52

147 Ibid, pp 18–19

148 Ibid, p 14

149 Ibid

150 Letter from SPBPT to J Allan, Avanti Architects, November 2007; Dubowitz left for Italy, Deffenbaugh graduated and Lewis started teaching at the Scott Sutherland School of Architecture in Aberdeen

151 Note on file, 24 December 2009, HES files, HGG/A/SH/19 (loose file)

152 Correspondence from Buildings at Risk, Scottish Civic Trust to Argyll and Bute Council, 15 September 2008, HES files, HGG/A/SH/19, part 4

153 P Miller, 'Marquis Wants to Save A-list Seminary', *The Herald*, 14 November 2007; R Olcayato, 'Will Bute Battle Bloxham for Cardross?', *Building Design*, 9 November 2007, pp 8–9

154 P Miller 'Church willing to sell A-listed building for a nominal sum', *The Herald*, 11 December 2008

155 Letter from Historic Scotland to K Crilley, 26 October 2007; letter from Urban Splash to Historic Scotland, 12 November 2007, HGG/A/SH/19, part 4

156 P Miller, 'Church Willing to Sell A-listed Building for a Nominal Sum', *The Herald*, 11 December 2008

157 P Miller, 'Developer Puts in Offer to Give St Peter's a Makeover', *The Herald*, 2 November 2007, p 10

158 Miller, 'Church Willing to Sell A-listed Building for a Nominal Sum'

159 T Kemp, 'Saviour Found for Derelict Seminary', *Lennox Herald*, 2 January 2009; Urban Splash, 'St Peter's Seminary', 2008–9; note on file, March 2010, HES files, HGG/A/SH/19 (loose file)

160 Author correspondence with A Farquhar, 9 June 2016

161 Miller, 'Church Willing to Sell A-listed Building for a Nominal Sum'

162 Letter from A Farquhar to L Fabiani, 24 March 2008, HES files, HGG/A/SH/19 (loose file). A London-based arts educational organisation ACAVA had also shown an interest in the former ruin in late 2007, note on file, 13 November 2007, HES files, HGG/A/SH/19 (loose file)

163 HLF Scotland press release, '£4.2m funding to save St Peter's College', 23 March 2016, hlf.org.uk

164 Figures from NVA, 3 June 2016

165 Isi Metzstein, *The Times*, 18 January 2012; 'Isi Metzstein', *The Guardian*, 23 January 2012; A MacMillan, 'Isi and I' and 'An Amazing Mastery of Light: A Celebration of the Architecture of MacMillan/St Peter's and Metzstein', *RIAS Quarterly*, spring 2012, pp 33, 34–43; 'The Master: A Tribute to Andy MacMillan', *Building Design*, 18 August 2014; J Macauley 'Professor Andy MacMillan', *Architectural Heritage Society of Scotland Magazine*, autumn 2014, p 5; 'RIAS Honours Partners of MacMillan and Metzstein at Ceremony in NMS', *Architects' Journal*, 6 November 2014; G Benson, 'Andrew MacMillan', Twentieth Century Society Magazine, 2015, p 63

166 R Roscher, cited in 'St Peter's: Seminal Seminary', *Urban Realm*, 9 July 2015

167 Note on file, November 2009, HES files HGG/A/SH/19 (loose file)

168 'St Peter's, Cardross', note on file, 21 December 2011, p 9, HES files, HGG/A/SH/1197, part 1; A Farquhar, G van Noord and R Roscher, 'Kilmahew/St Peter's Commission Plan', May 2010

169 Farquhar, van Noord and Roscher, 'Kilmahew/St Peter's Commission Plan'; ERZ Limited, 'Kilmahew/St Peter's, Preliminary Draft Report', August 2011; and ERZ Limited 'Kilmahew/St Peter's, Masterplan Summary Document', November 2011

170 Author correspondence with A Farquhar, 9 June 2016

171 J Glenday,' Hinterland: Seeing the Light', *Urban Realm*, 22 April 2016

172 ERZ Limited, 'Kilmahew/St Peter's, Masterplan Summary Document', pp 22–5

173 *Helensburgh Advertiser*, 18 April 2012

174 NVA and Avanti Architects, 'Kilmahew/St Peter's, Cardross, Design Statement, Application for Planning and Listed Building Consent', January 2013; 'Kilmahew/St Peter's, Cardross, Schedule of Works Planning Submission', 28 November 2012

175 NVA, 'Kilmahew/St Peter's, Cardross, Design Statement, Application for Planning and Listed Building Consent', January 2013

176 G van Noord (ed), *To Have and Hold: Future of a Contested Landscape*, 2011, p 51; note on file, 24 September 2009 and 24 December 2009, HES files, HGG/A/SH/19 (loose file)

177 A Farquhar, quoted in 'Lottery Cash to Save St Peter's Seminary in Cardross', BBC News online 5 December 2013, www.bbc.co.uk/news/uk-scotland-glasgow-west

178 *Helensburgh Advertiser*, 23 January, 2014

179 G Stamp, 'St Peter's Seminary in Cardross – Better Off a Ruin?', *Apollo Magazine*, 10 October 2015

180 The project was funded through Grigor's Lighthouse Achievement Award in 2005 and a Creative Scotland Award in 2006, Grigor, *Space and Light Revisited*

181 '£4.2m funding to save St Peter's College', 23 March 2016, hlf.org.uk

182 G Murray, 'Beyond Venice', and I Gilzean, in 'Conservation and Preservation (debate excerpts)', in van Noord, *To Have and to Hold*, pp 36, 50; J Allan, 'Poetry and Pragmatism, Restoring St Peter's Seminary', in van Noord, *To Have and to Hold*, p 28; E Hollis in conservation with A Farquhar (June 2011), in van Noord, *To Have and to Hold*, p 54; E Hollis, 'Anxious Care and Unsightly Aids', in van Noord, *To Have and to Hold*, p 108

183 R Moore, 'St Peter's Seminary – A Second Coming for Scotland's Modernist Masterpiece?', *Guardian*, 17 January 2015

184 I Gilzean, 'To Have and to Hold', in van Noord, *To Have and to Hold*, p 112

185 NVA, 'Hinterland, Kilmahew/St Peter's, A Future Reclaimed', leaflet, 2016

186 'St Peter's: Seminal Seminary', *Urban Realm*, 9 July 2015, urbanrealm.com

187 A Farquhar in conservation with E Hollis (June 2011), in van Noord, *To Have and to Hold*, p 100

188 I Gilzean, author interview, 13 May 2016

189 A Farquhar, in van Noord, *To Have and to Hold*, p 82; author correspondence with A Farquhar, 9 June 2016; 'St Peter's Seminary Subject of Heritage Talk', *Helensburgh Advertiser*, 2 February 2015

190 Note on file, 24 September 2009, HES files (HGG/A/SH/19 loose file)

191 C Ramaswamy, 'Saving St Peter's Seminary', *Scotsman*, 2 September 2011, pp 20–1; P Miller, '£450,000 Grant could Help Save A-listed Seminary', *The Herald*, 29 April 2009

192 Miller, '£450,000 Grant could Help Save A-listed Seminary'

193 'Cash Boost for Seminary', *Helensburgh Advertiser*, 18 April 2012; 'Helensburgh Councillors Approve Funding for Seminary', *Helensburgh Advertiser*, 21 January 2014; 'Cardross Seminary to Host Arts Festival', *Helensburgh Advertiser*, 15 February 2015

194 'Work on Historic Woods Start', *Helensburgh Advertiser*, 20 May 2010; 'Cardross Seminary Plans are On Track', *Helensburgh Advertiser*, 31 August 2013

195 Moore, 'St Peter's Seminary – A Second Coming?'

196 J Glenday, 'Hinterland: Seeing the Light', *Urban Realm*, 22 April 2016

197 'Hinterland Effect', *Helensburgh Advertiser*, 24 March 2016

198 A Farquhar, 'Hinterland, St Peter's', *Architectural Heritage Society of Scotland Magazine*, spring 2016, pp 15–18

199 A Farquhar, 'The Hinterland Manifesto', in NVA, 'Hinterland, Kilmahew/St Peter's, A Future Reclaimed', 2016

200 Glenday, 'Hinterland: Seeing the Light', *Urban Realm*, 22 April 2016

201 Glenday, 'Hinterland: Seeing the Light'; for more specialist performance art reviews see M Begg, 'NVA: Hinterland', *Total Theatre*, 18–27 March 2016, totaltheatre.org.uk, and C Berger, 'Performance Review: Hinterland, NVA', *Scottish Journal of Performance*, June 2016, pp 125–9

202 J MacMillan, 'Visual Art Review: Hinterland, St Peter's Seminary, Cardross', *Scotsman*, 21 March 2016

203 A Radcliffe, 'Review: Hinterland – St Peter's Seminary, Cardross', *The Times*, 21 March 2016

204 M Brown, 'Hinterland Celebrates the Beauty of a Derelict Architectural Masterpiece – Review', *Telegraph*, 20 March 2016; E Hopkirk, 'High Rise and Hinterland: Modernism's Morality Plays', *Building Design*, 24 March 2016; M Wade, 'Masterpiece Shines out of Darkness', *The Times*, 11 March 2016

205 Glenday, 'Hinterland: Seeing the Light'

206 L Gardner, 'Hinterland Review – Alchemy of Light and Sound brings St Peter's Back to Life', *Guardian*, 22 March 2016

207 J Alexander Durnan, 'To Ruin a Ruin?', *The Drouth*, 55, summer 2016, pp 28–35

208 See above reviews, and see also: 'Cardross Seminary Ruins to Host Public Arts Festival', *Helensburgh Advertiser*, 15 December 2015; D Pollock, 'Hinterland, St Peter's Review', *Big Issue*, 23 March 2016; C Massie, 'The Embarrassing Story of Scotland's Most Important Twentieth Century Structure', *The Spectator*, 27 February 2016; L Campbell, 'Hinterland gets Festival off to a Dramatic Start', *The List*, 21 March 2016

209 I Gilzean interview with author, 13 May 2016; cited in 'Hinterland', bbc.co.uk/news/uk-scotland-glasgow-west-35833744, 18 March 2016; Glenday, 'Hinterland: Seeing the Light'

210 *Helensburgh Advertiser*, 2 February 2015; edition.cnn.com, January 2015

211 '£4.2m funding to save St Peter's College', 23 March 2016, hlf.org.uk

212 'Hinterland effect', *Helensburgh Advertiser*, 24 March 2016

213 Glenday, 'Hinterland: Seeing the Light'

214 A Farquhar, 'Hinterland, St Peter's', *Architectural Heritage Society of Scotland Magazine*, spring 2016, pp 15–18

Conclusion

1 Author interview with I Metzstein, 26 August 1996

2 GKC practice archive, undated paper by Metzstein, 'The Land of Green Ginger'; interview with Metzstein, 26 August 1996

3 Interview with I Metzstein, 26 August 1996

4 *Independent*, 21 December 1994, p 22; *The Herald*, 29 October 1994

Timeline

Archbishops of Glasgow since 1922

1922–43 Archbishop Donald Mackintosh

1945–63 Archbishop Donald A Campbell

1964–74 Archbishop James Donald Scanlan

1974–2001 Archbishop Thomas Joseph Winning

2002–12 Archbishop Mario Conti

2012–present Archbishop Philip Tartaglia

Cardross Seminary Chronology since 1945

1945
Evacuation of students and staff from St Peter's College, Bearsden, to St Joseph's College, Mill Hill, England, to allow repairs to be made.

23 May 1946
Destruction of St Peter's College, Bearsden, by fire during dry rot repairs.

5 October 1946
Move of students and staff to Darleith House.

1948
Abortive bid, by Archbishop MacDonald of St Andrews and Edinburgh, to buy the Royal Hotel, St Andrews, for conversion into a national seminary and training college for male Catholic teachers. The Archdiocese of Glasgow acquires Kilmahew House and estate.

16 September 1948
Move of theology students to Kilmahew House (leaving philosophy students still at Darleith).

April 1953
Beginning of discussions between Jack Coia and the Archdiocese on extension to Kilmahew House; first (unrealised) scheme by Coia and McRoberts.

April 1956
Continuing discussion between Gillespie, Kidd & Coia (GKC) and Archbishop Campbell over initial scheme.

June 1959
Preparation of GKC drawings for second design.

February 1960
Exploration work under supervision of W V Zinn, consultant engineers.

1 March 1960
Arrival of machinery for construction of retaining wall.

June 1960
Construction of model.

October 1960
Transplantation of trees from site by students.

30 November 1960
Cutting of first sod by Archbishop Campbell.

17 April 1961
Beginning of construction of retaining wall, by contractors Hunter & Clark.

May 1961
Official appointment of Zinn as engineers for project.

July 1961
Alterations (to reduce cost) to design of sanctuary block.

November 1961
Alterations (to reduce cost) to design of main block; reduction in total estimated cost from £486,010 to £349,800.

8 November 1961
Completion of retaining wall.

25 December 1961
Convocation of Second Vatican Council.

January 1962
Beginning of structural revisions to classroom block.

29 April 1962
Commencement of pile driving.

15 June 1962
Acceptance of main building contract by James Laidlaw & Sons.

January 1963
Further alteration to sanctuary designs.

24 January 1963
Death of Monsignor Treanor, Rector of St Peter's College.

March 1963
Appointment of Father Michael Connolly as Rector.

April 1963
Move of Father McRoberts from his post at St Peter's to St Charles, Carstairs.

April 1963
Completion of main block foundations, and beginning of construction of first floor; delay to work by bad weather.

22 July 1963
Death of Archbishop Campbell.

August 1963
Alteration of convent block design.

August 1964
Beginning of alteration work to existing house.

September 1964
Completion of shell of main block.

8 September 1964
Laying of foundation stone in sanctuary by Archbishop Scanlan.

late 1964
Beginning of internal fitting out of convent block.

April 1965
Introduction of overtime working by Laidlaw to accelerate work.

12 April 1965
Progress visit by Archbishop Scanlan.

8 December 1965
End of Second Vatican Council.

18 March 1966
Complaints by Laidlaw about lack of detailed drawings.

April 1966
Alterations to stable block.

May 1966
Screening of BBC documentary *Four Modern Buildings*.

1 October 1966
Beginning of use of new buildings (except classroom block) by students and staff.

30 November 1966
Inauguration ceremony and solemn opening of St Peter's.

February–December 1967
Further alteration to Kilmahew House.

2 April 1967
Opening of classroom block (with exception of the library).

21 September 1967
Coffins of Archbishop Eyre and Archbishop Campbell re-interred at St Peter's College, Cardross.

19 October 1967
RIBA Bronze Regional Award to GKC for design of college.

29 November 1969
Receipt by architects of final claim from clerk of works.

March 1971
Vatican announcement that 13,450 Catholic priests had abandoned the priesthood between 1964 and 1967.

22 June 1971
Final cost statement from McLernan & Whyte, quantity surveyors (£609,805 5s 8d, including £574,575 due to the main contractors), along with claim for prolongation of £23,928 16s 9d.

22 October 1971
Settlement of final certificate (but not prolongation claim) by diocese.

1971
Kilmahew House listed at Category B.

1972
Appointment of Monsignor McMahon as Rector (in succession to Father Connolly). Documentary film *Space and Light* produced by Murray Grigor.

May 1972
Conclusion of negotiations over finalisation of architects' account.

7 April 1973
Report by Monsignor McMahon on water ingress and other problems with new college.

September 1974
Collapse of roof over stairway in classroom block.

14 November 1974
Statement by GKC to Archdiocese, disclaiming 'professional liability' for problems of building.

24 December 1974
Promise by GKC to start repair work in early 1975.

September 1975
Withdrawal of Motherwell Diocese's students from Cardross, to attend Drygrange Seminary.

25 March 1976
Death of Archbishop Scanlan.

November 1979
Decision in principle to close Cardross Seminary; application by First Hospitality Corporation of America for change of use of the complex to a hotel.

February 1980
Official closure of St Peter's College; re-housing of Glasgow Province Seminary in the former Convent of the Franciscan Nuns of the Immaculate Conception, Briar Road, Newlands.

March 1980
Planning application (later withdrawn) for change of use to conference centre.

May 1980
Withdrawal of First Hospitality Corporation of America's planning application and offer of purchase.

August 1981
Death of Jack Coia.

1983
Archdiocese submits application to part demolish former seminary buildings (refused 1984).

1983–7
Former Cardross seminary buildings used by the diocese as a drug rehabilitation and detoxification centre.

1 November 1985
Opening of new interdiocesan Chesters College, Bearsden, responsible for training priests for the whole country except St Andrews and Edinburgh, and Aberdeen.

1986
Publication of *Jack Coia: His Life and Work*.

1987
Closure of drug rehabilitation centre in former seminary, owing to deterioration of building.

September 1987
Statutory listing of St Paul's Church, Glenrothes (1956): the first post-war GKC building to be listed.

1990
Archdiocese submits two applications: one to convert the main block into flats, and one to demolish the seminary buildings (both withdrawn). Former seminary buildings added to the Scottish Civic Trust's Buildings at Risk Register. Kilmahew House is damaged by fire.

1992
Preparation of (abortive) plans by the Walker Group for marketing and restoration of Cardross complex. DOCOMOMO Scotland formed.

22 September 1992
Upgrading of the former St Peter's College by Historic Scotland from Category B to Category A.

October 1993
Archdiocese, in partnership with Classical House, submits two conjoined applications: the first to convert the main block into six townhouses (including demolition of convent block) with 60 new houses to be built in the grounds; the second, to retain the former seminary buildings as a consolidated ruin pending future re-use, and 24 new houses in the grounds.

4 October 1993
Redesignation of Chesters College as Scotus College, national seminary for the whole of Scotland (closed 2009).

February 1993
Death of John Cowell.

May 1994
Both planning applications of 1993 refused, but Dumbarton District Council approved the consolidated-ruin proposal option (not acted upon).

September 1994
Market Assessment Report compiled by EDAW CR Planning for Dunbartonshire Enterprise.

November 1994
Permission to demolish Kilmahew House (gutted by fire in May) given by Dumbarton District Council.

1994
Publication of the first *Mac Journal*, devoted to GKC. Heritage Lottery Fund established.

March 1996
Appeal against the rejection of the 1993 application for 22 new houses refused.

1997
Publication of *Cardross Seminary: Gillespie, Kidd & Coia and the Architecture of Postwar Catholicism* by RCAHMS.

1997
Maintenance masterplan of former seminary and estate by Page and Park and landscape architects Ian White Associates (not actioned).

August 1998
Archdiocese and Classical House submit application for formation of 33 new house plots and new country park. Repairs to make safe the ruined seminary buildings proposed.

January 2000
Public enquiry held at Geilston Hall, Cardross, to hear evidence on the 1998 application (finally refused by Scottish Ministers in August 2000).

June 2001
Death of Cardinal Thomas Winning.

January 2004
Cardross Regeneration Trust (later renamed the St Peter's Building Preservation Trust, SPBPT) formed.

5 July 2004
Archdiocese and Classical House submit a three part planning proposal comprising: 28 new houses; the stabilisation of the former seminary buildings (report compiled by Clyde Design Partnership); and the creation of a community park with restoration of two listed bridges.

October 2004
SPBPT publicly withdraw support for the Archdiocese 2004 application.

Timeline

November 2005
The ruined Cardross voted by *Prospect* readers as Scotland's 'most important post-war building'.

November 2005
Two independent reports (by Montagu Evans, and Ryden) concluded that the applicants' 2004 stabilisation costings for the ruined seminary were not robust.

March 2006
Historic Scotland refuse 2004 listed building consent (new housing and park proposals eventually withdrawn in 2013).

January 2007
Historic Scotland fund a conservation report on the ruined seminary. Avanti Architects commissioned to carry out this work by the Archdiocese.

June 2007
SPBPT successfully nominate the ruined Cardross for inclusion in the World Monument Fund's 100 most endangered sites.

November 2007 – February 2008
Exhibition *Gillespie Kidd & Coia, Architecture, 1956–1987*, held at the national Scottish architecture centre, the Lighthouse in Glasgow (catalogue published 2007).

2007
Classical House withdraw from future development of the former seminary.

October 2008
St Peter's Seminary Conservation Assessment produced by Avanti Architects.

2008
Developers Urban Splash develop two schemes to re-use the ruined seminary as a hotel, and health and sports centre (withdrew interest in 2009 owing to global financial crisis). Public arts charity NVA curate public art element of unrealised schemes.

March 2008
NVA independently propose idea of the part-restored/part-ruined seminary buildings and the estate landscape becoming a publicly funded art venue.

2009
Murray Grigor's film *Space and Light Revisited* screened.

2009
NVA receive Scottish Arts Council grant to explore the potential of the ruined seminary as an arts venue: produce the Kilmahew/St Peter's Commission Plan in May 2010.

2010 – May 2016
Kilmahew/St Peter's project awarded a total of £7.45 million of funding from public bodies, including Argyll and Bute Council, Cosla, Creative Scotland, Heritage Lottery Fund, Historic Scotland and Scottish Government. In this period it also received £2.67 million in private donations.

November 2010
'To Have and to Hold' debate devoted to the ruined seminary (curated by NVA), forms part of the 12th Venice Architectural Biennale.

2011
Ownership (in principle) passed from Archdiocese to NVA.

2011
To Have and to Hold: Future of A Contested Landscape published.

2011
Kilmahew/St Peter's academic research network the Invisible College begins a three-year programme.

November 2011
Kilmahew/St Peter's, Masterplan Summary Document produced.

January 2012
Death of Isi Metzstein.

January 2013
Kilmahew/St Peter's, Cardross, Design Statement produced. NVA planning and listed building consent applications approved.

August 2014
Death of Andy MacMillan.

November 2014
Avanti Architects, ERZ Landscape Architects and NORD Architecture appointed as Kilmahew/St Peter's design team.

June 2015
Work begins on clearing and environmentally cleaning the former seminary buildings and site by contractors Reigart.

18–27 March 2016
The public art event *Hinterland* staged by NVA.

Select Bibliography

Religious and Social History

P F Anson, *The Catholic Church in Modern Scotland*, London, 1935

R Boyle and P Lynch (eds), *Out of the Ghetto? The Catholic Community in Modern Scotland*, Edinburgh, 1998

J M Bradley, *Ethnic and Religious Identity in Modern Scotland*, Aldershot, 1995

C G Brown, *Religion and Society in Twentieth-Century Britain*, London and New York, 2006

C G Brown, *Religion and Society in Modern Scotland*, Edinburgh, 1997

C G Brown, *The Death of Christian Britain*, London and New York, 2001

S Bruce, A Glendinning, I Paterson and M Rosie, *Sectarianism in Scotland*, Edinburgh, 2004

J Cooney, *Scotland and the Papacy*, Edinburgh, 1982

J Cumming and P Burns (eds), *The Church Now*, Dublin, 1980

J Darragh, *The Catholic Hierarchy of Scotland*, Glasgow, 1986

T M Devine (ed), *Irish Immigrants and Scottish Society in the Nineteenth and Twentieth Centuries*, Edinburgh, 1990

T M Devine (ed), *St Mary's Hamilton – a Social History*, Edinburgh, 1995

T M Devine (ed), *Scotland's Shame? Bigotry and Sectarianism in Modern Scotland*, Edinburgh, 2000

A Dickson and J H Treble (eds), *People and Society in Scotland III*, Edinburgh, 1992

D Forrester and D Murray (eds), *Studies in the History of Worship in Scotland*, Edinburgh, 1984

T Gallagher, *Glasgow, the Uneasy Peace*, Manchester, 1987

C Harvie, *No Gods and Precious Few Heroes*, Edinburgh, 1981

J Highet, *The Scottish Churches*, London, 1960

S K Kehoe, *Creating a Scottish Catholic Church: Catholicism, Gender and Ethnicity in Nineteenth-Century Scotland*, Manchester, 2010

R P McBrien, *Catholicism* (2 vols), London, 1980

R P McBrien (ed), *Encyclopedia of Catholicism*, New York, 1995

M McHugh, The Development of the Catholic Community in the Western Province, 1878–1962 (PhD thesis, University of Strathclyde), Glasgow, 1990

C Maclean and K Veitch (eds) *Religion: Scottish Life and Society, A Compendium of Scottish Ethnology*, East Linton, 2006

D McRoberts (ed), *Modern Scottish Catholicism, 1878–1978*, Glasgow, 1979

G Scott-Moncrieff, *Catholic Edinburgh*, Glasgow, 1961

M T R B Turnbull, *Cardinal Gordon Joseph Gray: A Biography*, Edinburgh, 1994

B Wicker, *Culture and Liturgy*, London and New York, 1963

Architectural History

N Bingham, E Harwood, K Powell and A Powers, *The Twentieth Century Church*, Exhibition booklet, 1997

Archdiocese of Chicago, *Environment and Art in Catholic Worship*, Chicago, 1986

L Campbell, *Coventry Cathedral*, Oxford and New York, 1996

L Campbell, M Glendinning and J Thomas (eds), *Basil Spence: Buildings & Projects*, London, 2012

R Close and A Riches, *The Buildings of Scotland: Ayrshire and Arran*, New Haven and London, 2012

K Cruft, J Dunbar and R Fawcett, *The Buildings of Scotland: Borders*, New Haven and London, 2006

A L Drummond, *The Church Architecture of Protestantism,* Edinburgh, 1934

J Gifford, *The Buildings of Scotland: Fife*, Harmondsworth, 1988

J Gifford, *The Buildings of Scotland: Perth and Kinross*, New Haven and London, 2007

J Gifford, *The Buildings of Scotland: Dundee and Angus*, New Haven and London, 2012

J Gifford, *The Buildings of Scotland: Highlands and Islands*, Harmondsworth, 1992

J Gifford, *The Buildings of Scotland: Dumfries and Galloway*, Harmondsworth, 1996

J Gifford and F A Walker, *The Buildings of Scotland: Stirling and Central Scotland*, New Haven and London, 2002

J Gifford, C McWilliam and D Walker, *The Buildings of Scotland: Edinburgh*, Harmondsworth, 1984

M Glendinning, *Rebuilding Scotland: The Post War Vision, 1945–1975*, East Linton, 1997

M Glendinning, *Modern Architect: The Life and Times of Robert Matthew*, London, 2008

M Glendinning and A Mackechnie, *Scottish Architecture*, London, 2004

M Glendinning, R MacInnes, A MacKechnie, *A History of Scottish Architecture,* Glasgow, 1996

J Gold, *The Practice of Modernism: Modern Architect and Urban Transformation, 1954–1972*, London and New York, 2007

P Hammond, *Towards a Church Architecture,* London, 1962

G Hay, *The Architecture of Scottish Post-Reformation Churches,* Oxford, 1957

K Kaspar, *New German Architecture,* London, 1956

G E Kidder Smith, *The New Churches of Europe,* London, 1964

I G Lindsay, *The Scottish Parish Kirk,* Edinburgh, 1960

P Long and J Thomas (eds), *Basil Spence: Architect*, Edinburgh, 2008

J Macaulay and C Hermansen (eds), *Mac Journal One: Gillespie Kidd & Coia,* Glasgow, 1994

R Maguire and K Murray, *Modern Churches of the World*, London, 1965

C McKean, *The Scottish Thirties,* Edinburgh, 1987

Colin McWilliam, *The Buildings of Scotland: Lothian*, Harmondsworth, 1978

E D Mills, *The Modern Church,* London, 1956

National Monuments Record of Scotland, Reginald Fairlie manuscript collection, 1933–55

P Nuttgens, *Reginald Fairlie,* Edinburgh, 1959

R Proctor, *Building the Modern Church: Roman Catholic Church Architecture in Britain, 1955 to 1975*, Farnham, 2014

J Rodger (ed), *Gillespie, Kidd & Coia: Architecture 1956–1987,* Glasgow, 2008

R W K C Rogerson, *Jack Coia,* Edinburgh, 1986

B Schotz, *Bronze in my Blood,* Edinburgh, 1981

F A Walker, *The Buildings of Scotland: Argyll and Bute*, New Haven and London, 2002

D M Watters, *Cardross Seminary: Gillespie, Kidd & Coia and the Architecture of Postwar Catholicism*, Edinburgh, 1997

E Williamson, A Riches and M Higgs, *The Buildings of Scotland: Glasgow,* New Haven and London, 1990

St Peter's College: Practice Drawing List

This list of drawings (1960–7) was compiled by the author in 1996. The archive was gifted by Isi Metzstein and Andy MacMillan to Glasgow School of Art in May 2001 and is now housed in the school's archives.

Key to List

UNC – unclassified drawing

n/t – no title

n/s – no scale

f.s. – full scale

p – pencil

i – ink

ci – coloured ink

cp – coloured pencil

[All drawings are on tracing paper, except where indicated]

Main Block and General Complex

number	date	description
KS133	Mar 1961	Insc: 'elevations, boundary wall retaining 1/8" ' [p/i]
KS134	Mar 1961	Insc: 'plan of retaining wall 1/16" ' [p/1]
KS134	Mar 1961	Insc: 'plan of retaining wall, revised Oct 1961 1/16" ' [p/i]
CC600000	Dec 1961	Insc: 'block plan & site plan 1/16" ' [p/1]
CC600001	Dec 1961	Insc: 'cloister floor plan 1/8" ' [p/i]
CC600001A	Dec 1961	Insc: 'library floor plan' [i]
CC600002	Dec 1961	Insc: 'ground floor plan 1/8" ' [i]
	Dec 1961	Insc: 'common room plan 1/8" ' [i]
CC600002A	Dec 1961	Insc: 'first floor plan 1/8" ' [i]
CC600003A	Dec 1961	Insc: 'classroom floor plan' [i]
CC600004	Dec 1961	Insc: 'second floor plan 1/8" ' [i]
CC600005	Dec 1961	Insc: 'third floor plan 1/8" ' [i]
CC600001	Jun 1964	Insc: 'cloister floor plan 1/8" ' [p/i]
CC600002	Jun 1964	Insc: 'ground floor plan 1/8" ' [p/i]
CC600003	Jun 1964	Insc: 'first floor plan 1/8" ' [p/i]
CC600004	Jun 1964	Insc: 'second floor plan 1/8" " [p/i]
CC600005	Jun 1964	Insc: 'third floor plan 1/8" ' [p/i]
CC600007	Dec 1961	Insc: 'section through chapel' [p/i]
CC600008	Dec 1961	Insc: 'section through sanctuary 1/8" ' [p/i]
CC600009	Dec 1961	Insc: 'section through refectory, section C-C 1/8" ' [pi]
CC600010	Dec 1961	Insc: 'key section A-A' [p/i]
CC600011	Dec 1961	Insc: 'section though classroom 1/8" ' [p/i]
CC600012	Dec 1961	Insc: 'east elevation 1/8" ' [p/i]
CC600013	Dec 1961	Insc: 'south elevation 1/8" ' [p/i]
CC600014	Dec 1961	Insc: 'west elevation 1/8" ' [i]
CC600015	Dec 1961	Insc: 'north elevation 1/8" ' [p/i]
CC600017	Mar 1962	Insc: 'setting-out plan, piling' [p/i]
CC600018	Jun 1962	Insc: 'excavation, foundation & retaining layout 1/8" ' [p/i]
CC600032	Jul 1962	Insc: 'section showing existing ground levels' [p/i]
CC600033	Jun 1962	Insc: 'section showing existing ground level' [p/i]
CC600048	Oct 1962	Insc: 'west side chapels, plans, sections & elevations 1/4" ' [p/i]
CC600054	Nov 1962	Insc: 'section, ground floor slab 1/4–1'0" ' [p/i]
CC600096	Sep 1963	Insc: 'floor joists layout' [p/i]
CC600097	Oct 1963	Insc: 'north and south gables, precast concrete facing unit layout 3/8" ' [p/i]
CC600105	Oct 1963	Insc: 'sanctuary block sections 1/4" ' [p/i/cp]
CC600110	Oct 1963	Insc: 'sanctuary block sections 1/4" ' [p/i/cp]
CC600111	Oct 1963	Insc: 'sanctuary block sections 1/4" ' [p/i]
CC600125	Feb 1964	Insc: 'plans, wardroble layouts, first stage 1/8" ' [p/i]
CC600129	Mar 1964	Insc: 'sanctuary floor plan 1/4" ' [p/i]
CC600213	Nov 1964	Insc: 'west elevation, window layout 1/4" ' [p/i/cp]
CC600214	Dec 1964	Insc: 'window elevation / east elevation 1/4" ' [i]
CC600246	Apr 1965	Insc: 'elevations, finishes to internal galleries 1/4" to 1" 10" ' [i]

CC600416	no date	n/t, plan, with key Insc: gas supply / soil & waste / water supply / electricity cable / rainwater / tile drains. n/s [p/i]
UNC	Mar 1962	Insc: 'plan showing road, sewer & ground levels 1/16" = 1ft' signed: 'D A Donald Wishart, Civil Engineers, 223 West Regent Street, Glasgow' pencil on linen-backed paper.
UNC	no date	Insc: 'St Peter's College, Kilmahew, Cardross, plan as proposed' n/s, pencil on linen-backed paper.
UNC	no date	Insc: 'east elevation' n/s [p/i]
UNC	no date	n/t, south elevation, n/s [i]

Main Block Details

number	date	description
CC600	Oct 1966	Insc: 'sacristy fitments, centre dresser 1" & 1 1/2" ' [p/i]
CC600	no date	Insc: 'detail sanctuary roof 1/4" ' [p/i]
CC600	no date	Insc: 'refectory lectern 1/2" ' [p/i]
CC600	no date	Insc: 'chapel & refectory door details 1 1/2" ' [p]
CC600	Oct 1966	Insc: 'sacristy fitments, centre dresser 1/2" & f.s.' [p]
CC600	no date	Insc: 'stool 1/4 f.s. details' [p/cp]
CC6000156	Apr 1964	Insc: 'window details, typical door panel section, f.s.' [p/i]
CC600016	Mar 1962	Insc: 'sewage disposal plant, section through 1/4" ' [p/i]
CC600019	Jun 1962	Insc: 'excavation, foundation & retaining details' n/s [p/i]
CC600020	Jun 1962	Insc: 'excavation, foundation & retaining details' n/s [p/i]
CC600021	Jun 1962	Insc: 'excvation, foundation & retaining details' n/s [p/i]
CC600022	Jun 1962	Insc: 'excavation, foundation & retaining details' n/s [p/i]
CC600031	Jul 1962	Insc: 'boiler house layout 1/8" ' [p/i/cp]
CC600037	Aug 1962	Insc: 'drainage details, manholes & drains 1/2" & 1" ' [p/i]
CC600038	Aug 1962	Insc: 'typical section through vaults 1/2" & 1" ' [p/i]
CC600040	Aug 1962	Insc: 'details, refectory, gable & kitchen link 1/2" ' [p/i]
CC600041R	Aug 1962	Insc: 'boiler house drainage 1/4" ' [p/i]
CC600042	Nov 1962	Insc: 'boiler room, cold water supply 1/4" & 1" [p/i]
CC600043	Sep 1962	Insc: 'boiler house, details duct positions 1/4" [p/i]
CC600044	Sep 1962	Insc: 'detail boiler house access stair' n/s [p/i]
CC600045	Sep 1962	Insc: 'details, opening, ground floor slab 1/4" & 1/2" ' [p/i]
CC600046	Oct 1962	Insc: 'details, entrance hall wall 1/4" &1/2" ' [p/i/cp]
CC600050	Nov 1962	Insc: 'drainage details' n/s [p/i]
CC600053	Nov 1962	Insc: 'boiler room cold water supply 1/4" & 1" ' [p/i]
CC600055 R1	Nov 1962	Insc: 'ground floor plan 1/8"–1'0" ' [p/i]
CC600063	Feb 1963	Insc: 'foundation layout, cloister level 1/4" ' [p/i]
CC600064	Feb 1963	Insc: 'plan of brickwork, cloister level 1/4" ' [p/i]
CC600065	Feb 1963	Insc: 'brickwork details, cloister level 3/8" ' [p/i]
CC600066	Feb 1962	Insc: 'elevation of brickwork, cloister level 1/4" ' [p/i]
CC600067	Dec 1963	Insc: 'details of main exterior stair, west side cloister 1/4" & 1/4 f.s.' [p/i]
CC600068	Mar 1963	Insc: 'main staircase, details of beam 1 1/2" [p/i]
CC600069	Mar 1963	Insc: 'main stair details' n/s [p/i/cp]
CC600070	Apr 1963	Insc: 'gallery & gutter unit details 1 1/2" & 1/4 f.s.' [p/i/cp]
CC600071	Apr 1963	Insc: 'toilets, precast details 1 1/2" ' [p/i]
CC600072	Apr 1963	Insc: 'north gable details' n/s [p/i]
CC600073	Apr 1963	Insc: 'gallery precast details 1 1/2" ' [p/i]
CC600074	Apr 1963	Insc: 'gallery & gutter details 1 1/2" ' [p/l/cp]
CC600075	Apr 1963	Insc: 'section through gallery with end detail 1 1/2" ' [p/i]
CC600076	Apr 1963	Insc: 'gable window details 1 1/2" & 1/4 f.s. ' [p/i/cp]
CC600077	Apr 1963	Insc: 'south gable, part gable elevations' n/s [p/i]
CC600078	Apr 1963	Insc: 'high level windows f.s.' [p/i]
CC600079	Apr 1963	Insc: 'toilets, high level window details 1 1/2 ' [p/i]

Drawing List

CC600080	May 1963	Insc: 'details gable frame 1"' [p/i/cp]
CC600081	May 1963	Insc: 'details, gable frame 3/8"' [p/i]
CC600082	May 1963	Insc: 'details, gable frame 3/8"' [p/i]
CC600083	May 1963	Insc: 'details, north gable escape stair chimney flue 3/8" & 1/4"' [p/i]
CC600085	May 1963	Insc: 'north gable, escape stair, chimney flue, east elevation 3/8"' [p/i]
CC600086	May 1963	Insc: 'north gable, escape stair chimney flue section C & D 3/8"' [p/i]
CC600087	Jun 1963	Insc: 'north gable escape stair, chimney flue details 3/8"' [p/i]
CC600090	May 1963	Insc: 'drainage, soil waste from columns 1" & 1/8"' [p/i]
CC600091	May 1963	Insc: 'gable & gutter flashing details 1 1/2"' [p/i/cp]
CC600095	Sep 1963	Insc: 'setting out & drainage plan 1/8"' [p/i]
CC600106	Oct 1963	Insc: 'sanctuary block sections 1/4" scale' [cp]
CC600112	Oct 1963	Insc: 'sanctuary block sections 1/4"' [p/i/cp]
CC600113 R1	Oct 1963	Insc: 'roof joists layout 1/8"' [p/i]
CC600114	Nov 1963	Insc: 'roof details 1"' [p/i]
CC600117	Nov 1963	Insc: 'details of gallery finish 1/4 f.s. & 1"' [p/i]
CC600119	Dec 1963	Insc: 'details of gutter unit finish & flashings 1/4 f.s.' [p/i]
CC600120	Dec 1963	Insc: 'detail flashings, gutter & gallery, 1/4 f.s.' [p/i]
CC600122	Feb 1964	Insc: 'setting out, sanctuary block, revised' n/s [p/i]
CC600126	Feb 1964	Insc: 'details, stage 1, wardrobe units 1"' [p/i]
CC600129 R1	Mar 1964	Insc: 'sanctuary floor plan, 1/4"' [i]
CC600137	Mar 1964	Insc: 'details, stage 1 wardrobes & partitions at toilets 1"' [p/i]
CC600140 R1	Mar 1964	Insc: 'details, east spiral staircase, sanctuary block 1" & 1/2"' [p/i]
CC600154	Apr 1964	Insc: 'window details, typical section f.s.' [p/i]
CC600155	Apr 1964	Insc: 'window details, typical door section, f.s.' [p/i/cp]
CC600160	May 1964	Insc: 'window details, convector unit in cell f.s.' [p/i]
CC600161	May 1964	Insc: 'sanctuary block window openings, details 1/2" 1/4"' [p/i]
CC600162	Jul 1964	Insc: 'detail cloister to sanctuary duct 1/4"' [p/i/cp]
CC600173 R2	Aug 1964	Insc: 'details, west stair sanctuary floor level 1/2"' [p/i]
CC600174	Aug 1964	Insc: 'details, west stair sanctuary 1/2" section' [p/i]
CC600175	Aug 1964	Insc: 'details, west stair sanctuary sections 1/2"' [p/i]
CC600179	Sep 1964	Insc: 'external window details f.s.' [p/i]
CC600180	Sep 1964	Insc: 'typical plan, section & internal & external elevation 1" to 1'0"' [p/i]
CC600181	Sep 1964	Insc: 'f.s. details, external panel' [p/i/cp]
CC600182 R1	no date	Insc: 'f.s. details for window' [p/i]
CC600183	Sep 1964	Insc: 'details of windows' n/s [p/i]
CC600187A	Oct 1964	Insc: 'window details, convector cabinet' n/s [p/i]
CC600196	Oct 1964	Insc: 'cell details 1 1/2" & f.s.' [p/i/cp]
CC600197	Oct 1964	Insc: 'sacristy window details f.s.' [p/i]
CC600198	Oct 1964	Insc: 'study bedroom details 1"' [p/i]
CC600199	Oct 1964	Insc: 'wardrobe details, f.s. & 1 1/2"' [p/i]
CC600201	Nov 1964	Insc: 'toilet windows, additional details, f.s.' [p/i]
CC600202	Nov 1964	Insc: 'toilet windows, elevation & section 1"' [p/i]
CC600203	Nov 1964	Insc: 'toilets, sections 1" to 1'0"' [p/i]
CC600204	Nov 1964	Insc: 'toilet, sections 1" to 1'0"' [p/i]
CC600205	Nov 1964	Insc: 'toilet details, plan 1"' [p/i]
CC600207A	Mar 1965	Insc: 'toilets, heating unit details, f.s.' [p/i]
CC600208	Nov 1964	Insc: 'cell, full size details' [p/i]
CC600210	Nov 1964	Insc: 'window details, doors from internal galleries f.s. & 1"' [p/i]
CC600211	Nov 1964	Insc: 'detail layout wardrobe unit 1 1/2"–1ft' [p/i]
CC600212 R1	Nov 1964	Insc: 'cell, full size detail of cabinet over wash hand basin' [p/i]
CC600220A	Sep 1965	Insc: 'table desk for SBR 1" & 1/2 f.s.' [p/i]
CC600232	Mar 1965	Insc: 'first floor, south end, details of framing 1" to 1'0"' [p/i]
CC600232	Mar 1965	Insc: 'bookcase to S.B.R. 1" to 1'0" f.s. & f.s.' [p/i/cp]
CC600235	Mar 1965	Insc: 'toilets, convector details 1" to 1'0"' [p/i/cp]

CC600245	Apr 1965	Insc: 'finish to internal galleries 1" to 1'0" ' [p/i]	CC600303	Apr 1966	Insc: 'screens, refectory handrail & connector 1" ' [p/i]
CC600249	May 1965	Insc: 'west stair sanctuary sections 1/2" ' [p/i]	CC600304	no date	Insc: 'main block screens, detail' n/s [p/i]
CC600250	May 1965	Insc: 'west stair sanctuary elevation 1/2" ' [p/i]	CC600305	Apr 1966	Insc: 'chapel & refectory screens 1/4"=1'0" ' [p/i]
CC600252	Aug 1965	Insc: 'east side chapels, plan, sections, elevation 1" ' [p/i]	CC600306	Apr 1966	Insc: 'chapel, refectory screens 1/4 f.s.' [p/i]
CC600261	Jul 1965	Insc: 'west stair sanctuary, plan at first floor exterior gallery & classroom floor level 1/2" to 1'0" ' [p/i]	CC600307	Apr 1966	Insc: 'stair handrail detail 1 1/2" ' [p]
			CC600317	Jun 1965	Insc: 'sacristy fitments f.s. sections' [p/i]
CC600261	Jun 1965	Insc: 'staircase details 1/2" ' [p/i]	CC600318	Jun 1965	Insc: 'sacristy fittings, f.s. details & 1/2" ' [p/i]
CC600261A	no date	Insc: 'handrail & balustrade details 1/2" ' [/cp]			
CC600263	Jul 1965	Insc: 'sanctuary roof shrine, section 1/2" ' [p/i]	CC600319	no date	Insc: 'sanctuary block, window at externs chapel 1" & 3" ' [p]
CC600265	Jul 1965	Insc: 'section, sanctuary roof shrine 1/2" ' [p/l]	CC600322	no date	Insc: 'confessional partition & door details 1/4" & 3" ' [p]
CC600267	Jul 1965	Insc: 'side chapel details 1" ' [p/i]	CC600409	no date	n/t, toilets n/s [p/i]
CC600268	Aug 1965	Insc: 'east side chapels, roof plan 1" & 1'0" ' [p]	CC600411	no date	Insc: 'toilets, first, second, third floor plan' n/s [p/i]
CC600269	Aug 1965	Insc: 'east side chapels, details of glazing, revision No.1, 1/4 f.s.' [p/i/cp]	CC600414	no date	Insc: 'section through sewage disposal unit 1/4" ' [p/i]
CC600270	Aug 1965	Insc: 'east side chapels, details of glazing, revision No.1, 1/4 f.s.' [p/i/cp]	CC600418	no date	Insc: 'second floor toilets plan' n/s [p/i]
CC600272	Aug 1965	Insc: 'details sanctuary roof showing position of rooflight 1/4" = 1'0" ' [p/i/cp]	CC600419	no date	Insc: 'third floor toilets plan' n/s [p/i]
			CC600420	no date	Insc: 'first floor toilets plan' n/s [p/i]
			CC600642	Aug 1962	Insc: 'boiler house details, sump & pump 1 1/2"' [p/i]
CC600278	Dec 1965	Insc: 'sanctuary rooflight details 1/2 f.s. plans & sections' [p/i/cp]	CC660	no date	Insc: 'plans, existing lift well detail 1/2" ' [p/i]
CC600286	Dec 1965	Insc: 'sanctuary rooflight details 1/2 f.s. sections & plan north' [p/i]	UNC	Jan 1963	Insc: 'detail of R.W. outlets to gutter units 1/2 f.s.' [p/i/cp]
CC600287	Jun 1965	Insc: 'ground floor screen details 1/8 f.s.' [p]	UNC	no date	n/t detail section with sketches showing existing house and walls n/s [p/i]
CC600288	no date	Insc: 'chapel seating details 1/4 f.s.' [p/i/cp]			
CC600288A	no date	Insc: 'chapel seating 1/4 f.s.' [p/i]	UNC	no date	Ins: 'details of R.W. outlets to BALC units 1/2 f.s.' [p/i/cp]
CC600289	no date	Insc: 'chapel seating 1/4 f.s. details' [p/i]	UNC	no date	Insc: 'plan, elevation & section, refectory heating cabinet' n/s [p/i]
CC600292	Feb 1966	Insc: 'ground floor screen details 1/4 f.s. 1/2" & 1/4" ' [p/i/cp]	UNC	no date	Insc: 'tabernacle drawing for Mr Coia architeck [sic]' signed 'Gill and Son, Dublin' n/s coloured ink wash on linen-backed paper.
CC600296	no date	Insc: 'refectory tables, 1/2" & 3"–1'0" ' [p/i]			
CC600301	Mar 1966	Insc: 'internal screens 1/4" & 1" scale details' [p/i]			
CC600302	Mar 1966	Insc: 'internal screens elevation 1/4" ' [p/i]	UNC	no date	Insc: 'refectory balustrading, chapel screen details' n/s [p/i]

Convent Block, Kitchen Block, & Existing House

number	date	description
CC169	no date	Insc: 'section through refectory & community room 1/2" ' [p/i]
CC171	no date	Insc: 'section through corridor & refectory 1/2" ' [p/i]
CC600	Aug 1965	Insc: 'shelving details, existing house' n/s [p/i]
CC600	Dec 1967	Insc: 'sisters oratory, alter details 1" ' [p/i]
CC600	1967	Insc: 'convent oratory, details, light fitting 1/4" & 1/4 f.s.' [p/i]
CC600	Sep 1967	Insc: 'convent oratory, existing house, details, bench seating 1/4 f.s.' [p/i]
CC600	no date	Insc: 'convent oratory, exiting house, layout 1" ' [p/i]
CC600	Feb 1967	Insc: 'convent oratory in existing house 1/4" ' [i/cp]
CC600	no date	Insc: 'convent oratory, existing house, stall seating details 1/4 f.s.' [p/i]
CC600	no date	Insc: 'kitchen fittings details f.s. & 1 1/2" rep 1'0" ' [p/i]
CC600004A	Dec 1961	Insc: 'convent upper floor plan' n/s [i]
CC600005A	Dec 1961	Insc: 'convent roof plan' n/s [i]
CC600006	Dec 1961	Insc: 'roof plan, convent, existing house, classroom block 1/8" ' [i]
CC600092	Aug 1963	Insc: 'revised convent plan 1/8" ' [p/i]
CC600098	Oct 1963	Insc: 'section & elevation, convent block 1/8" ' [p/i]
CC600099	Oct 1965	Insc: 'convent block,sections 1/4" ' [p/i]
CC600100	Oct 1963	Insc: 'ground floor plan, convent block 1/4' [p/i]
CC600101	Oct 1963	Insc: 'convent block, first floor plan 1/4" ' [p/i]
CC600102	Oct 1963	Insc: 'convent block, plumbing details 1/4" ' [p/i]
CC600103A	Oct 1963	Insc: 'convent block, brickwork, setting out' n/s [p/i]
CC600103B	Oct 1963	Insc: 'convent block, brickwork, setting out 1"= 1ft' [p/i]
CC600116	Nov 1963	Insc: 'precast concrete details, convent block 1" & 1/4" ' [p/i/cp]
CC600141	Mar 1964	Insc: 'roof details, convent block 1/4", to be read with drawing No. CC600114, showing main block roof'[p/i]
CC600142 R1	Mar 1964	Insc: 'details, first floor "balters" & flooring & layout, stage 1 wardrobes 1/4" ' [p/i/cp]
CC600144 R1	Mar 1964	Insc: 'convent block, details, low roof 1/4" to 1" ' [p/i/cp]
CC600145	Dec 1964	Insc: 'convent block, details, ground floor joist 1/4" ' [p/i/cp]
CC600146	Mar 1964	Insc: 'convent block, details, wardrobe units Stage One, 1" ' [p/i]
CC600147 R1	Apr 1964	Insc: 'setting out windows, parlour 2, convent block 1" ' [p/i]
CC600148 R1	Apr 1964	Insc: 'convent block, community room, setting out windows 1" ' [p/i]
CC600149 R1	Apr 1964	Insc: 'convent block, setting out windows, parlour 1, 1" ' [p/i]
CC600150 R1	Apr 1964	Insc: 'convent block, 'office', setting out windows 1" ' [p/i]
CC600151 R1	Apr 1964	Insc: 'convent block, pantry kitchen, setting out windows 1" ' [p/i]
CC600152 R1	Apr 1964	Insc: 'setting out windows "refectory", convent block 1" ' [p/i]
CC600153	Apr 1964	Insc: 'details, window openings, convent block 1/2 f.s. 1/8 f.s.' [p/i]
CC600163	no date	Insc: 'revise layout of existing house, ground floor plan' n/s [p/i]
CC600164	no date	Insc: 'revise layout of existing house, first floor plan' n/s [p/i]
CC600165	no date	Insc: 'revise layout of existing house, second floor plan' n/s [p/i]
CC600166	no date	Insc: 'revise layout of existing house, third floor plan' n/s [p/i]
CC600167	no date	Insc: 'section through refectory & community room 1/2" ' [p/i/cp]
CC600168	Jul 1964	Insc: 'convent block details, community room & refectory roof junction 1" ' [p/i]
CC600184A	Sep 1964	Insc: 'detail, junction of convent with old house 1/2" ' [p/i]
CC600185A	Sep 1964	Insc: 'section through junction at old house 1/2' [p/i]
CC600186	Sep 1964	Insc: 'window details, convent block, refectory, community room, parlours, office pantry f.s. 1/2 f.s. 1" ' [p/i]
CC600187	Oct 1964	Insc: 'convent block, first floor windows, elevation, plan 1" & 1/4" ' [p/i]
CC600188	Oct 1964	Insc: 'convent block, window details f.s.' [p/i/cp]

CC600189	Oct 1964	Insc: 'convent block, window details f.s.' [p/i/cp]		CC600227	Jan 1965	Insc: 'convent block, door to heating unit 1" to 1'0" ' [p/i]
CC600190	Oct 1964	Insc: 'convent block, windows details f.s.' [p/i]		CC600227	Dec 1964	Insc: 'existing house, wardrobe fittings, rector's bedroom 1 1/2" to 1'0" & f.s.' [p/i/cp]
CC600191	no date	Insc: 'convent block, first floor partition details 1/4 f.s. to 1" to 1'0" ' [p/i]		CC600228	Mar 1965	Insc: 'convent block, internal elevations, 1/2' [p/i]
CC600192 R1/R2/R3	Oct 1964	Insc: 'convent block, layout of toilet area 1" to 1'0" ' [p/i]		CC600229	Mar 1965	Insc: 'convent block, internal elevations 1/2" ' [p/i]
CC600193 R1	Oct 1964	Insc: 'convent block, toilet area, sections 1" to 1'0" ' [p/i]		CC600236	Mar 1965	Insc: 'convent block, nuns' bedrooms 4, 5 & 6, plans & sections 1" to 1'0", revision 1' [p/i/cp]
CC600194 R1 /R2	Nov 1964	Insc: 'guest bathroom, plan, section, 1" to 1'0" & 1/4 f.s.' [p/i]		CC600237	Apr 1965	Insc: 'convent block, nun's bedroom f.s. plan of heating unit' [p/i/cp]
CC600195 R1	Oct 1964	Insc: 'convent block, window details 1" ' [p/i]		CC600238	Apr 1965	Insc: 'convent block, nuns' bedrooms 4, 5 & 6, full size details' [p/i]
CC600200	Oct 1964	Insc: 'convent block, toilet area, windows to north, plan 7 sewing room, detail at exterior door, full size details' [p/i/cp]		CC600239	Apr 1965	Insc: 'convent block, guest bedroom, plans, section 1" to 1'0" ' [p/i]
				CC600240	Apr 1965	Insc: 'convent block, nuns' bedrooms 1, 2 & 3 plans & sections 1" to 1'0" ' [p/i/cp]
CC600215	Dec 1964	Insc: 'convent block, door & link screens, detail, elevations & sections 1/2" ' [p/i]		CC600241	Apr 1965	Insc: 'plan at first floor 1/4" to 1'0" ' [p/i/cp]
CC600216	Dec 1964	Insc: 'convent block details, doors & window, elevation & sections 1" ' [p/i]		CC600253	Jun 1965	Insc: 'stair to first floor, sections 1/2" to 1'0" ' [p/i]
CC600217	Dec 1964	Insc: 'convent block, details, f.s. window, screens & doors' [p/i/cp]		CC600254	Jun 1965	Insc: 'convent block, stair to first floor elevation 1 1/2" to 1'0" ' [p/i]
CC600218	Dec 1964	Insc: 'convent block, details, door & screen f.s.' [p/i/cp]		CC600255	Jun 1965	Insc: 'stair to first floor, section 1/2" to 1'0" ' [p/i]
CC600219	Dec 1964	Insc: 'convent block, details, screens f.s.' [p/i/cp]		CC600256	Jun 1965	Insc: 'sections, first floor 1/2" & 1'0" ' [p/i]
CC600221	Apr 1965	Insc: 'convent block, nun's bedroom f.s. plan of cupboard & heating unit' [p/i/cp]		CC600257	Jun 1965	Insc: 'section through sewing room, library & study, section first floor 1/2" to 1'0" ' [p/i/cp]
CC600222 R1	Dec 1964	Insc: 'convent block. section through cupboard to nun's bedroom, full size details' [p/i]		CC600258	Jun 1965	Insc: 'convent block, stair to first floor plan 1" to 1'0" ' [p/i]
				CC600259	Jun 1965	Insc: 'stair to first floor section 1" to 1'0" ' [p/i/cp]
CC600223	Dec 1964	Insc: 'convent block, nuns' bedroom, section through heating cabinet, full size details' [p/i/cp]		CC600260	May 1965	Insc: 'section through study & storage unit 1" to 1–0" ' [p/i/cp]
CC600226	Feb 1965	Insc: 'convent block, details, external doors f.s.' [p/i]		CC600271	Aug 1965	Insc: 'convent block, nun's bedroom f.s. details bookcase & ceiling' n/s [p/i]
CC600227	Mar 1965	Insc: 'convent block, heating cabinets f.s. & 1" ' [p/i/cp]		CC600273	Aug 1965	Insc: 'convent block / sewing area 1/2 f.s. details of convector unit' [p/i]

CC600273	Aug 1965	Insc: 'convent block, pantry, kitchen office, details of fitments 1/4 f.s.' [p/i/cp]
CC600274	Aug 1965	Insc: 'convent block, community room & refectory, plan, sections 1/2 f.s.' [p/i]
CC600274	Aug 1965	Insc: 'external work details, forecourt entrance 1/8" & 1/2" ' [p/i]
CC600274A	Nov 1965	Insc: 'convent block, community room fitment, modification 1" & 1/2 f.s.' [p/i]
CC600275	Aug 1965	Insc: 'convent block refectory, plan, section, elevations 1" ' [p/i/cp]
CC600293	Feb 1966	Insc: 'kitchen layout 1/4" ' [p/i]
CC600294	Feb 1966	Insc: 'kitchen block, foundation plan 1/4" ' [p/i/cp]
CC600295	Feb 1966	Insc: 'kitchen block, kitchen layout 1/4" ' [p/i/cp]
CC600296	no date	Insc: 'kitchen details, north elevation 1/2" ' [p/i]
CC600298	Mar 1966	Insc: 'kitchen block, cross-section 1/2" ' [p/i]
CC600299	Mar 1966	Insc: 'kitchen block, cross section 1/2" ' [p/i]
CC600300	Mar 1966	Insc: 'kitchen block, long section 1/2" ' [p/i]
CC600310	Apr 1966	Insc: 'kitchen block link details 1/4" f.s. & 1/2" ' [p/i]
CC600311	Apr 1966	Insc: 'kitchen block, kitchen details, screens to servery & external links' n/s [p/i]
KS64	Jan 1960	Insc: 'proposed utilisation of existing house 1/16" ' [p/i]
UNC	no date	n/t, ink sketch of existing bridge, elevation & plan n/s [i]
UNC	no date	Insc: 'plan of kitchen block' n/s [p]
UNC	no date	n/t, elevation, kitchen block n/s [p]
UNC	no date	n/t, detail, existing house elevation n/s [p]
UNC	no date	n/t, detail of Kilmahew House. n/s [p]
UNC	no date	Insc: 'section 5–5' n/s [p/i]
UNC	no date	Insc: 'section through retaining wall 1"–1'0" ' [p]
UNC	no date	n/t , elevation, kitchen block n/s [p]
UNC	no date	n/t, section [i]

Classroom Block Drawings

number	date	description
CC600	no date	Insc: 'common room scheme 1 × 1 1/2' [p/i]
CC600	no date	Insc: 'rooflights 1/4 f.s. & f.s [p/i]
CC600	no date	Insc: 'upper floor details 1/2". 1'0" ' [p/i]
CC600	Oct 1966	Insc: 'partition details 1" ' [p/i]
CC600	Oct 1966	Insc: 'details, door & partitions 1" ' [p/i]
CC600023 R1	Nov 1961	Insc: 'library precast concrete mullions & columns 1/8" ' [p/i]
CC600024	Jul 1962	Insc: 'main columns profile 1" ' [p/i]
CC600026	Nov 1962	Insc: 'main stair detail 1/2" ' [p/i]
CC600036	Mar 1964	Insc: 'details, main staircase 1" ' [p/i]
CC600049	Nov 1962	Insc: 'amended dimensions floor plans 1/8"
CC600051	Nov 1962	Insc: 'section 3/8" ' [p/i]
CC600059	Jan 1963	Insc: 'library floor plan & link 1/4" ' [p/i/cp]
CC600089	May 1963	Insc: 'shuttering on classroom slab soffit 1/4" ' [p/i]
CC600093	Sep 1963	Insc: 'common room floor slab 1/4" ' [p/i]
CC600118	Dec 1963	Insc: 'details of outlets to common room, external gallery 1/4 f.s. & 1/4" '
CC600121	Jan 1961	Insc: 'duct details, cloister to library 1/4" ' [p/i]
CC600123	Feb 1964	Insc: 'details, heating pipes, library floor 1" ' [p/i]
CC600130	Mar 1964	Insc: 'section & detail of columns and main beams 1" & 1/4" ' [p/i]
CC600132	Mar 1964	Insc: 'main outline 1"& 1/4" ' [p/i]
CC600133	Mar 1964	Insc: 'elevations & section through walls of classroom block 1/4" & 1" ' [p/i]
CC600138	Mar 1964	Insc: 'roof 1/4", superseded: see drawing 234' [p/i]
CC600139	Mar 1964	Insc: 'details roof (preliminary) 1/2" ' [p/i]
CC600231	Mar 1965	Insc: 'details, outlets from edge beam 1/8" & 1" ' [p/i]
CC600251	May 1965	Insc: 'common room floor, stair to external gallery 1" to 1'0" ' [p/i]
CC600282	no date	Insc: 'layout of roof boarding 1/4". 1' 0" ' [p/i]

CC600283	no date	Insc: 'roof details 1 1/2". 1'0" ' [p/i]		UNC	no date	n/t, ground-floor plan, ink / colour wash sketch
CC600308	April 1966	Insc: 'details of main stair 1 1/2". 1'0" ' [p/i]		UNC	no date	n/t, ground-floor plan, ink / colour wash sketch
CC600309	Aug 1965	Insc: 'details, main stair 1" = 1'0" ' [p/i]		UNC	no date	n/t, plan of cloister level, ink sketch
CC600310	no date	Insc: 'library floor, fluorescent lighting layout' n/s [p/i]		UNC	no date	n/t, second-floor plan, ink / colour wash sketch
CC600314	May 1966	Insc: 'library windows, 1/4 f.s. details' [p/i]		UNC	no date	n/t, second-floor plan, ink / colour wash sketch
CC600315	May 1966	Insc: 'library window details 1" & 1/2" ' [p/i]		UNC	no date	n/t, section of main block & site plan, ink / colour wash sketch
CC600403	no date	Insc: 'ventilators to upstands 3" & f.s.' [p/i]		UNC	no date	n/t, section through classroom block, ink sketch
CC600403	no date	Insc: 'library – common room stair, plans & section 1/2" ' [p/i]		UNC	no date	n/t, section through main block, ink sketch
CC600405	no date	Insc: 'classroom sections' n/s [p/i]		UNC	no date	n/t, site plan, ink / colour wash sketch
CC600412	Nov 1965	Insc: 'rooflights, 1/4 f.s. & f.s.' [p/i]		UNC	no date	n/t, section, ink sketch
CC600413	Nov 1965	Insc: 'rooflight details' n/s [p/i/cp]		UNC	no date	n/t, section, ink sketch
UNC	no date	n/t, section [p/i]				
UNC	no date	n/t, section [p/i]				
UNC	no date	n/t, detail n/s [p]				
UNC	no date	n/t, section n/s [p]				
UNC	no date	Insc: 'details of seating & writing surface' n/s [p/i]				
UNC	no date	Insc: 'lecture room seating 1/2 f.s. details of supports' [p/i]				
UNC	no date	n/t, details of seating n/s [p/i/cp]				
UNC	no date	Insc: 'lecture room seating layout 1, 1/4" ' [p/i]				

Display Drawings

number	date	description
UNC	no date	n/t, section of main block, ink / colour wash sketch
UNC	no date	n/t, classroom block & kitchen block section, ink sketch
UNC	no date	n/t, first-floor plan, ink / colour wash sketch
UNC	no date	n/t, first-floor plan, ink / colour wash sketch
UNC	no date	n/t, ground & first-floor plan, ink / colour wash sketch
UNC	no date	n/t, ground-floor plan
CC600414	no date	n/t, ground-floor plan, ink sketch
UNC	no date	n/t, ground-floor plan, ink sketch
UNC	no date	n/t, ground-floor plan, ink / colour wash sketch

Acknowledgements

This book is a substantially updated and expanded edition of the monograph *Cardross Seminary*, originally published in 1997 by the Royal Commission on the Ancient and Historic Monuments of Scotland (RCAHMS). St Peter's was originally chosen as the subject for two reasons: firstly, it was recognised as a key monument of postwar Scottish Modern architecture, designed by Scotland's leading Catholic church architects, Gillespie, Kidd & Coia; and secondly, the proposals for the demolition of the ruined complex had prompted RCAHMS to carry out an extensive photographic survey in 1994.

Historic Environment Scotland (HES) has chosen in 2016 to update that original history of St Peter's Seminary to cover the two decades since the previous edition. Additionally, its publication contributes to the Year of Innovation, Architecture & Design 2016, and marks 50 years since the 1966 opening of the extended St Peter's College, Cardross. The book now updates the story of the building's slow decline, and examines the extraordinary protracted battle (over 20 years) to salvage the ruined remnants of the former college. Finally, it records the completion of the first phase of the part-restoration project for its re-use as a cultural centre, begun in 2015, and concludes in March 2016 with the staging of *Hinterland* – a public art event by NVA, which officially opened the former seminary buildings to the general public.

The text of this book has been written by Diane Watters and edited by Miles Glendinning (Scottish Centre for Conservation Studies, University of Edinburgh), with a final section by Angus Farquhar.

For the preparation of this new book HES would like to thank Miles Glendinning, Penny Lewis, Angus Farquhar and NVA. At HES, Ranald MacInnes and Aonghus Mackechnie also provided guidance. The book was designed by Oliver Brookes. James Crawford and Christine Wilson efficiently managed the process through to publication, and image preparation was carried out by Derek Smart. The following individuals originally provided valuable help in the preparation of the 1997 book (through recollections and/or commenting on the text): Isi Metzstein, Mary McHugh, John McCaffrey, John Durkan, Father John Fitzsimmons, Father James Foley and Robert W K C Rogerson.

HES would also like to thank Neil Baxter, Stuart Bryce, Monsignor Charles Burns, Ian Campbell, John Deffenbaugh, Dan Dubowitz, Kate George, Angus Gilmore, Ian Gilzean, Jocelyn Grant, Mark Lodge, Raymond McCluskey, Christine McWilliam, Donna Maguire, Susannah O'Rourke, David Page, Robert Proctor, Johnny Rodger, Catherine Stevenson, Linda Sutherland, Mairi Sutherland and Susannah Waters.

The following members of HES staff also assisted in the work: Robert Adam, Alex Adamson, Iain Anderson, Zoe Ballantine, Alasdair Burns, Isobel Fry, Simon Green, Neil Gregory, Anne Martin, Andrew Nicoll, Clare Sorensen and Steve Wallace.

Angus Farquhar, NVA

My contribution to this book reflects a decade long collective effort to bring about the resuscitation of Kilmahew/St Peter's. The words accompanying the photo essay are a distillation of many conversations, debates and arguments that have taken place with the core team throughout the intervening years. Thanks are due to John Allan, Rolf Roscher, Clare Simpson, Brian McGinlay, Ellen Potter and Peter Boyden for additional material, James Crawford and James Johnson for judicious text and photo editing and the photographers for their contributions. Many thanks to all within NVA and wider afield who have helped us to reach this point. At times it has been a muddy slog, but like all great journeys, the moments when light breaks through darkness and you glimpse greater vistas make each step taken worthwhile.

Editorial Notes

Unless otherwise specified, the contents of this volume are Crown Copyright.

Each illustration is accompanied by a caption that includes, when known, the collection from which the image is sourced and a unique HES identification number. Copies of HES material are available to view and purchase online at www.canmore.org.uk.

CC references denote drawings from the original Gillespie, Kidd & Coia archive, held by Glasgow School of Art. A full list of these drawings with descriptions can be found in the St Peter's College: Practice Drawing List Appendix.

Index

85A collective 181

Aachen, Corpus Christi Church 35
abandonment, St Peter's College 118, 120, 128–9, 133
Abbey Church, Fort Augustus 23
Abercrombie, Patrick 32
Aberdeen, St Mary's Cathedral 39
Aberdeen Diocese 121
Abrahams, Tim 164
Abronhill, Cumbernauld *16*
accommodation block *see* main block
Addyman Archaeology 168
Ahmedabad, Millowners' Association Building 109
Airdrie
    St Andrew's Church 47
    St David's Church 47
Alberti, Leon Battista 29
Alison & Hutchison & Partners 58, *58*
Allan, John
    Avanti assessment team 165, 168
    Lighthouse exhibition 165
    NVA and 174, 175, 179, 185, 194
    see also Avanti Architects
altars
    building plan-types 54–5
    central in liturgy 37, 39, 52
    consecration 214
    Kilmahew House convent oratory 78
    Our Lady of Good Counsel Church, Dennistoun 54
    St Benedict's Church, Drumchapel 55
    St Charles's Church, Kelvinside 56
    St Mahew's Chapel 114
    St Margaret's Church, Clydebank 58
    St Mary's Cathedral, Aberdeen 39
    St Paul's Church, Glenrothes 53
    St Peter's College 90, *93–5*, 121
        chapel viewed from *91*
        graffiti near *226, 229*
        Hinterland 234, *244*
        ruins/remnants of *150, 205*, 214, *214*, 234
        side and lower altars 90, 108, 109, 122, 234, *244*
        tabernacle 214

    water ingress 138, 139
Anderson, Robert Rowand 27, 63
    see also Rowand Anderson, Kininmonth & Paul
Andrews Weatherfoil 112
Anson, Peter F 23, 26, 46
Apostolic Constitution Maxime Interest 14
Archdiocese of Glasgow 12, 13–14, 50
    church building programme 15, 25, 27–9, 31, 126
        GKC 15, 20, 28–9, 43–6, 47–8, 50–1, 54–8
        repairs/restorations 154
        St Aloysius Church 41, 45
        Ward's role 16–17
    community size 13, 14
    finances 14, 126, 128, 140
    Kilmahew estate *72*, 77, 129, 140, 148
    reorganisation 14
    St Peter's College 128, 129, 146, 149
        abandonment/closure 128, 133
        Avanti Architects' report 168
        blamed for neglect of 142, 148, 149, 162, 164
        building problems 127
        Classical House plans for 140–1, 149, 156, 160–1, 162, 163
        drug rehabilitation centre 129, *129*, 133
        First Hospitality Corporation of America plans for 133
        Kilmahew House fire 142
        listed building 138
        NVA plans 174
        planning for 19, 20, 70, 121
        student numbers 123, 126, 128
        Urban Splash proposal 173
        valuations 128, 144, 149, 150
        Walker Group plans for 140
        see also Crilley, Ken
    Second Vatican Council reforms 17, 18, 121
Archdiocese of St Andrews and Edinburgh 14, 54, 70, 121
Architectural Association 156
Architectural Heritage Society of Scotland 152
Architectural Policy Unit 147, 165
Arden House 4
Ardrossan
    Park Parish Church 31
    St Peter in Chains Church 45, *45*
Argyll and Bute Council 146
    St Peter's College
        1998 planning application 149, 150

2004 planning application 160, 162
Classical House offer 161
NVA plans 174, 178
ARM Architects 160
Arran
Brodick 4
St Molios' Church 22, *22*
Arrochar, St Peter and Paul's Church 47–8
art in churches
Coia on 136
see also Schotz, Benno
art works theme, St Peter's College *see* cultural centre
artificial lighting, St Peter's College 87, 98, 100, 109
Avanti Architects
St Peter's College 146
conservation assessment 150, 162, 168, *168*, 172, 173, 175
NVA plans 175, 178, 179, *180*, 194
see also Allan, John
Ayton 4

Babylon Hotel, Nice 109
Baines, Mark
GKC staff 64, 132
Lighthouse exhibition 148, 165
Mackintosh School of Architecture 132, 139
Metzstein's dialogue with 139
on GKC's work 135, 139, 164
Themes & Variations exhibition 140, 156
balconies, St Peter's College 82, 87, 90, *115*
Banham, Reyner 34, 115
Bannockburn, Our Lady and St Ninian's Church 28
Barley, Nick 161, 174
Barrett, Gerry 51
BBC 23, 115, 122
Bearsden
Chesters College (later Scotus College) 121, 127, 128
St Peter's College 70
destroyed by fire 4, 12, 68, 70
Eyre and 112, 113
organ 90
Beaux-Arts architecture 27, 28, 29, 40, 42, 43, 45
bedrooms, St Peter's College 4, 76, 127, *156*, 202, 218, *228*
beehive cells 107
Bell, Alexander D *21*, 58

Bellshill Maternity Hospital, Lanarkshire 62, *63*
Benson, Gordon 156, 165
Bentley, John Francis 28
Bernat Klein Studio, Selkirk 33
billiard room, Kilmahew House 73
Bishopbriggs, St Matthew's Church 47
Bishops' Conference of Scotland 12
Blackwell's Music Shop 64
Bloxham, Tom 173
Bo Bardi, Lina 226
BOAC offices, Glasgow 64, *65*
Bohm, Dominikus 45
Bo'ness, St Mary's Church 54
Bordeaux House 164
Bottrop, Holy Cross 55
Bourdon Building, Glasgow School of Art 65
Boyd, Lesley 160
Boyle, Rory 181, 234
bridges
Kilmahew estate 77, 160, 178, 194, *199*
St Peter's College 82, *84*
Brodick 4
Broek and Bahama 115
Brooke Miller Partnership 154
Brown, Rev. David 138
Brucefield Church of Scotland, Whitburn 59, *59*
Brutalism 115, 205
Bunton, Sam 47
Burnet, J J
Beaux-Arts architecture 27, 43
Metzstein and MacMillan compared to 156
RIBA Gold Medal 63
St Molios' Church 22, *22*
St Philip's Episcopal Church 28
Burnet, John (senior) 4, *72*, 77
Burns, John William 4, 77
Burns, Monsignor Charles 73
Bute, Marquess of 25, 70, 173

Ca d'Oro Building, Glasgow 43
cabins, St Peter's College 178
Cairns & Ford 59
Caithness, Dunnet Parish Church 25
Calderwood, East Kilbride 31

Cambridge, Robinson College 46, 64–5, 139
Campbell, Alexander Buchanan 43, 51
Campbell, Archbishop Donald 12, 14, *14*
    church building 15, 50
    death 17, 112
    McRoberts and 71–2
    re-interments 113–14, 128
    St Mahew's Chapel opening 25
    St Peter's College 19, 70, 74, 110, 112, 114, 123, 126
    Ward and 16, 17
Campbell and Hislop 40
Campbell, J A 27
camping facilities, St Peter's College 178
Canna, Protestant church 22, *22*
car park, St Peter's College 178
Cardross Community Council 140, 152, 161, 164
Cardross Golf Club 77, 152
Cardross Regeneration Trust 156, 160, 161
    see also St Peter's Buildings Preservation Trust
Carmyle, St Joachim's Church 48
Carstairs, St Charles 74
Casa d'Italia, Glasgow 128
Casot, Lucy 185
Castlemilk
    St Margaret Mary's Church 29
    St Martin's Church 54, 154
Catholic Church 12–19
    Constitution on the Sacred Liturgy 18, 37, 121
    Decree on Priestly Formation 19, 122
    Dogmatic Constitution on the Church 18
    Liturgical Movement 37, 42, 54
    Oath Against Modernism 17, 214
    Pastoral Constitution on the Church in the Modern World 18
    problems 8, 126–7, 186
    reforms 6, 8, 17–19, 120, 121, 136
        see also Second Vatican Council
    schools 14, 15, 29, *29*
    see also Archdiocese of Glasgow; Archdiocese of St Andrews and Edinburgh; priests' training
Catholic Heritage Commission 141
Catholic Pavilion, Empire Exhibition 26, 43, 45, 46, *46*, 48, 50
ceilings, St Peter's College 84, 178
Centre for Contemporary Arts, Glasgow 159
chain, St Peter's College 205, *222*
Chalmers, Peter MacGregor 22, *22*, 27

chapels 74
    Catholic Pavilion, Empire Exhibition 46
    Kilmahew House 73
    La Tourette 109
    Notre Dame du Haut *11*, 39, 54
    Robin Chapel, Edinburgh 25
    Robinson College 64
    St Columbkille's Church, Rutherglen 45
    St Mahew's Chapel *23*, 25, 71, 114
    St Mary's Chapel, Duntocher 31
    St Peter's College, Cardross 4, 62, 73, 82, *83*, 84, 87, 90, *91–3*, *95*, 104, 106, 107, 202, 205
        1st design 72, 74
        Eyre and Campbell's re-interment 114
        furniture and fittings 104
        Hinterland 241
        in use 113, 121–2, 127, 128
        Le Corbusier influence 109
        NVA plans 178, 194, 218
        performance/maintenance 127
        sanctuary rooflight from *107*
        side chapels *69*, 74, 84, 87, 107, 109, 122, *132*, *182*, 205, *218*
        Urban Splash scheme *171*
        vault collapse 218
        water ingress 113, 127
    SS Ninian Martin and John RC Church, Whithorn 26
Chesters College (later Scotus College), Bearsden 121, 127, 128
Christ the King Church, Glasgow 29
Christ's Church, Dunollie 25
Church of the Holy Family
    Oberhausen 56
    Port Glasgow 48, *48*
Church of the Holy Name, Cumbernauld 36
Church of the Immaculate Conception, Glasgow *29*, 31
Church of St Mary of the Assumption, Bo'ness *55*
Church of Scotland
    architecture 22, 23, 26, 31, 59
    Brucefield, Whitburn 59, *59*
    Canna 22, *22*
    commissioning procedure 53
    Livingston 36
    St Andrew's Parish Church, Edinburgh 26, *26*, 27
Civic Trust 136, 141, 152
Clare, John 142
Classical House

1993 proposal 140, 173
1998 proposal 149, 150
2004 proposal 156, 160, 162
Historic Scotland and 161
Urban Splash proposal 173
withdrawal from projects 146, 172
classroom block, St Peter's College 4, *69*, 76, 77–8, *98*, *98*, 100, *100*, 106, 205
    Avanti Architects' report 168
    condition analysis 168
    construction 110, 111, 112
    derelict *147*, *154*, 202, *202*
    furniture and fittings 104
    graffiti *230*
    Hinterland 234, *234*, *241*
    in use *118*, 127
    Kilmahew House *100*, 127
    materials 108
    NVA work 175, 178, *182*, *247*
    problems 127
    roof lights 100
    stairs 98, 100, *102–3*, *206*, *210*
        common room 100, *102–3*, 128
        external 77, 100
        Hinterland 234
        roof collapse 127
    steps to 84
classrooms, Kilmahew House 73
cloister, St Peter's College 74, 82, *82*, 84, 106, 205, *225*
    columns 107
    Hinterland 234
    library access 100
    materials 108
    natural lighting 87
    see also walkways, St Peter's College
closure, St Peter's College 118, 120, 128–9, 133
Clyde Design Partnership 160
Clydebank
    St Eunan's Church 47
    St Margaret's Church 53, *56*, 57–8
Clydebelt (environmental group) 152
Coatbridge, St Kevin's Church 47
Coia, Gaetano 47
Coia, Jack 40–1, 42–3, *42*, 46–7
    Catholic faith 50
    church buildings 27, 45, 47, 48, 50, 52–3, 54, 55

St Anne's, Dennistoun 28–9, 45
    St Laurence's, Greenock 48, *48*
death 65
East Kilbride housing 50
MacMillan and 47, 48, 50, 51, 53, 143
Metzstein and 47, 50, 51, 52–3, 143
religious art in churches 136
    see also Schotz, Benno
RIBA Gold Medal 51, 63–4
Rogerson's book on 42, 43, 135, 140, 143
role in designs 165, 168
St Peter's College
    1st design 50, 72–3, *73*, 74
    construction delays 111
    Grigor's documentary 128
    problems 128
    role in design 70, 143, 152, 156
    visits to 73, 128
Stamp's opinion of 156
see also Gillespie, Kidd & Coia
Coia, Jacqueline 143
Coia, John 47
Colinton Mains Church, Edinburgh 25, 27
Colmer, Stephen 160
common room, St Peter's College 4, 98, 100, *102–3*, *121*, 128, 178
concelebration 121–2
conference centre, proposed for St Peter's College 133
Congar, Yves 17
Conlon, C R 25
Connelly, Monsignor Tom 140, 152
Connolly, Father/Rev. Michael J 74, 114, *120*, 123
conservation 6, 8, 23, 25
    Cumbernauld 154
    GKC's work 133–6, 138, 152, 154
    Modernist architecture 8, 118, 133–6, 139, 152, 187
    St Peter's College 120, 129, 132, 133, 136, 138, 140–1, 142–88
        Avanti Architects' assessment 150, 162, 168, *168*, 172, 173, 175
    see also listed buildings
consolidated ruin/mothballing option, St Peter's College 120, 129, 140, 141, 142, 149, 150, 178
Constitution on the Sacred Liturgy 18, 37, 121
Conti, Archbishop Mario 156, 175
convent block, St Peter's College 80, *80*, *182*
    Avanti Architects' report 168

construction 111–12, *114*
furniture and fittings 112
Hinterland 242
La Tourette and 109
materials 80, 108
NVA plans 178
oratory 78, *78*, 104
planning and design 4, 72, 73, 74, 76, 77, 78, *78*, 80, 106, 109
proposed demolition 134, 140
vandalism 162
Cooney, John 125
Cooper, Malcolm 161, 162, 178
Copcutt, Geoffrey 34, *34*, 62
Cordiner, Thomas S 15
Bearsden college alterations 70
church buildings 29, *29*, 31, 48
Kilmahew House library furniture 72
Corpus Christi Church, Aachen 35
corridor, St Peter's College 82
Cosla/Scottish Government Regeneration Capital Grant Fund 178–9
costings, St Peter's College 72, 110, 114
see also valuations
Council of Trent 19, 104, 120
country park proposals, Kilmahew estate 142, 150, 152, 160, 172
courtyard, St Peter's College 78, 82, 84, 104, 106, 109
Coventry Cathedral 39, *39*, 48
Cowell, John 47, 50, 51, *71*, 147
St Peter's College
role in design 51, 69, 70, 116
role unacknowledged 143, 152, 165
weathertightness problem 127
Craigsbank Parish Church, Edinburgh 59
Crawford, Hugh Adam 45, 46
Creative Scotland 147, 174, 175, 178
Crilley, Ken 147, 150, 152, 160
Crosbie, William 45
Cruft, Kitty 134
crypts
La Tourette 109
St Peter's College 4, 90, *96*, *108*
derelict 202
Eyre and Campbell's re-interment 114
Hinterland 234
reuse by NVA 195

windows 205
cultural centre
St Peter's College 6, 142, 144, 174
see also NVA
Culzean Castle 196
Cumbernauld 31, 53
Catholic population 16
church buildings 35–6, *36*, 55, 57, 152, 154
heritage/conservation 154
housing 16, *16*, 34, 60
Sacred Heart Church 55, 57, 152, 154
St Mungo's Church 35, *36*
schools 60, *60*, 62
Town Centre 34, *34*, 62, 63, 106, 133
Cumbernauld College 62, *62*
Cumbernauld Free Church 36
Cunningham, John *120*

Dalbeth Cemetery 113
Dalkeith, Easthouses Church 26, 27
Dalziel North Church, Motherwell 27
Darleith House 4, 70, 72, 73
Davidson's Mains, St Margaret's Church 31
Davis Duncan Partnership 140
Davison, John 36
Dawson, Archibald *42*, 45
decoration, St Peter's College 77
Decree on Priestly Formation 19, 122
Deffenbaugh, John *158*, *159*, 160, 162
demolition
Kilmahew House 6, 120, 129, 134, 140, 141, 142, 149
site after 6, *130–1*, *146*, *147*
proposed for St Peter's College buildings 133, 134, 138, 140, 175
Dennistoun
Our Lady of Good Counsel Church 54–5
St Anne's Church *27*, 28–9, 43, 45
Devine, Bishop Joseph *120*, 152
dining rooms/refectories
Bourdon Building, Glasgow School of Art 65
Kilmahew House 73, 74
St Peter's College
1st design 74
convent block 80, *80*

derelict *152*

furniture and fittings 104

glazed screens 87, *87*

in use 122, 127

Kilmahew House inspiration for 73

lectern *104*

NVA plans 178, 194

partitions 87

planning and design 4, 32, 72, 82, 84, 87, 104, 106, 107, 202, 205

vaults 90, 218

visitors in *121*

Diocese of Aberdeen 121

Diocese of Motherwell 14, 54, 126, 127, 128, 152

Diocese of Paisley 14

DOCOMOMO (Documentation and Conservation of the Modern Movement) 133, 135, 138, 139, 141

Dogmatic Constitution on the Church 18

Doughty, Gordon 152

drawing room, Kilmahew House 73

drug rehabilitation centre, St Peter's College 6, 129, *129*, 133

Drumchapel

St Benedict's Church 54, 55, *56*, 135, *135*, 136

St Laurence's Church 25

Drygrange House 70

Drygrange Seminary 126

see also St Andrew's College, Drygrange

DTA (architects) 152

Dubovitz, Dan 147, *150*, *154*, 158–9, 160

Duerden, Patrick 161, 164

Dumbarton

Round Riding Road 61

St Michael's Church 48

Dumbarton District Council 133, 138, 140, 141, 142

Dumfries, St Teresa's Church 31

Dunbartonshire Enterprise 142

Duncan, Thomas 59

Dunfermline, St Leonard's Parish Church 22

Dunnet Parish Church, Caithness 25

Dunollie, Christ's Church 25

Duntocher, St Mary's Chapel 31

Durkan, Dr John 123

Durnan, J Alexander 184

East Kilbride *31*, 32

Freeland Lane 50

Murray 1st Development 50, *50*

St Bride's Church *41*, *57*

campanile demolition 57, *57*, 135

Coia on liturgical arrangements 53

design 55, 56–7

in *Architectural Review* 114

restoration 154

East Kilbride Development Corporation 47, 50

East Lothian, Nunraw Abbey 74

Easterhouse, St Benedict's Church 55, 136, 152, 154

Easthouses Church, Dalkeith 26, 27

Edinburgh

Colinton Mains Church 25, 27

Craigsbank Parish Church 59

Longstone Parish Church 25, 27

National Library of Scotland 26

Nuffield Transplantation Unit *32*, 33

Reid Memorial Church 25

Robin Chapel 25

St Andrew's Church 26, *26*, 27

St Margaret's Church 31

St Mary's Cathedral *21*, 58

St Patrick's Church 45

St Philip's Episcopal Church 28

St Salvador Episcopal Church 25

see also Archdiocese of St Andrews and Edinburgh

Edinburgh University 65, 116

Ednie, Caroline 156

Elders Departmental Furniture Store, Glasgow 104

Elie parish church, Fife 22

Empire Exhibition

Catholic Pavilion 26, 43, 45, 46, *46*, 48, 50

Palace of Industries North 45–6

Encyclical Mediator Dei 37

English Heritage 134, 161

Erskine, Ralph 165

ERZ (landscape architects) 175, 179, 193

Exhibition of Church Architecture 114

Eyck, Aldo van 106

Eyre, Archbishop Charles Peter 14, 27, 112, 113, 128

Fabiani, Linda 163, 178
Faifley, St Joseph's Church 54, 55
Fairlie, Reginald 22–3, *23*, 25, 26, 45, 54
Fairlie, Reginald, & Partners 15, 23, 25, 26, 70
Falkirk
    St Francis Xavier Church 26
    St Mary of the Angels Church 55–6
Farquhar, Angus *184*
    background 192
    Hinterland 181
    St Peter's College 185
        NVA 147, 174, 175, 178, 179, 192–3
        site safety 180
Farrow, Mr 114
Feast of Christ the King 37
Ferguson, Patricia 163
Fernie, Ian 138
Festival of Britain 50
Fife, parish churches 22
A Film for Cardross: Resurrection Cycle 160
First Hospitality Corporation of America 133
Fitzsimmons, Father John 18, 123, 127, 128
flats, proposed use for St Peter's College 133
floors/flooring, St Peter's College 84, 87, 127
Florence, Santa Maria Novella 29
Foley, Father James 18, *120*, 123, 128
footbridge *199*
Forbes Leith, Father 23
Fort Augustus, Abbey Church 23
Fort William, Immaculate Conception Church 22
Forum group 106
foundation stone, St Peter's College 112, *115*
Freeland Lane, East Kilbride 50
Fry, E Maxwell 51
Fuller, Buckminster 226
Fulton, H M 112
Functionalism 32–3, 51, 154, 187
furniture and fittings, St Peter's College 87, 104, 107, 112, 122, 128

Gaff Gillespie & Kidd 40
Gale, Iain 165
Gallagher, Frank *121*
Gallagher, Michael 180
Galston, St Sophia's Church 27, 28
Gerrard, John 141
Gibberd, Frederick *37*, 39
Gilchrist, Jim 160, 161, 164
Gillespie, John Gaff 40, 51
Gillespie, Kidd & Coia 40–65
    archive 72, 76, 77, 110, 139, 156, 165
    Bellshill Maternity Hospital 62, *63*
    BOAC offices, Glasgow 64, *65*
    Catholic Pavilion, Empire Exhibition 26, 43, 45, 46, *46*, 48, 50
    church architects 19, 35, 37, 39, 42, 50–9, 164
        Archdiocese of Glasgow 15, 20, 28–9, 43–6, 47–8, 50–1, 54–8
        listed buildings 135–6, 148, 149, 152, 154
    Church of the Holy Family, Port Glasgow 48, *48*
    Church of St Mary of the Assumption, Bo'ness 55
    community buildings 34
    conservation 133–6, 138, 152, 154
    Cumbernauld College 62, *62*
    exhibitions of work 140, 148, 163, *163*, 165, 168
    hospitals 51, 62, *63*
    housing 46, 48, 50, *50*, 60–1
    Hull University halls of residence 61, 64
    Industrial Power Exhibition 48, 50
    Knightswood Secondary School, Glasgow 46
    Mackintosh's influence on 46, *46*, 48, 51, 64, 65, 107, 110, 205
    Modernist architecture 31, 40, 42, 45–6, 48–65, 139, 156, 187
        Catholic Pavilion 26, 45, 46, *46*, 48
        churches 12, 20, 40, 42, 45, *45*, 48, 50, 53–9, 136
        see also St Bride's Church, East Kilbride
        housing 48
        Iconic Modernism 65, 132, 146, 154, 188
        megastructures 34, 64
        schools 61–2
        see also St Peter's College, Cardross
    Our Lady of Good Counsel Church, Dennistoun 54–5
    Our Lady and St Francis Church, Glasgow 135
    Palace of Industries North 45–6
    publicity 70, 114–16
    Robinson College, Cambridge 46, 64–5, 139
    Round Riding Road, Dumbarton 61
    Sacred Heart Church, Cumbernauld 55, 57, 152, 154
    St Andrew's Church, Airdrie 47
    St Anne's Church, Dennistoun *27*, 28–9, 43, 45

St Benedict's Church, Drumchapel 54, 55, *56*, 135, *135*, 136
St Benedict's Church, Easterhouse 55, 136, 152, 154
St Bride's Church, East Kilbride *41*, *57*
    campanile demolition 135
    Coia on liturgical arrangements 53
    design 55, 56–7
    in *Architectural Review* 114
    restoration 154
St Charles's Church, Kelvinside 55, 56, 135
St David's Church, Airdrie 47
St Eunan's Church, Clydebank 47
St Joachim's Church, Carmyle 48
St Joseph's Church, Faifley 54, 55
St Kevin's Church, Coatbridge 47
St Laurence's Church, Greenock 48, *48*
St Margaret's Church, Clydebank 53, *56*, 57–8
St Maria Goretti, Glasgow 48
St Martin's Church, Castlemilk 54, 154
St Mary of the Angels Church, Falkirk 55–6
St Mary's Church, Bo'ness 54
St Matthew's Church, Bishopbriggs 47
St Michael's Church, Dumbarton 48
St Patrick's Church, Greenock 43, *43*, 45, 53
St Patrick's Church, Kilsyth 55, *56*, 57, 152, 154
St Paul's Church, Glenrothes *52*, 53, 54, 58, 135
St Paul's Church, Shettleston 48
St Peter in Chains, Ardrossan 45, *45*
St Peter and Paul's Church, Arrochar 47–8
schools 15, 46, 51, 60, *60*, 61–2, *61*
Spence and 48
Wadham College, Oxford 51, 64
see also St Peter's College
Gillespie, Neil 154
Gilzean, Ian 165, 174, 179, 180
GKC *see* Gillespie, Kidd & Coia
Glasgow
    BOAC offices 64, *65*
    Ca d'Oro Building 43
    Casa d'Italia 128
    Catholic church architecture 14, 15, 17
    Centre for Contemporary Arts 159
    Christ the King Church, King's Park 29
    Church of the Immaculate Conception *29*, 31
    Elders Departmental Furniture Store 104
    Gorbals *13*, 32
    Heron House *33*
    Hidden Gardens 193
    high-rise flats *13*
    Howford Special School 60
    Immaculate Heart of Mary Church, Springburn 31
    Industrial Power Exhibition 48, 50
    King's Park Secondary School 61, *61*
    Knightswood Secondary School 46
    Leon Shop 43
    Lourdes Secondary School 31
    Our Lady of Good Counsel Church, Dennistoun 54–5
    Our Lady and St Francis Church 135
    Protestant church architecture 27
    St Aloysius Church 41, 45
    St Alphonsus Catholic Church 27
    St Andrew's Cathedral 71, 114
    St Anne's Church, Dennistoun *27*, 28–9, 43, 45
    St Augustine's, Milton 25
    St Benedict's Church, Drumchapel 54, 55, *56*, 135, *135*, 136
    St Benedict's Church, Easterhouse 55, 136, 152, 154
    St Charles, Carstairs 74
    St Charles's Church, Kelvinside 55, 56, 135
    St Columba's Church, Maryhill 43, 45
    St Columbkille's Church, Rutherglen 43, 45
    St Eunan's Church, Clydebank 47
    St Francis Catholic Church *13*, 27
    St Joachim's Church, Carmyle 48
    St Laurence's Church, Drumchapel 25
    St Margaret Mary's Church, Castlemilk 29
    St Margaret's Church, Clydebank 53, *56*, 57–8
    St Margaret's Episcopal Church, Newlands 27
    St Maria Goretti 48
    St Martin's Church, Castlemilk 54, 154
    St Matthew's Church, Bishopbriggs 47
    St Patrick's Church 27
    St Patrick's Church, Kilsyth 55, *56*, 57, 152, 154
    St Paul's Church, Shettleston 48
    St Teresa of Lisieux Church, Possilpark 29, *29*
    St Thomas the Apostle Church, Riddrie 31
    St Vincent Street Church *33*, 48, 142
    schools 46, 60, 61, *61*
    Vocation Exhibition 114, 125
    see also Archdiocese of Glasgow; Bearsden
Glasgow Art Club 55
Glasgow School of Architecture 40
Glasgow School of Art 46, 47, 64, 65, 77, 110, 143
    Bourdon Building 65

GKC's archive 72, 76, 77, 110, 139, 156, 165
Mackintosh, Charles Rennie 46, 64, 65, 142, 143
Glasgow University 65
glazing *see* natural lighting, St Peter's College
Glendinning, Miles 133, *136*, 154, 168
Glenrothes 31, 53
St Columba's Church 35, *35*
St Paul's Church *52*, 53, 54, 58, 135
Gorbals, Glasgow *13*, 32
Grace, Father Piers 53
graffiti 160, 193, 195, 226
Graham, J Gillespie 4
Grant, J, Ltd 104
Gray, C 25
Gray, Charles 23, 70
Gray, Archbishop Joseph 53, 57
Greenock
St Andrew's Church 71
St Laurence's Church 48, *48*
St Patrick's Church 43, *43*, 45, 53
Gretna, St Ninian R C Church 28, *28*
Grigor, Murray 128, 147, 159–60, 165, 179

Haddow, T Harley, and Partners *21*
Hagia Sophia 27
hall, St Peter's College 82, 84, 87
Hall Kirk, Livingston 25
Hamilton, Lanark County Buildings *31*
health spa, proposed use of St Peter's College *171*, 173
Henket, Hubert-Jan 138
heritage *see* conservation
Heritage Lottery Fund 147, 149, 152, 154, 162
Lighthouse exhibition 165
St Peter's College, NVA plans 174, 178, 180, 185
Heron House, Glasgow *33*
Hidden Gardens, Glasgow 193
High Mass, St Peter's College *120*
Hinterland 6, *8*, 144, 175, 180–1, *181*, 184–5, 195, 234, *234–45*
Hinterland Manifesto 246
Historic Buildings Council 140
Historic Scotland 134
listing of buildings 134, 150, 154
GKC churches 135, 152, 154
St Peter's College 129, 138, 152, 187

St Peter's College 147, 149–50
1993 proposal 140, 141, 150
1998 proposal150 152, 160
2004 proposal 160–1, 162, 163
Avanti Architects report 168, 172
HS blamed for neglect of 146
Kilmahew House demolition 142
listing 129, 138, 152, 187
NVA plans 174, 178
Urban Splash scheme 173
see also Cooper, Malcolm; Hume, John; MacInnes, Ranald
historicist architecture 25, 27, 28
see also Traditionalist architecture
Hodgkinson, Patrick 139
Hollis, Edward 179, 195
Holy Cross, Bottrop 55
Holy Trinity, Wester Hailes 59
Hopkirk, Elizabeth 184
Hoskins Architects *171*
Hoskins, Gareth 173–4
hotel, proposed use of St Peter's College 133, 173
housing
Cumbernauld 16, *16*, 34, 60
East Kilbride 50, *50*
GKC 46, 48, 50, *50*, 60–1
proposals for Kilmahew/St Peter's 140, 149, 150, 152, 160, 173, 178
see also cabins
Houston, James, & Son 31
Howford Special School, Glasgow 60
Hull University halls of residence 61, 64
Hume, John 135, 150
Hunter & Clark 110
Hutchestown flats, Glasgow *13*
Hyslop, Fiona 163, 178, 184

Ian White Associates 149
Iconic Modernism 146, 154, 187
GKC's influence 65, 132, 148, 154, 158, 159
Immaculate Conception Church, Fort William 22
Immaculate Conception, Church of the, Glasgow *29*, 31
Immaculate Heart of Mary Church, Springburn 31
Industrial Power Exhibition, Kelvin Hall 48, 50
Invergarry, St Finnan's Church 23, *25*

Invisible College 175, 180, *181*, 195

John XXIII, Pope *14*, 18
Johnson, James 181, 195, 214
Justice, T, & Sons 104

Kahn, Louis 33
Kelly, Hugh *121*
Kelvin Hall
    Industrial Power Exhibition 48, 50
    Vocation Exhibition 114, 125
Kelvinside, St Charles's Church 55, 56, 135
Kennedy, Thomas Warnett 26, 43, 45, 46, 48
Keppie Planning 160
Kerr, H F 27
Kidd, William A 40, 42
Kildrum, Cumbernauld
    housing 60
    St Mungo's Church 35, *36*
Kildrum Parish Church, Cumbernauld 35, *36*
Kildrum Primary School, Cumbernauld 60, *60*
Kilmahew burn 77, 196, *200*
Kilmahew Castle 77, 150, 152, 160, 196
Kilmahew estate 77, 144, 148, 196
    Archdiocese of Glasgow *72*, 77, 129, 140, 148
    bridges 77, 160, 178, 194, *199*
    map *72*
    NVA and *145*, 148, 175, *180*, 194, 195, 196
    pre-war population 152
    proposals for 142
        country park 142, 150, 152, 160, 172
        hotel 173
        housing 140, 149, 150, 152, 160, 173, 178
    St Mahew's Chapel *23*, 25, 71, 114
    walled garden 77, 178, *180*, 193, 196, *196*
        proposed housing 140, 149, 160, 178
    see also landscaping
Kilmahew House *72*, 73, *78*, *116*, 140, *146*
    1948 move to 4, 70
    1949–50 alterations 125
    convent accommodation 73, 78, *78*
    demolition 6, 120, 129, 134, 140, 141, 142, 149
    site after *6*, *130–1*, *146*, *147*
    fires 6, *141*, 142
    GKC's extension *see* St Peter's College, Cardross
    kitchen 78, *78*, 138
    landscaping 77, 196
    library 72, 73, 74, 123
    listed building 129, 133, 138
    McRoberts' proposals 25, 70, 72, *73*, 74
    NVA plans 178, 202
    offices 73, 74, 106
    original design 4, 77
    refectory/dining room 73, 74
    Urban Splash scheme for site *172*
    valuation 128
Kilmahew Lake *200*
Kilsyth, St Patrick's Church 55, *56*, 57, 152, 154
King's Park, Christ the King Church 29
King's Park Secondary School, Glasgow 61, *61*
Kinloch, Ronald 148, 149
kitchens
    Kilmahew House 78, *78*, 138
    St Peter's College 122, 142
        construction 111, 112
        demolition 138, 175
        link to 84, 106
        materials 108
        NVA plans 175, 178
        planning and design 76, 77, 80
Knightswood Secondary School, Glasgow 46
Koolhaas, Rem 164
Kung, Hans 17, 18

Laidlaw, James, & Sons 110–11, 115
Laird, Michael, & Partners 47
Lamb, Fiona 194
Lanark County Buildings, Hamilton *31*
landscaping
    Kilmahew House 77, 196
    St Peter's College 78, 104
        NVA plans 149, 175, 178, 180, 196
Law and Dunbar-Naismith 36
Law, Graham 36
Le Corbusier 33, 34
    influence on GKC's work 54, 106

Index

St Peter's College 108, 109, 115–16, 164, 195, 205
    La Tourette *108*, 109, 164, 205
    Metzstein's praise for 51
    Millowners' Association Building 109
    Notre Dame du Haut *11*, 39, 54, 109
    Unité d'Habitation 106, 108
Le Havre, St Joseph 39
Leon Shop, Glasgow 43
Leslie, William 59
Leuchars, parish church 22
Lewerentz, Sigrud 115
Lewis, Penny 147, 174
    Cardross Regeneration Trust/St Peter's Buildings Preservation Trust 156, 158–9, *159*, 160, 161, 162, 164
    Metzstein and 148
    on Lighthouse exhibition 168
libraries
    Kilmahew House 72, 73, 74, 123
    St Peter's College 98, 100, 123, 128, 178
Lighthouse Exhibition 148, 163, *163*, 165, 168, *181*
lighting *see* artificial lighting, St Peter's College; natural lighting, St Peter's College
Lindsay, Ian G 23, *23*, 25, *25*, 54, 71, 134
listed buildings 133, 134–6, 150, 154
    GKC churches 135, 148, 152, 154
    Kilmahew estate bridges 160
    Kilmahew House 129, 133, 138
    Modernist architecture 118, 133–6, 139, 152, 187
    St Peter's College 135
        Historic Scotland and 129, 138, 152, 160, 162, 163, 187
        under Kilmahew House listing 129, 133, 138
        upgrade to A-listing 138, 140, 141, 143, 187
    Spence, Basil 134
    see also conservation
Liturgical Movement 37, 42, 54
Liverpool, Metropolitan Cathedral of Christ the King *37*, 39
Livingston 25, 36, 58, *58*
Loan, Douglas 140, 141
London, St Joseph's College 70
Longstone Parish Church, Edinburgh 25, 27
Loos, Adolf 109
Lorimer, Hayden 195
Lorimer, Hew 23
Lorimer, Robert 28
Lourdes Secondary School, Glasgow 31
lower church, St Peter's College 90, 107, 108, 109

Lutomski, Mieroslaw 47, 51, 53, 54

McAnally, Alexander 15, 29, *29*
Macauley, Catriona 180
McCaffrey, John 13–14, 18, 41, 126
MacCallum, Charles 51, 70, 139, 143
McCarron, Richard 58
McCrorie, Helen 158
McCulloch, James 152
MacDonald, Archbishop 70
MacDougall (formerly Thomson), Leslie Grahame 21, 25, 32
McGarvey, Seamus 179
McGill, Bishop *125*
McGinlay, Brian 175, 179, 194
Macgregor, Alex 47
McHugh, Dr Mary 126
MacInnes, Ranald 133, 135, 147, 163, 178
Mackay, John *120*
McKean, Charles 41
Mackintosh, Charles Rennie 139, 156
    Glasgow School of Art 46, 64, 65, 142, 143
    Grigor's film 128
    Hill House 107
    influence on GKC 46, *46*, 48, 51, 64, 65, 107, 110, 205
    Modernist architecture 46
    Windyhill 104
Mackintosh, Archbishop Donald 43, 45
Mackintosh School of Architecture 65, 132, 139, 143, 154
McLellan, Sadie 57
McLernan & Whyte 110
McMahon, Father James D *120*, 121, 123, 125, *125*, 127, 128, 142
MacMillan, Andrew 47, *71*, 139–40, 154, *158*, *162*, 163, 164, 165
    Catholic liturgy 53
    control during construction 65, 202
    death 175
    GKC archive 156
    interviews with 109, 156
    Lighthouse exhibition 165
    Mackintosh School of Architecture 65, 132, 139, 154
    role in design 42, 50, 51, 139, 156
        churches 48, 53, 54
        St Peter's College 50, 69, 70, 106, 110, 116, 132, 138, 142, 143, 152, 165, 168, 188
    St Peter's College

preservation 147–8, 173–4, 184
    water ingress 161
  Scottish Design Awards 164
  Stamp and 109, 148, 156
McMillan, Joyce 184
Macpherson, Archibald 23, 28, 41, 45
McRoberts, Father David 23, 25, 70–2, 74
  Eyre and Campbell's re-interment eulogy 114
  St Peter's College 72–3, *73*, 74, 123
  Ward and 71, 72, 74
McWilliam, Colin 26–7
Maguire, Robert 35, 56
main block
  St Peter's College 4, 74, *88*, *115*, 202, 205
    artificial lighting 100
    Avanti Architects' report 168
    balconies 82, 87, 90, *115*
    construction *69*, 111, *111*, 112, *112*, *113*, 114
    corridor 82
    dereliction *132*, *166*, 168, *208*, *210*, *212*
    first floor *212*, *224*
    graffiti *228*
    Hinterland *234*, *241*, *242*
    links 80
    materials 108
    NVA's work 175, 178, *182*, *188*, *208*, *210*, *212*, *218*, *220*
    performance/maintenance 127
    planning and design 76, 77, 80, 82, *83*, 84, 87, 104, 106, 107
    proposals for reuse 140, 173
    sanctuary block and 76, 77, 90, 107, *107*
    stabilisation/consolidation 160–1, 175
    stairs *208*, *218*
    see also chapels; cloister, St Peter's College; dining rooms/refectories; students' rooms
Maitland, J Steel 72
Malevich, Kazimir 181, 234
Mansfield, Susan 168
Marseilles, Unité d'Habitation 106, 108
Maryhill, St Columba's Church 43, 45
materials, St Peter's College 77, 82, 87, 100, 104, 108–9
Matta-Clark, Gordon 218
Matthew, J F 25
Matthew, Robert H 32, 33, 64, 65, 164
  see also Robert Matthew Johnson-Marshall (RMJM)
megastructures 34, 61, 62–3, 64, 106, 187

Cumbernauld Town Centre *34*, 62, 106
  Heron House *33*
Menart, C J 41, 45
Metropolitan Cathedral of Christ the King, Liverpool *37*, 39
Metzstein, Isi 47, 51, 65, *71*, 139–40, *158*, *162*, 163, 164
  control during construction 65
  death 132, 175
  Edinburgh University 65
  GKC archive 156
  Hinterland 184
  interviews with 69, 109, 148, 156, 164, 165
  King's Park Secondary School *61*
  Lewis and 148
  Lighthouse exhibition 165
  Mackintosh and 110
  Mackintosh School of Architecture 65, 132, 139, 154
  megastructures 62–3
  Modernist architecture 65, 154, 187
  on Baines 139
  on Le Corbusier 51
  Reiach's Kildrum design 59
  role in design 42, 50, 51, 139, 156, 165, 168
    churches 52–3, 54
    St Peter's College 50, 62–3, 69, 70, 74, 106, 110, 116, 132, 138, 142, 143, 152, 165, 188
    schools 61, *61*
  St Peter's College
    conservation/reuse 132, 139, 142, 147–8, 173, 184, 187
    retrospective accounts of 69, 74, 77, 106, 108, 109, 110, 147, 148, 187, 205
  Scottish Design Awards 164
  Stamp and 109, 143, 148, 156
  Themes & Variations exhibition lecture 156
Metzstein, Saul 165
Mickel, Derek 54
Miller, John 140
Millowners' Association Building, Ahmedabad 109
Milton, St Augustine's 25
Modernist architecture 20, 25–9, 31–9, *31*, *32*, 60, 109, 187
  conservation 8, 118, 133–6, 139, 152, 187
  GKC 31, 40, 42, 45–6, 48–65, 139, 156, 187
    Catholic Pavilion 26, 45, 46, *46*, 48
    churches 12, 20, 40, 42, 45, *45*, 48, 50, 53–9, 136
    see also St Bride's Church, East Kilbride
    housing 48
    Iconic Modernism 65, 132, 146, 154, 188

megastructures 34, 64
schools 61–2
see also St Peter's College, Cardross
listed buildings 118, 133–6, 139, 152, 187
Mackintosh 46
Metzstein on 65, 154, 187
Postmodernism and 154
schools 61–2
see also Bo Bardi, Lina; DOCOMOMO (Documentation and Conservation of the Modern Movement); Iconic Modernism
Moncur Memorial Church, Orkney 25
Monro, Sir Hector 133, 142
Montagu Evans 162
Moore, Rowan 179
Morris & Steadman 134
Mortimer, Jack 45, 48
mothballing/consolidated ruin option, St Peter's College 120, 129, 140, 141, 142, 149, 150, 178
Motherwell, Dalziel North Church 27
Motherwell Diocese 14, 54, 126, 127, 128, 152
Muirhead & Sons 112
Murphy, Richard 163
Murray 1st Development, East Kilbride 50, *50*
Murray, Keith 35, 56
Museum of Modern Art, Oxford 65
Musgrave, Lucy 136, 138

Nagele church 115
National Library of Scotland, Edinburgh 26
National Trust 25
natural lighting, St Peter's College 108
classroom block 98, 100
cloister 87
convent block 80, *242*
crypt 205, *222*
kitchen block 80
links 80
lower church 109
main block 84, 87, *87*
sanctuary block 87, 90, 107
see also roof lights, St Peter's College
New Churches Research Group (NCRG) 35, 53, 54, 56
New Facade exhibition 159

New Towns 16, 31, *31*, 35, 58, 133, 154
see also Cumbernauld; East Kilbride; Glenrothes; Livingston
Newlands
St Margaret's Episcopal Church 27
St Peter's College move to 121, 128
Newman Association 18
Noord, Gerrie van 175, 179, 193
NORD Architecture 175, 179, 194
Northumberland, Seaton Delaval Hall 179
Notre Dame du Haut, Ronchamp *11*, 39, 54, 109
Novak creative studio 181
Nuffield Transplantation Unit, Edinburgh *32*, 33
Nugent, Father Kenneth 47, 50, 121, 122, 141
Nunraw Abbey, East Lothian 74
nursing home, proposed use of St Peter's College 133
Nuttgens, Patrick 23, 115
NVA 192–4
12th Architectural Biennale, Venice 178, 179
Allan, John, and 174, 175, 179, 185, 194
Gilzean's support for 165
Kilmahew estate *145*, 148, 175, *180*, 194, 195, 196
St Peter's College 6, 144, 145, 147, 150, *168*, 173–85, *176*, *180*, 193–5, 202, 205
altar 214
chapels 178, 194, 218
classroom block 175, 178, *182*, 247
clean up 218
Heritage Lottery Fund 174, 178, 180, 185
landscaping 175, 178, 180, 196
main block 175, 178, *182*, *188*, *208*, *210*, *212*, *218*, *220*
site donated to NVA 148
see also Farquhar, Angus; *Hinterland*

Oath Against Modernism 17, 214
Oberhausen, Church of the Holy Family 56
offices
Kilmahew House 73, 74, 106
St Peter's College
convent block 80
NVA 178
oratory, St Peter's College 78, *78*, 104
organ loft, St Peter's College 90
Our Lady of the Assumption and St Meddan, Troon 22
Our Lady of Good Counsel Church, Dennistoun 54–5

Our Lady of Lourdes, Pontarlier 54
Our Lady and St Francis Church, Glasgow 135
Our Lady and St Francis School 61–2
Our Lady and St Ninian's Church, Bannockburn 28
Our Lady of Sorrows, South Uist 58
Our Lady Star of the Sea, Tayport 22, *23*
Our Lady's High School, Cumbernauld 62
Oxford
    Museum of Modern Art 65
    Wadham College 51, 64

Page, David 149
Page and Park 149, 150, 154
Paisley, Russell House 72
Paisley Diocese 14
Palace of Industries North, Empire Exhibition 45–6
Park Parish Church, Ardrossan 31
Parr, James, & Partners 58
partitions, St Peter's College 87
Pastoral Constitution on the Church in the Modern World 18
Paterson, A N 40
Paterson, John L 33
Paterson, Toby 147, 159
Paul VI, Pope 118
pavilion, St Peter's College, NVA plans 178
Perret, Auguste 39
Pitlochry, St Bride's Church 58
Pius X, Pope 17, 214
Pius XI, Pope 37
Pollen, Father 23
Pontarlier, Our Lady of Lourdes 54
Port Glasgow, Church of the Holy Family 48, *48*
Possilpark, St Teresa of Lisieux Church 29, *29*
Postmodernism 64, 65, 154, 187
Powers, Alan 156
preservation *see* conservation
Prestonpans, St Gabriel Church 58
Prestwick, St Nicholas Church 27
priests' training 19, 120, 123, 125–6, 128
    St Peter's College and 63, 104, 121, 122
Pritchard, Walter 45
Proctor, Robert 39, 48, 53, 54, 109, 165
Programme for Priestly Formation 120, 123
publicity, GKC 70, 114–16

Pugin & Pugin 23, 27, 45, 48

Quinn, James *120*

Radcliffe, Allan 184
Rahner, Karl 17, 18
ramp, St Peter's College 106, *118*, 205, 234
RCAHMS 134
refectories *see* dining rooms/refectories
Reiach, Alan 26, 32, 35, *36*, 59
Reid Memorial Church, Edinburgh 25
Reigart (contractors) 181, 218
Renton, Stuart 35
retaining walls, St Peter's College 77–8, 110, *232*
RIAS Scottish Thirties project 134
Richards, John 33
Riddrie, St Thomas the Apostle Church 31
Robert Matthew Johnson-Marshall (RMJM) 154
    see also Matthew, Robert H
Robin Chapel, Edinburgh 25
Robinson College, Cambridge 46, 64–5, 139
Rodger, Johnny 165, 168
Roehampton maisonettes 108
Rogers, Ian 47, 51
Rogerson, Robert W K C 42, 43, 48, 135, 143
Roman Catholic Church *see* Catholic Church
Rome, Scots College 71, 113, 128
Ronchamp, Notre Dame du Haut *11*, 39, 54, 109
roof lights, St Peter's College
    classroom block 100
    hall 87
    sanctuary block 90, 107, *107*, 110, 202, 205
roofs, St Peter's College
    Avanti Architects' report 168
    NVA plans 178, 202
    problems 127
        see also water ingress
    sanctuary block 107, *107*, 110, *147*, 162, 168, 178
Roq et Rob project 34
Roscher, Rolf 175, 179, 184, 193, 194
Rosewell, St Matthew's Church 28
Round Riding Road, Dumbarton 61

Rowand Anderson, Kininmonth & Paul 59, *59*
    see also Anderson, Robert Rowand
Royal Fine Art Commission for Scotland 139
Royal Scottish Academy of Music and Drama 179
Russell Diplock Architects 36
Russell House, Paisley 72
Russell, Mike 162, 163
Rutherglen 25, 43, 45
Ryan, Columba 18
Ryan, James *121*
Ryden (estate agents) 162

Sacred Heart Church, Cumbernauld 55, 57, 152, 154
sacristy
    Kilmahew House 73
    St Peter's College 90, *96*, 104, 195, 205
        Hinterland 234
St Aloysius Church, Glasgow 41, 45
St Aloysius College 41
St Alphonsus Catholic Church, Glasgow 27
St Andrews 70
St Andrew's Cathedral, Glasgow 71, 114
St Andrew's Church
    Airdrie 47
    Edinburgh 26, *26*, 27
    Greenock 71
    Livingston 58, *58*
St Andrew's College, Drygrange 159
    see also Drygrange Seminary
St Andrews University 70
    St Salvator's Chapel Choir 181
St Anne's Church, Dennistoun *27*, 28–9, 43, 45
St Augustine's, Milton 25
St Benedict's Church
    Drumchapel 54, 55, *56*, 135, *135*, 136
    Easterhouse 55, 136, 152, 154
St Bride's Church
    East Kilbride *41*, 57
        campanile demolition 57, *57*, 135
        Coia on liturgical arrangements 53
        design 55, 56–7
        in *Architectural Review* 114
        restoration 154
    Pitlochry 58

St Charles, Carstairs 74
St Charles's Church, Kelvinside 55, 56, 135
St Columba's Church
    Glenrothes 35, *35*
    Livingston 36
    Maryhill 43, 45
St Columbkille's Church, Rutherglen 43, 45
St David's Church, Airdrie 47
St Eunan's Church, Clydebank 47
St Finnan's Church, Invergarry 23, *25*
St Francis Catholic Church, Glasgow *13*, 27
St Francis Xavier Church, Falkirk 26
St Gabriel Church, Prestonpans 58
St Joachim's Church, Carmyle 48
St Joseph, Le Havre 39
St Joseph's Church, Faifley 54, 55
St Joseph's College, London 70
St Kevin's Church, Coatbridge 47
St Laurence's Church
    Drumchapel 25
    Greenock 48, *48*
St Leonard's Parish Church, Dunfermline 22
St Mahew's Chapel *23*, 25, 71, 114
St Margaret Mary's Church, Castlemilk 29
St Margaret's Church
    Clydebank 53, *56*, 57–8
    Edinburgh 31
St Margaret's Episcopal Church, Newlands 27
St Maria Goretti, Glasgow 48
St Martin's Church, Castlemilk 54, 154
St Mary of the Angels Church, Falkirk 55–6
St Mary of the Assumption, Church of, Bo'ness 55
St Mary's Cathedral
    Aberdeen 39
    Edinburgh *21*, 58
St Mary's Chapel, Duntocher 31
St Mary's Church, Bo'ness 54
St Matthew's Church
    Bishopbriggs 47
    Rosewell 28
St Michael's Church, Dumbarton 48
St Molios' Church, Arran 22, *22*
St Mungo's Church, Cumbernauld 35, *36*
St Nicholas Church, Prestwick 27
St Ninian 26
St Ninian R C Church, Gretna 28, *28*

St Patrick's Church
    Edinburgh 45
    Glasgow 27
    Greenock 43, *43*, 45, 53
    Kilsyth 55, *56*, 57, 152, 154

St Paul's Church
    Glenrothes *52*, 53, 54, 58, 135
    Shettleston 48

St Peter in Chains Church, Ardrossan 45, *45*

St Peter and Paul's Church, Arrochar 47–8

St Peter's Buildings Preservation Trust 146–7, 161, 162, 164
    as Cardross Regeneration Trust 156, 160, 161
    Avanti Architects' report 168, 172
    banner on St Peter's 163
    Lewis's role 148, 156, 162
    Prospect magazine March 2006 *159*, 164

St Peter's College, Bearsden 70
    Eyre and 112, 113
    fire at 4, 12, 68, 70
    organ 90

St Peter's College, Cardross 4, 68–117, *116*, *130–2*, *137*, 146, *147*, 154, *159*
    1st design 50, 70, 72, *73*, 74, 77, 82
    2nd design 59–60, 74–109, *75*, *76*, *77*, *78*, *80*, *82–3*, *84*, *87*, *88*, 114, 115–16, 134
    altars 90, *93–5*, 121
        chapel viewed from *91*
        graffiti near *226*, *229*
        Hinterland 234, *244*
        ruins/remnants of *150*, *205*, 214, *214*, 234
        side and lower altars 90, 108, 109, 122, 234, *244*
        tabernacle 214
        water ingress 138, 139
    balconies 82, 87, 90, *115*
    bridge 82, *84*
    ceilings 84, 178
    chain 205, *222*
    chapels 4, 62, 82, *83*, 84, 87, 90, *91–3*, *95*, 104, 106, 107, 202, 205
        1st design 72, 74
        externs chapel 90
        Eyre and Campbell's re-interment 114
        furniture and fittings 104
        Hinterland 241
        in use 113, 121–2, 127, 128
        Kilmahew House chapel and 73
    Le Corbusier influence 109
    NVA plans 178, 194, 218
    sanctuary rooflight from *107*
    side chapels *69*, 74, 84, 87, 107, 109, 122, *132*, *182*, 205, 218
    Urban Splash scheme *171*
    vault collapse 218
    water ingress 113, 127
    see also altars

classroom block 4, *69*, 76, 77–8, 98, *98*, 100, *100*, 106, 205
    Avanti Architects' report 168
    condition analysis 168
    construction 110, 111, 112
    derelict *147*, *154*, 202, *202*
    furniture and fittings 104
    graffiti *230*
    Hinterland 234, *234*, *241*
    in use *118*, 127
    Kilmahew House *100*, 127
    materials 108
    natural lighting 98, 100
    NVA work 175, 178, *182*, *247*
    roof lights 100
    stairs 100, *102–3*, 127, *206*, *210*, 234
    steps to 84

cloister 74, 82, *82*, 84, 106, 205, *225*
    columns 107
    Hinterland 234
    library access 100
    materials 108
    natural lighting 87
    see also walkways, St Peter's College

closure 118, 120, 128–9, 133

Coia, Jack
    1st design 50, 72–3, *73*, 74
    construction delays 111
    Grigor's documentary 128
    problems 128
    role in design 70, 143, 152, 156
    visits to 73, 128

common room 4, 98, 100, *102–3*, *121*, 128, 178

conservation 120, 129, 132, 133, 136, 138, 140–1, 142–88

construction 64, *69*, 109–14, *111*

context 31–9

convent block 80, *80*, *182*
    Avanti Architects' report 168

construction 111–12, *114*
furniture and fittings 112
Hinterland 242
La Tourette and 109
materials 80, 108
natural lighting 80, *242*
NVA plans 178
oratory 78, *78*, 104
planning and design 4, 72, 73, 74, 76, 77, 78, *78*, 80, 106, 109
proposed demolition 134, 140
vandalism 162
costings 72, 110, 114
see also valuations
courtyard 78, 82, 84, 104, 106, 109
Cowell's role 51, 69, 70, 116
unacknowledged 143, 152, 165
weathertightness problem 127
crypt 4, 90, *96*, *108*
derelict 202
Eyre and Campbell's re-interment 114
Hinterland 234
natural lighting 205, *222*
reuse by NVA 195
windows 205
decoration 77
dining rooms/refectories
1st design 74
convent block 80, *80*
derelict *152*
furniture and fittings 104
glazed screens 87, *87*
in use 122, 127
Kilmahew House inspiration for 73
lectern *104*
NVA plans 178, 194
partitions 87
planning and design 4, 32, 72, 82, 84, 87, 104, 106, 107, 202, 205
vaults 90, 218
visitors in *121*
drug rehabilitation centre 6, 129, *129*, 133
Farquhar's exploration 193
floors/flooring 84, 87, 127
foundation stone 112, *115*
furniture and fittings 87, 104, 107, 112, 122, 128

Grigor's film 128
hall 82, 84, 87
Hinterland 6, *8*, 144, 175, 180–1, *181*, 184–5, 195, 234, *234–45*
Iconic Modernism 148
Kilmahew House *see* Kilmahew House
kitchen block, natural lighting 80
landscaping 78, 104
NVA and 149, 175, 178, 180, 196
Le Corbusier's influence 108, 109, 115–16, 164, 195, 205
listed building 135
Historic Scotland and 129, 138, 152, 160, 162, 163, 187
under Kilmahew House listing 129, 133, 138
upgrade to A-listing 138, 140, 141, 143, 187
lower church 90, 107, 108, 109
MacMillan and
design 50, 69, 70, 106, 110, 116, 132, 138, 142, 143, 152, 165, 168, 188
preservation 147–8, 173–4, 184
water ingress 161
McRoberts and 72–3, *73*, 74, 123
main block 4, 74, *88*, *115*, 202, 205
artificial lighting 100
Avanti Architects' report 168
balconies 82, 87, 90, *115*
construction *69*, 111, *111*, 112, *112*, *113*, 114
corridor 82
dereliction *132*, *166*, 168, *208*, *210*, *212*
first floor *212*, *224*
graffiti *228*
Hinterland *234*, *241*, *242*
links 80
materials 108
natural lighting 84, 87, *87*
NVA's work 175, 178, *182*, *188*, *208*, *210*, *212*, *218*, *220*
performance/maintenance 127
planning and design 76, 77, 80, 82, *83*, 84, 87, 104, 106, 107
proposals for reuse 140, 173
sanctuary block and 76, 77, 90, 107, *107*
stabilisation/consolidation 160–1, 175
stairs *208*, *218*
materials 77, 82, 87, 100, 104, 108–9
Metzstein and
conservation/reuse 132, 139, 142, 147–8, 173, 184, 187
design 50, 62–3, 69, 70, 74, 106, 110, 116, 132, 138, 142,

143, 152, 165, 188
  retrospective accounts of 69, 74, 77, 106, 108, 109, 110, 147, 148, 187, 205
Modernist architecture 4–5, 6, 20, 31, 33, 40, 61, 62–3, 74, 104, 106, 107, 108, 172, 187, 188
  Bo Bardi and 226
  Metzstein's comments 62–3, 65
  revaluation 8, 118, 129, 133, 136, 138, 141, 142, 181
NVA and 6, 144, 145, 147, 150, *168*, 173–85, *176*, *180*, 193–5, 202, 205
  altar 214
  chapels 178, 194, 218
  classroom block 175, 178, *182*, *247*
  clean up 218
  Heritage Lottery Fund 174, 178, 180, 185
  landscaping 149, 175, 178, 180, 196
  main block 175, 178, *182*, *188*, *208*, *210*, *212*, *218*, *220*
  site donated to NVA 148
opening 113, *117*
pavilion, NVA plans 178
performance/maintenance 64, 127–8, 133, 149, 187
  water ingress 113, 127, 128, 138–9, 161
ramp 106, *118*, 205, 234
retaining walls 77–8, 110, *232*
roof lights
  classroom block 100
  hall 87
  sanctuary block 90, 107, *107*, 110, 202, 205
roofs
  Avanti Architects' report 168
  NVA plans 178, 202
  problems 127
  see also water ingress
  sanctuary block 107, *107*, 110, *147*, 162, 168, 178
sacristy 90, *96*, 104, 195, 205
  Hinterland 234
sanctuary block 4, 87, 90, *93–6*, *200*
  artificial lighting 100
  closure 128
  construction *69*, 111
  derelict *132*, *147*, 150, 202, 205, *214*
  design 76, 107, 109, 110, 205
  entrance at night *125*
  foundation stone 112, *115*
  graffiti *220*, *227*, *233*
  Hinterland 234

  in use 113, 127
  La Tourette and 109
  main block and 76, 77, 90, 107, *107*
  materials 108
  natural lighting 87, 90, 107
  NVA plans 178
  ramp 106, *118*, 205, 234
  roof 107, *107*, 110, *147*, 162, 168, 178
  roof light 90, 107, *107*, 110, 202, 205
  stairs *210*
  Urban Splash scheme *171*
  water penetration 127
  see also altars; chapels
staff and students 120
stairs 82, 84, 87, *96*, 106, 205
  classroom block 77, 98, 100, *102–3*, 127, 128, *206*, *210*, 234
  escape 82, 108, 109
  Le Corbusier's influence 109
  main block *208*, *218*
  materials 108
  performance/maintenance 127
  sanctuary *210*
students' rooms 4, 76, 127, *156*, 202, 218, *228*
  furniture and fittings 87
tabernacle 78, 90, *93*, 234
topping out *71*
valuations 128, 144, 149, 150
walkways 82, 106, 108
  see also cloister, St Peter's College
water ingress 113, 127, 128, 138–9, 161
Watters and Glendinning at *136*
St Peter's College, Newlands 121, 128
St Peter's Seminary Conservation Assessment 150, 162, 168, *168*, 172, 173, 175
St Philip's Episcopal Church, Edinburgh 28
St Salvador Episcopal Church, Edinburgh 25
St Salvator's Chapel Choir, St Andrews University 181
St Sophia's Church, Galston 27, 28
St Teresa of Lisieux Church, Possilpark 29, *29*
St Teresa's Church, Dumfries 31
St Thomas the Apostle Church, Riddrie 31
St Vincent Street Church, Glasgow *33*, 48, 142
Salmon & Son & Gillespie 40
Saltire Society 25, 71
sanctuaries 28, 31, 39, 57

Catholic Pavilion, Empire Exhibition 46
St Charles, Kelvinside 56
St Laurence's, Greenock 48
St Paul's Church, Glenrothes 54
sanctuary block, St Peter's College 4, 87, 90, *93–6*, 200
   artificial lighting 100
   closure 128
   construction *69*, 111
   derelict *132*, *147*, *150*, 202, *205*, *214*
   design 76, 107, 109, 110, 205
   entrance at night *125*
   foundation stone 112, *115*
   graffiti *220*, *227*, *233*
   Hinterland 234
   in use 113, 127
   La Tourette and 109
   main block and 76, 77, 90, 107, *107*
   materials 108
   natural lighting 87, 107
   NVA plans 178
   ramp 106, *118*, 205, 234
   roof 107, *107*, 110, *147*, 162, 168, 178
      Avanti Architects' report 168
      NVA plans 178
   roof light 90, 107, *107*, 110, 202, 205
   stairs *210*
   Urban Splash scheme *171*
   water ingress 127
   see also altars
Sanctuary video installation 158
Santa Maria Novella, Florence 29
Scandinavian Furnishings 104
Scanlan, Archbishop James Donald 18, 55, *125*
   appointment 17
   church finances 17, 126
   St Bride's Church, East Kilbride 56, *57*
   St Peter's College 112, *115*, 126
      building problems 127
      foundation stone laying 112, *115*
      inauguration 68, 113, 159
      RIBA Bronze Regional award 116
      staff changes 123
   Ward and 17
Schillebeeckx, Edward 17, 18
schools
   Catholic Church 14, 15, 29, *29*

Cumbernauld 60, *60*, 62
GKC 15, 46, 51, 60, *60*, 61–2, *61*
Howford Special School, Glasgow 60
Kildrum Primary School, Cumbernauld 60, *60*
King's Park Secondary School, Glasgow 61, *61*
Knightswood Secondary School, Glasgow 46
Lourdes Secondary School, Glasgow 31
Modernist architecture 61–2
Our Lady and St Francis School 61–2
Our Lady's High School, Cumbernauld 62
Schotz, Benno 45, 47, 53, 56
Schwarz, Rudolf 35, 37, 45, 55, 56
Scobie, Rev. Andrew 140, 152, 164
Scots College, Rome 71, 113, 128
Scott-Moncrieff, George 23
Scottish Arts Council 165, 174, 194
Scottish Catholic Renewal Movement 18, 123
Scottish Civic Trust 136, 141, 152
Scottish Enterprise Dunbartonshire 161
Scottish Episcopal Church 31, 36
Scottish Government/Executive 147, 150, 152, 174, 178
   Hinterland funding 181
Scottish Historic Building Trust 141–2
Scottish Lay Action Movement 18
Scottish Modern Movement 65
Scottish Parliament 147
Scottish Television 115
Scotus College *see* Chesters College (later Scotus College)
SCRM *see* Scottish Catholic Renewal Movement
Seaton Delaval Hall, Northumberland 179
Second Vatican Council 17–19, 126, 214
   Constitution on the Sacred Liturgy 18, 37, 121
   effect on church design 39, 52, 57
   McRoberts' views 71, 74
   Oath Against Modernism withdrawal 214
   St Peter's College and 8, 63, 118, 120–1, 123, 186
Senn, Rainer 54
SHBT *see* Scottish Historic Building Trust
Sheridan, John 140, 162
Shettleston, St Paul's Church 48
Simmons, C E 28, *28*
Simpson, James 160
Sisters of St Joseph of Newark 73
Skye, 'The Storr' 192
Smithson, Alison and Peter 33
Soulis Technologies 160

South Uist, Our Lady of Sorrows 58
SPBPT *see* St Peter's Buildings Preservation Trust
Spence, Basil *13*, 164
    Coventry Cathedral 39, *39*, 48
    GKC and 48
    listed buildings 134
    St Andrew's Church, Edinburgh 26, *26*, 27
    SS Ninian Martin and John RC Church, Whithorn 26
sports centre, St Peter's College 173
Springburn, Immaculate Heart of Mary Church 31
SS Ninian Martin and John RC Church, Whithorn 26
staff, St Peter's College *120*, 123
stairs
    Kilmahew House 73
    St Peter's College 82, 84, 87, *96*, 106, 205
        classroom block 77, 98, 100, *102–3*, 127, 128, *206*, *210*, 234
        escape 82, 108, 109
        Le Corbusier's influence 109
        main block *208*, *218*
        materials 108
        performance/maintenance 127
        sanctuary block *210*
Stamp, Gavin
    Coia's role in design 143
    control of narratives 165
    GKC's churches 56
    Kilmahew House demolition 142
    Lewis's adaptation of discourse 158
    Lighthouse exhibition 165
    Mackintosh School of Architecture lecturer 132, 139
    Metzstein and MacMillan and 109, 148, 156, 165
    St Benedict's Church demolition 135
    St Peter's College and 136, 138, 139, 141, 142–3, 146, 158, 161, 174
Steffann, Emil 45
Stephenson, Derek, and Partners *33*
Stevenson, Father 23
Stirling University 33, 116
Stirton, Paul 133, 141
Strathnaver Church, Sutherland 25
Stronsay, Moncur Memorial Church 25
students, St Peter's College *120*, *122*
students' rooms, St Peter's College 4, 76, 127, *156*, 202, 218, *228*
Supple, Philip 181
Sussex University 116

Sutherland, Strathnaver Church 25
Sutherland, John 31
swimming pool, St Peter's College, Urban Splash scheme *171*

tabernacle, St Peter's College 78, 90, *93*, 234
Tait, Thomas S 45
Tarbolton, H O 25
Tartaglia, Archbishop Philip 175
Tayport, Our Lady Star of the Sea 22, *23*
teaching block *see* classroom block, St Peter's College
Team 10 32–3
Themes & Variations exhibition 156
Thirties Society 135
Thistle Foundation 25
Thompson, Alexander *33*
Thomson, Alexander 48, 59, 142, 156
Thomson, Bishop Francis *125*, 126
Thomson (later MacDougall), Leslie Grahame 21, 25, 32
'To Have and to Hold' debate 179
Traditionalist architecture 21–7, 32
    Coventry Cathedral 39
    Drygrange House 70
    McRoberts' approach 71
    St Paul's Church, Glenrothes 54
    St Peter's College 1st design 74
    see also historicist architecture
training of priests 19, 120, 123, 125–6, 128
    St Peter's College and 63, 104, 121, 122
Treanor, Monsignor Charles 70, 73, 74, 123
Troon, Our Lady of the Assumption and St Meddan 22
Tschumi, Bernard 214
Twentieth Century Society 141, 146, 161, 162, 164, 168

Urban Splash 146, 161, *171*, *172*, 173–4, *173*

valuations, St Peter's College, Cardross 128, 144, 149, 150
Vanbrugh, John 179
Vatican II *see* Second Vatican Council
vaults, St Peter's College 205
    convent block 106

damage and repair 172, 178, 181, 193, 218
main block 82, 84, 87, 106–7, 160
sanctuary floor 90
Vocation Exhibition, Kelvin Hall 114, 125

Wadham College, Oxford 51, 64
Walker, David 134
Walker Group report 136, 138, 140, 149
walkways, St Peter's College 82, 106, 108
see also cloister, St Peter's College
walled garden 77, 178, *180*, 193, 196, *196*
proposed housing 140, 149, 160, 178
Walsh, Bishop 39
Walsh, James *120*
Ward, Bishop James 16–17, 18, *19*, 20
Coia and 50, 70
Eyre and Campbell's re-interment 114
McRoberts and 71, 72, 74
St Peter's College 17, 70, 72, 74, 110, 112, 113, 123, 126, 127
Wark, Kirsty 165
water ingress, St Peter's College 113, 127, 128, 138–9, 161
Watters, Diane *136*
Welch, Herbert A, and Hollis 40
Wester Hailes, Holy Trinity 59
Westminster Cathedral 28
Wheeler, Anthony 35
Whiston, P, & McRobie 31
Whiston, Peter 31, 35, 74
White, Very Rev. John 31
Whitham, David 133
Whithorn, SS Ninian Martin and John RC Church 26
Whyte, Prof James 35, 54
Williams, Bede 181
Wilson, Colin St John 139, 165
Wilson, Hugh 36
Wilson, Michael 140, 142, 152
windows *see* natural lighting, St Peter's College
Winning, Archbishop Thomas Joseph 18, 123, *125*, 126, 128, 138, 149
Womersley, Peter *32*, 33, 134
World Monument Fund 188
Wright, Frank Lloyd 205
Wright, Sandy 64

Wylie, George 165
Wylie and Lochhead 104, 112

Zeidler, Cordula 161, 162
Zinn, W V 74, 76, 108, 110–11

School of Art

The Gillespie, Kidd and Coia archive at The Glasgow School of Art comprises approximately 18,000 items. This material mainly dates from 1953, when Isi Metzstein and Andy MacMillan took over the majority of the practice's design work, to 1987 when the company closed. At this point, the archive was moved to GSA, where Metzstein and MacMillan had both studied and taught, MacMillan becoming Head of the Mackintosh School of Architecture in 1973. The archive was officially gifted to GSA in 2001 and has since been catalogued, conserved and made accessible to the public.

Unfortunately, the majority of the company's earlier records, dating back to the late nineteenth century, had earlier been destroyed, partly as a result of paper salvage work during the Second World War, and partly due to damage caused by a burst water pipe in 1956. However, the archive material covering the 1950s–1980s is incredibly comprehensive, providing detailed documentation for the firm's modernist designs for churches, housing and educational buildings. During this period the company mainly worked on projects based in Glasgow and the West of Scotland but their work also included buildings for organisations such as the University of Hull, University of Cambridge and the Museum of Modern Art in Oxford.

The archive is divided into sections relating to each project, plus general office paperwork. In turn, each project consists of job files: correspondence between the architects, clients and contractors, plus invoices, quotes and accounts; images, the vast majority of which are black and white and show the finished buildings, both exterior and interior; and architectural drawings, from site plans, floor plans, sections and elevations to details for joinery, brick work and fittings. Researchers can therefore track the history of a project from initial proposal to completed work. In the case of St Peter's Seminary, Cardross, the archive holds 24 job files of paperwork, c70 photographs, c200 contact sheets and over 450 negatives, plus 400 architectural drawings.

Further information about the archive, including a selection of digitised images can be viewed on GSA's Archives and Collections website www.gsa.ac.uk/archives. The archive can also be viewed in person by prior appointment. Please contact the Archives and Collections service for more information.

Susannah Waters
Archives and Collections Manager

Archives and Collections
The Glasgow School of Art
www.gsa.ac.uk/archives
archives@gsa.ac.uk
+44 (0)141 353 1418

NVA

NVA's mission is to make powerful public art that reconnects people to their built and natural heritage. Established in Glasgow in 1992, the organisation has produced many dynamic interventions in unusual landscapes over the past twenty years. NVA's practice uses creative learning and environmental innovation, involving audiences in physically redefining urban and rural settings, revealing how places shape and are shaped by people. The name NVA takes its inspiration from *nacionale vita activa*, the Ancient Greek ideal of a lively democracy where actions and words, shared amongst a community of equals, bring new thinking into the world.

Recent commissions include Ghost Peloton for the Grand Depart of the Tour de France in 2014, and Speed of Light, a signature contribution to the 2012 Olympics staged at the Edinburgh International Festival. NVA transformed Arthur's Seat using bespoke radio controlled light-suits activated by 3,000 hill runners, animating the mountain with trails of choreographed patterned light. Speed of Light has toured internationally with productions in Japan, England and with ultra-runners in an epic crossing of the Ruhr in Germany.

NVA developed its first permanent work, the Hidden Gardens, behind Tramway in Glasgow in 2003. It is Scotland's first sanctuary garden dedicated to peace, linking up different faith groups in the city in a secular setting. It has won numerous awards over the last twelve years.

www.nva.org.uk

St Peter's College, Cardross